942.31

Wiltshire Record Society

(formerly the Records Branch of the Wiltshire
Archaeological and Natural History Society)

VOLUME XXVII

FOR THE YEAR 1971

Impression of 400 copies

WILTSHIRE RETURNS
TO THE
BISHOP'S VISITATION QUERIES
1783

EDITED BY

MARY RANSOME

DEVIZES

1972

ISBN: 0 901333 04 2

THIS VOLUME IS PUBLISHED WITH THE HELP
OF A GRANT FROM THE LATE MISS ISOBEL
THORNLEY'S BEQUEST TO THE UNIVERSITY OF
LONDON

Set in Times New Roman 10/11 pt.

PRINTED IN GREAT BRITAIN BY
THE GLEVUM PRESS LTD.,
GLOUCESTER

CONTENTS

PREFACE

THE SOCIETY is indebted and expresses its warm thanks to the Salisbury Diocesan Registrar (Mr. Alan M. Barker) for permission to publish the documents that form the text printed below; to the County and Diocesan Archivist (Mr. M. G. Rathbone) and the Assistant Diocesan Archivist (Miss Pamela Stewart), in whose care the documents are, for making them available; to the Institute of Historical Research, University of London, for keeping the documents so that Miss Ransome could work on them in its library; to the trustees of the Isobel Thornley Bequest for a most generous grant towards the cost of printing; and particularly, of course, to Miss Ransome for undertaking the edition and completing it promptly.

Miss Ransome wishes to record her warm personal thanks to Miss Pamela Stewart, Mr. D. A. Crowley, and Mr. K. H. Rogers for their kind and expert help in solving a variety of problems; and in particular to Miss Elizabeth Crittall, Editor of the *Victoria History of Wiltshire*, who made available the typescript of parish histories not yet published, and who has generously shared her wide knowledge of Wiltshire in many informal and useful conversations.

The documents here published relate rather to the diocese of Salisbury than to the county of Wiltshire. At the time of their compilation Berkshire was part of the diocese, and when Miss Ransome began work on her edition in 1969 it was thought possible that the Berkshire returns might be included. Their inclusion, however, would have required a much larger volume, and one that would have been beyond the Society's financial means. Inquiries made in 1970 suggested that the organizations in Berkshire concerned with historical records and their publication were unable to share in the expense of a larger volume, and so with some reluctance it was decided to confine the volume to the Wiltshire returns.

CHRISTOPHER ELRINGTON
May 1972

ABBREVIATIONS OF TITLES CITED IN THE NOTES

Alum. Cantab.	J. and J. A. Venn, *Alumni Cantabrigienses*
Alum. Oxon.	J. Foster, *Alumni Oxonienses*
Benson and Hatcher, *Salisbury*	R. Benson and H. Hatcher, *Old and New Sarum or Salisbury* (1834) (part of Hoare's *Modern Wilts.*)
Clergy Books, 1783	Salisbury Diocesan Record Office, Clergy Books, 1783
Complete Peerage	G. E. Cockayne, *Complete Peerage*, ed. Vicary Gibbs and H. A. Doubleday
D.N.B.	*Dictionary of National Biography*
Gents. Mag.	*Gentleman's Magazine*
Hoare, *Mod. Wilts.*	Sir Richard Colt Hoare, *Modern Wilts.* (1822-37)
Liber Regis	*Liber Regis or Thesaurus rerum Ecclesiastiarum*, ed. J. Bacon (1786)
Lond. Mag.	*London Magazine*
Pembroke Papers	*Pembroke Papers*, I. 1734-80, II. 1780-94; *Letters and Diaries of Henry tenth Earl of Pembroke and his circle*, ed. Lord Herbert (1942, 1950)
Sarum Dioc. R.O.	Salisbury Diocesan Record Office
V.C.H. Wilts.	*Victoria County History of Wiltshire*
W.A.M.	*Wiltshire Archaeological and Natural History Magazine*
Wilts. Inst.	Sir Thomas Phillips, *Institutiones Clericorum in Comitatu Wiltoniae* (1825)
Wilts. Top. Coll.	*Topographical Collections of John Aubrey*, ed. J. E. Jackson (1862)
Worcs. Hist. Soc.	Worcestershire Historical Society

INTRODUCTION

THE MANUSCRIPT

The present volume contains the returns made by the Wiltshire clergy at the primary visitation of Bishop Barrington in July 1783. Following the practice which had by the mid 18th century become general, Barrington sent out in advance of his visitation a list of questions addressed to the officiating clergy in all the parishes under his jurisdiction, with an explanatory letter and a printed form on which their answers were to be made. The completed forms were subsequently bound up into three volumes—two containing the parishes in Wiltshire and one those in Berkshire. The volumes, which have had their folios numbered in a single sequence, are in the Diocesan Record Office at Salisbury. They have half-calf bindings and marbled end-boards, each volume being 11½ inches high and 9¼ inches broad. Included in the two volumes of Wiltshire parishes are fourteen Berkshire parishes, and a note inside the front cover of the Berkshire volume states that these have been bound up with the Wiltshire parishes by mistake. The parishes are bound in alphabetical order, which has not, however, been strictly kept.

Each parish return consists of two double sheets, folded to form eight pages. Pages 1 and 2 are filled by the bishop's letter (with the names of parish and deanery filled in by an official) and the list of places and times of visitation and confirmation; pages 3 to 8 contain the queries, printed on the left-hand side, with space left for the answers, and with the postscript at the end. At the foot of page 8, on the right-hand side, is the address, 'To the officiating minister, rector, or vicar of —,' the name of the parish being filled in by an official. The whole eight pages were presumably folded, with the address outside. In some returns the bishop's letter, with the names of the parish and deanery, is missing and the names have been written across the top of the answers, always in the same hand—presumably again by an official.

The handwriting of the answers varies greatly, ranging from small, neat, scholarly hands and beautiful italic script, through free but well formed hands, to unformed, childish scrawls. The majority, however, are clear and easy to read. There is little variation in the spelling and few spelling mistakes, but certain archaic forms are used by most of the clergy. Some returns have no signature, and a considerable number of those that were signed by curates do not name the incumbents.

EDITORIAL METHOD

The returns printed below are confined to Wiltshire, and omit all those for Berkshire. Each parish has been given a serial number, printed before the name of the parish in bold type. Following the name of the parish are the number of the folio on which the return for the parish begins and the name of the rural deanery. The bishop's letter and the queries are printed at the beginning of the text, and are not repeated in each return; for ease of understanding the returns, the queries have also been printed at the back of the volume on a sheet which folds clear of the other pages. The more complex queries, and where appropriate the answers to them, have been subdivided with letters in square brackets, for greater clarity.

The text has been edited by extending some abbreviations, by adopting others as standard even where they are not used in the manuscript, and by rationalizing the spelling, the use of initial capital letters, the expression of sums of money and of dates giving the day of the month, and, where possible, the punctuation. The inconsistent use in the manuscript of figures and words to express numbers has been left unaltered other than in sums of money and dates, partly because of the impossibility of achieving a consistent usage that would retain the actual words (as distinct from the written symbols) of the original returns. Words underlined in the manuscript are printed in italics. The spelling of surnames and place-names has been kept as in the manuscript, except in the headings to each return. In those headings a form in the manuscript that is markedly different from the modern form is given in brackets. The deanery names are also printed in their modern forms; the manuscript usually omits an 'e' from Chalke, Malmesbury, Potterne, and Wylye.

Other editorial additions and corrections to the text are enclosed in square brackets.

Footnotes are used to indicate the absence of the bishop's letter from the beginning of a return, to supply missing names of curates and incumbents, and generally for purposes of identification, explanation, and cross-reference. The missing names are taken from the Clergy Books for 1783 in the Diocesan Record Office; the names of colleges and dates of matriculation enable the reader to refer to the relevant entries in J. Foster's *Alumni Oxonienses* and J. and J. A. Venn's *Alumni Cantabrigienses*.

THE BISHOP

Shute Barrington was one of the aristocratic bishops who were increasing in number in the second half of the 18th century.[1] He was the youngest son of the first Viscount Barrington, and his eldest brother, the second viscount, was Secretary at War during the war of American Independence. After Eton and Oxford he became, through his brother's influence, chaplain in ordinary to George III at the age of twenty-six, and a canon successively of Christ Church, Oxford, St. Paul's, and Windsor. He became bishop of Llandaff in 1769, was translated to Salisbury in 1782, and in 1791 to Durham, one of the richest sees, which he held until his death at the age of ninety-one in 1826.

[1] The following account of Barrington's career is based on *D.N.B.;* George Townsend, 'Memoir of the late Bishop of Durham', prefixed to *Theological Works of the first Viscount Barrington* (1828); C. J. Abbey, *The English Church and its Bishops* (1887), ii. 220–3.

During his nine years at Salisbury he seems to have been an efficient and energetic bishop. The importance he attached to confirmation can be seen in his letter to the clergy sent out with the visitation queries in 1783, enclosing copies of 'a few plain questions and answers on the subject of the sacred rite' to be distributed by the clergy among their parishioners. His visitation charge, later printed, is refreshingly sensible and direct. 'My resolution,' he said, 'is never to select any curious topic of speculation, unconnected with the purposes of these meetings; . . . Little solicitous about the elegance of composition, I am anxious in the extreme to deliver my sentiments with simplicity and freedom.' He stressed the importance of a clergyman's own personal behaviour, as well as diligence in carrying out his duties, especially in a period when 'shameless profligacy, avowed libertinism, infidelity and superstition in every shape are making a most alarming progress.' He enlarged upon the vital importance of residence or, where economic circumstances made this impossible, a wise choice of curates and emphasized the rule that no one should employ a curate from another diocese without informing the bishop. He urged the necessity, in the interest of the clergy themselves, of having clear terriers, and evidently sent out directions prescribing the form in which they should be drawn up. The whole tone and content of the charge is simple, evangelical, and practical.[2]

Barrington spent large sums of money on improvements to the bishop's palace at Salisbury, employing the architect James Wyatt. Draining operations were undertaken to make the palace less damp, and the cathedral churchyard, described by a visitor in 1782 as 'like a cow common', was also drained and levelled and part of it enclosed in the palace grounds. Unfortunately Wyatt's alterations to the cathedral were less happy, involving much destruction, roundly denounced at the time and since. 'These important alterations (by some called improvements)', wrote Sir Richard Colt Hoare in 1824, 'called forth the pens and just animadversions of various lovers of antiquity', including Horace Walpole.[3] The bishop seems to have been on good terms with Salisbury corporation, co-operating in their plans for the rebuilding of the Council House, involving the demolition of the bishop's guildhall, in 1785,[4] and he is said to have done much for the poor in the diocese.

As a churchman Barrington was a staunch Protestant of the evangelical school. He was a friend of Hannah More, who often visited him at his country house at Mongewell, near Wallingford. He was much opposed to any further concessions to Roman Catholics which might result in their return to political power, and he considered that the corruption of the Church of Rome was one of the main causes of the French Revolution. Nevertheless he was ready to allow Catholics toleration short of political power, and offered hospitality

---

2 *A Charge delivered to the clergy of the diocese of Sarum at the primary visitation of that diocese in the year 1783, by Shute, Lord Bishop of Sarum* (Oxford, 1783). The supplementary answers for Maddington, **131** below, represent an attempt to meet the bishop's requirement of a terrier.

3 *V.C.H. Wilts.* vi. 78; addenda to S. H. Cassan, *Lives and Memoirs of the Bishops of Sherborne and Salisbury* (1824). For a forthright denunciation by a modern writer see R. L. P. Jowitt, *Salisbury* (1951), p. 27.

4 *V.C.H. Wilts.* vi. 121.

and financial help to French bishops and clergy fleeing from the revolution. He published various tracts and sermons, several attacking Catholic doctrine, but he was in no sense a scholar. George Townsend, his chaplain in his old age, considered that 'his published works were characterized by sound judgment, clearness of expression, and fervent piety' and that he was 'more distinguished for the exemplary discharge of his duties, for piety and well-regulated benevolence, than for eminent talents or extensive knowledge.'[5] Though not, perhaps, a very interesting person, Barrington seems to have been widely respected by his contemporaries. 'He has been unfortunate in that his steady progress up the ladder of preferment is remembered when his blameless character and unaffected piety are forgotten.'[6]

PREPARATIONS FOR THE VISITATION

Barrington was confirmed as bishop of Salisbury in August 1782, and by the following May preparations were being made for his primary visitation. The visitation was to be combined with a confirmation tour, and the registrar, Joseph Elderton, urged the necessity of having gaps between the confirmations at the various centres, to avoid too great a strain upon the bishop. Barrington considered this unnecessary but Elderton pointed out that Bishop Hume had been taken ill during his last visitation and been obliged to omit Berkshire, so that no confirmations had been held there since 1776. Numbers were therefore likely to be very large.[7] The dean, thanking the bishop for giving the clergy in his peculiars (which would not be visited) the opportunity to bring their parishioners for confirmation, also referred to the likelihood of large crowds, especially in Berkshire, and in the end the registrar's plans were accepted. He now set about organizing accommodation at the various visitation centres for the bishop and his officials and servants, collecting information about the state of the roads between one centre and another, and preparing for the bishop's use lists of benefices and beneficed clergy.[8] Barrington was staying at Mongewell and on 3 July Elderton wrote to him to offer a choice of lodgings in Salisbury during the visitation there. He could stay either with 'Mr. Goddard, the grocer in the market place . . . with his commodious dining-room and bed chambers' or with Mrs. Shergold at the King's Arms. The registrar then drew up, and on 5 July sent out, letters to all the innkeepers at whose inns the bishop and his retinue proposed to stay. They were to provide not only accommodation for the bishop and his party, but also 'for the entertainment of his clergy' after the visitation. Accommodation must also be provided for the registrar and his staff, 'and likewise proper apartments for the office business of the registrar and his clerks. Your answer, acknowledging

[5] 'Memoir of the late Bishop of Durham,' pp. xlvi–xlvii.
[6] M. G. Jones, *Hannah More* (1952), p. 65.
[7] Sarum Dioc. R.O., Misc. Vis. Papers, 8: J. Elderton to Mr. Burn, 29 Apr. 1783.
[8] Ibid.: Note from dean, n.d.; list of roads. For the itinerary and the visitation and confirmation centres see below, p. 16.

the receipt of this letter, by the first post, is expected, and will oblige.'[9] Arrangements had to be made for the visitation sermons preached at each centre by one of the clergy of the neighbourhood. Apparently the practice was to nominate three for each centre, 'so that if one is excused, two remain to be applied to.'[10] Finally the notices of the places and dates of visitation and confirmation, directions about the proceedings, the bishop's letter to the clergy, with the list of questions and forms for the answers, had to be sent out to all the clergy. The visitation queries had become largely standarized by this period and Barrington's questions do not differ significantly from those sent out by other 18th-century bishops.[11]

CHURCH SERVICES

The returns printed in this volume give a vivid picture of the diocese, though not a complete one. All the Berkshire parishes have been omitted, and even for Wiltshire the returns are not complete. The diocese contained a number of 'peculiars' where the bishop had no visitorial jurisdiction. In some of them the dean had such jurisdiction, in others the dean and chapter, the treasurer, or the precentor. In all, the peculiars numbered about twenty. Further, there are no returns for another nine parishes which were not peculiars. Either these returns were mislaid or, perhaps more likely, the clergy concerned, through negligence or disinclination, did not send them in.[12] Nevertheless the returns are a valuable source of information about the Wiltshire clergy and their work in the late 18th century.[13]

The official standards set for the 18th-century clergy were not very exacting, and the Wiltshire clergy on the whole conformed to these standards reasonably well. They were weakest on the requirement laid down by the canons of 1604 to hold two services every Sunday. Of the 232 parishes making returns only 93 (about 40 per cent) met this requirement, though another 8 had two Sunday services in the summer only, and 3 more had two services every other Sunday. Wilcot had two every other Sunday in summer; and the two parishes in Cricklade, St. Sampson and St. Mary, both served by the same curate, had a system whereby there were two services every other Sunday at St. Sampson and one service on the alternate Sunday at St. Mary. On the other hand only

[9] Sarum Dioc. R.O., Misc. Vis. Papers, 8: Elderton to the bishop, 3 July; draft letter to innkeepers, 5 July.

[10] Ibid.: Elderton to Mr. Burn, 29 Apr.

[11] They may be compared with, e.g., those of Bishops Wake and Gibson at Lincoln in 1706 and 1723, Lincoln Rec. Soc. iv (1913); Bishop Secker at Oxford in 1738, Oxfordshire Rec. Soc. xxxviii (1957); and Archbishop Herring at York in 1743, Yorks. Arch. Soc. Rec. Ser. lxxi (1928).

[12] Bishopstone (Chalke), Brixton Deverill, Charlton (Potterne), East Kennet, Fifield Bavant, Kellaways, Kingston Deverill, Leigh Delamere, West Overton. The vicar of Charlton was presented by the churchwardens for neglect of his duties: Sarum Dioc. R.O., Churchwardens' presentments, 1783.

[13] See the discussion of the returns by Dr. Anne Whiteman in V.C.H. Wilts. iii. 50–2.

five parishes,[14] all very small, fell below the standard of one service every Sunday and this must be set against the fact that fewer than half the parishes fulfilled the canonical requirement. The rest of the record is much better. A surprising number of churches had services on weekdays, especially on Good Friday, Christmas day when it fell on a weekday, and Ash Wednesday, and some also on the Mondays following Easter and Whit Sundays. Only 60 parishes never had weekday services, the reason most commonly given being that all the parishioners were working people who could not attend church on weekdays. The canons of 1604 required the celebration of Holy Communion at least three times a year, and the general standard aimed at in the 18th century was at least four times a year, on the three great festivals and after harvest.[15] About 73 per cent of the Wiltshire parishes had four or more celebrations a year, and only two—Bremilham and Pertwood—fell below the canonical minimum of three. At Bremilham the parish appears to have been in a general state of decay and on the rare occasions when Communion was celebrated a chalice had to be borrowed from Foxley; while at Pertwood the parish was so small that the canonical number for Communion could rarely be obtained. This is a good record for a predominantly rural area. The 18th-century bishops were anxious to encourage catechizing, and in this field also the record of the Wiltshire clergy is respectable. In just over 70 per cent of the parishes some attempt at least was made, most frequently in Lent but often at other times, generally in the summer. There are, however, many references to poor attendance, to unsuccessful attempts to make the parishioners send their children, and to the small number of children able to read. In 68 parishes there was no catechizing at all, the reason generally being that 'no one attends'. In some cases the gap was filled by schools where the children were taught the catechism. But in as many as 155 parishes there were no schools of any kind and in a number of others only very small private schools or small charitable bequests for teaching a few children to read.

Comparison of the general efficiency of the Wiltshire clergy with their exact contemporaries in the dioceses of Worcester and Oxford shows a remarkably uniform picture.[16] The proportion of churches having two services every Sunday was almost exactly the same in Wiltshire and the diocese of Worcester, but higher in Oxford, where the majority had two services. Of the Worcester churches 82 per cent had celebrations of Holy Communion four times a year against 73 per cent in Wiltshire, and Worcester also had a rather better catechizing record; but Wiltshire had a much better one for weekday services.

DISSENT

Answers to queries 7 and 8, on the numbers of dissenters, atheists, and habitual absentees from church, give the impression that dissent was not a

---

[14] Burcombe, **32**; Great Chalfield, **37**; Ditteridge, **69**; Norton **150**; and Pertwood, **157**.

[15] N. Sykes, *Church and State in England in the 18th Century* (1934), p. 250.

[16] See '*State of the Bishopric of Worcester, 1782–1808*' (Worcs. Hist. Soc. N.S. vi), p. 9; Diana McClatchley, *The Oxfordshire Clergy, 1777–1869* (1960), p. 80.

serious problem except in a very few parishes;[17] that convinced atheists were few and far between but habitual absentees all too numerous. One hundred and fifty-eight parishes claimed to have no dissenters at all. Twenty parishes had a few Catholics, generally only one or two families, only four reporting any significant numbers. Of these, Tisbury, Donhead St. Andrew, and Ansty chapel[18] are all close to Wardour Castle, where the Catholic Lord Arundell had a chapel and a resident priest. The fourth parish, Stourton, contained Lord Stourton's residence, Bonham House, where there was a private chapel. Protestant dissent was more widespread but again numbers were small except in the cloth-making towns of Bradford, Devizes, Malmesbury, Trowbridge, and Wilton, and the weaving village of North Bradley, where dissenters were numerous. There were also fair numbers in Salisbury, in St. Thomas's parish but with a meeting-house in St. Martin's, and at Marlborough. Five villages reported numbers which were perhaps large in proportion to the total population.[19] Methodists and Moravians were present in 37 parishes. The returns tend to be vague about their numbers but, perhaps predictably, Methodism seemed to flourish in the places where Protestant dissent was also strong; for example in Bradford, Trowbridge, and Wilton. There was a large Moravian congregation and chapel at Tytherton, in the parish of Bremhill. Twelve parishes reported Methodist chapels, including Tisbury, which, for its size, was a hotbed of nonconformity of every kind. There was a tendency among the clergy to regard Methodists as unfortunate and deluded rather than wicked. The vicar of Sutton Benger referred to parishioners who attended the nearby Methodist meeting at Christian Malford as 'regular, well-meaning, but mistaken people.' The returns for Heddington and Stanton St. Bernard referred to '2 or 3 deluded people called Methodists', and the vicar of Preshute said indulgently that some of his poorer parishioners 'steal now and then to the Methodist meeting-house at Marlborough'. The vicar of Avebury, however, took a sterner view and considered that they were assisted by the devil in gaining proselytes.

Many clergy ignored the question about parishioners who 'profess to disregard religion and absent themselves from the public worship of God', and some appeared to be almost shocked by the first half of the question. 'I do not know that there are any who *professedly* disregard religion,' wrote the curate of Wroughton **(80)**, 'but there are many who commonly absent themselves from public worship.' At Hilmarton 'some do absent themselves from divine worship through profaneness and irreligion'; Enford had its share of 'practical atheists'; Christian Malford had 'many Sabbath-breakers'. In a large number of parishes absentees from church were numerous, despite the efforts of the clergy.[20] The vicar of Avebury lamented the evil effects of alehouses, and condemned the 'trifling excuses' of absentees in his other parish of Winterbourne Monkton. Poverty and the want of suitable clothing

[17] On the history of dissent in Wiltshire, see *V.C.H. Wilts.* iii. 87–98, on Roman Catholicism, and 99–147, on Protestant nonconformity.
[18] Included in the return for Baverstock, **11.**
[19] Corsley, **59**; Longbridge Deverill, **65**; Downton, **72**; Grittleton, **95**; and Tisbury, **198.**
[20] See North Bradley, **24**; Corsley, **59**; Patney, **156**; Upton Lovell, **205**; and many others.

were mentioned as reasons in several parishes[21] and at Rodbourne Cheney 'age and infirmities.' On the other hand many clergy praised the regularity of their parishioners[22] and the vicar of Milton Lilborne was happy to inform the bishop that 'I have no complaint to make against any of my parishioners'.

THE PARISH CLERGY

The 262 clergy, incumbents and curates, seem to have been, on the whole, a very ordinary group of clergymen. Socially the majority came from the gentry and professional classes, though the exact proportion cannot be calculated because no information on the subject is available for some 56 clergy.[23] There were no sons of peers; 82 at least were sons of 'gentry' and another 57 sons of clergymen. It is safe to say that over 60 per cent of them were of the gentry or professional classes. Between 70 and 75 per cent had degrees, the great majority from Oxford, and a few more had been to one of the universities but had not taken a degree. There were a few outstandingly distinguished men among them. Benjamin Blayney, rector of Poulshot, was a notable Hebrew scholar who later became Regius Professor of Hebrew at Oxford; Charles Daubeny, vicar of North Bradley, published a number of theological works said to anticipate in some ways the Tractarian movement; James Stonhouse, rector of Great and Little Cheverell, was notable both as a medical practitioner and as an evangelical preacher, and was the original of Hannah More's 'Shepherd of Salisbury Plain'.[24] Joseph Townsend, rector of Pewsey, was a man of many parts. A geologist, he had also studied medicine, and published *The Physician's Vade Mecum*, theological and travel books, and *Free Thoughts on Despotic and Free Governments* (1781). With five other clergy he was a member of the Committee of Correspondence set up in Wiltshire, as in most English counties, in 1780 to support the county petitions criticizing excessive government expenditure and demanding moderate parliamentary reform.[25] A number of clergy were doctors of divinity, several were or had been fellows of their colleges. John Keble, vicar of Poulton, had the distinction of being the father of the eminent Tractarian; and George Wells, rector of Manningford Bruce and curate of North Newnton, was clearly a 'character', who regarded the visitation queries as so much bureaucratic red tape.[26]

The most notorious defect of the 18th-century church was pluralism, and the non-residence which resulted from it. The returns give, superficially, a bad impression of the Wiltshire clergy in this respect, but a closer examination

[21] Sherrington, **175**; Sutton Mandeville, **193**; Wootton Rivers, **228**.

[22] e.g. Chiseldon, **45**; Fovant, **88**; Stockton, **188**; Upavon, **204**.

[23] Social classification is based on the description of the father in *Alum. Cantab.* and *Alum. Oxon.*

[24] See *D.N.B.* for all these men.

[25] *Copies of the Proceedings of the General Meetings of the County of Wilts.* (1780). The other five clergy who were members of the committee were William Bowles and John Harington (Stratford-sub-Castle, **190**), Henry Kent (Urchfont, **207**), Richard Pococke (Mildenhall, **140**), and Edward Polhill (Milston, **141**).

[26] See North Newnton, **146**.

improves the picture a good deal. Of the 232 parishes making returns, only 90 were served by a resident incumbent, but 39 more were served by a resident curate, so that a little over half the parishes were served by resident clergy.[27] A further 80 parishes were served by an incumbent or curate living not more than 5 miles away from the church, and in fact no parish was served by clergy living much more than 10 miles away.[28] The one exception was Chippenham, where the vicar, though sometimes resident, admitted that he lived most of the time in Kent because of 'very material family concerns.' He did not say what arrangements he made for services in his absence, and no curate is mentioned in the Clergy Books for 1783. Pluralism was much the most frequent reason for non-residence. Of the 262 clergy 124 were pluralists in the sense of holding or serving more than one cure. Of these, 68 were incumbents holding two livings,[29] 25 were incumbents serving a second church as curate, making a total of 93. In addition, 31 curates were serving two or more churches. Here, as with non-residence, the picture is not quite as black as it appears. Of the 93 pluralist incumbents, 36 held one living outside Wiltshire, all but 6 in adjoining counties. All but 15 resided on one or other of their cures. All the 31 'pluralist' curates were serving churches close to each other, but a complicated situation could sometimes arise, as, for example, in the parishes served by two brothers, James and John Evans. At Fovant the rector, Dr. Thomas Eyre, lived in the rectory, which he had made into a summer residence,[30] but apparently did not serve the church, and the return was made by his curate, James Evans, recently appointed master of the city grammar school in Salisbury, where he lived. He was also curate of Teffont Evias, about 2 miles from Fovant, where the rector was a pluralist and resided on his other living at Odstock. Evans was assisted at Teffont Evias by his brother John, who was curate of Hindon and of Pertwood, about a mile apart, and who lived partly at Hindon and partly at Fovant. A study of the times of services at the various parishes suggests that the Evans brothers, and especially John, led a strenuous life on Sundays. John took morning service at Teffont every Sunday at 10.0, with a sermon every other Sunday. He then had a journey of 4 or 5 miles to Hindon, where he took a service (with a sermon) at 11.30 and an afternoon service at 3.30. Every other Sunday he took a service at Pertwood (where the parish contained only one family) at 1.0, returning to Hindon for the 3.30 service. Meanwhile James would travel from Salisbury to Fovant, 9 or 10 miles, for morning service (with sermon) at 10.30 and afternoon service at 2.0; then 2 miles to Teffont for the afternoon service there (with sermon every other Sunday) at 3.15, returning afterwards to Salisbury. As he had only recently been appointed to the city grammar school, it is to be hoped that this exhausting programme was a temporary one.

[27] The proportion of resident and non-resident incumbents was almost exactly the same in 1783 in Worcester and Oxford dioceses: see above, n. 16.

[28] The distances given by the clergy in the returns appear to be generally accurate, though naturally tending to minimize distances when they lived away from their cures.

[29] This figure may be too low, as there are several incumbents the reason for whose non-residence is not certain.

[30] *Pembroke Papers*, ii. 365.

Pluralism was not the only reason for non-residence. In some parishes there was no parsonage house, in others it was too small, dilapidated, damp, or in an unhealthy situation.[31] Bremilham, where 'my parsonage house is made a pig-sty of by Farmer Bennet of Cowitch', was an extreme case. Other clergy pleaded ill-health, their own or of members of their family, this being often combined with complaints about the house. The rectors of All Cannings and of Castle Eaton both found the damp situation of their parsonages bad for their health and could live in them only in the summer; and the vicar of Longbridge Deverill found winter residence in Bath 'for the benefit of the waters' essential for his health. Eleven clergy were also schoolmasters, whose duties sometimes involved non-residence and therefore to some extent prevented the proper performance of their parochial duties. James Evans, curate of Fovant and Teffont Evias, as already mentioned, lived in Salisbury; so did John Skinner, vicar of Shrewton, as he was master of the choristers' school, and his parish was served by a curate. Others, for instance James Mayo, vicar of Avebury and Winterbourne Monkton and master of Calne grammar school, and Thomas Huntingford, rector of Corsley and master of Warminster school, were able to live near enough to their churches to carry out their duties reasonably well. Only three schoolmasters were complete absentees from their parishes: William Williams, vicar of Marden, and master of Blackheath grammar school; James Charters, vicar of Broad Chalke and Bower Chalke and under-master at Rugby; and Thomas Bromley, vicar of Stanton St. Bernard and assistant master at Harrow. Other reasons for non-residence were residence at Oxford or Cambridge as fellow or tutor of a college, and the holding of canonries and prebends, or other ecclesiastical offices, either at Salisbury or elsewhere.

How far was this extensive pluralism due to real economic need? The returns give no information about the values of livings, except in a few cases where the clergy mention the matter, generally to complain of the inadequacy of their incomes. A Diocese Book of the early 18th century in the Diocesan Record Office gives the 'estimated' values of livings, sometimes with later additions, and so, in many cases, does John Bacon's *Liber Regis*, the 1786 edition of Ecton's *Thesaurus Rerum Ecclesiasticarum*. Bacon clearly took most of his 'reputed values' from the Diocese Book, but in some cases he gives a different and rather higher figure.[32] Values were rising during the 18th century,[33] so that the figures in the Diocese Book must be presumed to be lower than the values obtaining in 1783. Even allowing for this, there was undoubtedly a large number of very poor livings in Wiltshire in 1783. Over

---

[31] e.g. Heddington, **100**; Lydiard Tregoze, **130**; Norton, **150**.

[32] Values quoted in this Introduction are from the Diocese Book, repeated by Bacon. unless otherwise stated. They are generally the gross annual values. Ecton's work also gave the patrons of livings, and the many later editions were much consulted by clergy in search of preferment. See, for example, *Diary of Thomas Wilson, 1731–7 and 1750*, ed. C. L. S. Linnell (1964), p. 182.

[33] Some livings improved as a result of inclosure; a few (e.g. **201**) became poorer. Further details of most of the inclosures mentioned in the answers may be found in *Wilts. Inclosure Awards*, ed. R. E. Sandell (Wilts. Rec. Soc. xxv).

a hundred were probably worth less than £100, many of them £50 or less. In the returns themselves North Newnton and Poulton were each said to be worth only £20, and Winterbourne Earls only £10. Twenty-five livings were worth more than £200, four were worth more than £300. In the early years of the 19th century, when ecclesiastical reforms were being carried out, £150 was usually regarded as the dividing line between modest comfort and poverty.[34] Judged by this standard, pluralism in Wiltshire was being used to supplement an inadequate income by 41 of the 68 incumbents holding more than one living and by 17 of the 25 incumbents serving a second parish as curate. There is little information in the returns about curates' stipends, but the 31 curates serving two cures undoubtedly did so to avoid financial hardship.[35] Thus out of the total 124 cases of plurality of all kinds, 89 can be regarded as the result of economic necessity, and in some cases pluralism would still barely produce an adequate income. Thomas Meyler, for example, remarked of his two livings, Preshute (£80) and Marlborough St. Peter (£30), that one provided bread and cheese and the other a place to eat and sleep. Even if the figures were under-estimates, the livings can hardly have provided much more, particularly as he employed his son as curate to assist him at Marlborough, where the standard of services was exceptionally high.

There is, however, another side to the picture. Nine incumbents held two livings each of which was worth over £150, and of the 25 livings worth more than £200, 12 were held by pluralists. Some of these provide excellent examples of the importance, as a means of ecclesiastical advancement, of family connections, chaplaincies to peers, or tutorships to their sons. Perhaps the most interesting of all the Wiltshire pluralists was Nathaniel Hume, vicar of Bremhill and of West Kington, both livings in the gift of the bishop. Hume was the nephew of Bishop John Hume,[36] Barrington's predecessor, and his career provides a striking example of the ladder of preferment available in the 18th century for those with an influential patron. He became rector of St. Lawrence Jewry, London, in 1762 and a prebendary of St. Paul's the following year, his uncle then being dean of St. Paul's. The uncle became bishop of Salisbury in 1766 and in 1776 the nephew, still keeping his London living, became prebendary and vicar of Winterbourne Earls and for a few years master of St. Nicholas Hospital. In 1780 he gave up his London living to hold two of the bishop's better livings, Compton Bassett and West Kington; and in 1782 he resigned Compton Bassett and moved to Bremhill, the most valuable of all the bishop's livings,[37] where he remained until his death in 1804. In 1799 he exchanged West Kington for Brixton Deverill, of slightly lower value, with William Douglas, whose father, John Douglas, was by that time bishop.

[34] W. L. Mathieson, *The English Church and Reform, 1815–1840* (1923), p. 22.
[35] Only four returns mention curates' stipends: Aldbourne, £40, with house, £10; North Newnton, £20 7s.; Maddington, and Stanton St. Bernard (given under Heddington), each £20: see **1; 146; 131; 100.**
[36] Not brother, as implied in the obituary notice of Thomas Henry Hume, the bishop's only son, which refers to Nathaniel Hume as his uncle: *Gent. Mag.* (1834), i. 663. This mistake has been followed by later writers. See below, n. 39.
[37] 'About £200 clear' in Diocese Book; £400 in Bacon.

Hume was a canon of Salisbury and became precentor in 1774. The return for Bremhill was made by himself, in a neat and scholarly hand. He resided partly at Bremhill and partly at Salisbury and kept a curate. West Kington was served as curate by the rector of the adjoining parish of Nettleton. Hume's obituary notice in the *Gentleman's Magazine* described him as 'a gentleman endeared to all who knew him by the long and constant exercise of all the milder virtues, and whose loss is generally regretted.'[38] His brother John, who had succeeded him as master of St. Nicholas Hospital, held West Lavington, another of the bishop's livings, served for him by a curate, till 1783, when he exchanged all his English preferments for the deanery of Derry with his former schoolmate at Westminster, Edward Emily.[39]

The bishop had in all 20 livings in his gift in Wiltshire and was by far the largest ecclesiastical patron in the diocese. Of his other Wiltshire livings, Aldbourne was held, non-resident, by the son of the diocesan registrar and another five were held by various diocesan and cathedral officials; Potterne and Brixton Deverill by Arthur Coham, archdeacon of Wiltshire, who divided his time between the two and kept a curate at the latter; St. Edmund's, Salisbury, by the sub-dean, who resided; Shrewton by John Skinner, master of the choristers' school, and Idmiston by Edward Moore, formerly master of the city grammar school, both of whom were vicars of the cathedral. Shrewton was served by a curate, but Moore managed to serve Idmiston in combination with his duties at the cathedral. Monkton Farleigh and Warminster, each worth less than £100, were held by pluralists with adequate but not rich livings elsewhere; and Boscombe, the two Chitternes (All Saints and St. Mary), Littleton Drew, and Marlborough St. Peter, all poor livings, by pluralists whose incomes would otherwise have been very inadequate. Of the remaining bishop's livings—Compton Bassett, Inglesham, Poulshot, and Fisherton de la Mere—only the last was held by a non-resident. Most of these appointments had been made by Bishop Hume and they compare favourably with Bishop Hurd's use of his patronage in the diocese of Worcester at about the same period.[40]

Apart from the Crown, the most important lay patron in Wiltshire was the earl of Pembroke, as a result of the acquisition of Wilton Abbey by his family at the Dissolution. The most valuable of his 10 livings, Bishopstone (deanery of Chalke), for which there is no return, was held by his cousin, William Neville, non-resident and rector of Burghclere, Hants.[41] Two of the better Pembroke livings, Chilmark and Fovant, were held by Dr. Thomas Eyre,

[38] *Record of Old Westminsters*, ed. G. F. Russell Barker and Alan Stenning, i. 493; W. Dodsworth, *Salisbury Cathedral* (1792), p. 235; *Wilts. Inst.* ii, *passim;* Hoare, *Mod. Wilts.* v. 97; *Gent. Mag.* (1804), lxxiv. 484.

[39] See **123.** In the *Cartulary of St. Nicholas Hospital*, ed. C. Wordsworth, John Hume is described as the bishop's son and Nathaniel Hume as the bishop's brother, and incorrect dates of death are given for both of them. Both were the sons of James Hume M.D., of Oxford, brother of Bishop Hume: *Record of Old Westminsters*, i. 493; *Alum. Oxon.; London Magazine* (1766), p. 688.

[40] *Bishopric of Worcester, 1782–4* (Worcs. Hist. Soc. N.S. vi), p. 13.

[41] Clergy Books, 1783; *Pembroke Papers*, ii. 80. Bacon gives £300 as the value.

Lord Pembroke's chaplain and adviser on patronage matters. Returns for both these parishes were made by curates. Four more of the Pembroke livings were held by members of the Hawes family, relations of Henry Hawes, former rector of Wilton and 'much in favour' with Lord Pembroke's father. Fugglestone and Wilton were held by John Hawes, whose health appears to have been poor, and both were served by curates, Fugglestone by John's son Henry. This Henry Hawes was himself vicar of North Newnton, another Pembroke living, and of West Knoyle, a chapel appendant to it, both of them served by curates. Another Henry Hawes, son of the former rector of Wilton, held the Pembroke living of Little Langford.[42] This was served for him by a neighbouring clergyman, Hawes himself being resident curate of Box. Lord Pembroke's three remaining livings were all held by men connected with the education of his son. Henry Hetley, vicar of South Newton, had been Lord Herbert's tutor; Thomas Bromley, vicar of Stanton St. Bernard, had been his housemaster at Harrow, where he was still an assistant master; and the rector of Wylye, John Dampier, was the son of Thomas Dampier, formerly lower master at Eton, who had recommended the historian William Coxe to accompany Lord Herbert on a European tour.[43] Hetley served South Newton himself, though resident in Salisbury; Stanton St. Bernard and Wylye were both served by curates.

Finally, it must be emphasized that the returns are particularly valuable for the vivid impression they give of many individual clergy and their personal problems. James Mayo, vicar of Avebury, is a well-meaning bore who becomes human in his anxiety lest the new bishop should disapprove of his residence at Calne as master of the grammar school, a job that is tedious to him but necessary for the support of his fourteen children; 'many of them are young, and must, without an uncommon interposition of the divine providence, be left unprovided for' when their father dies.[44] Algernon Frampton, rector of Tockenham, is worried about his health and about a disagreement with his parishioners over tithes which renders it impossible for him to draw up a new terrier. He is most anxious that the bishop should understand his difficulties.[45] James Stonhouse, rector of Great and Little Cheverell, is unable to give the exact date of his institution because 'having been obliged to pack up that with many other papers of importance, letters, etc. in boxes on account of the number of workmen in my house; therefore cannot without very great inconvenience unpack and sort such a multiplicity of papers at present.'[46] Timothy Meredith, vicar of Wootton Bassett, would like the bishop's opinion

---

[42] *Pembroke Papers*, ii. 353, Dr. Thomas Eyre to Lord Herbert, 5 July 1787. In the same letter Fugglestone was said to be worth £300, Wilton £170, and Little Langford £100. The corresponding values in the Diocese Book are £200, £160, and £80.

[43] *Pembroke Papers*, ii. 46, 82; *Eton College Reg.* 1753–90, ed. R. A. Austen-Leigh, p. 145. Coxe himself later became rector of Fugglestone. The whole subject of Lord Pembroke's ecclesiastical patronage, especially in North Newnton and Stanton St. Bernard, where prebends were involved, is one of considerable complication and interest, which the present editor hopes to study further.

[44] See **9.** 17.

[45] See **201,** letter to bishop.

[46] See **39,** after 20.

on the situation of one of his parishioners, Mrs. Mary Stanley, whose husband was transported for fourteen years, and 'no intelligence having been received . . . for upwards of seven years, the said Mary wishes to know if she is at liberty to marry another.'[47] A rather different matrimonial problem weighs upon the mind of John Eyre, curate of Wylye; two of his parishioners, whom he refused to marry because one might be the son of the other's half-sister, have got married in the next parish. What can he do about it? He is also worried about the 'profanation of the Lord's day in my parish' by the sale there of the *Salisbury Journal* on Sundays, and by the obstinate refusal of the recipients of a parish charity to wear the prescribed badges.[48] Thomas Huntingford, rector of Corsley, deplores the use of the communion table 'for the transaction of parish business at vestries,' and other deficiences in church equipment;[49] and James Neale, curate of Aldbourne, a disappointed man, 'next March 1784 a curate 40 years', tried to start a school for poor families, but has had to give it up and has 'brought trouble on myself by the undertaking.'[50] Some of the returns have an air of self-righteousness;[51] but by and large they present a picture of simple, worthy men doing their best, often in very difficult conditions. Even the rich pluralists were, with some exceptions, doing their duty in at least one of their livings, though in vastly more comfortable circumstances. Some seventy-five years separate the returns from Trollope's Barsetshire novels, but they provide precursors both of Mr. Crawley of Hogglestock and of Archdeacon Grantley.

[47] See **227.** 19.
[48] See **230.** 14, 19.
[49] See **59.** 19.
[50] See **1.** 16.
[51] e.g. Sopworth, **181**; Stratton St. Margaret, **191**; Winterslow, **224.**

WILTSHIRE RETURNS TO THE BISHOP'S VISITATION QUERIES

[The bishop's letter sent, with the list of places and times of visitation and confirmation, to each parish].

To the officiating minister, rector, vicar, or curate of the parish of —— in the deanery of —— and diocese of Salisbury.

Reverend Sir,

I desire you to return written answers to the following queries, on the blank spaces near or under them, and deliver the same, signed with your name, and sealed up, to my chaplain, at my ensuing visitation.

I have caused articles of enquiry to be sent to the churchwardens of your parish, as a rule and direction by which they are to make their presentments; and I request you to put them in mind of the obligations they are under to do it, in a religious conformity to the oath they have taken.

As I purpose to confirm, in the course of my visitation, such young persons as are of the age of fifteen years or upwards, and duly qualified for that rite, you will give notice of such my intention in your parish church, on the Lord's day after you receive this letter; and also, at the same time, you will read an exhortation which accompanies this; and repeat it on the Lord's day immediately preceding the confirmation. You are likewise desired to distribute among those who are to be admitted to confirmation the few plain questions and answers on the subject of the sacred rite, of which I have sent what I hope will prove a sufficient number for your young parishioners. I earnestly recommend it to you to instruct them in private, as well as in public; and to exhort them to entertain a due sense of the obligations they are under to fulfil their baptismal vow; and of the happiness they will enjoy in this life, and be entitled to in a better, from a conscientious performance of those duties which necessarily result from a religious observance of the promises made at confirmation.

Acquaint those who are to be confirmed that it is expected they come to church with such dispositions as may lead them to behave with decency during the whole of the service; and to make the proper answers as directed in the liturgy; to depart orderly; and to return to their respective places of abode as early in the day as possible.

You will prepare a list of those persons whom you think qualified to partake of this rite, and deliver the same to my chaplain, before eight o'clock on the morning of the confirmation; and to each person in your list you are desired to give a ticket with his or her name written thereon, together with the name of your parish, in the following or like words, subscribed with your own name; *Examined and approved - A.B. rector, vicar, or curate of* —— which ticket each person must bring with him to the church; and without it none will, on any account, be admitted to confirmation.

There will be no prayers before the confirmation; but you are requested to attend yourself, with your parishioners, by eight o'clock in the morning, in some convenient place near the church, till the name of your parish be called; which will be done alphabetically.

I am, Reverend Sir,
Your sincere friend and brother
S. SARUM

20 May 1783

Places and times of visitation and confirmation.

July	19	Windsor	Saturday	Confirm
	20	Reading	Sunday	Confirm inhabitants
	21	ditto	Monday	Visit and confirm
	22	Newbury	Tuesday	Visit and confirm
	23	Wallingford	Wednesday	Confirm
	24	Abingdon	Thursday	Visit and confirm
	25	Farringdon	Friday	Confirm
	26	Swindon	Saturday	Confirm
	27	Marlborough	Sunday	Confirm inhabitants
	28	ditto	Monday	Visit and confirm
	29	Malmesbury	Tuesday	Confirm
	30	Chippenham	Wednesday	Visit and confirm
	31	Devizes	Thursday	Visit and confirm
Aug.	1	Bradford	Friday	Confirm
	2	Warminster	Saturday	Confirm
	3	Salisbury	Sunday	Confirm inhabitants
	4	ditto	Monday ⎱	Visit and confirm
	5	ditto	Tuesday ⎰	
	6	Ludgershall	Wednesday	Confirm
	7	Hungerford	Thursday	Confirm
	8	Wantage	Friday	Confirm

[*Queries, sent with the bishop's letter to each parish. The letters in square brackets have been added to the text of both queries and answers, for greater clarity.*]

Q.1. [a] How often and at what hours upon the Lord's day is divine service, both prayers and preaching, performed in your church or chapel? [b] If divine service be not performed twice every Lord's day, what is the reason?

Q.2. Is divine service performed in your church or chapel upon any weekdays, holidays, or festivals that happen on weekdays?

Q.3. Do you perform divine service as incumbent, or as curate, of your parish?

Q.4. [a] Do you serve any other cure? If so, what cure, and how many, and [b] at what distance are the cures you serve from one another? [c] Are you duly licensed to the cure which you serve?

Q.5. How often in the year is the holy sacrament of the Lord's Supper administered in your church or chapel? And at what times of the year?

Q.6. [a] What number of communicants have you, generally, in your parish? [b] In particular, what was the number which communicated at Easter last? [c] Was it greater or less than usual?

Q.7. [a] Are there any reputed papists in your parish, or chapelry, and how many and of what rank? [b] Have any persons been lately perverted to popery, and by whom and by what means? [c] Is there any place in your parish, or chapelry, in which they assemble for divine worship, and where is it? [d] Doth any popish priest reside in your parish, or resort to it? And by what name doth he go? [e] Is there any popish school kept in your parish?

Q.8. [a] Are there any Presbyterians, Independents, Anabaptists, or Quakers in your parish or chapelry? And how many of each sect? And of what rank? [b] Are there any other places made use of for divine worship, than such as are used by the above-mentioned sects? [c] What are the names of their teachers, and are they all licensed as the law directs? [d] Is their number greater or less of late years than formerly, according to your observation, and by what means? [e] Are there any persons in your parish who profess to disregard religion, or [f] who commonly absent themselves from all public worship of God?

Q.9. [a] Do your parishioners duly send their children and servants, who have not learned their catechism, to be instructed by you? [b] And do you either expound to them yourself, or make use of some printed exposition, and what is it? [c] At what particular seasons of the year, and in what language, are the young persons of your parish, or chapelry, catechized?

Q.10 [a] Have you a register book of births and burials duly kept, and in good preservation? [b] And do you regularly make your returns of births and burials into the registrar's office, as the canon requires? [c] How far back does your register of births and burials go?

Q.11. Is there a register book duly kept, according to the directions of the Act of Parliament against clandestine marriages?[1]

[1] Lord Hardwicke's Marriage Act, 1753, 26 Geo. II, c. 33.

Q.12. [a] Are there any chapels of ease in your parish? What are the names of them? [b] How often are there prayers and sermons in them? [c] Have they any estates or funds particularly appropriated to their maintenance? [d] How far distant are they from the parish church? [e] By whom are they served? [f] Have you any ruinated chapels in which there is no divine service performed?

Q.13. [a] Have you a true and perfect account or terrier of all houses, lands, tithes, pensions, and profits, which belong to you as minister of your parish? [b] Hath a duplicate thereof been laid up in the bishop's registry? [c] Hath there been, since that was done, any augmentation made of your living? [d] And hath an account of such augmentation been transmitted thither also?

Q.14. [a] Is there any free school, alms-house, hospital, or other charitable endowment in your parish? And for how many, and for what sort of persons? [b] Who was the founder? And who are the governors or trustees? [c] What are the revenues of it? Are they carefully preserved, and employed as they ought to be? Are the statutes and orders made concerning it well observed? [d] Have any lands or tenements been left for the repair of your church, or for any other pious use? [e] Who has the direction and management of such benefactions? And who takes an account of and conducts them?

Q.15. [a] Are the churchwardens in your parish chosen every year in the *Easter* week? [b] How are they chosen? By the minister and parishioners together, or one by the minister and the other by the parishioners?

Q.16. [a] Is there (or has there been founded) any public school in your parish? [b] Is there any charity school in your parish? How is it supported? By voluntary subscription, or by a settled endowment? Is it for boys or girls, and for how many? [c] What are the children taught? More particularly, [d] is care taken to instruct them in the principles of the Christian religion, and to bring them regularly to church? [e] And are they also lodged, fed, and clothed? [f] And how are they disposed of when they leave school? [g] Does your school flourish? And if not, for what reasons?

Q.17. [a] Do you constantly reside upon this cure, and in the house belonging to it? [b] If not, where, and at what distance from it, is your usual place of residence? [c] How long in each year are you absent? [d] And what is the reason for such absence?

Q.18. By whom, and to what uses, is the money given at the offertory disposed of?

Q.19. Is there any matter relating to your parish or chapelry of which it may be proper to give me information?

Q.20. What is your place of residence, and the nearest post town?

P.S. They who by illness, or any other just cause, are prevented from attending the visitation, are requested to send their answers by those persons who attend for them; or by the post, in covers, not weighing above two ounces, to the bishop, at *Mongewell-House*, Wallingford, Berks. It would be an additional satisfaction to the bishop, if his clergy, at the end of these queries, would write the dates of their collation, or institution; of their deacon's and priest's orders; and their degrees.

1 ALDBOURNE[2] f.1   D. Marlborough

1. The stated service on the Lord's day is prayers and sermon that begin at half past ten in the morning—second prayers in the afternoon. Service begins at three. But at my commencing curate I observed that the servants who could not attend in the morning were numerous, and hearing that formerly there used to be an afternoon sermon for which I was told £20 a year was allowed, I have constantly preached twice but never received any stipend.

2. On some holidays there is service performed, as in the weeks of the three great festivals. On Ash Wednesday and Good Friday I usually preach.

3. As curate. Stipend £40 a year out of which the curate pays the window tax. The vicarage house is considered as £10 a year.

4. I serve no other parish. I never thought myself adequate to the duty of one parish.

5. Every month, on the first Sunday, and on the three great festivals.

6. Above an hundred. At Easter last I believe we had eighty, more or less. I think the communicants are decreasing.

7. We have no papists or popish chapels.

8. We have no dissenters. No meetings whatever, in licensed houses; but I believe in one house a journeyman weaver called a Methodist reads to a few people, perhaps ten or a dozen, who all come to church. We have persons who may be said to be practical atheists, and we have a number of ragged poor who will not come to church unless they have decent apparel.

9. I cannot induce them to send young people to be instructed. I have vainly attempted it. The season for catechizing is the six Sundays in Lent. I have duly catechized, till this last Lent. As I proposed during the summer once more to endeavour to instruct them effectually by collecting them, if I could, in the vestry on week days, I omitted the Lent catechizing. I used no exposition but my own in the afternoon sermon.

10. The register is duly attended. The returns made regularly. The register goes back as far as 1636.

11. There is.

12. No chapels of ease.

13. Mr. Elderton[3] has a terrier. According to orders I drew up an exact terrier and sent it with the approbation of parishioners to the registrar to be signed by his son and to have a duplicate with the parish register, but [it] has not been returned.

14. There is a school over the church porch. Now disused. If any endowment it's lost. There is a benefaction of [blank] annually from Upham farm to be distributed by churchwardens. But I believe irregularities attend the distribution.

---

[2] Two separate letters, one addressed to 'Aldbourn' the other 'Aldbourne'. The return to the first, **1,** is made by the resident curate, to the second, **2,** by the vicar, resident in Bath, and also signed by the curate. The curate's return has a sad and disappointed tone; the vicar's is more cheerful and praises the curate's zeal. There are no serious discrepancies between the two returns.

[3] The vicar, John Elderton, 1756–1832. Trinity Coll. Oxford 1771. Son of Joseph Elderton, diocesan registrar. Curate of Monkton Farleigh, **144.**

15. The minister chooses one, the parish the other churchwarden annually in Easter week.

16. None. The brutal ignorance of the labouring people induced me to attempt to found and endow a reading, writing, and working school for poor families. I began a building, but I had not powers to finish my design, but brought trouble on myself by the undertaking.

17. I have constantly resided in the vicar's house.

18. We never have a farthing given, neither can I persuade the officers of the parish ever to approach the communion.

19. I have many. But I doubt my judgement with respect to propriety.

20. Aldbourn, Wilts. Ramsbury nearest post town.

29 October 1783. James Neale[4] of Pembroke Hall, Cambridge Took the degree of M.A. July 1743. Ord. D. by Dr. Gibson, bishop of London, and licensed 10 March 1744. Ord. P. by Dr. Secker, archbishop of Canterbury, 2 June 1751.

Next March 1784 a curate 40 years.

2 ALDBOURNE f.9   D. Marlborough

1. The customary service is prayers and sermon in the forenoon half past ten; in the afternoon prayers only at three; there used to be £20 a year formerly allowed by the parish for a sermon in the afternoon, but the present curate who hath resided for eleven years last past hath voluntarily preached a sermon in the afternoon (as well as the forenoon) without any stipend or allowance for the same.

2. The present curate ever since he came to Aldborne hath performed divine service and preached sermons on Christmas day, Good Friday, and Ash Wednesday, and performed divine service (without a sermon) on two other days in Christmas week, Easter week, and Whitsun week.

3. The present curate performs divine service as curate and has resided eleven years in that capacity in the vicarage house.

4. He serves no other cure; hath no particular licence to serve this cure; hath been in priest's orders and officiated for about thirty years.

5. The holy sacrament of the Lord's Supper is duly administered in this parish church on Christmas day, Easter day, Whitsunday, and the first Sunday in every month of the year.

6. There were only thirty communicants when the present curate entered on this cure, but now and for ten years past there have been and are one hundred communicants and upwards; though it so happened that a less number, not many more than eighty, communicated last Easter.

7. There is not one papist or reputed papist known of in this populous parish.

8. No professed sectary or dissenter from the established church is at present declaredly so in this parish: about 23 years ago there was a congregation of Independents; their place of divine worship was then burnt down and never was rebuilt. The members came to the parish church and have continued to do so. There are numbers of the poor who refrain from attending the public

---

[4] 1722–92. Pembroke Coll. Cambridge 1739. Classical and biblical scholar: *D.N.B.*

service from want of raiment—some who are habitual Sabbath breakers. The farmers and people of good condition, in point of circumstance, are constant frequenters of the public service.

9. The parishioners do not duly send their children and servants who have or have not learned their catechism to be instructed. The curate occasionally expounds the catechism in an afternoon's sermon; during the six Sundays in Lent, the children of the parish are catechized, agreeable to the rubric, in the vulgar tongue.

10. There is a parish register book of births and burials duly kept in the parish church and in good preservation, and due return is made of births and burials into the registrar's office. The register books go back as far as 1636.

11. There is.

12. There is no chapel of ease or ruinated chapel in this parish.

13. Knows of no terrier in parish preservation but there is a full and perfect terrier, or terriers, in the bishop's registry.

14. Over the church porch there is a room, with a fireplace and forms, where, formerly, a school used to be kept; but there is no trace of any endowment thereof, if such there ever was.

15. The churchwardens in this parish are chosen every year in the Easter week, one by the minister and the other by the parishioners.

16. There is no public or charity school in this parish.

17. The present curate constantly resides in the vicarial house, and has resided therein for eleven years last past. The vicar resides at Bath, and serves the cure of Monkton Farley, near Bath, in the diocese of Sarum, for Mr. Peter Gunning, the rector.

18. Although there has been so considerable an increase of communicants since Mr. Neale came to this parish, there has been no offertory; and he is sorry to mention that the farmers in general, or very few of them, or the churchwardens, do not accustom themselves to receive the sacrament.

19. None that occurs materially to the recollection.

20. The nearest post town to Aldborne is Ramsbury near Marlborough.

John Elderton, vicar of Aldbourn

James Neale A.M., curate of Aldbourn

John Elderton, of Trinity College Oxford, ord. D. by the bishop of Sarum at his palace 28 September, 1772. Ord. P. by the bishop of London at the Chapel Royal 30 May 1773.

James Neale ord. D. by Edmund, bishop of London, at London 10 March 1744. Ord. P. by Thomas, bishop of Oxford, at Christchurch, Oxford, 2 June 1751.

3 ALLINGTON f.25   D. Amesbury

1. At half after eleven and half past three. Never has been served twice a day.

2. Christmas day, Good Friday, fast days, and thanksgiving days.

3. As a curate.[5]
4. Amesbury, three miles and half distance. Not licensed.
5. Christmas, Easter, and Whitsuntide.
6. Four or five the usual number. Last Easter [blank].
7 & 8. All of the established church.
9. Those who attend are usually catechized in Lent.
10. [a] We have a proper register book. [c] No further back than 1766.
11. There is such a book kept.
12. No such thing.
13. The rector is absent, I am but lately come to the curacy and cannot properly answer this question.
14. No such things.
15. Only one churchwarden. Chosen by the parish.
16. No such things.
17. My place of residence is at Amesbury, three miles and half distance.
18. No money given.
19. Nothing.
20. Amesbury, Wilts.
   I have been ordained about four years.

Henry Lewis[6]

4 ALL CANNINGS f.33   D. Avebury
1. Twice. Prayers with sermon at 11 in morning and prayers at 4 in afternoon.
2. On the principal feasts and fasts.
3. As incumbent.
4. No other cure.
5. Four times. Easter day, Whitsunday, 1st Sunday after Michaelmas, and Christmas day.
6. About thirty.
7. None that I know of.
8. None particularly that I know of.
9. The children are publicly examined in the church six Sundays every year beginning generally on Trinity Sunday.
10. There are register books duly kept, and returns regularly made.
11. A register book according to the Act of Parliament.
12. One at Etchilhampton, one mile distant from All Cannings, served by the Rev. Mr. George Jaques[7] twice each Sunday from Lady day to Michaelmas and once from Michaelmas to Lady day.
13. A terrier delivered up. No augmentation.
14. None.

---

[5] Rector, Lucy Berkeley. Probably New Coll. Oxford 1733; resident rector of Great Witley and rector of Acton Beauchamp, Worcs. Lord Craven, patron of Allington, was related to the Berkeley family: *Complete Peerage.*

[6] Curate of Amesbury, **6.**

[7] Hertford Coll. Oxford 1766. Son of Henry Jacques, curate of Poulshot, **159**; rector of Hazelbury, worth £12 *per annum*, church demolished: Clergy Books, 1783.

15. One by minister, one by the parish.

16. None.

17. I reside part of the year in the parsonage house, the dampness of the situation not agreeing with my constitution, and I keep a constant resident curate.

18. None collected.

19. None.

20. All Cannings near Devizes.

John Fullerton LL.B.[8] Ord. D. 26 April 1755. Ord. P. 27 July 1755. Instituted 12 June 1770.

5 ALTON BARNES f.41   D. Avebury

1. I perform divine service twice every Sunday, which in the morning usually begins at eleven o'clock, in the afternoon at three.

2. I perform divine service on the holidays at the three great festivals and on Good Friday.

3. As incumbent.

4. None.

5. Four times, viz. at Christmas, Easter, and Whitsuntide, and on the first Sunday after Michaelmas.

6. There are generally from nine to twelve communicants and as far as I can recollect nine at Easter last.

7. None.

8. None. The people generally attend the public worship of God and seem not to show any disregard to religion.

9. The parishioners have not regularly sent their children and servants for instruction; the more respectable part have no children; the lower part are not taught to read.

10. Yes. The register goes back as far as the year 1593.

11. Yes.

12. None.

13. There is no terrier of the living in my possession nor has it been possible to make one at present, the ground being covered with corn.

14. None.

15. There is one churchwarden chosen annually by my consent and approbation.

16. None.

17. During the short time I have been the incumbent of this parish I have resided eight months in each year and in the parsonage house.

18. No offertory.

19. None.

20. At Alton Barnes near Devizes.

[8] Emmanuel Coll. Cambridge 1749.

John Brereton A.M.[9] rector of Alton Barnes
I was ord. D. 20 Dec. 1767. Ord. P. 18 Dec. 1768 by the lord bishop of Oxford at Christchurch, Oxford, and instituted to the rectory 3 June 1778.

J.B.

6 AMESBURY f.49   D. Amesbury

1. The service is performed at Amesbury little before ten in the morning and at two in evening.
2. Christmas day, Good Friday, fast days, and thanksgiving days.
3. As curate.[1]
4. Allington, three miles and half distance. Not licensed.
5. Christmas, Easter, and Whitsuntide.
6. Four or five and twenty the usual number, but last Easter and Whitsuntide above thirty.
7 & 8. All of the established church.
9. Those who attend are always catechized once or twice in Lent.
10. [a] We have a proper register book. [c] No further back than 1757.
11. There is such a book kept.
12. No such thing.
13. There is neither parsonage house nor glebe land, but a small vicarage house.
14. No such things.
15. The minister choose one, the parish the other churchwarden in Easter week.
16. No such things.
17. I live in the house belonging to this cure.
18. To the poor of the parish.
19. Nothing.
20. At Amesbury, Wilts.
I have been ordained about four years.

Henry Lewis[2]

7 ASHLEY f.57   D. Malmesbury

1. Once, at ten o'clock in the morning.
2. Never.
3. Curate.[3]
4. [a] Malmesbury. [c] I am.
5. Three times, viz. Christmas, Easter, and Whitsuntide.
6. Four. The same number every time since I served it.
7. None. No place. No popish priest or school.
8. [a] Not one dissenter in the parish of any denomination. [e] Not any that I know of.

[9] Queen's Coll. Oxford 1762.
[1] Clergy Books, 1783, give Henry Richards as perpetual curate (possibly Exeter Coll. Oxford 1763) and Mr. Lewis as sub-curate.
[2] See **3.**
[3] H. Strong: see **133.**

9. I read catechetical lectures in Lent. I catechize the children in Lent.
10. The register book is in good preservation.
11. I have not seen any.
12. None.
13. There is an old terrier lodged in the registrar's court. No augmentation.
14. None.
15. Only one churchwarden.
16. None.
17. I reside at Malmesbury.
18. The money is given.
19. I do not know of any.
20. Malmesbury, which is a post town.
 Thomas Ripley A.M.,[4] rector of Ashley. Ord. D. 11 June 1775 and ord. P. 26 May 1777. Instituted to Ashley 18 March 1782.

8 ASHTON KEYNES f.65   D. Cricklade
My Lord,
 As the Rev. Mr. Thomas, the present curate,[5] has lately been at Oxford to keep terms for his degree and is obliged to go from thence to Wales on business, have taken upon myself to answer the following queries according to the best of my knowledge, from information I have received from him and the parishioners.
 I am, my Lord, your most dutiful son and servant
 T. Wickes.
1. Prayers and preaching are performed every Sunday morning at 10 o'clock and prayers every Sunday afternoon from Lady day to Michaelmas. Prayers and preaching also at the chapel of the Leigh once every Sunday throughout the year.
2. Divine service is performed in the church upon all holidays and festivals.
3. Divine service is performed by the Rev. Mr. Thomas, curate.
4. He serves no other cure and is not licensed, as he intends to leave it soon.
5. The sacrament of the Lord's Supper is administered four times in the year.
6. There are generally between 20 and 30 communicants.
7. There are no reputed papists in the parish.
8. Nor Presbyterians, Independents, Anabaptists, nor Quakers but great numbers who absent themselves from all public worship.
9. The curate catechizes all such children and servants as are sent to him for that purpose every Wednesday and Friday in Lent.
10. There is a parish register book of births and burials.
11. And also a register book for marriages, according to the Act of Parliament.
12. There is one chapel called the Leigh; prayers and preaching are performed there once every Sunday throughout the year by the curate of Ashton Keynes. It is one computed mile distant from Ashton Keynes.
13. I have an attested copy of a terrier made in the years 1683 and 1704, taken

---

[4] 1752–1813. St. John's Coll. Cambridge 1771.
[5] Clergy Books, 1783, give 'Mr. Campbell' as curate. Mr. Thomas appears to be only temporary: see answer 4.

from the bishop's registry; by which it appears that there were at that time
8 tenements or houses belonging to the vicarage; all which, through the
carelessness or neglect of former incumbents, have been possessed by different
persons for many years, upon payment of 3 or 4 shillings yearly, though
worth as many pounds; some of which have also been sold by word of mouth,
and descended from father to son, without any other contract, lease, or title
than the above verbal agreement. By virtue of an Act of Parliament passed
in the year 1777[6] there was an inclosure of a large common and by which the
value of the living was much augmented, and almost a general exchange of
the vicar's glebe lands, but no terrier or account of these has been yet transmitted to the bishop's registry and it will require much time and pains to get
a true account of them.
14. [a] There is no free school, alms-house, nor hospital that I know of in the
parish. [d] It appears by the terrier that there was a church house belonging
to the maintenance of the church, out of which was paid only 2 shillings per
year to the lord of the manor; which house was taken down about six years
ago by the lord of the manor and no consideration has been paid for it.
There was likewise a small parcel of land belonging to the same.
15. The churchwardens of the parish are chosen every year in the Easter week,
one by the minister and the other by the parishioners.
16. There is no public school nor charity school in the parish.
17. The curate constantly resides in the parish, near the church, except when
he keeps terms at Oxford.
18. [Blank]
19. [Blank]
20. I reside at Tetbury in the county of Glocester.

T. Wickes[7]

T. Wickes B.A., A.M., D.D. Ord. D. 21 Aug. 1748. Ord. P. 21 July 1751.
Instituted to the vicarage of Tetbury in the county of Glocester 29 Jan 1778.
Ditto to the vicarage of Ashton Keynes, Wilts., 13 May 1783.

9 AVEBURY f.73   D. Avebury
1. Divine service—prayers and preaching—once every Lord's day alternately
with the church of Winterborne Monkton, united to Avebury *per favor* of the
Lord Chancellor Hardwicke, the patron of both, and Dr. Sherlock, diocesan
—at the expense of the present incumbent (near £100) about the year 1747[8]
—both churches being so situate—at the distance of 3 quarters of a mile from
each other—that the inhabitants of both parishes may conveniently attend
the services of both churches—the present bishop of Bath and Wells—then
rector of Compton—being one of the commissioners.[9]
2. Prayers and homilies read on weekdays after the three principal festivals
—as also on some other holy days. [*Continues on a separate sheet attached to
the return.*] To be added to A. 2nd. About the year 1740 Whitfield and the

[6] 17 Geo. III, c. 139.
[7] Thomas Croome Wickes, patron and incumbent; Pembroke Coll. Oxford 1743.
[8] Union dated 24 April 1747: Sarum Dioc. R.O., Diocese book.
[9] Charles Moss, rector of Compton Bassett 1743–50.

Wesleys broke forth from the University, and—compassing heaven and earth to gain proselytes—maintained, among other things, in their preachings, that the Church of England, or rather the *clergy* of the Church of England, had totally departed from the pure doctrine of the Gospel, and particularly those that were contained in her homilies—which, as they and their followers asserted, were wholly laid aside and absolutely sunk into oblivion—to obviate which objection, as far at least as respected myself, the obsolete usage or practice or custom of reading homilies, on certain occasions, in the church, was revived, with good effect, by me, who was then curate to my father, at Avebury—an essential blow being thereby given to the growth and establishment of Methodism in that parish. James Mayo, vicar, 28 July 1783.

3. I perform the divine service of this church as incumbent.

4. I serve no other church or cure but the united church of Winterborne Monkton as above mentioned.

5. The holy sacrament is administered in this church four times in the year viz. Christmas, Easter, Whitsuntide, or the next Sunday after according as the alternate service happens, and the nearest Sunday to St. Michael, before or after.

6. The number of communicants in this parish is generally about 40—which was nearly the number at Easter last—and has been nearly the same during the course of 40 years last past.

7. There are no reputed papists in this parish—there have been no persons lately perverted to popery—no place in this parish where papists assemble for divine worship—no popish priest—no popish school in this parish.

8. There are no Presbyterians, Anabaptists, or Quakers in this parish—two or three families (one of the rank of farmers, the others poor) who may be said to be of the Independent denomination who would have dwindled and sunk to nothing long before this time had it not been for the unseasonable encouragement and support unfortunately given them, some years ago, by that arch-miser old Caleb Bailey[1] of Barwick, in this neighbourhood, who, when he could keep his unrighteous Mammon no longer, by his last will and testament, bequeathed all his personals, to a considerable amount, in trust for the purpose of supporting meeting-houses of the Independent denomination, particular regard being had to this at Avebury. The present teacher's name is Davis, an inhabitant of the town of Marlborough—whether licensed or not I cannot learn. There is also one other unlicensed house occasionally made use of for preaching by a person whose name is Winter,[2] who is also an inhabitant of the town of Marlborough—some years ago, if I mistake not, expelled from some hall in Oxford—of the sect called Methodists, who maintain that they are predestinated and elected and therefore must and shall, most certainly and unconditionally, be saved without works or without any labour or application of their own—the great enemy of souls of course assisting them in gaining proselytes—yet am happy to inform your Lordship that of this sect the number is far less than formerly, owing, I trust, in some measure to my

[1] Bequest in 1749 to help those 'who shall preach or study to be fit to preach to congregations of the Presbyterian, Baptist, or Independent denominations': *V.C.H. Wilts.* iii. 123.

[2] Cornelius Winter, a convert of Whitefield's: *V.C.H. Wilts.* iii. 131 sqq. See **136**.

attending to the advice of Dr. Sherlock, when my diocesan, concerning these men, viz. that we should refrain from them and let them alone, rather *living* than *preaching* against them—'giving none occasion to the adversary to speak reproachfully, and taking diligent heed, in all things, that the ministry be not blamed.' There are 4 persons in this parish who, though not professedly, yet by their life and conversation, disregard religion, and who therefore commonly absent themselves from all public worship, viz. one who was formerly an alehouse-keeper or landlord, and 3 others who now live in that abandoned state and who, as we may suppose, are against all religion because all religion is against them—which remarkable instance plainly evinced the truth of the observation, often made, namely that alehouses are the bane of the nation, both with regard to the spiritual as well as temporal estate of the inhabitants thereof—as the keepers of them must, of necessity, be the patrons and promotors—the examples, abettors, and encouragers of all irreligion and iniquity in order to support themselves and families. What a pity it is then that the government of so good and pious a prince, whose rectitude of mind and integrity of heart must make him abhor and detest all manner of vice and wickedness, cannot be supported without giving so much countenance to the enemies of religion, by granting so many licences to public houses.

9. Finding that those of my parishioners who keep *servants* could not be prevailed on so far as to use their influence and authority as to cause them to attend on catechizing, I have been obliged to content myself with instructing children only—after the second lesson in the afternoon, on the Lord's day, in the summer season, making use of no printed exposition, but expounding and explaining extempore, or rather memoriter from Archbishop Wake, Bishop Burnet, etc. and endeavouring to lead them to an understanding thereof by means of the *Catechism broke into Short Questions*, the author of which was—as I think I have been informed—a clergyman of this neighbourhood. [3]

10. A register book of births and burials is duly kept, and returns regularly made of births and burials into the registrar's office—or at least at the visitation—but not always so well authenticated as they ought to be by being signed by the minister and churchwardens, as the canon, I think, requires—and without which they are of no great weight in a court of justice.

11. A register book, according to the directions of the Act of Parliament against clandestine marriages, is duly kept.

12. There are no chapels of ease in the parish.

13. The copy of a terrier of the house, lands, tithes, etc. belonging to me, as the minister of this parish, extracted out of the registry of the lord bishop of Sarum, bearing date 5 May 1682, is now in my possession—but as there have been some alterations and improvements made in the lands of late years,

---

[3] Two widely used expositions of the Catechism, William Wake's *Principles of the Christian Religion explained, in a brief commentary on the Church Catechism* (1700), and Gilbert Burnet's *Exposition of the Church Catechism for the use of the diocese of Sarum* (1710), are frequently mentioned in the answers to this query. *The Catechism broke into short questions* was perhaps by James Stonhouse, rector of Great Cheverell and author of a number of religious tracts. See **123**. 13.

by means of an exchange, a more true and perfect terrier shall be transmitted to the registry as soon as it can be prepared.

14. There is no free school—properly so called—no alms-house, no hospital, or any other endowment of that sort, in this parish. No lands or tenements left for the repair of the church—or any other pious use.

15. The churchwardens, in this parish, are generally chosen every year in the Easter week, with very few exceptions for many years past, one by the minister, the other by the parish.

16. There is no public school, properly so called, in this parish, only a small charity school, supported partly by voluntary subscriptions, partly by a settled endowment—the whole about £8 per annum—for 8 boys and 8 girls —or rather 16 children whether boys or girls—who are taught and instructed in reading, writing, and in the grounds and principles of the Christian religion —care being taken, by the master, to bring them regularly to church.

17. After spending the greatest part of my youth, for near twenty years, in a constant residence at Avebury, I have, by the indulgence of my diocesans, particularly Dr. Thomas and Dr. Hume (which indulgence I now humbly pray for a continuancy of from your Lordship) resided, for some years past, in this town of Calne, in consequence of my being honoured with a nomination or appointment to an endowed school here (salary £50 per annum) of which Lord Shelburne, Sir Edward Bayntun, Sir James Long, Mr. Ambrose Goddard, Mr. Heneage, etc. are the trustees, and which I was, as it were, under an indispensable necessity of accepting, and of submitting to the laborious employment of school teaching, for the support of a numerous family, consisting of no less than 14 children. Whom God preserve! and towards whom, together with their tender and affectionate mother, I humbly presume most earnestly to entreat your Lordship to look hereafter with a charitable and compassionate eye—when it shall please God to remove me from them—as I am advancing in years—as the high price of provisions and the great burthen of taxes render my income comparatively small—as many of my children are young, and must, without an uncommon interposition of the divine providence, be left unprovided for—my present income being scarce adequate for the most economical disbursements.

18. The money given at the offertory is disposed of by the minister, chiefly to the aged poor and needy, particular regard being had to those who frequent the communion—not absolutely excluding the sick, at the same time, who appear to be in great distress though perhaps they may not have been communicants—especially if they are disposed to become such during their illness.

19. If any other matter relating to this parish should hereafter occur of which it may be proper to give your Lordship information, the opportunity and encouragement intimated in this query of communicating the same to your Lordship, from time to time, and in due time, will be thought an honour by, my Lord, your Lordship's most dutiful and most faithful humble servant,

James Mayo, vicar of the united churches of Avebury and
Winterborne Monkton
Calne, 24 July 1783

20. Calne, a post town between Marlborough and Chippenham, Wilts.

First instituted to the vicarage of Avebury in the year 1746—but proceeding no further in the university than the degree of B.A.—consequently not being qualified to apply for a dispensation—the vicarages of Avebury and Monkton *united* being at the same time considered as above value in the King's Book— was re-instituted to Avebury with Monkton—on a cession or rather avoidance, occasioned by my possessing myself of the small rectory of Ditcharidge, otherwise Ditchbridge—by instrument bearing date 1 July 1767.[4] Deacon's orders bearing date 17 June 1739. Priest's orders bearing date 25 Sept 1743.

James Mayo A.B.[5]

10 BARFORD ST. MARTIN f.81   D. Chalke

1. Prayers and a sermon every Sunday morning at 11 o'clock, and prayers at $\frac{1}{2}$ past 2 o'clock in the afternoon.
2. Service is performed on all the great festivals, but not on any other common weekdays.
3. I perform it as incumbent.
4. I serve no other cure but my own church.
5. Four times in every year, Easter, Whitsuntide, Michaelmas, and Christmas.
6. The number last time about 30, which is more than double what used to be.
7. None that I know of.
8. There are no dissenters that I know of, but several profligate people who do not attend divine service.
9. My custom is to catechize the children in Lent, and the better sort of the inhabitants send their children to church for that purpose.
10. I have a register book of the births and burials, but not legible farther back than 1632.
11. There is a book kept according to the Act.
12. There are no chapels of ease in my parish, nor any funds for that purpose.
13. I have made out as correct a terrier as I could of the mansion and lands belonging to the living; no augmentation since.
14. No free school, alms-house, or hospital. There is a benefaction of £5 a year paid by Lord Pembroke for the repair of the church.
15. Every Easter Tuesday. One by the minister, the other by the parish.
16. There is no school in the parish.
17. I constantly reside in the parsonage house.
18. The money is disposed of by the minister, to help the industrious inhabitants, who keep themselves from the parish.
19. None that I recollect.
20. Barford near Wilton.[6]

---

[4] Under the Canons of 1604 an M.A. was required as a justification for a dispensation for plurality. An Act of 1529 (21 Hen. VIII, c. 13) required the holder of a benefice of the annual value of £8 or more to obtain a dispensation to hold a second benefice. The value of the second benefice was immaterial. The combined value of Avebury and Winterbourne Monkton in the King's Book was £14; Ditteridge, £2 8s. 9d.
[5] Queen's Coll. Oxford 1734.
[6] No signature; rector, John Honywood.

11 BAVERSTOCK f.97 D. Chalke

[*Written across the foot of the first page:*] No queries, directions, or other papers having been sent from your Lordship, or at least none having come to the minister of Compton Chamberlaine, I therefore include Compton in these answers.[7] The chapelry of Ansty has an exempt jurisdiction and is a perpetual curacy.

1. Prayers and preaching once only from custom, as well as at Compton Chamberlaine and at Ansty. Morning and evening service at each of these hours in this order: Baverstock at 10, Compton at half after eleven, Ansty $\frac{1}{2}$ after two; alternate, Ansty $\frac{1}{2}$ after 10, Baverstock at one, Ansty [*recte?* Compton] $\frac{1}{2}$ after two.

2. Service at Compton 3 days after Christmas, 2 days after Easter Sunday, and Whitsunday, and on Good Friday.

3. As curate of Compton, Baverstock, and Ansty.

4. I serve Baverstock, Compton $1\frac{1}{2}$ mile from it, and Ansty near 5 miles from each. I have no licence.

5. Four times at each: at Christmas, Easter, Whitsunday, and Michaelmas.

6. At Baverstock at Easter 13. At Compton as near as I can recollect about 20. At Ansty about 20.

7. There is no papist either in Baverstock or Compton.

8. There are no dissenters or sectarists of any denomination in Baverstock or Compton. At Ansty some reputed papists, the chapelry being in the neighbourhood of Wardour,[8] where they resort to worship, but all of low degree. A woman a reputed papist keeps a school but teaches only the children of reputed papists. I don't know that I have had more than two perverted to popery in 25 years, and they married papists. Their number in all is 47.

9. I catechize in each of my cures, have constantly done it every year for 25 past at Ansty. I frequently give the catechumens different printed expositions suited to their different ages, and expound the catechism from the pulpit to them and the congregation. The exposition partly collated and partly my own.

10. There is a register of births and burials in each parish. Compton commences from 1538, Baverstock from 1714. Annual returns are made.

11. Yes.

12. No.

13. This I can't answer.

14. None.

15. There is only one churchwarden in each parish chosen at Easter by the parish.

16. No public or charity school in either.

17. No, I reside near 4 miles from Ansty and near 9 from Baverstock and Compton. I am never absent more than one Sunday in a year and not in every year.

18. There are no offerings at the communion.

[7] A return for Compton Chamberlayne, **55**, was, however, made by the rector. There are no serious discrepancies between the two returns.
[8] Seat of the Catholic Lord Arundell.

19. [Blank]
20. Donhead near Shaftesbury.
   Ord. D. at Oxford 1756. Ord. P. at Sarum 1758. A.B. Merton College 1756.[9]
   On sending the citation and directions relating to the terrier to the rector of
Baverstock I received the following answer, which I copy, 'I beg leave to
return the latter with this particular request, that you will be pleased to
promise that it shall be executed, if necessarily required from the rector so far
distant from Baverstock, as soon as an accurate survey of the premises can be
effected. To be present at his Lordship's primary visitation is impossible.
                     E. May,[1] Ilfracombe near Barnstaple, Devon'

12 BERWICK ST. JAMES f.105   D. Wylye
1. Divine service is performed once every Lord's day both prayers and
preaching at 11 in the morning and 2 in the afternoon alternately. It has never
been customary to perform service oftener.
2. It has never been customary to perform divine service on any weekdays
except Christmas day when it falls on a weekday.
3. As curate.[2]
4. I serve Stapleford about a mile from Berwick. I have no licence.
5. The sacrament is administered at Christmas, Easter, and Whitsuntide.
6. About 16 commonly at Easter which is nearly the whole number of
communicants.
7. None.
8. None.
9. I have catechized and prepared the children and servants for confirmation.
It has not been customary for the parishioners to send them to me at any
particular season for that purpose.
10. There is a register of marriages kept according to the Act of Parliament.
[This is the answer to No. 11, misplaced.]
11. [Blank]
12. None.
13. None.
14. None.
15. There is one churchwarden chosen by the parish.
16. None.
17. I reside in Salisbury, 8 miles from Berwick.
18. None collected.
19. None.

[9] No signature. Curate, Thomas Smith; Merton Coll. Oxford 1751.
[1] Emmanuel May, 1736–1804. Exeter Coll. Oxford 1753. Vicar of Ilfracombe. Clergy Books,
   1783, have the following note for this parish: 'Rector non-resident. House in very bad
   condition. Complaints of neglect. Curate's stipend said to be small, and time of service
   inconvenient.'
[2] Vicar, James Burch. Perhaps Balliol Coll. Oxford 1754.

20. Salisbury, 8 miles from Berwick.

George Trenchard,[3] curate
Ord. D. by the bishop of Oxford 20 Dec. 1778. Ord. P. by ditto 21 May 1780.

13 BERWICK ST. JOHN f.115[4]   D. Chalke

1. Twice on Sundays, viz. at half past ten and at three in the afternoon.
2. On the two holidays after Christmas day, on Good Friday, on the Monday after Easter, and after Whitsunday.
3. As incumbent.
4. I serve no other.
5. On Christmas day, the first Sunday in Lent, on Easter day and Whitsunday, at Michaelmas, and sometimes about 5 November.
6. Between twenty and thirty usually.
7. None, but the Hon. Mr. Arundell only.
8. There are several Presbyterians in the parish, but no place of divine worship for them, or any other sectaries.
9. The children come regularly to be catechized, after Whitsuntide, when the days are long, and I make use of an exposition drawn up by myself.
10. I have a register book of births and burials, from which I make returns regularly into the office, beginning from 1550.
11. There is.
12. None.
13. I have, and a duplicate thereof hath been sent to the bishop's registry. And no augmentation hath been of late made.
14. There is not any free school, alms-house, or hospital in the parish.
15. Of the two churchwardens chosen at Easter, one is chosen by the minister and the other by the parishioners.
16. There is no such public school.
17. I reside in my parish, constantly, except a few weeks perhaps at Bath, for the benefit of my health.
18. There is no collection made.
19. None at all.
20. At Berwick St. John near Shaftesbury.

Ed. Rolle,[5] instituted in 1755. Ord. D. in 1731, ord. P. in 1732. And B.D. in 1771.

14 BERWICK ST. LEONARD f.121   D. Chalke

1. Divine service, both prayers and preaching, is performed once in the day, generally about noon, at Berwick St. Leonard, and once every Lord's day in the chapel of Sedgehill which is annexed to it.[6] The parish of Berwick St. Leonard consists of only a farm-house and three or four cottages, and is very near to Hindon and Fonthill Bishop.

[3] Perhaps Merton Coll. Oxford 1773.
[4] Letter missing.
[5] Edward Rolle, 1705–91. New Coll. Oxford 1723. *Alum. Oxon.* gives B.D. in 1758.
[6] Served by a different curate: see **173.**

2. Only on Sundays.
3. As curate.[7]
4. Two others: Fonthill Gifford and Fonthill Bishop. The latter parish adjoins to Berwick St. Leonard, and the churches are only half a mile asunder. Not licensed by the bishop.
5. Four times: at Easter, Whitsuntide, Michaelmas, and Christmas.
6. [a] Seldom more than five or six. [b] The usual number attended.
7. None.
8. None. [e] There are none.
9. There are at present only three or four children in the parish, and those in their infancy.
10. [a] I have. [b] I do. [c] The register of births goes back to the year 1723; the register of burials to the same period.
11. There is.
12. None.
13. I have not, and must leave the question to the rector.
14. None.
15. The parish being so very small, there is seldom more than one church-warden chosen, which is in the Easter week.
16. None.
17. [a] I do not. [b] At Chicklade, an adjoining parish to this and the two Fonthills. [c] Never absent longer than a few days.
18. As the communicants consist chiefly of the lower class of people, it has not been the custom to collect any money.
19. No other matter that I know.
20. Chicklade, near Hindon.
                    John Thaine Frowd,[8] curate of Berwick St. Leonard
     Ord. D. 25 Sept. 1774 and ord. P. 22 Sept. 1776.

15 BEECHINGSTOKE [Betchingstoke] f.129   D. Avebury
1. Once a day at half past ten or two o'clock.
2. On all festivals and holidays when I think there is a probability of having any congregation.
3. As incumbent.
4. I serve the cure of Huish, distant six miles from Stoke.
5. Four times in the year. At Christmas, Easter, Whitsunday, and Michael-mas.
6. From eight to twelve persons. At Easter last the number was nearly the same as usual.
7. There are none.
8. There are none.
9. [a] They do not. [c] In the summer season; in the English language.
10. [a, b] I have a register book regularly kept. [c] To the year 1671.
11. There is a register book as required by the Act of Parliament.

[7] Rector, Michael Bridges; resides in Norfolk: Clergy Books, 1783. 1718–1807. St. John's Coll. Cambridge 1737. In 1783 he was incumbent of three Norfolk parishes.
[8] 1752–1826. Oriel Coll. Oxford 1770.

12. There are none.
13. I have not. If required I will provide a terrier at a season when the land can be properly measured. There has been no augmentation.
14. There is none.
15. They are. One by the minister and one by the parishioners.
16. There is none.
17. I do.
18. By myself to objects that I deem worthy.
19. There is none.
20. Bechingstoke near Devizes.
    Charles Mayo LL.B. [9] Instituted to the rectory of Bechingstoke 7 Feb. 1779. Ord. P. March 1775.

Charles Mayo

16 BIDDESTONE f.137   D. Malmesbury
    The Visitation at Chippenham, Wednesday 30 July.
1. At eleven o'clock and three alternately. This service has always been usual, the benefice very small.
2. Only the greater festivals, and that since my own incumbency, the inhabitants being engaged in their daily labour.
3. As incumbent.
4. I serve another small cure, my own likewise at about 4 miles distance, viz. Littleton Drew.
5. At Easter, Whitsuntide, Michaelmas, and Christmas.
6. About twenty. They are increased nearly double.
7. No.
8. Few or no dissenters but more who absent themselves.
9. In general they do. I expound to them myself in the mother tongue yearly between Easter and Whitsuntide.
10. The register books are regularly kept and the returns regularly made by myself. The oldest register of Bidstone I know goes back to the year 1688. That of Slaughterford to 1700.
11. There is.
12. No chapels of ease. Two ruinated chapels, one at Bidstone St. Peter, the other at Slaughterford.
13. I have with the assistance of the respectable part of the parishioners obtained (I believe) a much more certain terrier than any preceding and which is here sent. But some deficiences remain with respect to the discrimination of the distinct (though indeed inconsiderable) parish of Bidstone St. Peter. No augmentation, though till I took to it the whole hath not exceeded in general £35 per annum. It is since raised, during a *temporary* agreement.
14. None.
15. Yearly at Easter. One by the minister, the other by the parishioners.
16. No.
17. There is no parsonage house but a cottage set forth in the terrier. I reside

[9] 1751–1829. Queen's Coll. Oxford 1767. Rector of Huish, **106.**

about a mile distant at Corsham alms-house, where I read daily prayers to the almspeople (in number six) and attend to instruct such a limited number of free boys as shall offer my salary—£20 per annum. But the better sort of people are above the charity and the lower unable to afford the loss of their children's labour.

18. These offerings were introduced here by the present incumbent who distributes them in beef to 20 poor families at Christmas.

19. Not that I now recollect.

20. At Corsham near Chippenham, Wilts.

Charles Page[1]

Degree and deacon's orders (I believe) 1761. Priest's orders 1766. Institution 1766. Collation 1774.   C.P.

17 BISHOPSTROW f.145   D. Wylye

1. Divine service is performed twice every Lord's day unless anything very particular happens to prevent it. Prayers in the morning at half past ten, prayers and preaching in the afternoon about half past two.

2. Divine service is generally performed in my church on holidays, if a sufficient number appear to make a congregation; which does not always happen as I often meet only the clerk at the church. Passion week is regularly observed, with a sermon on Good Friday.

3. I perform divine service as incumbent.

4. I do not serve any other cure.

5. The holy sacrament is administered four times in the year: Christmas day, Easter day, Whitsunday, and the Sunday next after St. Michael.

6. The number of communicants are generally about fourteen. I cannot ascertain the exact number which communicated last Easter.

7. Not one reputed papist in my parish. No place in my parish in which they assemble for divine worship. No popish priest resides in my parish, nor resorts to it, neither is there any popish school kept in my parish.

8. There are no Presbyterians, Independents, Anabaptists, or Quakers in my parish. No place made use of for divine service but the church, and is generally attended by a very full and decent congregation. There are some who do not attend the public worship so frequent as could be wished, but none, that I know of, who profess to disregard religion.

9. They do not, but have desired them for the future duly to send them to me, and I will do my endeavour privately to instruct them that they may be able to make a good appearance in the public church in the time of Lent, the usual time of catechizing. Have made use of no particular exposition, but do at times in my sermons endeavour to explain parts of the catechism.

10. The register books of births and burials are duly kept and in good preservation; and the returns of births and burials are regularly made into the registrar's office. The register goes back to the 25 March 1686.

11. There is a register book duly kept according to the direction of the Act of Parliament against clandestine marriages.

[1] Queen's Coll. Oxford 1755. Rector of Littleton Drew, **125.**

12. There is no chapel of ease in the parish. We have only one church, which is in good condition.

13. Have no account of any houses, lands, tithes, pensions, or profits. Have *now* endeavoured to procure a perfect account of everything belonging to me as minister of this parish and will take care that the same be laid up in the bishop's registry.

14. We have no free school, alms-house, hospital, or other charitable endowment in the parish. We have no lands or tenements left for the repair of the church, or for any other pious use.

15. The churchwardens are chosen every year in the Easter week, one by the minister, the other by the parish.

16. There never was any public school founded in this parish; neither is there any charity school here.

17. I have constantly resided in my parish and in the house belonging to the rectory till the latter end of the year 1782 to the May following, during which time my health obliged me to make Bath my residence, being so much afflicted with the gout as to disable me from doing the duty of my church; but took particular care to have my church regularly supplied morning and afternoon by a neighbouring clergyman;[2] and the dampness of my situation in the winter, occasioned by the water-meadows that surround me, was another reason of my absence.

18. To the poor and sick of the parish, as occasions offer.

19. I do not know of any other that deserves your Lordship's attention.

20. I reside on my living and in the house belonging to it, which is distant from Warminster one mile, a post town.

Instituted to this living 23 Oct. 1767. Ord. D. by the bishop of Bristol in the cathedral of Christchurch, Oxford, 2 Feb. 1753. Ord. P. by the bishop of Oxford in the cathedral church of Christ in Oxford 9 June 1754. Took my M.A. degree in the university of Oxford 13 Nov. 1754.

Thomas Fisher,[3] rector of Bishopstrow in the county of Wilts. 28 July 1783

18 BLUNSDON ST. ANDREW f.153   D. Cricklade

1. Once, according to ancient usage.

2. No; and in a small parish of about 4 farms, 1 gentleman's house, and 1 cottage, few can attend, hardly on Ash Wednesday, or Good Friday.

3. As curate to the Rev. Mr. Travell.[4]

4. At Rodbourne Cheney, about two miles distant.

5. At Easter, Whitsuntide, and Christmas. Four generally attend.

6. Commonly about four; which I think was the number both the last times.

[2] Clergy Books, 1783, give 'Mr. Huntingford' as curate. Probably Thomas Huntingford, rector of Corsley, **59,** and curate of Brixton Deverill.

[3] Merton Coll. Oxford 1748. Also vicar of Norton Bavant, **151,** served for him by the rector of Sutton Veny, **208.**

[4] Ferdinando Tracy Travell, rector. 1740-1808. Wadham Coll. Oxford 1757. Rector of Upper Slaughter, Glos.

7. No.
8. No.
9. There have yet been no children to send since I have served, perhaps there may be in about another year.
10. Yes. It begins in 1653.
11. Yes.
12. No.
13. I am not informed.
14. No.
15. There is but one, chosen by the parishioners.
16. No.
17. I reside on my own cure at Rodbourne about two miles off. There is no house for the incumbent.
18. None given.
19. I am not certain.
20. Mr. Travell resides at Upper Slaughter near Northleach.[5]

19 BOSCOMBE f.161   D. Amesbury
1. At half after ten and two. Never has been served twice on the same day in the memory of man.
2. Christmas day, Good Friday, feast days, and thanksgiving days.
3. As curate.[6]
4. Bulford, four miles distance. Not licensed.
5. Christmas, Easter, and Whitsuntide.
6. Four or five the usual number. Last Easter [*blank*]
7 & 8. All of the established church.
9. Those who attend are usually catechized in Lent.
10. We have a proper register book but by some accident it has been mislaid so that I cannot just now tell how far it goes back.
11. Such a book is kept.
12. No such things.
13. The rector is absent, I am but lately come to the curacy and cannot properly answer this question.
14. No such things.
15. Only one churchwarden, chosen by the parish.
16. No such things.
17. Sometimes in the parsonage house, sometimes at Amesbury.
18. No money given.
19. Nothing.
20. Amesbury, Wilts.
   I have been ordained about twenty-four years and am a M.A.
                                                             W. Cropley[7]

[5] No signature. Curate, John Nelson. Vicar of Rodbourne Cheney, **166.**
[6] Rector, John Nairn. Perhaps Emmanuel Coll. Cambridge 1758. Non-resident rector of Pertwood, **157.**
[7] William Cropley: Clergy Books, 1783.

20 BOWER CHALKE f.169 D. Chalke
1. Once a day at one o'clock. The living is so small, and having three different churches to preach at renders it impracticable to have prayers above once a day.
2. No.
3. As curate.[8]
4. Yes, Broad Chalk and Alvedeston, the former a mile off, the latter about four. I am not licensed to the cure.
5. Four times in the year, viz. Easter, Whitsuntide, Michaelmas, and Christmas.
6. Generally twenty, seldom more or less.
7. There are none.
8. None.
9. They are sent to be catechized on Sundays in the summer season, in the English language. Having three different churches to preach at, the time will not permit to make use of any exposition.
10. Yes, and do regularly make returns; the births as far back as 14 May [17]02, burials as far back as 16 May 1702.
11. There is.
12. There are none.
13. [*Blank*]
14. There are none.
15. Every year in the Easter week; the one by the minister, the other by the parishioners.
16. There are none within the parish.
17. I reside upon the cure but not in the house belonging to it.
18. None given.
19. No.
20. Broad Chalk near Sarum.[9]

21 BOX[1] f.177 D. Malmesbury
1. Twice every Lord's day, sermon always in the forenoon.
2. On Easter Monday and Tuesday, Whit Monday and Tuesday, Good Friday and Christmas day, and at other festivals when a congregation can be procured.
3. As curate.
4. No.
5. Monthly and on all the great festivals.
6. At the festivals about twenty-five, at the monthly sacrament 15 or 16.
7. None.
8. No sectaries of any denomination whatever.

[8] Vicar, James Charters or Chartres. Also vicar of Broad Chalke. 1754–1823. King's Coll. Cambridge (patrons of both livings) 1773.
[9] No signature. Curate, 'Mr. Evans'.
[1] This return is made in two different hands. The vicar, in addition to writing his name, ordination dates, etc., has also written the answers to queries 13, 16, and 19 and his address at query 20. The rest of the return was presumably made by the curate.

9. A numerous congregation every Lord's day, the children are regularly and duly catechized at all times of the year.
10. A register book in good preservation, from the year 1644.
11. Yes.
12. None.
13. A terrier is deposited in the registry on 10 Dec. 1677 since which no augmentation.
14. No alms-house or hospital.
15. Yes, one by the minister, the other by the parish.
16. A charity school in a flourishing state for thirty boys and girls. As to instruction, only in the principles of the Christian religion, writing, arithmetic, etc. The master whereof has an house to reside in and lands to the value of £2 yearly. Trustees the vicar and heirs of George Speke, Giles Eyre, and Samuel Webb. Will of Lady Rachel Speke dated [figures crossed out] 1707.
17. Constantly in the parish.
18. By the minister's churchwarden, generally, to the use of the second poor. [2]
19. Nothing.
20. Samuel Webb, the vicar, Winford, Somerset, near Bristol. Henry Hawes, curate, Box near Bath.

Samuel Webb M.A., [3] vicar, ord. D. 19 March 1756 by the bishop of Oxford. Ord. P. 25 Sept. 1757 by the bishop of Bath and Wells. Instituted to the vicarage of Box 17 Nov. 1774.

Henry Hawes A.B., [4] curate of Box

22 BOYTON f.185   D. Wylye
1. Twice, viz. prayers at half after ten in the morning, sermon and prayers at half after two in the afternoon.
2. On certain festivals.
3. As curate. [5]
4. [a] None. [c] No.
5. Four times, viz. Christmas, Easter, Whitsuntide, and St. Michael.
6. About fifteen; rather more at Easter last than usual.
7. None.
8. None.
9. No.
10. [a] Yes. [c] From 1712 to the present time.
11. Yes.

[2] i.e. those not receiving parish relief.
[3] Probably Trinity Coll. Oxford 1750.
[4] Wadham Coll. Oxford 1759. Rector of Little Langford, **119,** served by the rector of Steeple Langford. A member of Wilton corporation and son of Henry Hawes, a former rector of Wilton. Dr. Eyre (of Chilmark and Fovant) described him as 'poor Hawes with a family of six children' and as 'looking like a primitive Christian, which is not much the line of the clergy in these days': *Pembroke Papers*, ii. 353, 434.
[5] Rector, Dr. Coventry Townsend Powys Litchfield (or Lichfield) 1740–1810. Magdalen Coll. Oxford (patrons of the living) 1758. Vicar of Honington, Warws. Fellow of Magdalen and resident there: *State of the Bishopric of Worcester, 1782–1804* (Worcs. Hist. Soc N.S. vi), p. 171.

12. None.
13. Incompetent, being curate only.
14. None.
15. At Easter, by the minister and parishioners.
16. A charity school for boys and girls, supported by the voluntary bounty of a gentleman in the parish, but terminable at his pleasure. [c] Reading and writing. [d] Yes. [e] No.
17. No, but at Bapton, about two miles distant.
18. None given.
19. None that I know.
20. Bapton near Heytesbury.

Henry Davis B.A.[6]

23 BRADFORD f.193   D. Potterne
1. Divine service is performed twice every Lord's day, beginning at half past ten in the morning and at three o'clock in the afternoon.
2. On Wednesdays and Fridays and all holidays and festivals.
3. As curate.[7]
4. I have not taken a licence.
5. Monthly throughout the year.
6. The number of communicants are not diminishing, nor were they less than usual last Easter.
7. Very few, and those of little reputation without any place of worship or priest.
8. Of almost every denomination under Heaven innumerable. There are also two Methodist meetings supplied by a variety of teachers.
9. No ! ! !
10. Our registers of births and burials are kept in very good preservation as far back as the year 1579, and our returns regularly made into the registrar's office.
11. Yes.
12. There are six chapels of ease in this parish, (viz.) Holt, Atworth, Wraxall, Winsley, Westwood, Stoke, served alternately by the Rev. Mr. Glynn and the Rev. Mr. Paris.[8]
13. I have not seen any terrier, nor hath any augmentation of the living been made of late years.
14. There are two hospitals here, one founded by the lord of the manor for three old women and still under his direction; the other endowed by John Hall Esq. with an annuity of £40 per annum net paid out of an estate called Packscroft farm in the parish of Steeple Ashton, for the support of four poor

[6] Wadham Coll. Oxford 1775.
[7] Vicar, Dr. Walter Chapman. Probably Pembroke Coll. Oxford 1729. A scholar and eloquent preacher and a friend of Dr. Johnson: W. H. Jones, *Bradford-on-Avon*, 121.
[8] According to Clergy Books, 1783, Atworth and Holt were served by Mr. Glynne (rector of Great Chalfield, 37), South Wraxall, Limpley Stoke, Winsley, and Westwood by Mr. Paris.

men now under the government of the countess of Bristol, and both the foundations are properly supported.

15. The churchwardens are chosen annually in the Easter week, one by the minister, and the other by the parishoners.

16. There is a charity school kept in the churchyard, supported by the donations of several benefactors, as may be seen in the inscriptions in the front of the organ gallery.

17. My seat is near the centre of the town.

18. This money is distributed by the clerk and myself to relieve the wants of the most distressed inhabitants.

19. [*Blank*]

20. Bradford is a post town.

Admitted to the degree of B.A. in Michaelmas term 1780 as member of Christ Church Oxford. My deacon's orders are dated 24 Sept. 1780. Letters of priest's orders dated 26 May 1782.

Benjamin Richardson[9]

24 NORTH BRADLEY f.201   D. Potterne

1. Divine service is performed twice every Sunday. Prayers and sermon once a day, and prayers with an occasional lecture on the catechism in the other part of the day at 10 o'clock morning and 2 in the afternoon.

2. Upon every Friday; there are prayers also on Wednesdays and Fridays in Lent and every day in the Passion week and chief holidays.

3. As incumbent.

4. No.

5. The sacrament is administered upon the 4 grand festivals. Also upon the first Sunday in every month.

6. The number of communicants amount in general to about 40.

7. No papist, nor popish priest residing in the parish.

8. There are many dissenters, chiefly Baptists. Their teachers are chiefly weavers, who take up the business for the day. Whether they are licensed or not the minister cannot say. With respect to those who disregard religion, and absent themselves from all public worship, of such alas! the number is beyond any calculation; and of these not a few who have wilfully resisted every endeavour of their minister to bring them to a better disposition.

9. They cannot be persuaded to do it. The minister appointed prayers every Friday, with the design that the children should be brought to church for the purpose of being instructed in the catechism after service, but he has not succeeded.

10. [a] Yes. [b] Yes. [c] The register book goes back to about the year 1720.

11. Yes.

12. There are none.

13. There is a terrier; but not so perfect as one could be wished.

14. There is no free school nor any charitable endowment in the parish, nor any benefaction of any kind appropriated to the repair of the church.

[9] 1759–1832. Christ Church Oxford 1777. The Clergy Book has the comment 'a coxcomb' against his name.

15. The churchwardens are chosen every Easter week, one by the minister, the other by the parishioners.

16. There neither is, nor ever has been, so far as can be known, any charity school of any kind in the parish.

17. The minister constantly resides in the vicarage house. The minister cannot take upon him to say how long in each year he has been absent; but this he can safely say, that he wishes to be resident as much as possible. This year he has been absent one month in the spring.

18. The money is reserved by the minister in order to be distributed together with some addition of his own at Christmas, in clothing, cheese, and coals to such as are judged proper objects.

19. Nothing, but what I trust the churchwardens will present to your Lordship.

20. North Bradley near Trowbridge, Wilts.

The Rev. Charles Daubeny[1] was collated to the vicarage of North Bradley 4 Oct. 1777. He was ord. D. 19 Dec. 1773 and ord. P. 27 Dec. 1773. His degree is *Bachelor of Civil Law*, in the university of Oxford.

25 BREMILHAM f.209   D. Malmesbury

[*Written on the margin of the letter:*] Received the instructions 19 June. Sent the instructions for confirmation to Mr. Bennet the 29. [*Written under the address:*] Mr. Lyne of the Light my churchwarden.[2]

1. Divine service is performed every Sunday by myself beginning at two o'clock in the afternoon.

2. We have no divine service upon any weekdays, holidays, or festivals.

3. Divine service is performed by me as rector.

4. I serve no other cure.

5. The holy sacrament hath been administered but once since my institution,[3] and then was obliged to borrow from Foxley the communion plate. Here is no surplice.

6. We had no sacrament last Easter.

7. We have no reputed papists nor popish priest, nor popish school in my parish.

8. The principal absentee from all public worship of God is John Bennett of Cowitch.

9. My parishioners don't send their children nor servants to be instructed in their catechism.

10. We have no register book.

11. We have no register book against clandestine marriages.

---

[1] 1745–1827. Oriel Coll. Oxford 1762. Archdeacon of Sarum 1804. He spent large sums of his own money on improving the church and on charitable works in the parish and was the author of many theological works: *V.C.H. Wilts.* viii. 228; *D.N.B.* Clergy Books, 1783, also mention a curate, Mr. Spencer, for whom see Winkfield, **218**, of which he was rector.

[2] Edmund Lyne of Lea (or 'the Ligh') and Cleverton; 'the Light' was probably Lea. The churchwardens' presentment was, however, signed only by John Bennett (presumably John Bennett of Cowage referred to below, queries 8 and 17), who made the standard presentment 'All things well': Sarum Dioc. R.O., Churchwardens' presentments, 1783.

[3] i.e. since 1760: *Wilts. Inst.* ii. 79.

12. We have no chapels of ease in my parish.
13. We have had £200 added by the governors of Queen Anne's Bounty[4] which brings me in £4 per annum to my living.
14. There is no free school, alms-house, hospital, or any other charitable endowment in my parish.
15. This year my churchwarden Mr. Lyne was chose by myself on Easter Monday.
16. We have no school in my parish.
17. My parsonage house is made a pigsty of by Farmer Bennett of Cowitch.[5] My present residence is at Westport about a mile from Cowitch.
18. Here is no offertory money to dispose of.
19. None I know of.
20. My place of residence is at Westport joining to Malmesbury.[6]

26 BREMHILL f.221   D. Avebury
1. Prayers and a sermon in the morning between 10 and 11 o'clock, and prayers in the evening about 6 o'clock in summer, in winter no evening service on account of the duty at Highway and the distance. At Highway evening service and a sermon between 2 and 3 o'clock.
2. On the state holidays, Monday and Tuesday in Easter and Whitsun weeks, and the holidays after Christmas day.
3. As incumbent. I have also a curate,[7] being resident part of the year at Salisbury.
4. None but Highway, a parish annexed to Bremhill distant about 6 miles.
5. At Bremhill at the 3 great festivals, and Michaelmas; at Highway on the 3 great festivals.
6. At Bremhill generally about 20, at Easter last between 20 and 30; at Highway seldom more than 4 or 5.
7. None.
8. There is a Quakers' meeting-house now disused: about 3 or 4 Quakers in the parish. A Moravian chapel at Titherton, an hamlet in this parish, about 50 of the members of which are parishioners. 2 teachers, Timms and Sutcliffe.[8] They have a large congregation, but whether increased of late years I cannot tell.
9. Catechizing has been for a long time disused, but I have revived it since I came to the living.
10. Yes.
11. Yes.
12. Highway a parish annexed; there is also a chapel at Foxham, distant

---

[4] In 1766: Hodgson, p. 415.

[5] Pevsner, under Foxley, notes 'mortuary chapel at Cowage Farm (i.e. the former church of Bremilham). Only the nave stands, with its bellcote': *Buildings of England: Wiltshire* (1963), p. 224.

[6] No signature. Rector, Daniel Freer. Died 1793: *Wilts. Inst.* ii. 97. Perhap Trinity Coll. Oxford 1735. There is clearly some personal drama behind this return.

[7] Mr. Palmer, who also served Highway chapel.

[8] See also **27**.

about 4 miles, endowed by a private person with £3 a year, but being no part of the original endowment, and the stipend by no means adequate, it has been for several years given up.

13. Having been not long possessed of this vicarage, I have not yet had sufficient time to make out a proper terrier, it being a very complicated business on account of a late inclosure, but will do it as soon as I can; I find some old terriers.

14. None.

15. Every Easter week. One by the minister, one by the parishioners.

16. None.

17. When not in residence as canon of Sarum, I reside here in my vicarage house.

18. Either by myself or curate to such objects as we think deserving.

19. Not to my knowledge.

20. Bremhill near Calne.

Nathaniel Hume,[9] vicar of Bremhill. Collated 2 March 1782. Ord. D. 23 Sept. 1759. Ord. P. 2 March 1760.

27 BRINKWORTH f.237   D. Malmesbury

1. Every Sunday morning at 11, evening at 3. Sermon in the morning.

2. On holidays and festivals. Wednesdays and Fridays in Lent.

3. As rector.

4. I serve no other cure while resident. My curate[1] serves no other cure.

5. At Easter, Whitsuntide, Michaelmas, and Christmas.

6. From about 12 to 20, the same number nearly as for years past.

7. None.

8. Our parish a few years ago swarmed with sectaries; at present they are few in number. We have one Independent meeting-house that is seldom used, and one Moravian but whether licensed or not I cannot say. The Independent minister's name is Mr. Cadman, the Moravian Mr. Sutcliffe.[2] My audience in general is from 150 to 200.

9. Always during Lent and often in the afternoon in summer.

10. There is, and we do as is required.

11. There is.

12. We have none.

13. We have.

14. We have neither free school, alms-house, or hospital, but there was a donation of 20s. a year given by Lady Howard to buy Bibles and Common Prayers by the direction of the minister. There is £5 a year left by will by a Mr. Wickes to be disposed by the churchwardens only for teaching ten poor children to read, and £10 a year by the same gentleman for the use of the poor of the parish by the minister and churchwardens every Christmas. It has hitherto been duly paid.

[9] 1732–1804. Christ Church Oxford 1752. Nephew of John Hume, bishop of Salisbury 1766–82. For his various preferments see above, p. 11-12.
[1] Clergy Books, 1783, give 'Mr. Brook' as curate.
[2] See also 26.

15. Yes. One by the minister, the other by the parishioners.
16. No other than what is already mentioned. I myself give £5 5s., the parishioners give £5 5s. more towards instructing the poor children, in reading.
17. I have regularly resided every year, since the first I was inducted to the living, some months. In my absence the curate has a bed in the parsonage house. I have another living (Wellow) in the diocese of Winchester where I perform duty when not resident at Brinkworth.
18. Money is seldom collected. When any is collected it is distributed among the poor who attend.
19. Nothing that I know of.
20. Brinkworth near Malmesbury.
   J. Penton A.M.[3] Ord. D. 28 Feb. 1768. Ord. P. 25 Sept. 1768. Instituted to the rectory of Brinkworth 17 May 1780.

28 BROAD CHALKE f.245   D. Chalke
1. [a] Once a day, at ten o'clock. [b] The living being so small, and having three different churches to preach at, renders it impracticable.
2. No.
3. As curate.
4. Yes, Bower Chalk, and Alvediston, the former a mile distant, and the other five miles. Am not licensed to the cure.
5. Four times in the year, viz. Easter, Whitsuntide, Michaelmas, and Christmas.
6. About twenty in general, Easter perhaps a few more.
7. There are none.
8. None.
9. They are sent to be catechized on Sundays in the summer season, in the English language; having three different churches to preach at, time will not permit to make use of any exposition etc.
10. Yes, and do regularly make returns. The births as far back as 23 July 1703 and the burials as far as 23 July [17]03.
11. There is.
12. There are none.
13. [Blank]
14. There are none.
15. Every year in the Easter week, the one by the minister, the other by the parishioners.
16. There are none in the parish.
17. I reside upon the cure but not in the house belonging to it.
18. None given.
19. No.
20. Broad Chalk near Sarum.[4]

[3] John Penton, Trinity Coll. Cambridge 1762.
[4] No signature. See **20.**

29 BROMHAM f.253   D. Avebury

1. Divine service is performed twice every day of the Lord.
2. Divine service cannot be attended on weekdays by labouring people without great injury to their families.
3. I perform, and ever have since I have been in orders as incumbent.
4. No.
5. The holy sacrament is administered thrice in the year, viz. at the three great festivals.
6. Between thirty and forty: last Easter the same, less generally at Whitsuntide.
7. No papists in my parish, none perverted to popery, no place in my parish where they assemble for divine worship, no popish school.
8. There are no Presbyterians, Anabaptists, and but four Quakers who are poor people. There is a place erected for their worship to which they resort from other places. There are no persons who profess to disregard religion, but too many who in works deny it and absent themselves from all public worship in common with the rest of the kingdom.
9. The generality of the parish are so poor as not to be able to afford time to have their children instructed in reading; as soon as they are old enough, they are sent out to plough or spin for their living; so that I have been obliged to distribute halfpence every Sunday to these poor children to bring them to church, by which means they have learned by memory the Lord's Prayer, the Creed, and the Ten Commandments.
10. The register books are duly kept and returned. They go back to the time of the Reformation.
11. There is.
12. None.
13. I have a true and perfect account of houses, lands, tithes, and profits which belong to me, a duplicate whereof I am told is laid in the bishop's registry. There has been no augmentation since.
14. There is an alms-house supported by Sir Edward Bayntun[5] at his own pleasure; no lands or tenements left for repairs but by a church rate.
15. Chosen in Easter week, one by the minister and the other by the parishioners.
16. There is no public school or charity school but two or three private ones.
17. I constantly reside upon this cure and in the house belonging to it. I now am never absent nor have been one whole year put together these forty-five years; and then I have taken care to have it supplied when secular affairs have forced me to London.
18. The money is disposed to the greatest objects of distress.
19. I know of none.
20. Bromham near Devizes.

Ord. D. and P. 1734. Instituted to Yatesbury 1735, to Bromham 1741.

J. Rolt A.M.[6]

---

[5] Sir Edward Bayntun-Rolt, formerly Rolt, of Spye Park, patron of the living and brother of the rector. For this charity see *V.C.H. Wilts.* vii. 186.

[6] John Rolt, 1712–93. Merton Coll. Oxford 1736. Rector of Yatesbury, **231**, served by the curate of Compton Bassett, **54**.

30 BROUGHTON GIFFORD f.261 D. Potterne

1. Divine service is performed twice every Lord's day in the summer and once in the winter; sermon in the afternoon only. Service begins at eleven, and at half, or three quarters, after two.
2. Divine service performed on saints' days during the summer.
3. As incumbent.
4. No other cure.
5. The sacrament of the Lord's Supper is administered four times in every year; viz. at the three great festivals and on the Sunday after Michaelmas day.
6. The greatest number about fourteen or sixteen; at Easter last not more than twelve; and the number seems to decrease.
7. No papist or reputed papist in this parish. No popish priest resident in the parish, nor any popish school kept. No place in which they assemble for divine worship.
8. There are in this parish Presbyterians, Independents, Anabaptists, Methodists, Moravians, sectarists of almost every denomination, several of whom never appear at church. The rest, though occasionally coming there, are more constant frequenters of unlicensed meeting-houses, and spend much of their time, to the great detriment and poverty of their families, in going after ignorant *itinerant* preachers.
9. The parishioners are negligent in sending their children to be catechized, the time usual for doing which in this parish is on the Sundays in Lent.
10. A register book of births and burials is duly kept, and in good preservation. A return of births and burials is regularly made at the bishop's or archdeacon's visitation.
11. A register book duly kept, according to the direction of the Act of Parliament against clandestine marriages.
12. No chapel of ease in this parish.
13. The exact terrier is transmitted to the bishop, a copy whereof is kept.
14. No free school or other charitable endowment in this parish.
15. Two churchwardens chosen annually at Easter, one by the rector, the other by the parishioners.
16. No public school or charity school in the parish.[7]
17. Reside in the parsonage house.
18. Money collected at the offertory which amounts to a few shillings immediately given to the poor who attend.
19. Nothing else material deserving particular information.
20. Nearest post town to Broughton Gifford is Melksham.

Robert Addams Hickes A.M.,[8] rector of Broughton Gifford

31 BULFORD f.269 D. Amesbury

1. The service at Bulford is generally performed either at eleven or one but never twice on the same Sunday; it has never been customary.

---

[7] £500 was, however, given in 1782 for founding a school: *V.C.H. Wilts.* vii. 58.
[8] Probably St. John's Coll. Oxford 1752.

2. The parish consists chiefly of labouring people and except on Christmas day and Good Friday or a general fast or thanksgiving no service is performed on weekdays.
3. I am appointed to do the duty by Edmund Southby Esq., impropriator.
4. I serve the curacy of Boscombe at four miles distance and I have no licence.
5. The sacrament is administered at Christmas, Easter, and Whitsuntide.
6. The usual number of communicants are from six to ten, at Easter last eight.
7. I believe all the inhabitants of Bulford are of the established church.
8. Few country churches are better attended.
9. Those who attend are instructed in their catechism in Lent.
10. The register book goes no further back than 1776.
11. There is such a book kept.
12. No such thing.
13. There is neither parsonage house nor glebe land.
14. No such thing.
15. The minister chooses one, the parish the other churchwarden in Easter week.
16. No such things.
17. I generally reside at Amesbury, sometimes at Boscombe.
18. No money is given.
19. Nothing.
20. At Amesbury, Wilts.
I have been ordained about twenty-four years and a M.A.

W. Cropley[9]

32 BURCOMBE f.277   D. Chalke
1. Divine service is performed every other Sunday at one o'clock.
2. Divine service is not performed on any holiday or festival.
3. As minister.
4. I serve Wishford, distance about three miles.
5. The holy sacrament is administered three times in the year, Christmas, Easter, and Whitsuntide.
6. Number of communicants about thirty.
7. None.
8. None.
9. The parishioners are catechized in the English language.
10. The register book of births and burials is duly kept. Returns regularly made.
11. A register book is kept according to the directions of the Act of Parliament.
12. None.
13. There is neither house or land which belong to the minister. The small tithes amount to £11. The prior of Burcombe[1] gives £4 more.
14. No free school, alms-house, or other charitable endowment.

[9] See **19**.
[1] This presumably refers to the master, or prior, of St. John's hospital, Wilton, to which the church was appropriated in 1347: Hoare, *Mod. Wilts.* i, Branch and Dole hundred, 151.

15. The churchwardens are chosen every year by the parishioners.
16. No public school.
17. I do not reside upon the cure—no house. Usual place of residence at Wishford, about three miles distant.
18. None collected.
19. I know of no matter proper to give your Lordship information.
20. Wishford, Sarum.
   J. W. Birch,[2] minister. Ord. D. 1764. Ord. P. 1770. Degree B.D.

33 BUTTERMERE f.285   D. Marlborough
1. Divine service is performed at 11 o'clock in the winter, at 2 o'clock in the summer.
2. On Christmas day.
3. As incumbent.
4. I serve Combe, Hants, where I reside. The churches of Buttermere and Combe are at two miles distance.
5. Four times in the year.
6. Very few communicants.
7. No papist.
8. No Presbyterian, Independent, Anabaptist, or Quaker.
9. [Blank]
10. There is a register book of births and burials, but, the old one being lost, it goes back only to the year 1727.
11. Yes.
12. No chapel of ease.
13. No terrier.
14. No free school.
15. The inhabitants consist wholly of farmers and labourers; there are three only of the former living in the parish at present and they serve offices in turn.
16. No public school.
17. I reside in my vicarage house of Combe, Hants, which is the adjoining parish.
18. No money given at the offertory.
19. [Blank]
20. Combe near Hungerford.
   Thomas Baker M.A.[3] Ord. D. 18 Sept. 1763. Ord. P. 17 June 1764. Instituted to the rectory of Buttermere 31 Oct. 1772.

34 CALSTONE f.293   D. Avebury
1. Once a day morning and afternoon alternately at 11 and 3 o'clock. Occasional duty at neighbouring churches.
2. Not on weekdays, unless on Christmas day and Good Friday.
3. As incumbent.

---

[2] Queen's Coll. Oxford 1757. Rector of Wishford, **225,** and of Ashbury, Berks.: Clergy Books, 1783.
[3] Merton Coll. Oxford 1757. Vicar of Tidcombe, **199,** served by the curate of Chute.

4. I often do duty at another church, but am not the curate thereof. About a mile distance.

5. 3 times in the year, viz. on Christmas day and on Easter and Whitsunday.

6. There are but four houses in the parish. The number at Easter was seven, less than usual.

7. None.

8. None.

9. There are but few children in the parish. None sent to be catechized.

10. I register in a book of my own the few births and burials. They have at times been returned as the canon requires when there has been a number. The register goes no further back than my own time, about 22 years.

11. A register is lately kept.

12. None.

13. Your Lordship's enquiry has occasioned me to draw up a terrier which is a true and perfect one to the best of my knowledge, with the augmentation[4] to my living annexed, which will be delivered in. I know nothing of any terrier before my time.

14. None.

15. There is only one churchwarden, who is chosen yearly in the Easter week by the minister and parish.

16. None.

17. I reside in the parsonage house and am very seldom absent from my living.

18. No offertory but from my own family.

19. None that I know of.

20. At Calstone near Calne.

Instituted to the rectory 3 Nov. 1758. Ord. D. 18 Dec. 1743. Ord. P. 23 June 1745. M.A. Queen's, Oxford.

Thomas Heath[5]

35 CASTLE COMBE f.301   D. Malmesbury

1. Prayers are read at eleven o'clock in the morning, and at two in the afternoon. After the evening prayers follows a sermon.

2. Divine service is performed every saint's day at eleven in the morning, and on every other day for which an Epistle or Gospel is appointed.

3. As incumbent.

4. I serve no other cure.

5. Four times, viz. on Christmas day, on Easter day, on Whitsunday, and on the Sunday after Michaelmas.

6. Seldom more than twelve; which, I believe, was about the number last Easter. But I was at that time too ill to do any duty myself.

7. There is not one papist in this parish.

---

[4] £200 from Queen Anne's Bounty in 1723: Hodgson, p. 415.
[5] Queen's Coll. Oxford 1738. Vicar of Hilmarton, **101**, served by a resident curate.

8. We have none of any sect but Methodists; who about 20 years ago obtained from my predecessor in the manor a plot of ground, on which (contrary to their solemn verbal declarations before the execution of the lease) they built a meeting-house; which house is licensed. On this lease there are now two lives. There is no settled teacher. Some itinerant attends almost every Sunday and sometimes on a weekday. The number of attendants there is, I believe, much the same as from the beginning. There are several in my parish who, I have reason to think, commonly absent themselves from all public worship of God.

9. They never send their children for this purpose but when called upon so to do. I expound the catechism in a course of sermons. I choose the longest days in the year for this duty of catechizing, which is done in the mother tongue.

10. I answer the two first branches of this query in the affirmative; with respect to the last, here is no register that goes further back than 1653. From time to time it has been pretty regularly kept.

11. There is.

12. Here is no chapel of ease.

13. I have an authentic terrier of the lands, tithes, and profits belonging to the rector, which was taken in A.D. 1737. But whether there be a duplicate in the bishop's registry, I know not. A more full and particular terrier has just now been taken, and will be delivered in today at your Lordship's visitation.

14. See the answer to Q.16.

15. The two churchwardens are always chosen at the time mentioned, one by the minister, the other by the parishioners; this is the ancient custom.

16. There is an endowment left by one Parry, for the teaching of ten poor children of this parish, boys and girls indiscriminately, to read the scriptures. In strictness they are to be discharged at the age of seven years. The sum left by will was £100 but payment was delayed by the executor so long that the interest amounted to £20 more. For which entire sum of £120 an ancestor of mine gave a real security upon his estate here for the payment of £5 per annum for ever. This annuity has never failed to be paid punctually, either by my predecessors or myself, by quarterly payments. But the trust, I believe, has by some negligence been suffered to expire. And the nomination of the master or mistress is now left to the lord of the manor. In which capacity I do all I can to answer the purpose of the benefactor. The original deed of security is laid up in the parish chest.

17. I reside constantly upon this cure, not in the parsonage house but in the manor-house, which is equally near the church; or, however, the difference is very small.

18. It is always distributed by the minister among such paupers of the parish as he thinks most deserving and most in want of assistance.

19. Nothing more than what is expressed in the terrier.

20. Castle Combe near Chippenham, Wilts.

Richard Scrope D.D.[6] was instituted to the two rectories of Tubney and Aston Tirrold, Berks. (the former under value), 5 Aug. 1766 on the presentation of the president and scholars of Magdalen College in Oxford. And on 18 Dec. 1777 he was, upon his own petition, as patron, instituted to the rectory of Castle Combe, Wilts., having previously obtained a dispensation for holding the last mentioned rectory with that of Aston Tirrold. This last instrument bears the date 15 Dec. 1777. The said Richard Scrope was ord. D. 22 Dec. 1751 and ord. P. 24 Sept. 1752.

Richard Scrope. Castle Combe, 30 July 1783

36 CASTLE EATON f.309   D. Cricklade
1. I read prayers and preach in the morning at eleven o'clock; read prayers in the afternoon at three o'clock.
2. It is a small country parish, and no congregation would attend on week-days, except a few particular ones.
3. As incumbent.
4. No, I serve no other church.
5. I administer the sacrament four times in the year, viz. Christmas, Easter, Whitsuntide, and about Michaelmas.
6. The number of communicants last Easter day was 23 or 24, rather more than usual.
7. None.
8. None. I know of no persons who profess to disregard religion; there are a few who too often absent themselves from the public worship of God.
9. I hear the children their catechism six Sundays in the year, beginning the first Sunday after Whitsunday and make use of an exposition printed at Oxford, which I think a good one. The author's name is not to it.
10. [a, b] Yes, and the returns duly made. [c] 1549.
11. Yes, duly kept.
12. None.
13. I have made a terrier.
14. None.
15. The churchwardens are chosen at Easter, one by the minister, the other by the parishioners.
16. None, nor any endowment or provision of that sort.
17. I reside at my living in the parsonage house the summer season, the remainder of the year at Fairford 3 miles from it, on account of its being a very low and wet place, and not agreeing with my health.
18. No collection is made, as I found no such custom.
19. None at all.

[6] 1749–87. Oriel Coll. Oxford 1747. He was unable to attend the visitation. 'I am still very weak, and unable to bear the least degree of fatigue, or much company,' he wrote to the bishop. 'Besides, my habit is so exceedingly relaxed, particularly in this hot weather, that I am sure I could not possibly support myself . . . Other parts of my duty I find myself equally unable to perform.' He was represented and his confirmation candidates presented by his assistant, James Pidding, rector of the neighbouring parish of Yatton Keynell, **232:** Sarum Dioc. R.O., Misc. Vis. Papers, 8.

20. In my parsonage house, Castle Eaton, the summer season, in the winter at Fairford, which is the nearest post town.

Instituted 8 June 1762. Ord. D. 24 Sept. 1758. Ord. P. 1 June 1760. Degree, M.A.

Lancelot Kerby,[7] rector

37 GREAT CHALFIELD f.317[8]   D. Potterne

Incumbent of Great Chalfield's answers to the following queries respecting his cure.

1. Divine service, viz. prayers and preaching, hath been performed, for time immemorial in my church, two Lord's days out of three; on one part of the day. Every third Lord's day it is wholly omitted. When it is in the forenoon, it begins about 10. In the afternoon at half after 2 o'clock. The reason why divine service hath not usually been performed twice every Lord's day, I apprehend, is because the rectory doth not afford the incumbent a competent maintenance.

2. Divine service hath never been usually performed on any weekday in my church.

3. As incumbent.

4. Besides my own church, I serve the cure of Holt and Atworth chapels, in the parish of Bradford; to which I am duly licensed. The former is at the distance of one mile, the latter about 3 miles from my church.

5. The Lord's Supper is administered 3 times in the year viz. Easter, Whitsuntide, and Christmas.

6. The number of communicants last Easter and for many years past has been nearly equal, viz. 9 or 10.

7. There is no popish meeting, school, nor person of the popish communion.

8. There is no meeting-house belonging to any description of dissenters, and but one dissenter in my parish. There are none who profess to disregard religion; but some there are who too commonly absent themselves from public worship.

9. There being very few inhabitants, it hath never been usual publicly to catechize, in my parish.

10. We have such a register book, as far back as the reign of Henry VIII, from which returns are regularly made.

11. We have a register book of this description.

12. There are no chapels of ease nor ruinated chapels.

13. A duplicate of a terrier of my rectory was delivered to the registrar in the year 1671: since which my benefice hath been augmented with £400;[9] an account of which hath been transmitted to the registry.

14. There is no charitable endowment, nor benefactions left for pious uses.

15. There is only one churchwarden chosen every Easter week by the parishioners.

16. There has never been any such school founded in my parish.

[7] Trinity Coll. Oxford 1753.
[8] Letter missing.
[9] In 1776: Hodgson, p. 416.

17. There is no house belonging to the minister. My constant residence is at Holt, about one mile from my church.
18. The communicants being most of them poor, there has never been any collection at the communion.
19. Nothing else proper to be communicated to your Lordship.
20. My residence is at Holt, the nearest post town to which is Bradford.

Clement Glynn A.B.[1] of Hertford College, Oxford. Ord. D. 1755. Ord. P. 1758. Instituted to the rectory of Chalfield Magna 1762.

38 GREAT CHEVERELL f.323   D. Potterne

1. As I could not answer this question satisfactorily either to your Lordship or myself in so small a compass I took the liberty of explaining the nature of the duty in a letter to your Lordship;[2] and am much obliged to your Lordship for your very kind reply.
2. There is none, nor ever was [in] the late incumbent's time except on Christmas day.
3. As the incumbent.
4. None but my other parish of *Great* [*recte* Little] Cheverel, which is adjoining to *Little* [*recte* Great] Cheverell.
5. At Easter, Whitsuntide, Michaelmas, and at Christmas, both in this, and likewise at my other parish. Eight times in the two parishes.
6.

1781	Easter 22	Whit. 28	Mich. 28	Christmas 26
1782	*	34	29	23
1783	35	29		

   * I did not count them, as something happened to prevent it.
7. [a] None. [d] No. [e] No.
8. [a] Not one. [e] I know of none so *very abandoned.* [f] I am grieved to say too many, notwithstanding my remonstrances, but much less than formerly.
9. [a] In general they do. [b] I use the Church Catechism broke into short questions in my examination of the *little* children, adding occasionally such questions, and remarks as *then* occur to me for the benefit of the elder. After this I speak to the audience in general for about a quarter of an hour, explaining at large and enforcing such passages of the catechism as the children have that evening repeated. [c] In spring and also in autumn for six Sundays successively. [d] In English. I *give* some of them Lewis's Exposition of the Catechism[3] to read at home.
10. [a] I have. [b] I do every year at the visitation. [c] From 15 May 1654.
11. There is.
12. [a] There are none. [f] None.
13. [a] I have. [b] There is. [c] No.
14. [a] None. [d] None.
15. They are. One by the minister, the other by the parishioners.

---

[1] Hertford Coll. Oxford 1751.
[2] This letter has not been traced.
[3] John Lewis, *The Church Catechism explain'd by way of question and answer and confirmed by Scripture proofs* (1700 and many later editions).

16. [a] There has not. [b] In answer to this question I have enclosed Mr. Townsend's will relating to it,[4] which I procured from Doctors' Commons, and printed, having been denied a copy of these clauses from Mr. Wadman of Imber, the executor. For many years no children have been sent there. The school-house is now in a ruinous condition, and nothing left in the will for the support of it. There are (the effect of your Lordship's queries I presume) three children sent lately. I put twenty children to school at my own expense to a very good schoolmaster, who lives in Great Cheverell.

17. [a] I reside in the parsonage house of *Little* Cheverell eight months in the year. My curate, Mr. Roots, and his wife live in my parsonage house at Great Cheverell. [c] Four months. [d] Being advanced in life (now in my 68th year) and this situation at the foot of the downs being very bleak, I am obliged to remove in the winter season, and I then reside at Bristol Wells.

18. None has ever been collected, as the parish consists of cottagers, and very poor farmers.

19. If there were I should think it my duty to acquaint your Lordship.

20. At *Little* Cheverell; and the nearest post town is Devizes.

James Stonhouse,[5] rector of Great Cheverell

I was presented to this living by the present earl of Radnor 5 Dec. 1779, and inducted on 12 Feb. 1780; but as to the date of *institution* I cannot ascertain it having been obliged to pack up *that* with many other papers of importance, letters, etc. in boxes on account of the number of workmen in my house; therefore cannot without very great inconvenience unpack and sort such a multiplicity of papers at present. I took my Doctor of Physic's degree on 14 Jan. 1745, and was of St. John's College Oxford.

My curate Mr. Roots[6] was ordained 17 Oct. 1779 by the present bishop of Bangor, nominated to the curacy of Letterston. He was ordained priest on 24 Sept. 1780 by the present bishop of Winchester, then bishop of Worcester, being curate to Mr. Rollins of Pershore in that county,[7] which was too laborious for him. He has been with me about two years, and an half. He is of Trinity College, Cambridge, but has not yet taken any degree.

39 LITTLE CHEVERELL[8] f.331   D. Potterne

1. As I could not answer this question satisfactorily either to your Lordship or myself in so small a compass I took the liberty of explaining the nature of the duty in a letter to your Lordship; and am much obliged to your Lordship for your very kind reply.

---

[4] See **39. 2.**

[5] 1717–95. St. John's Coll. Oxford 1733. A noted doctor and evangelical preacher and author of a number of devotional tracts. Lecturer at All Saints' Clifton and well known in Bristol society. A friend of Hannah More: *D.N.B.;* M. G. Jones, *Hannah More* (1957), p. 10; and a number of other references to him.

[6] William Roots, admitted to Trinity Coll. Cambridge as a '10 year man', 1781. Also curate of Coulston, **56.**

[7] John Rawlins, vicar of St. Andrew, Pershore, with Holy Cross curacy and the chapels of Bricklehampton, Besford, Defford, Pinvin, and Wick: *State of the Bishopric of Worcester, 1782–1804* (Worcs. Hist. Soc. N.S. vi), 107.

[8] Separate queries, but the answers almost exactly the same as for Great Cheverell, **38.**

2. There is none, nor ever was in the time of the three last incumbents except on Christmas day, till by the will of James Townsend Esq., *proved* in the year 1730, ten shillings were appropriated for a sermon to be preached every Good Friday in this church which is done accordingly; but *very few* attend, as no notice is taken of that day by the working people of this neighbourhood, whose bread depends on their labour.

3. As the incumbent.

4. None but my other parish of *Great* Cheverell, which is adjoining to *Little* Cheverell.

5. At Easter, Whitsuntide, Michaelmas and at Christmas, both in this, and likewise at my other parish. Eight times in the two parishes.

6.

1781	Easter 35	Whit. 33	Mich. 34	Christmas 28
1782	22	34	31	22
1783	32	24		

7. [a] None. [d] No. [e] No.

8. [a] Not one. [e] I know of none so *very abandoned*. [f] I am grieved to say too many, notwithstanding my remonstrances, but much less than formerly.

9. [a] There are not so many as I could wish and as there ought to be, but I believe as many as there are generally in parishes of this size.
[b] I use the Church Catechism broke into short questions in my examination of the *little* children, adding occasionally such questions, and remarks as *then* occur to me for the benefit of the elder. After this I speak to the audience in general for about a quarter of an hour, explaining at large and enforcing such passages of the catechism as the children have that evening repeated.

10. [a] I have. [b] I do every year at the visitation. [c] From 8 May 1654.

11. There is.

12. [a] There are none. [f] None.

13. [a] I have. [b] There is. [c] No.

14. There are none.

15. They are. One by the minister, and the other by the parishioners.

16. [a] No. [b] No.

17. [a] I reside in the parsonage house eight months in the year. [c] Four months. [d] Being advanced in life, and this situation at the foot of the downs being very bleak, I am obliged to remove, during that time, and then reside at Bristol Wells.

18. None has ever been collected, as this parish is so circumstanced that none can afford to give: chiefly cottagers, and a few farmers, who are renters.

19. If there were I should think it my duty to acquaint your Lordship.

20. At *Little* Cheverell; and the nearest post town is Devizes.

James Stonhouse, rector of Little Cheverell
I was presented to this living by the late earl of Radnor 4 May 1764, and *inducted* on 8 July 1764. But as to the date of *institution* I cannot ascertain it having been obliged to pack *that* with many other papers of importance, letters, etc. in boxes on account of the number of workmen in my house; therefore cannot without very great inconvenience unpack and sort such a multiplicity of papers at present. I took my Doctor of Physic's degree on 14 Jan. 1745, and was of St. John's College Oxford.

My curate Mr. Roots was ord. D. 17 Oct. 1779 by the present bishop of Bangor, nominated to the curacy of Letterston. He was ord. P. on 24 Sept. 1780 by the present bishop of Winchester, then bishop of Worcester, being curate at Pershore in that county. He has been with me about two years and half, strongly recommended by the incumbent Mr. Rollins, whose duty was too laborious for him. He is of Trinity College, Cambridge, but has not yet taken any degree.

40 CHICKLADE f.339 D. Chalke
1. The service was but once on the Lord's day before my residence, since which (at present having no other cure) I have had it twice during the summer, at 11 o'clock in the morning, and 3 in the afternoon. The sermon alternately.
2. Upon Good Friday.
3. As incumbent.
4. At present I serve no other cure.
5. Four times in the year, at Christmas, Easter, Whitsunday, and Michaelmas.
6. There are about 100 inhabitants only, including men, women, and children, consequently the number of communicants are small, about 10 or 12 generally; at Easter in particular there were only 10 owing to the principal family in the parish being absent.
7. No papists.
8. None. [e] Two or three only.
9. Before I resided in the parish there was no school in it—consequently but very few of the children as yet can say their catechism—as soon as they have learned it I shall take care to hear them, and expound to them from Archbishop Wake and Bishop Ken's expositions.
10. There was no register book properly kept when I first came into the parish in the year 1780. The parish have since provided one, and the births and burials are duly registered.
11. Yes.
12. None.
13. The parish has been lately inclosed by Act of Parliament,[9] a copy of which Act was sent to the late bishop. The plan and award is kept in the parish church.
14. None.
15. The churchwardens are chosen every year in the Easter week, one by the minister and the other by the parishioners.
16. None.
17. I constantly reside upon this cure but not in the parsonage house. The house I reside in was given me by the patron for that purpose, the parsonage house being too small. The house I reside in is about a hundred yards distant from the church and is in the parish. I never absent myself from my cure above a month or five weeks, and that for the purpose of sea bathing once a year.
18. By the minister and churchwardens to the poor.

[9] 21 Geo. III, c. 14.

19. I do not recollect any.
20. Chicklade. The nearest post town is Hindon.
Rev. Benjamin Blatch[1] is standing for his LL.B. degree, Oxford. Instituted to the rectory of Chicklade 26 Sept. 1780. Ord. D. 15 March 1772. Ord. P. 20 Sept. 1772.

41 CHILMARK f.353   D. Chalke
1. Divine service has been regularly performed every Lord's day; at half an hour after ten in the morning and at a quarter before three in the afternoon.
2. Divine service has not been customarily performed on any weekdays, but at the greater festivals: the inhabitants are mostly of the laborious class, and ordinary business would prevent their attendance on other days.
3. As curate to the Rev. Dr. Eyre.[2]
4. I serve no other church, and am not licensed to Chilmark, being only engaged to serve the duty for a short space of time, till a gentleman is admitted to holy orders.
5. The holy sacrament has been always administered four times a year, particularly at the greater festivals.
6. There have been generally about fourteen communicants; last Easter, as near as I can learn, there were about 17 or 18.
7 & 8. From careful enquiries, I can hear of no persons in the parish who differ from the established church. [e] I know of no person in the parish deserving this distinction.
9. Three or four Sundays every year, but at no particular season, it has been usual to instruct the children in the Church Catechism, in the vulgar tongue. It has been continued this summer, and expounded by the assistance of Archbishop Secker's lecture;[3] further I have taken every convenient occasion to preach on different parts of the catechism.
10. The register is duly kept, and the returns regularly made. The register commences in the reign of Charles II.
11. Such a register is duly kept and in good preservation.
12. There are no chapels in the parish.
13. There is a perfect terrier which bears the date 1704 signed by the minister and churchwardens. The living has undergone no alterations since the date of the terrier. [*On a separate sheet of paper:*] On the terrier: The rector is in possession of a very perfect terrier, the duplicate of which is lodged in the bishop's court. The terrier was made *anno* 1704, signed by the minister, churchwardens, and some of the inhabitants. Since that time the living has undergone no alterations. J. Bumpsted, curate. Chilmark, 3 Aug. 1783.
14. There is no free school in the village, or any other but a very inconsiderable day school.

---

[1] St. Edmund Hall Oxford 1767.
[2] Dr. Thomas Eyre, St. John's Coll. Oxford 1748. Rector of Fovant, **88,** and chaplain to Lord Pembroke, the patron of both livings. There are many references to him and letters from him in both volumes of *Pembroke Papers.*
[3] Thomas Secker, *Lectures on the Church Catechism,* published posthumously, 1769.

15. The churchwardens are chosen every Easter Monday; one by the minister, the other by the parishioners.

16. There is no public school in the parish.

17. Till within these few weeks the rector has resided in the parsonage house; since which, being on the point of resigning the cure, have not removed from the place I have hitherto resided in, viz. Wilton, 8 miles from Chilmark.

18. It has never been customary at Chilmark to collect alms at the administration of the holy sacrament.

19. Nothing that I can inform myself of.

20. I reside at Wilton near Salisbury.

J. Bumpsted, curate of Chilmark. Ord. D. 21 May 1720. Ord. P. 24 Dec. 1720.

Rev. Dr. Eyre, rector

42 CHILTON FOLIAT f.361   D. Marlborough

1. Divine service is performed in the parish church of Chilton Foliat, twice every Lord's day (viz.) both prayers and preaching at eleven in the forenoon, and prayers only at three in the afternoon.

2. Divine service is usually performed at Chilton upon no other weekdays but *Christmas day*, *Good Friday*, and *Fridays* in Lent, but this *latter* is at the option of the minister.

3. As curate. [4]

4. The present curate of Chilton serves no other church, nor is he licensed to the cure.

5. The holy sacrament of the Lord's Supper is administered at Chilton four times in the year, namely upon the three great festivals and the Sunday nearest the feast of St. Michael the Archangel.

6. The number of communicants has generally within the last seven years amounted to about 40. Last Easter their number seemed to be rather increasing.

7. None.

8. There are no professed sectaries of any denomination in the parish except one Quaker and his family consisting of nine persons. But there are many who absent themselves though not entirely yet in general from the public worship of God.

9. The parishioners do not send their children and servants to be instructed in their catechism by the curate. But there is in the village a charity school where the children of the poor are well instructed in reading, writing, and the Church catechism and brought to church every Lord's day in Lent to be examined publicly by the minister.

10. There is a register book of births and burials, but in no very good preservation, except for the last ten or fifteen years. The returns, as the curate believes, have been regularly made into the registrar's office. The first page of the oldest register extant bears date *anno domini* 1598.

11. There is.

[4] Rector, Dr. Edward Popham. See Lacock, **117**, of which he was vicar.

12. [a] None. [f] None.

13. The curate humbly presumes that this quere may be more satisfactorily answered by the rector than by him. All that he can say is that the edifices upon the living are in excellent repair and the temporal interests of the church well attended to.

14. The curate humbly presumes that the answer to these queres as far as the parish of Chilton is concerned will come more properly under the 16th article of enquiry. [d] None.

15. They are. One by the minister, and the other by the parishioners.

16. There is a charity school founded for about 20 boys and girls, who are taught reading, writing, accompts, and their catechism. They are provided with books but not clothed, nor is there any other resource for them upon leaving school than their own industry. The revenues of the school which amount to something more than £20 per annum are at present under the management of Mr. Bigg, a gentleman of honour and character. And the attention and diligence of the present master make the the school more respectable than in former years.

17. The curate does not reside in the parsonage house nor within the parish but at Hungerford, something short of 2 miles distant from the cure. The reason for non-residence is that he is master of the grammar school at Hungerford.

18. The money collected at the offertory is deposited in the church chest and annually at Christmas disposed of to clothe or otherwise relieve distressed family or families who receive no assistance from the parish, at the discretion of the minister and churchwardens.

19. I know of none, my Lord.

20. Hungerford, Berks.

Edward Meyrick,[5] was ord. D. by the present lord bishop of Bath and Wells, when bishop of St. David's, at his palace of Abergwilly 15 Aug. 1773. Ord. P. in the same place by the present lord bishop of Ely, when bishop of St. David's, 14 Aug. 1774.

43 CHIPPENHAM f.369   D. Malmesbury

1. Prayers and sermon every Sunday morning at ten o'clock, evening prayers at four in the summer and three in the winter unless prevented by extra duty at the chapel at Titherton.

2. Wednesdays and Fridays in Lent, every Friday, holiday, and festival in the year.

3. As incumbent.

4. None except my own chapel of Titherton three or four miles distant from the parish church.

5. The first Sunday in every month and on Christmas day, Easter day, and Whitsunday.

---

[5] Perhaps the Edward Meyrick of Hungerford whose son Edward Graves matric. Queen's Coll. Oxford 1795.

6. Between twenty and thirty in general, at Easter double that number, the same as usual.

7. Only one family, a relation of Lord Arundel's; none to my knowledge have been converted to popery; a chapel in Mr. Arundel's house, the priest resides with him, by name of Smith. No popish school.

8. A few of each sect, of no considerable rank. One Methodist meeting, Moore the name of the teacher, but whether licensed or not cannot say. Salter, the Presbyterian teacher and licensed according to law. The number about the same as usual since I have been incumbent. [e, f] Of the former I cannot be certain but have many that absent themselves from all public worship.

9. They do not. I catechize children belonging to the schools at different times in the year and endeavour to explain in my discourses some particular parts but have never expounded the whole at any particular part of the year or made use of any printed exposition.

10. [a] Yes. [b] Yes. [c] A hundred and fifty years.

11. Yes.

12. [a] One, Titherton-Lucas. [b] Prayers and sermon every Sunday except the first in the month and those Sundays that I am obliged to omit on account of the badness of the roads and shortness of the days in the winter season. [c] All the tithes of the place were given to the vicar of Chippenham in 1772. [d] Three or four miles. [e] By myself. [f] None.

13. None.

14. [a] A free school for twelve boys. [b] T. Woodroffe; the bailiff of the borough and vicar for the time being. [c] Yes. [d] There is a terrier in the registry of the lord bishop of Sarum made 1671 giving an account of the lands and leases belonging to the church. [e] Some feoffees have the management of them; no account hath passed for many years and I believe the parish receive[s] little or no benefit from them.

15. Yes, one by the minister, the other by the parishioners.

16. [a] No. [b] A school for girls founded by Mr. Lock, a vicar of Chippenham. A field was purchased with the money and lets for £5 5s. per year. The children are taught to read and write. I examine them every year in their catechism, they are brought to church, but neither lodged, fed, or clothed; in general go into service.

17. [a] I reside in the vicarage house but not constantly. [b] At Lewisham in the county of Kent about one hundred miles distance. [c] Very material family concerns.

18. By myself, and generally given to the greatest objects either in meat, bread, or clothing.

19. [Blank]

20. Chippenham.

Mr. Dalby was instituted to the vicarage 7 March 1777. Ord. D. 29 Dec. 1769 and ord. P. 23 Dec. 1770 at Christ Church Oxford. M.A.

Thomas Weekes Dalby,[6] vicar of Chippenham

[6] Christ Church Oxford 1765.

44 CHIRTON [Chirkton] f.377   D. Potterne
1. Divine service, both prayers and preaching, is performed once only on the Lord's day, in the morning and evening alternately. The morning service begins at ten o'clock, the evening service at three o'clock. Mr. Clarke pleads custom and the smallness of the income as reason why service is but once on a Lord's day.
2. On Christmas day only.
3. As curate.
4. I serve my parish of Wilcot and the cure of Wilsford. Wilcot is 5 miles and Wilsford 2 miles from Cheriton. The distance from Wilcot to Wilsford is 4 miles.
5. Three, viz. Christmas day, Easter Sunday, Whitsunday, or the Sundays next after those festivals.
6. [a] 14 or 15. [b] 14.
7. There is no reputed papist in this parish, nor do I know or believe that resort to it.
8. There are no dissenters in this parish, nor is there any place made use of for public worship besides the church, from which several commonly absent themselves.
9. The young persons have duly attended the times I have catechized this summer in the English language. I expound to them by the assistance of Lewis's catechism.
10. We have a register of baptisms and burials with paper leaves. I am informed that regular returns of baptisms and burials have been made into the registrar's office. The register goes back to 1579.
11. Yes.
12. [a] No. [f] No.
13. Mr. Clarke tells me there is a terrier dated 14 Feb. 1704/5 in the registry (of which he has a copy) and that an augmentation of £2 per annum has been since made to the vicarage, but that no account of such augmentation has been transmitted to the registry.
14. [a] No free school, alms-house, or hospital in this parish. [d] No.
15. The churchwardens are chosen yearly in the Easter week by the parishioners.
16. No.
17. I reside on my living at Wilcot, which place is 5 miles from Cheriton.
18. No money is collected.
19. I do not know of any.
20. Wilcot is my place of residence; Pewsey is the nearest post town.
                                              T. Markes,[7] curate

Deacon's orders of the above vicar bear date 23 Sept. 1770; priest's 22 Sept. 1771. Institution 1 Nov. 1781. Resides at Horningsham, near Frome, Wilts.
                                              Samuel Clarke,[8] vicar

[7] Thomas Markes. See Wilcot, **215**, of which he was vicar.
[8] Also curate of West Knoyle, **116**. The vicar's name etc. are in a different hand from the rest of the return.

45 CHISELDON f.385   D. Marlborough

1. Half hour after 10 in the morning, three in the afternoon alternately. Twice not customary for a long time past; another church, at the distance of one mile and a half only, served with it.
2. On all holidays and on Wednesdays and Fridays throughout Lent in one or other of the parishes alternately.
3. As incumbent.
4. Liddington as incumbent likewise, the distance at about one mile and a half.
5. At the four customary or most normal seasons.
6. Rather under twenty. At Easter last 17.
7 & 8. No papist or dissenter in the parish. The congregation in general commendably numerous.
9. The children are catechized on Sundays, and on Wednesdays and Fridays throughout Lent, and attend commendably; a course of sermons on the catechism is preached on the Lent Sundays at least once in two years.
10. The register is very duly kept from the year 1717 inclusive, and an extract annually returned to the registrar's office.
11. There is.
12. Nothing to be said on any of the items of this query.
13. A pretty good one and as perfect as conveniently it can be made. Two duplicates thereof in the registry of different dates but not exactly corresponding. An inclosure of 1779 hath augmented the benefice about £25 per annum. The Queen's Bounty by estate and interest amounts to £14 per annum.[9] No return of these to the registry hath yet been made.
14. [d] An estate of about £7 per annum: the rent divided to twenty poor housekeepers equally at Christmas at the direction of the minister and lord of the manor.
15. The churchwardens are very regularly chosen at Easter, one by the minister the other by the parishioners.
16. A school for teaching twenty poor children to read supported by a voluntary subscription of £10 per annum. They are likewise instructed in the Church catechism and brought together to church on all holidays at least.
17. Constant residence for twenty years past in the vicarage house.
18. To the poor at the discretion of the minister.
19. Nothing at present occurs.
20. Chiseldon near Swindon, Wilts.

Richard Stock.[1] Instituted 29 June 1762. Ord. D. 24 Dec. 1749. Ord. P. 23 Dec. 1750, by Dr. Benson, bishop of Gloucester. Was admitted to the degree of M.A. 22 June 1748.

46 CHITTERNE ALL SAINTS f.393   D. Wylye

1. Once a day the two churches, viz. Chittern St. Mary and All Saints being very near to each other, having the same audience in both, therefore divine

---

[9] 1757. £200 grant by Thomas Calley and £200 by Queen Anne's Bounty: *V.C.H. Wilts.* ix. 20.
[1] William Richard Stock, Pembroke Coll. Oxford 1741. The signature is in a different hand from the rest of the return.

service, prayers and preaching, is performed alternately in each church at the hours of 10 and three.
2. Not upon all holidays and festivals, there being no hearers.
3. As curate.[2]
4. Yes, both Chitterns and Telsead, the former being within a quarter of a mile's distance of each other, and the latter three miles.
5. Four times, viz. on the three great festivals and Michaelmas.
6. About twenty in general but somewhat more last Easter and Whitsunday.
7. None at all.
8. No dissenters of any denomination whatever, except one Presbyterian; no dissenting place of worship, and but few absenters.
9. As many as are sent are catechized in Lent, and without any exposition.
10. Yes, which goes back as far as the year 1654.
11. Yes.
12. No.
13. Yes, and a duplicate thereof laid in the bishop's registry, and no augmentation made since.
14. None at all.
15. Yes, one by the minister and the other by the parishioners.
16. No.
17. Yes, but not in the vicarage house.
18. None given.
19. Nothing at all.
20. Chittern All Saints, Heytesbury the nearest post town.
   Ord. D. in 1779 and ord. P. in 1780.

Thomas Davies[3]

47 CHITTERNE ST. MARY f.401   D. Wylye
1. Once only, owing to the fewness of the inhabitants, at the hours of ten o'clock and three alternately.
2. Not upon all holidays and festivals, having no hearers.
3. As curate.
4. Yes, Chittern All Saints and Telsead, the former about a quarter of a mile and the other three miles distance.
5. Four times, viz. on the three great festivals and Michaelmas.
6. About fifteen in general but somewhat more last Easter.
7. None at all.
8. No dissenters of any denomination whatever, except one Presbyterian; neither any dissenting places of worship, and but few absenters.
9. As many as are sent, I catechize in Lent, without exposition.
10. Yes, and regular returns thereof made into the registrar's office. It goes back as far as the year [blank].
11. Yes.

[2] Vicar, Charles Gibbes. Probably St. Edmund Hall Oxford 1730. Vicar of Chitterne St. Mary, **47**, and curate of Marden, **138**, and resident at Urchfont. Father of George Gibbes of Woodborough and Patney, **226** and **156**.
[3] Perhaps Jesus Coll. Oxford 1770.

12. No.
13. Yes, and a duplicate thereof laid in the bishop's registry, and no augmentations made since.
14. None at all.
15. Yes, one by the minister and the other by the parishioners.
16. No.
17. [b] In the same village though not in the same parish.
18. None given.
19. Nothing at all.
20. Chittern All Saints, Heytesbury the nearest post town.

Thomas Davies, clerk[4]

48 CHOLDERTON [Choldrington] f.409   D. Amesbury
1. Eleven o'clock prayers and preaching. Prayers in the afternoon at 3 o'clock.
2. No.
3. As curate.[5]
4. [a, b, c] Yes, the curacy of Shipton,[6] a mile and half distant. [d] No.
5. Four times in the year, viz. Christmas, Easter, Whitsuntide, and Michaelmas.
6. About 12 or 14. At Easter about the same number.
7. [a] No. [b] No. [c] No. [d] No. [e] No.
8. No.
9. No.
10. [a] Yes. [b] Yes. [c] The register begins at 1652, and there is none to be found before that time.
11. Yes.
12. [a] None. [f] None.
13. There appears an old terrier dated 1677. But being found imperfect, a new one will be delivered to your Lordship, after the harvest is cleared that there may be a view taken of the lands.
14. No.
15. The parish consisting of only one farm, the churchwardens are continued.
16. There is a donation of £12 per annum left by Colonel Cracherode; of which £7 16s. is for the instruction of twelve poor children, £3 3s. given to the poor at Christmas, and £1 1s. for books.
17. No. At Kimpton, 4 miles distant.
18. The small collection that is made is disposed of by the curate among those poor that attend the sacrament.
19. No.
20. Kimpton near Andover, Hants.

B. Cane,[7] curate of Cholderton

49 CHRISTIAN MALFORD f.417   D. Malmesbury
1. Twice, at half an hour after 10 in the morning, and 3 in the afternoon.

---

[4] Curate and vicar the same as Chitterne All Saints, **46.**
[5] Rector, John Bradley. Perhaps Oriel Coll. Oxford 1752.
[6] Shipton Bellinger, Hants, diocese of Winchester.
[7] Basil Cane (Keene in Clergy Books, 1783). Oriel Coll. Oxford 1749. See also **82.**

2. Upon the days after the festivals of Christmas and Easter, upon Good Friday, and sometimes Ash Wednesday.

3. As incumbent.

4. None.

5. On the 3 great festivals.

6. [a] Between 20 and 30. [b] Generally much the same.

7. None as far as I know.

8. None, I believe, but Methodists, except perhaps a Moravian or two; and only one Methodist meeting *not licensed;* but several preachers, whose licences are unknown; the resident teacher not licensed.[8] Many sabbath-breakers, whom nothing but compulsion will, I fear, ever influence, and whose names will be returned whenever required.

9. The children are catechized annually in Lent; and on account of the number of schools and distribution of premiums are very numerous, I make use of no exposition in particular, sometimes Archbishop Secker's, at other times Dr. Clarke's.[9]

10. The register book is well preserved, and regularly kept and returned. The births and burials go as far back as the year 1653.

11. There is.

12. None.

13. There is a true original copy of the terrier in the bishop's registry of which I have a duplicate; I don't know how to make one more exact so have sent none; there has been an addition since of a small stable and waggon-house, but they are such trifling alterations as not to be worth mentioning. An augmentation has been made lately in my living of about £50 a year, an account of which may be transmitted, whenever required.

14. None.

15. Every year by the minister and parishioners alternately.

16. *3* supported chiefly by voluntary contribution. *1* for boys for writing and accompts. *2* others for either sex to learn reading, needlework, etc. When fit for service or apprenticeship, the parents dispose of them at pleasure.

17. I have resided almost constantly in my parsonage house for near 26 years.

18. By myself, chiefly to the necessitous communicants and sometimes to sick absentees.

19. Not to my knowledge.

20. Specified above, at my living of Christian Malford near Chippenham.
Collated to Christian Malford 16 Jan. 1756. Ord. D. by Bishop Pierce for Bishop Sherlock 1 Dec. 1755. Ord. P. by my father[1] 14 Jan. 1756. Oxon. made A.M. about 1753.[2]

[8] For the work of Whitefield, Rowland Hill, and Cornelius Winter at Christian Malford, see *V.C.H. Wilts.* iii. 131.

[9] Dr. Samuel Clarke's *Exposition of the Church Catechism* (1729).

[1] Edward Willes, bishop of Bath and Wells 1743–73.

[2] No signature. William Willes rector. Wadham Coll. Oxford 1747.

50 CLYFFE PYPARD [Cleeve Pepper] f.425 D. Avebury

1. Once every Sunday between ten and eleven and two and three alternately, having the care of another church.
2. Frequently.
3. As incumbent.
4. Winterbourne Bassett cure adjoining. Churches about two miles from each other. Not licensed.
5. Four times, viz. Easter, Whitsuntide, Michaelmas, and Christmas.
6. About 24, at Easter last 18, near as usual.
7. None, or any place of assembly for divine worship of that sort.
8. None. Other places are made use of for divine worship by a sect vulgarly called Methodists. The names of their teachers are one Shuter, Ways, Mills, Taylor, Sermon, Buttler, and Williams, etc. unknown to me. Not long sprung up before the house of Abel Greenaway was certified by the bishop's register 23 Jan. 1782. [*At top of last page in another hand:*] Jos. Elderton, registrar, 23 Jan. 1782, certificate to Abel Greenaway.
9. They do. I make use of the Church catechism (in the English language) at Lent and at some other times.
10. We have one duly kept, and in good preservation. Births and burials are regularly returned, and go as far back as 1683.
11. There is one.
12. There are none.
13. There appears to be an extract from the registry in 1704, but no augmentation since to my knowledge.
14. [a] There is a charitable endowment for 20 poor persons of £20 yearly, conducted by the officiating minister. [b] Mr. Thomas Spackman was founder, who left lands for that purpose. [d] I have never heard of any lands or tenements for the repair of the church, or any other pious use.
15. They are chosen one by the minister and the other by the parishioners.
16. There is a public school for boys and girls (at present) supported by the voluntary subscription of Mr. Thomas Spackman. They are taught the English language, writing, and accounts, are instructed in the liturgy of the Church of England every day, and come regularly to church. The school flourishes.
17. Constantly, not in the house belonging to it, but in a house adjoining the churchyard.
18. To the use of the poor.
19. None as I can recollect at present.
20. Clyffe Pypard near Wotton Bassett.

Deacon's orders 1761, priest's orders 1770. Clyff institution 1780. Draycott Foliatt institution 1780.

Edward Goddard[3], vicar

[3] Trinity Coll. Oxford 1741. Patron of the living. He was so dissatisfied with the incumbent presented in 1745 that he himself took orders and presented himself in 1780: *V.C.H. Wilts.* ix. 40. Rector of Draycot Foliat, **74,** also in the gift of the Goddard family, where there was no church, and curate of Winterbourne Bassett, **219.**

1 CODFORD ST. MARY f.433   D. Wylye

. Divine service is performed in this church twice on every Lord's day. Prayers and sermon at ten o'clock in the morning, and prayers at four in the afternoon.

2. No weekly prayers excepting holidays, which are always observed in this parish.

3. As curate.[4]

4. I serve another cure,[5] within a small distance of this parish, but have no licence.

5. The sacrament is administered in this church at four different times in the year, viz. at Easter, Whitsun, feast of St. Michael, and Christmas.

6. The number of communicants in this parish is, in general, about twenty, which was the number at Easter last.

7. We have no such persons within our parish, no place of divine worship for that purpose, nor any popish priest residing herein; neither have we any popish schools.

8. We have one Anabaptist only in this parish, who attends at their meeting which is at some distance from hence. We have none of the within mentioned sects, nor any teachers of the same. None that profess to disregard religion, but orderly and decently attend divine worship.

9. The children of this parish are generally catechized in Lent time, I expound to them myself, always in the English language.

10. We have a regular register book of births and burials duly kept, and a copy of the same sent in to the registrar's office every year. It goes back to the year 1612.

11. There is a register book of the same duly kept.

12. We have no chapels of ease or any such building whatever within my parish.

13. There is a terrier of all lands, tithes, etc. belonging to the rector enclosed herewith.

14. We have no free school, alms-house, nor any endowment whatever belonging to this parish.

15. The churchwardens are always chosen in the Easter week, by the minister and parishioners jointly.

16. We have no public school whatever in this parish.

17. I constantly reside upon this cure and never absent but when called upon business of moment, which seldom happens to me.

18. We have no such custom.

19. None to the best of my knowledge.

20. Codford St. Mary near Heytesbury.

    In testimony of the truth of the within mentioned particulars I have set my hand 24 July 1783.

                                           Henry Williams,[6] curate

---

[4] Rector, Dr. Thomas Smith. See Swindon, **194,** where he was resident vicar.
[5] Fisherton de la Mere, **85.**
[6] Probably also curate of Stockton. **188.**

52 CODFORD ST. PETER f.441   D. Wylye
1. In morning prayers and a sermon at half after ten. In afternoon prayers
at half after two.
2. Yes, on holidays.
3. Incumbent.
4. None.
5. Four times, viz. Christmas, Easter, Whitsun, and Michaelmas.
6. Generally about twenty.
7. None.
8. [a] None. [e] *Some, commonly.*
9. Servants regularly come. Children constantly catechized in Lent.
10. [a] Duly kept. [b] Yes. [c] 1681.
11. Yes, there is.
12. [a] *[Blank]* [f] None at all.
13. My rectory has been sometimes occupied, and sometimes let.
14. [d] *Some monies,* distributed at the discretion of minister and churchwardens.
15. Yes, one by the minister and the other by the parishioners.
16. None, excepting the minister's sending six children regularly to school at
his own charge.
17. I always reside on my rectory.
18. None given.
19. None.
20. Codford St. Peter near Heytesbury.
   Charles Thomas Kellow.[7] Ord. D. 1764. Ord. P. 1768. Instituted to the
rectory of Codford St. Peter *anno* 1777.

53 COLERNE f.449   D. Malmesbury
1. Divine service, both prayers and preaching, is performed once on every
Sunday at the hours of eleven in the morning and three in the afternoon,
alternately. I serve the curacy of Ditcheridge once in every fortnight, and on
the intermediate Sunday have frequently an opportunity of serving a friend
who may be ill or absent.
2. Never except on Good Friday and Christmas day when a sermon is
preached and the sacrament administered.
3. As incumbent.
4. The curacy of Ditcheridge, distant about one mile and half.
5. Four times in every year, viz. on Christmas day, Good Friday, Whitsunday, and the Sunday next before the feast of St. Michael.
6. At Christmas generally about twenty. On last Good Friday not more than
eight or nine. The number has been less of late than usual.
7. No papist or reputed papist.
8. None to my knowledge.
9. No person comes to me to be privately instructed. The children are

7 Trinity Coll. Oxford 1760.

catechized in the church in Lent or in the month of June when an exposition is read instead of the sermon for the day.
10. The register book is properly kept, and returns regularly made. It goes back to the year 1761.
11. There is.
12. No chapel of ease or ruinated chapel.
13. [Blank]
14. [Blank]
15. The churchwardens have been usually nominated, one by the minister, the other by the parishioners. The same churchwardens have been tacitly continued 6 or 7 years.
16. No charity school.
17. I reside constantly at Colerne but not in the vicarage house.
18. To the poorest of the people when sick or in distress.
19. Nothing, as I believe.
20. Colerne, Bath.
N. A. Bliss. Nathaniel Alsop Bliss[8] A.B. 10 Oct. 1769. Ord. D. 24 Dec. 1769. Ord. P. 26 May 1771. Instituted to Colerne 23 Feb. 1773. A.M. 5 July 1773.

54 COMPTON BASSETT f.457 D. Avebury
1. Divine service (prayers and preaching) is performed regularly every Sunday morning throughout the year, beginning usually about a quarter before eleven o'clock; and service twice a day (with prayers only in the afternoon) at 3 o'clock from the Sunday after Ascension day to Michaelmas. This has been the established practice in the parish for many years back.
2. Divine service is performed (but without a sermon) on Ash Wednesday, Good Friday, and Easter Monday in every year.
3. As incumbent.
4. I serve no other cure whatever.
5. Three times a year as follows, viz. Easter day, Whitsunday, and Christmas.
6. The communicants are generally about sixteen, but the number was considerably less at Easter last, owing to the casual absence of the two principal families from the parish, who when here seldom fail to communicate.
7. None, nor have any persons been lately perverted to popery, neither is there any place in the parish in which they assemble for worship. As to any popish priest either residing in or resorting to the parish, or any popish school kept here, I cannot learn there is either one or the other.
8. On diligent enquiry I do not find there are any of the sects mentioned in the question, neither are there in the parish any places for worship belonging to any other denomination of Christians.
9. I cannot speak with certainty to the articles of this question, having had

[8] New Coll. Oxford 1766. New College were the patrons of the living. The Clergy Books, 1783, give Dr. John Oglander, warden of New College, as 'rector, without institution, by a modern Act of Parliament', i.e. 5 Geo. III, c. 11 (Priv.) 1765, 'An Act for annexing the rectory of Colerne, in the County of Wilts., to the Office of Warden of the College of St. Mary, of Winchester in Oxford'.

the living little more than a year, during the greater part of which I have
been absent, obliged to it by an ill state of health and some necessary repairs
wanting in the parsonage house, which have not long been finished. I will
take strict care the duty of catechizing shall be duly performed in future, at
the accustomed season of Lent. *Bishop Wake's* will be the printed exposition
I intend making use of, and the examination will be in English.

10. There are two register books belonging to the parish: one, which is very
old, commencing A.D. 1558 and ending about 1680, has parchment leaves,
and considering its age is in decent preservation. The other is in tolerably
neat condition, and begins A.D. 1681. The returns of births and burials are
regularly made agreeably to the canon.

11. There is likewise a register book duly kept, according to the direction of
the Act against clandestine marriages.

12. No chapel of ease whatever, nor any which is ruinated.

13. On my induction your registrar sent me, pursuant to my letter for that
purpose, a terrier, bearing date 22 Jan. 1704, Michael Geddes, rector. This
instrument not only does not contain many particulars specified in the
question and which are detailed more at large in your Lordship's instructions
on this subject, but is now become in a manner useless, in consequence of an
inclosure in the year 1725, whereby the lands belonging to the rectory, and
which formerly lay in open common fields, were by certain allotments then
made in lieu thereof very much altered both in point of quantity and local
situation. The part of the glebe nearest to the house remains the same as
before. Your Lordship will please to excuse my not producing a terrier this
visitation, as I have not yet had the leisure to collect the proper materials, nor
the information necessary to authenticate such a writing.

14. In this parish there is neither free school, alms-house, hospital, or other
charitable endowment.

15. Yearly chosen in the Easter week; one churchwarden by the minister,
the other by the parishioners.

16. Only a small day school (unendowed) where reading, writing, etc. are
taught at a low price. The children are examined in the catechism once a
week, and are otherwise instructed in Christian principles. They attend
church, I believe, very constantly, at least those among the children whose
parents or relations live in the parish.

17. In answer to the first article in the question, I can only say I reside (in the
parsonage house) as much as my health and private circumstances will
permit. My absence uncertain, it may be about 5 months. My father lives in
The Grove at Highgate, where I may be heard of. In case I shall not be able
to keep a longer residence, I intend to put in a resident curate, with which
I hope your Lordship will be satisfied, as I am sure the parish will be.[9]

18. The sacrament money is disposed of by the minister for the relief of the
most necessitous poor in the parish.

19. Nothing besides what is already set down.

20. [*Blank*]

[9] Served by the curate of Yatesbury, **231**, who lived in Calne.

George Hayter,[1] rector of Compton Bassett. B.A. Exeter College, Oxford, 1775. Ord. D. 21 Dec. 1775 by Dr. Terrick, bishop of London. Ord. P. 21 Dec. 1776 by ditto. Collation to Compton Bassett 1 April 1782.

55 COMPTON CHAMBERLAYNE f.465   D. Chalke

1. Divine service is performed in the church at Compton Chamberlain once every Lord's day, alternately in the morning and afternoon; it is [not] performed twice on account of the small value of the living.
2. Divine service is [not] usually performed on weekdays, except on the more solemn occasions.
3. The cure is served by Mr. Smith,[2] as assistant to R. Head, who was instituted to the vicarage 9 June 1748.
4. With Compton Chamberlain Mr. Smith serves the adjoining cure of Baverstock.
5. The holy sacrament of the Lord's Supper is administered at Christmas, Easter, Whitsuntide, and Michaelmas.
6. At present I am not able to answer Q.6 with a proper degree of exactness; but have no reason to imagine that the number of communicants at Easter last was less than usual.[3]
7. I believe there are no reputed papists in the parish.
8. I do not know of any dissenters in the parish, nor of any persons who profess to disregard religion.
9. I presume the children are duly catechized.
10. A register book of births and burials is duly kept; and I presume returns thereof are made into the registrar's office. The register commenced in the year 1538 as I think, or at the original institution of registers.
11. A register book of marriages is duly kept.
12. There is no chapel of ease in the parish, nor any ruinated chapel.
13. Two terriers of Compton Chamberlain are in the bishop's registry. Augmentations to the value of £600 have been lately made to the living by the governors of the Bounty of Queen Anne,[4] and by Charles Penruddocke Esq., the patron. These are not yet inserted in the terrier, as a purchase is in view.
14. There is no free school, alms-house, or hospital in the parish nor do I know of any other charitable endowment, except what is mentioned in the terriers.
15. The churchwardens are chosen about Easter by the minister and parishioners.
16. There is no public school founded in the parish.

---

[1] Exeter Coll. Oxford 1771.
[2] Thomas Smith. See **11**, where Compton Chamberlayne is included in his return for Baverstock.
[3] See **11**, where the number of communicants at Compton Chamberlayne is given as about 20.
[4] In 1780 and 1783: Hodgson, p. 416.

17. I do not reside at Compton Chamberlain, but at Amesbury, a post town, twelve miles distant, for the convenience of serving the cures of Rowlston and Durrington.
18. No money is usually given at the offertory.
19. I know of no other matter belonging to the parish of which it may be proper to give your Lordship information.
20. Answered under Q.17.

R. Head M.A.,[5] vicar of Compton Chamberlain. Ord. D. 21 Sept. 1746. Ord. P. 20 Sept. 1747.

56 COULSTON [Cowlston] f.473   D. Potterne
1. Once every Lord's day in the parish church, generally a little before two o'clock, which time best suits the parishioners, on account of their large dairies; sometimes at eleven in the morning. The present rector found no other custom than is now complied with.
2. No.
3. As curate.[6]
4. [a] Yes, I am curate to Dr. Stonhouse, who is rector of Great and Little Cheverel. [b] The distance between the two churches of the Cheverels is less than one mile; from Great Cheverel to Coulston is two miles. [c] No.
5. Three times, namely Christmas, Easter, and Whitsuntide.
6. 1781 Christmas 10.
   1782 Easter 10; Whitsuntide 8; Christmas 10.   .
   1783 Easter 15; Whitsuntide 11.
   I commenced curate 20 June 1781.
7. [a] None. [c] No. [d] No. [e] No.
8. [a] Not one. [b] No. This parish contains but nine houses, six of which are cottages; hence I can easily discover who are absent; the greater part attend regularly.
9. I have twice endeavoured to catechize their children and servants, but none attended; on enquiry I am told the children are too young; and servants ashamed to expose their ignorance publicly.
10. [a] Yes. [b] Yes. [c] 1680.
11. Yes.
12. [a] No. [f] No.
13. Two are prepared, one of which will be delivered at the visitation, the other will be kept with the parish register.
14. No.
15. This parish continues the same person churchwarden for several years successively; one only, who is re-chosen every Easter by the parishioners.
16. No.
17. [a, b] I reside at the parsonage house at Great Cheverel, two miles from Coulston. [c] Not a day.

[5] Richard Head, 1723–1800. St. John's Coll. Cambridge 1742. Rector of Rollestone, **167**, and perpetual curate of Durrington, **75**.
[6] Rector, John Montagu. Perhaps University Coll. Oxford 1761 and fellow of All Souls. Also rector of Hilperton, **102**.

18. None collected.
19. I know of none.
20. Great Cheverel near Devizes.
Ord. D. 17 Oct. 1779. Or. P. 24 Sept. 1780. I am of Trinity College Cambridge but have not yet taken a degree.

William Roots,[7] curate. 28 July 1783

57 COLLINGBOURNE DUCIS f.481   D. Marlborough

1. Divine service is performed in my church twice every Lord's day, very extraordinary occasions excepted, viz. at 11 o'clock in the morning and at 3 in the afternoon. Prayers and preaching in the forenoon, only prayers in the afternoon.
2. Only on principal holidays or festivals that happen on weekdays. It has been dropped on other saints days for want of a congregation.
3. As incumbent.
4. I serve no other cure.
5. Four times in the year, at the 3 great festivals, and at Michaelmas.
6. Never more than twenty, seldom as many. Most communicants at Easter. Twenty was about the number last Easter.
7. None.
8. None. I know of no persons in my parish who *profess* to disregard religion. There are some who too often absent themselves from the public worship of God.
9. I catechize the children in the afternoon of Sundays between Whitsuntide and harvest. To the bigger ones I give Lewis's catechism, portions of which they learn by heart, and repeat to me at the same time.
10. I have, and the returns are duly and regularly made. The register goes back to 1653.
11. There is, and duly kept.
12. None.
13. I have in my possession a copy of an old terrier made in 1704. An exchange of lands lying in the common fields was made in the year 1775 by commissioners properly appointed. A true and exact account of the glebe lands belonging to the parsonage as settled by them will be delivered to your Lordship's registrar, together with an account of tithes, and all dues, etc. [*Written in the margin:*] An account and measurement of the glebe lands was taken in the year 1748.
14. There is no free school, alms-house, hospital, or other charitable endowment in my parish. I have in my hands £11 11s. transmitted to me by my predecessor as *charity money belonging to the parish;* whence it came, or to what uses to be applied, I have never been able to learn. The deposit has been kept sacred in my hands, and by way of interest for it, I have for five and twenty years past put 6 or 8 poor children to school, who are taught to read, and are instructed in the Church catechism.

[7] See **38**.

15. Our churchwardens are chosen every year in the Easter week, one by the minister, and the other by the parishioners.

16. There are none; nor any endowment or provision of that kind whatever.

17. I reside constantly upon my cure, and in the house belonging to it, except when I am necessarily obliged to be at another living which I have in the diocese of Winchester.[8] In my absence from hence I take care that the duty of this church and parish be properly done.

18. This is given by the minister to poor people who are communicants, or who have been communicants, but are hindered from attending the church by age and infirmities; and to any poor person who happens at the time to be sick in the parish.

19. I know of none.

20. At my parsonage house at Collingbourne Ducis. The nearest post towns are Pewsey, Wilts., and Andover, Hants.

William Tomlins A.M.[9] Ord. D. 20 Dec. 1741. Ord. P. 23 Dec. 1744. Instituted to the rectory of Collingbourne Ducis 1 May 1756.

58 COLLINGBOURNE KINGSTON f.489　　　　D. Marlborough

1. Divine service is performed alternately in the morning at eleven and in the afternoon at three as has been customary for many years, owing to the smallness of the living.

2. Divine service has not been performed in this church upon any weekdays, holidays, or festivals, Good Friday and Christmas day excepted.

3. Divine service is performed by Mr. Swayne,[1] my curate.

4. I understand Mr. Swayne officiates at his own church, Milton.

5. The holy sacrament is administered four times a year, viz. Christmas, Easter, Whitsuntide, and Michaelmas.

6. I am informed by Mr. Swayne that the number of communicants at Easter were about thirty, about the same number lately for some years past.

7. There are no reputed papists in the parish, neither doth any popish priest reside, nor is there any popish school kept in the parish.

8. There are no Presbyterians, Independents, Anabaptists, or Quakers in the parish. Mr. Swayne has not informed me that there are any persons who profess any disregard to religion living in the parish.

9. I have not heard that Mr. Swayne regularly catechizes the children.

10. There is a register book duly kept; returns are regularly made of births and burials into the registrar's office. It goes back to the year 1653.

11. There is a register book kept also against clandestine marriages.

12. There are no chapels of any kind in this parish.

13. There is a terrier belonging to this parish a duplicate of which has been laid up in the bishop's registry. There has been no augmentation made since the above has laid up in your Lordship's registry.

14. [a] There is no free school, alms-house, hospital, or other charitable endowment in the parish, consequently no governors etc. [d] There is a piece

8 Upham, Hants.
9 1709–88. St. Mary's Hall Oxford 1731. M.A. from King's Coll. Cambridge 1747.
1 John Swain, vicar of Milton Lilborne, **142.**

of land called Church acre lying in Southton Field value 15s. per annum, another acre in Aughton tything let for 9s. per annum for the use of the church under the direction of the churchwardens.

15. Churchwardens are chosen every year in the Easter week, one by the minister, the other by the parishioners.

16. There is not nor has there been founded in this parish any public or charity school.

17. I am a minor canon of the cathedral church of Winchester.

18. This is usually given to the poor communicants.

19. There is nothing relating to this parish that I could wish to inform your Lordship of.

20. I reside at Winchester.

Instituted 15 May 1770. Ord. D. 1768. Ord. P. 1769. B.A.

Nicholas Westcombe[2]

59 CORSLEY f.497   D. Wylye

[*Written across the top of the bishop's letter:*] The award for the terrier being not yet finally settled, the rector will transmit the particulars mentioned by his Lordship in his paper of directions the earliest opportunity.

[*Written at the foot of the letter:*] Before I had the honour of receiving this paper from his Lordship, I took occasion in my discourse on the Sunday when I read the Articles to tell my parishioners that the church would in future be more diligently attended to than it has been of late years, as his Lordship will observe in some of the answers to the following queries.

1. The church has not been served for many years back oftener than once on a Sunday, and that alternately morning and afternoon; the hours ½ past 10 and ½ past two. The reason I suppose to have been originally inattention, afterwards pleading custom, and thence concluding that because the church was served once for years back, therefore it ought not to be better served in future.

2. Only on Good Friday and Christmas day. But in future I purpose to serve the church twice in a week during Lent, all the Passion week, and the Mondays and Tuesdays in the Easter and Whitsun week.

3. As incumbent at Michaelmas next, when I shall be quit from my present engagement;[3] in the meanwhile, the church will be served by whatever assistants I can from time to time procure.

4. At the time mentioned in the last answer it is my intention to attend entirely to this church, and serve no other, because I am of the opinion that every parish should have divine service twice every Lord's day; the neglect of this in general has been a great cause of the increase of meeting-houses.

5. Hitherto it has been administered only on the 3 great festivals: but from Michaelmas next it is my intention to administer the sacrament regularly the first Sunday in every month, and in every other respect to restore the discipline of the church as nearly to its primitive institution as the difference of times will admit of.

---

[2] 1744–1813. Trinity Coll. Oxford 1763.
[3] Clergy Books, 1783, give 'Mr. Huntingford' as curate of Brixton Deverill. See also **17**.

6. About a score.

7. No papists in the parish, no popish chapel, nor priest. [e] None.

8. Presbyterians about 30 grown persons mostly of the lower class. Quakers none; Methodists about 12. The Methodists are Wesley's followers, have a licensed house, but no regular preacher. The Baptists have a licensed house, a regular preacher named Perrot licensed, and the Presbyterians attend a meeting-house standing in another parish. I am sorry to say that there [are] 10 or 12 families who live in total disregard to religion, and frequent no house of worship whatever.

9. Hitherto the parishioners have had no opportunities afforded them of having their children and servants publicly catechized. But it is my intention to catechize every Sunday, except on sacrament days.

10. [a] Yes. [c] To the year 1686.

11. Yes.

12. [a] No. [f] None.

13. None. The living hath been augmented by the late inclosing Act,[4] but the award is not yet finally settled.

14. None.

15. One churchwarden is chosen every year by the minister and parishioners from the overseers, who the next year becomes senior churchwarden, collects rates and pays all the church bills.

16. A dissenting minister, who preaches in another parish, keeps a school for writing and reading.

17. I purpose to reside there two months in the year, which is as much as my business at Warminster school will admit of. Warminster is not more than 4 miles distant from Corsley church, and so scattered are the houses of the last mentioned parish, that I am almost as near to some of them at my house in Warminster as if I resided at the parsonage house. Before the inclosing Act took lace the glebe of Corsley parish reached to within ½ a mile of Warminster church.

18. To the poor of the parish.

19. The communion table and appurtances are by no means in that decent condition which the sacredness of the place seems to require. It is not properly set apart for religious uses, but is made use of also for the transaction of parish business, at vestries. Neither the table, pulpit, or reading desk have any cloth to them, which by a word only from his Lordship would be ımmediately provided.[5] Farmers care not for these matters, and pay very ittle regard to decency in the house of God.

20. Warminster, a post town.

    Thomas Huntingford M.A.[6] Instituted 21 May 1783. Ord. D. 20 Dec. 1772. Ord. P. 15 June 1777. Both at Oxford.

[4] Warminster and Corsley Inclosure Act, 20 Geo. III, c. 36.

[5] Clergy Books note 'pulpit cloth, desk cloth, and communion cloth wanting'. These deficiencies were also presented by the churchwardens: Sarum Dioc. R.O., Churchwardens' presentments 1783.

[6] 1750–87. Trinity Coll. Oxford 1769. Master of Warminster school. At his death his widow and children were left in poverty and his brother, George Isaac (successively assistant master and warden of Winchester, bishop of Gloucester and Hereford), was nominated his successor at both Warminster school and Corsley by the marquess of Bath in order to provide for them: D.N.B. on George Isaac Huntingford.

60 CRICKLADE ST. MARY f.513 D. Cricklade

1. Every other Sunday in the afternoon, prayers and sermon. Divine service is served twice every Lord's day within the two parishes of St. Sampson and St. Mary, Cricklade, and the church of St. Sampson's is large enough to contain the inhabitants of both parishes, but the pews in general as well as the reading desk and pulpit is much out of repair, in Cricklade St. Sampson, the boards in some of them rotten and broke away from the earth, and if I have not been explicit in this particular in my presentment for Cricklade St. Sampson I wish to be so now.
2. At Cricklade St. Sampson's but not here.
3. Curate to Rev. Mr. Middleton.[7]
4. Eisey and St. Sampson.
5. Christmas, Easter day, Whitsuntide, and Michaelmas.
6. About eight or ten; at Easter perhaps about 12.
7. None.
8. None.
9. During Lent both here and at St. Sampson's.
10. Such a book is properly kept by me as curate.
11. There is.
12. None.
13. I suppose Mr. Middleton may have such a terrier.
14. [d] 100 acres on the common run let at about £70 a year left by Queen Elizabeth in exchange for some forest land solely at the disposal of bailiff, constable, and churchwardens for second poor; also about £30 a year in land at the discretion of minister, churchwardens, and overseers, part to be laid out in great coats; about £15 a year at the discretion of trustees appointed by the Chancellor. £5 a year by the will of the family of Jennours at Christmas at the discretion of the minister, all which I believe to be duly and properly applied in both parishes.
15. One by the minister, the other by the parish.
16. None.
17. In the vicarage house of St. Sampson.
18. No collection but at St. Sampson.
19. None.
20. Cricklade is a post town.
   Ord. D. at the White Hall Chapel, London, by the bishop of Ely 1771. Ord. P. at the cathedral of Gloucester 1775, in July.

E. Campbell[8]

61 CRICKLADE ST. SAMPSON f.521 D. Cricklade

1. Every Lord's day a quarter before eleven, in the morning prayers and sermon and prayers in the afternoon at three o'clock, when divine service is not required at Cricklade St. Mary.

[7] David Middleton. Perhaps Magdalen Hall Oxford 1778.
[8] Also curate of Eisey, **83.**

2. Divine service is performed on Wednesdays and Fridays, holidays and festivals.

3. As curate.[9]

4. At Eisey as curate, one short mile, and at Cricklade St. Mary adjoining to this parish.

5. At the four usual seasons, Christmas, Easter, Whitsuntide, and Michaelmas.

6. I judge between twenty and thirty, nearer thirty or perhaps more at Easter and Whitsuntide.

7. No papists or Roman Catholics as I ever heard of within eight miles of this place.

8. At one Thomas Batt's a shoemaker there is a meeting who call themselves Independents but are commonly called Methodists. The said Thomas Batt says he has a licence for his house or meeting taken out at Salisbury. [f] There is a man Gunne has or does not attend divine worship with any kind of propriety for these three years last past nor Deborah his wife, nor have either of them attended the sacrament for these six years upwards. [*This sentence is crossed out, but still legible.*]

9. Not so often as I could wish though I have given notice in the church that I should be willing from the beginning of Lent till Michaelmas ensuing to hear them. The smallpox has of late been some impediment, but our Church catechism is never omitted during Lent.

10. The office of making the returns of births and burials into the registrar's office is and has usually been done by the clerk of the parish; the parchment books for that purpose are in good order and are kept at my house as curate, the date of which for baptisms commences 1673 and for burials 1695.

11. A register book for marriages is kept according to the Act.

12. No chapel of ease; formerly one on the Widhill estate belonging now to the earl of Radnor but, service discontinued these fifty years, is become a ruinated place.

13. I suppose there is one in the possession of the vicar.

14. No alms-house nor hospital but formerly a free school endowed with £20 a year bequeathed by one Robert Jenner Esq., but no salary or master has been paid it during these last fifty years, though I am informed many of the charitable legacies left by him in other places are still kept paid, all which, I believe, are now paid out of the Widhill estate which of late is become the property of Lord Radnor.

15. The churchwardens are chosen every Easter Monday, one by me as representing Dr. Frome, the other by the parish.

16. See this quere answered against quere the fourteenth.

17. I constantly reside in the vicarage house.

18. To the most ancient poor widows and sometimes to the sick.

19. I recollect no other.

---

[9] Vicar, Dr. Thomas Frome. Merton Coll. Oxford 1754.

20. Cricklade, and a post town.
 Ord. D. at the chapel of White Hall 9 May 1771 and ord. P. at the cathedral of Gloucester in July 1775.

E. Campbell

62 CRUDWELL f.529[1]   D. Malmesbury

1. Once a day, morning and evening alternately, and alternating with the church of Hankerton, a vicarage contiguous to Crudwell and usually held by the rector of Crudwell, being in his patronage.
2. On such days as has been usual, on great festivals and fasts.
3. As incumbent.
4. I serve the church of Hankerton, distant one mile.
5. The sacrament is administered at least four times a year.
6. The number uncertain, sometimes considerable.
7. No papist in the parish.
8. No dissenters, of any denomination.
9. With moderate punctuality.
10. A register is duly kept and a copy returned to the registrar's office. The register goes back from the year 1659.
11. A marriage register is properly kept.
12. No chapel of ease.
13. I have not found any terrier in the parish, but am informed that there is an old terrier in the registry of Sarum.
14. There is a school for the instruction of seven children. The endowment is one field, let for £3 a year, and the school house and garden; founded by the duke of Kent, now under the direction of the earl of Hardwick, and has, I believe, for some time been committed to the inspection of the rector of Crudwell.
15. Two churchwardens chosen at Easter, one by the rector, the other by the parishioners.
16. Answered under article 14.
17. I reside constantly in the rectorial house.
18. The money is given by the rector to the poor.
19. I do not at present recollect any other matters worthy your Lordship's attention.
20. The nearest post town is Malmesbury.
 Ord. D. 27 June 1779. Ord. P. 19 Dec. 1779. Instituted 3 May 1782. A.M.

James Wiggett[2]

63 DAMERHAM[3] f.535   D. Chalke
1. Divine service is performed twice on the Lord's day: at ten in the morning and half past three in the afternoon.
2. It has not been customary to perform divine service on holidays.

[1] Letter missing.
[2] Perhaps Clare Coll. Cambridge 1773. Curate of Hankerton, **97**.
[3] In Hampshire since 1895.

3. As curate.[4]

4. I serve Martin which is a chapel of ease to Damerham. I am not licensed.

5. The sacrament is administered four times a year: at Easter, Whitsuntide, Michaelmas, and Christmas.

6. Before I entered upon the cure, the number of communicants were (as I am informed) between twenty and thirty. Last Easter about sixty communicated.

7. There is not a single papist in the parish.

8. There are no Independents, Anabaptists, or Quakers in the parish. There is a Presbyterian family but they now regularly attend the church. There are no persons who profess to disregard religion or commonly absent themselves from public worship.

9. They do, and I expound the catechism to them myself in Lent.

10. The register book of births and burials is duly kept and in good preservation. It goes back to the year 1600.

11. The register book, according to the directions of the Act of Parliament against clandestine marriages is duly kept.

12. Martin is a chapel of ease to Damerham and there are prayers and a sermon on every Sunday. There are tithes belonging to it, and it is distant from Damerham near three miles. The same curate serves the two churches.

13. There is no terrier in the parish.

14. There is neither free school, alms-house, hospital, or any other charitable endowment in the parish. No lands or tenements have been left for the repair of the church, or for any other pious uses.

15. The churchwardens are chosen every year in the Easter week, the one by the minister, the other by the parishioners.

16. There is no public school in the parish, nor ever has been.

17. I divide my time between Damerham and Salisbury.

18. It is not customary to collect money at the offertory.

19. There is no other matter I know of which it may be proper to give your Lordship information.

20. Salisbury.

Henry Rigby A.M.[5] Ord. D. 9 May 1763. Ord. P. 22 May 1766.

64 DAUNTSEY [Dantsey] f.543[6]   D. Malmesbury

1. Morning and evening alternately.

2. Sometimes on holidays; there is prayers read twice every day at the school, where any one may attend.

3. As incumbent.

4. None.[7]

[4] Vicar, Charles Mein Harries. Perhaps Jesus Coll. Oxford 1726. M.A. from King's Coll. Cambridge 1743.

[5] 1742–1817. Wadham Coll. Oxford 1759.

[6] Letter missing.

[7] But see query 17 and under Draycot Cerne, **73.** Clergy Books, 1783, also give him as curate of Kellaways (for which there is no return), held under sequestration by the vicar of Kemble: see **114.** He also did duty at Seagry, **171,** when the vicar was absent on account of his daughter's health.

5. Christmas, Easter, and Whitsuntide.
6. [a] [*Blank*] [b] More than usual.
7. None.
8. None. A few of the sect who call themselves Methodists, though fewer than usual.
9. The children are catechized at the free school by the master.
10. [a] Yes. [c] 1653, all in my possession.
11. Yes.
12. None.
13. Yes. My living has not been augmented since I have been rector.
14. There is a free school and alms-house for six poor people, and a schoolmaster who has £16 per annum and each poor person £5 4s. per annum. Endowed by the earl of Danby; under the direction of trustees, namely Sir James Tylney Long etc. etc., and the rector for the time being.
15. Yes, one by the rector and one by the parishioners.
16. Answered in the 14th Q.
17. I divide my time between my two parishes, this and Draycot Cerne.
18. To the sick and infirm, particularly those who attend the holy sacrament.
19. [*Blank*]
20. Draycot near Chippenham, Wilts.
    Collated 1757. *Vide* Draycot Cerne.

Francis Marius West,[8] rector of Dauntsey

65 LONGBRIDGE DEVERILL [Deverel Longbridge] f.549   D. Wylye
1. Prayers and preaching every Lord's day at half after ten in the morning; in the afternoon at the chapel of Monckton Deverel.
2. Divine service every Monday, Tuesday, and Thursday, at Deverel. No prayers on weekdays or holidays at Monckton.
3. I perform divine service as incumbent.
4. I do not serve any other cure.
5 & 6. The holy sacrament of the Lord's Supper is administered four times in the year: on Easter Sunday, Whitsunday, the Sunday after Michaelmas, and Christmas day; and at Monckton Deverel on the Sunday after each of the above days. There are generally between fifty and sixty communicants at Deverel, and between ten and fifteen at Monckton. The same number at each place last Easter as usual.
7. There is no papist nor reputed papist in my parish or chapelry.
8. There are about thirty families who are Presbyterians or Anabaptists, all of the lower class. No Quakers. No Independents. There is no place in the parish made use of for divine worship by any sect of dissenters. The number of dissenters is rather decreased. There are too many persons in the parish who seemingly profess to disregard religion by commonly absenting themselves from the public worship of God.
9. My parishioners never send their children or servants to be instructed by me; nor do they send them to church to be examined in the catechism or hear

[8] 1731–1800. Oriel Coll. Oxford 1748.

it expounded. I drew up an exposition of the catechism and took Archbishop Wake for my guide. I tried to examine the few children that came in Lent, but they were too young to profit by an exposition. I shall attempt it again next Lent.

10. There is a register book of births and burials duly kept, and in good preservation. The returns of births and burials are regularly made into the registrar's office. The register of births and burials goes as far back as 30 March 1682. There are some registers on loose pieces of parchment, but so defaced that little use can be made of them. They go as far back as the year 1561.

11. There is a register book duly kept, according to the directions of the Act of Parliament against clandestine marriages.

12. Monckton Deverel is a chapel of ease annexed to my living, but is a separate parish. Prayers and sermon every Lord's day in the afternoon. The estate belonging to it is mentioned in the terrier. It is distant from Deverel Longbridge about three miles. It is served by me as curate. There are no ruinated chapels.

13. I have a copy of a very imperfect terrier given in by Mr. William Crofts without date. He was buried the 1 June 1683. No other terrier that I know of has been transmitted to the bishop's registry. I have kept a regular account of the glebe and tithes belonging to the living but there have been such frequent exchanges of land in the parish; and there has been a design of exchanging the tithes from land, which would make such a total change in the living that I should have deferred sending a terrier till that was completed if I had not received your Lordship's directions to send one at the ensuing visitation.

14. There is an alms-house in my parish founded by Sir James Thynne, ancestor of the present Lord Weymouth, for six poor men and two women of the parish of Deverel Longbridge and Monckton Deverel, who are to be members of the Church of England, and of the age of sixty years at least. The number of trustees as settled by the endowment are eleven and to be renewed as often as the number shall be reduced to four. The present trustees are William Buckler, Esq., John Wadman Esq., William Chaffin Grove Esq., Edmund Lambert Esq., Rev. Charles Wake, LL.D., Mr. John Bennett. The revenue is an annuity or yearly rent-charge of £80 payable out of Lord Weymouth's manor and rents of Deverel Longbridge and Monckton Deverel, which is regularly paid and constantly applied as directed by the founder. The statutes and orders are punctually observed, and the charity is in a very flourishing state.

15. The churchwardens are chosen on Easter Monday, one by the vicar and the other by the parishioners.

16. There is no public school nor charity school founded in my parish.

17. I reside in the vicarage house, when my health will permit me. My winter residence is at Bath, where I go for the benefit of the waters.[9]

18. The money given at the offertory is disposed of, some by the church-wardens and some by myself, to poor families where any of them are sick.

[9] Clergy Books, 1783, give a curate, Mr. Goddard.

19. There is no other matter relating to my parish or chapelry of which it may be proper to give your Lordship information.
20. At Deverel Longbridge near Warminster, Wilts.

John Dobson,[1] vicar of Deverel Longbridge. Instituted 5 May 1760. Instituted to the vicarage of Market Lavington 14 March 1750. Ord. D. by Richard, bishop of St. David's, 7 Dec. 1750. Ord. P. by Joseph, bishop of Rochester, 3 March 1750 [? 1750/1]. Admitted to the degree of M.A. in the year 1749.

66 DEVIZES, ST. JOHN f.557   D. Potterne

1. Once every Sunday morning or evening. The morning at half past ten, the evening at three, both prayers and preaching alternately, the same congregation going to both churches.
2. On Mondays, Tuesdays, and Fridays every week and holidays if on those days or Saturdays.
3. As incumbent.
4. No; only the other church in this town belonging to this incumbency.
5. Six times, on the first Sunday in every other month and on the great festivals.
6. About eighty or ninety, rather more than usual at Easter communion.
7. [a] None. [b] None. [c] None. [d] None. [e] None.
8. There are many in the town of each sect, have each a meeting-house, are not of high rank. There is a Methodist meeting held in a private house where it is said many itinerant preachers hold forth, but cannot learn their names. It is said they are licensed. The number not greater, rather less, especially as to those of better rank, very few if any.
9. None but the schools, and most of the children of the town go to the schools, as there are several endowments. The children are catechized every Lent in time of service in the vulgar tongue. The minister sometimes preaches on the subject of the catechism.
10. Yes. The returns have been omitted sometimes, not being called for.
11. Yes.
12. [a] No. [f] No.
13. No. There are two in the bishop's registry. A house and garden added to it by Queen Anne's Bounty 7 years ago.[2]
14. Two alms-houses supported by the gift of [blank] and vested in the corporation. The writings lost but the corporation time immemorial have received and paid the endowment thereof.
15. Every year one by the minister and the other by the parishioners.
16. No public school but several endowments for boys and girls. The boys are taught reading writing and arithmetic and instructed in Lewis's explanation of the catechism, the girls reading and needlework. They are instructed in the principles of Christian religion, go regularly to church and go home to their parents when they leave school every day. The charities are as follows: 16

[1] Perhaps St. Mary's Hall Oxford 1743. Vicar of Market Lavington, **124,** served by the curate of West Lavington.
[2] And £200 in 1765: Hodgson, p. 417.

boys supported by a society of gentlemen called the Bear Club charity have a coat, waistcoat, breeches and that every year and are sometimes apprenticed; 20 boys supported by a legacy of £500, given by the will of Mr. Thomas Bencroft, trustees Rev. Dr. Stonhouse and Mr. Jacob Kerby, the will in their hands, for ever, no clothes, no apprenticeship; 10 boys supported by a legacy of £5 per annum for ever given by the will of Mr. [blank] Woodroffe, chargeable on lands in Chippenham now in possession of Mr. John Gale, the will with other deeds in the hands of the late Joseph Coburn Esq. or his assigns as mortgagees of part of the estate: 5 boys supported by a legacy of £2 10s. per annum for ever given by the will of Mr. Wild and paid by the chamberlains of the borough of Devizes, will in their hands, coat each year, but no apprenticeship; 6 boys supported by a legacy of £4 4s. per annum for ever, given by the will of Mr. Eyles and paid out of Salutation public house in Devizes, no clothes, no apprenticeship.
17. [a] Yes, yes.
18. By the minister to poor housekeepers, and when he visits the sick.
19. No.
20. Devizes, a post town.

Mr. Innes's[3] deacons orders dated 12 Sept. 1742. His priest's orders 23 Dec. 1744, his institution to Devizes 3 March 1774, to Stockton 9 March 1774.

67 DEVIZES, ST. MARY f.565   D. Potterne
1. Once every Sunday morning or evening. The morning at half past ten. The evening at three, both prayers and preaching alternately, the same congregation going to both churches.
2. On Wednesday and Saturday every week, and holidays, if they happen on Wednesdays or Thursdays.
3. As incumbent.
4. No, only the other church in this town belonging to this incumbency.
5. Six times, on the first Sunday in every other month.
6. About sixty; it is not administered in this church at Easter.
7. [a] None. [b] None. [c] None. [d] None. [e] None.
8. There are many in the town of each of those sectaries, each sect has a meeting-house. They are not of any high rank. Richard Fenner Presbyterian minister. [Blank] Dyer, Anabaptist. [Robert L— crossed out.] The number not greater, rather less, especially as to those of better rank; as there are many sectaries and some of those who profess themselves of the church go sometimes to the Independent meeting, where I am informed Methodists sometimes preach, it cannot be ascertained who commonly absent themselves from all public worship of God.
9. None but the schools, and most of the children go to the schools, as there are several endowments. The children are catechized every Lent in time of service in the vulgar tongue, and the minister sometimes preaches on the subject of the catechism.

---

[3] Edward Innes, Pembroke Coll. Oxford 1741. Rector of Stockton, **188**, served by a curate. The name and particulars of ordination are in a different hand from the rest of the return.

10. Yes. The returns have been sometimes omitted, not being called for.
11. Yes.
12. [a] No. [f] No.
13. No. There are two in the bishop's registry. A house and garden added to it by Queen Anne's Bounty seven years ago.
14. There are six girls supported by a legacy of £10 per annum for ever given by the will of Mrs. Powell, the money vested in the old South Sea annuity under the direction of the minister and churchwardens. Ten boys clothed, taught, and apprenticed by will of Mr. Thurman which will end in the year 1786. No alms-house or hospital. Some lands were left by one Smith the founder for the repair of the church, about £30 per annum under a feoffment; the feoffees have the sole management.
15. Yes, one by the minister, the other by the parishioners.
16. No, only a school house and several endowments for a certain number of boys and girls. The boys are taught reading, writing, and arithmetic, the girls reading and needlework; they are instructed in the principles of Christian religion, go regularly to church, all clothed, none fed, and go home to their parents when they leave school every day.
17. [a] Yes, yes.
18. By the minister to poor housekeepers as he sees occasion offer and when he visits the sick.
19. No.
20. Devizes, a post town. [4]

68 DINTON f.573   D. Chalke
1. Divine service is performed every Sunday, morning and afternoon. Prayers and sermon in the morning at eleven, and prayers in the afternoon at three.
2. Divine service is performed on Good Friday, Ascension day, Easter Monday and Tuesday, 5 November, 30 January, and Ash Wednesday.
3. I perform divine service as curate. [5]
4. I serve no other cure.
5. The holy sacrament of the Lord's Supper is administered four times in the year viz. Easter day, Whitsunday, Michaelmas, and Christmas day.
6. The number of communicants in general are ten or twelve. There were fewer than usual last Easter.
7. There are no reputed papists in the parish, nor any that have been perverted to popery.
8. There are no Presbyterians, Independents, Anabaptists, nor Quakers in the parish.
9. The parishioners send their servants and children to be catechized. The exposition I make use of is Lewis's. The season they are catechized in is Lent.
10. There is a register book of births and burials duly kept and in good

---

[4] No signature. See **66.**
[5] Vicar, William Deane. Vicar of Woolhampton and of Brimpton, Berks.: Clergy Books, 1783. Perhaps Trinity Coll. Oxford 1750.

preservation. The returns of births and burials are regularly made into the registrar's office. The register goes back as far as the year 1558.

11. There is a register book duly kept according to the Act of Parliament against clandestine marriages.

12. There is a chapel of ease in the parish called Teffont Magna. It is served by me every third Sunday in the afternoon. There are no estates or funds particularly appropriated to its maintenance. Teffont Magna is about a mile from Dinton.

13. [Blank]

14. There is no free school, alms-house, or other charitable endowment in the parish.

15. The churchwardens are chosen every year on Easter Monday. One is appointed by the minister, the other by the parishioners.

16. There is a public school for boys and girls in the parish but no charity school. The public school is under very good regulation.

17. I constantly reside upon the cure, and in the parsonage house.

18. There is no collection made.

19. I know of none.

20. Dinton. The nearest post town Wilton.

   Herbert Randolph LL.B.[6] Ord. D. 17 June 1764. Ord. P. 2 June 1765.

69 DITTERIDGE [Ditchridge] f.581   D. Malmesbury

1. Once every fortnight at the hours of eleven in the winter and twice in the summer as has been usual.

2. No.

3. As curate.[7]

4. Colerne.

5. Three times, viz. Easter day, the Sunday after Whitsunday, and the first Sunday after Christmas day.

6. Usually about six.

7. No papist.

8. None to my knowledge.

9. No person comes to me to be instructed. The children are catechized in the month of June.

10. We have a register book and returns are regularly made.

11. There is.

12. No chapel of ease.

13. [Blank]

14. No.

15. Elected at Easter.

16. No charity school.

17. At Colerne, distant about 1 mile and $\frac{1}{2}$.

18. To the poorest of the people.

---

[6] Probably Corpus Christi Coll. Oxford 1756.
[7] Rector, James Mayo. See Avebury, **9**, of which he was vicar.

19. Nothing as I believe.
20. Colerne, Bath.

N. A. Bliss[8]

70 DONHEAD ST. ANDREW f.589   D. Chalke
1. Prayers and a sermon at half past ten in the morning. Prayers at a quarter past two in the afternoon.
2. Not on weekdays but on some holidays.
3. As incumbent.
4. No.
5. At Easter, Whitsuntide, Michaelmas, and Christmas.
6. [a] In general about 25. [b] Thirty or upwards.
7. [a] Yes [Lord Arundell *crossed out*], a great number of no rank. [b] Not that I know of. [d] No. [e] No.
8. [a] There are Presbyterians [and a meeting-house *crossed out*] but I know not their numbers. [b] Not that I know of. [c] I know not. [d] I am but lately come to the parish, but am informed they diminish. [f] There are many absenters.
9. [But few have attended as yet *crossed out*.] None have ever attended for that purpose. I do not use any exposition. Lent is the general time, but being absent on account of health, I have catechized since that time, always in English.
10. [a] Yes. [b] Yes. [c] To the year 1653.
11. Yes.
12. [a] No. [f] At Easton there is the remains of an old chapel now turned into a barn.
13. [a] There is a terrier which I believe to be true. [b] I know not. [c] No.
14. [a] No. [d] No.
15. Yes. One by the minister and one by the parish.
16. No.
17. I reside constantly.
18. To the poor as I see occasion.
19. [I have *crossed out*.] I do not recollect any.
20. Lower Donhead, post town Shaftesbury, Dorset.

John Benet LL.D.,[9] rector. 1783

71 DONHEAD ST. MARY f.597   D. Chalke
1. Twice. Once at the church and once at the chapel with a sermon at each. Service begins at eleven and three. Morning service is alternate at each.
2. On Ash Wednesday, four days in the Passion week, with a sermon on Good Friday, on the festivals after Christmas, two days after Easter, Ascension day, two days after Whitsunday, and all state holidays.

[8] See **53**.
[9] St. Edmund Hall Oxford 1754.

3. As curate.[1]

4. No.

5. Four times, both at the church and chapel on the great festivals, and at Michaelmas.

6. I am not a priest, and the rector alone has administered the sacrament. I therefore cannot ascertain the number of communicants but am informed they are about 70.

7. There are, but no mass-house or popish priest; they go to Wardour, and no school.

8. There are some Presbyterians amongst the yeomanry; but no other sectarists, and these I am told lessen in number. They have a meeting-house in the parish to which the Presbyterians of the neighbouring parishes resort. Their teacher's name is Morgan, he lives at Tisbury.

9. I was absent during the Lent season at which time the rector served the church.

10. There is a register book of births and burials, and regular returns of each, I am informed, have been made into the registrar's office. It commences at 1653.

11. There is.

12. [a, b] One, viz. Charlton, served once every Sunday as mentioned in the first answer. [d] Near two miles from the church. [e] It is supported by the inhabitants of Charlton tithing.

13. This matter falls not under my cognizance, not being rector.

14. No free school, alms-house, nor hospital.

15. Two chosen annually, one by the minister and the other by the parishioners; the latter has the care of the chapel.

16. No public school or charity school.

17. I have resided constantly in the parish, but not in the parsonage house.

18. There are no offerings, I am informed, at the communion.

19. No.

20. Donhead near Shaftesbury.

Gilbert Jackson.[2] Ord. D. 28 Oct. 1781. A.B. 10 Oct. 1781.

72 DOWNTON f.605   D. Wilton

1. Divine service is performed, in Downton church, twice every Lord's day; begins at ten o'clock in the morning, and at three in the afternoon, excepting once a month, when I officiate in the afternoon at Nunton chapel, belonging to this parish, then there is no afternoon service here.

2. Only on Christmas day and three saints' days following, Ash Wednesday, Good Friday, the Monday and Tuesday in Easter week, and Monday and Tuesday in Whitsun week.

[1] Rector, Dr. Richard Jackson. 1701–96. Balliol Coll. Oxford 1720. Uncle to the curate, who represented him at the visitation. Although over 80, Dr. Jackson set out in May 1783 to escort the young son of Lord Torrington to join his father in Brussels: Sarum Dioc. R.O., Misc. Vis. Papers, 8, Richard Jackson to Joseph Elderton, the registrar, 5 May 1783.

[2] Lincoln Coll. Oxford 1776. He succeeded his uncle as rector in 1796.

3. As curate. [3]

4. I serve no other cure. I had a licence for my last curacy, in the diocese of Norwich, but have served this curacy for near nine years without being required to have a licence.

5. On the festivals of Christmas, Easter, Whitsuntide, and Michaelmas; and two sacrament Sundays each festival, on account of the number of communicants.

6. About one hundred and fifty. Last Easter as many as usual.

7. There are only three or four reputed papists in this parish, elderly persons of no rank. Papists have no place of worship, priest, or school in this parish; nor does their number increase.

8. There are no Quakers in this parish, but there are some Presbyterians, Independents, and Anabaptists. I cannot exactly ascertain the numbers of each sect; but, I suppose, they may all amount to fifty. They have two meeting-houses, but have no constant and settled teachers, and a great many of them now frequently attend divine service in the church. I know of no persons in my parish who profess to disregard religion, but fear there are too many who neglect it, and who too commonly absent themselves from public worship.

9. The parishioners, by my request, send their children to church to be catechized, generally every Wednesday in Lent, when I hear them repeat and explain to them the Church catechism and ask them some questions, all in the English language; and have frequently upwards of a hundred.

10. We have a paper register duly kept, and the oldest in tolerable preservation, beginning in the year 1602. But no return has been made into the registrar's office for some years, nor required. A copy of the register is now returned for the year 1782.

11. There is.

12. The chapel of Nunton, about four miles distant from Downton, is served by the minister of Downton the first Sunday in every month, in the afternoon; and morning and afternoon, four times in the year, when the sacrament is administered. There is no estate or fund appropriated for its maintenance, but Nunton is considered as appertaining to the parish of Downton, and pays vicarial tithes accordingly. No ruinated chapels.

13. I can make no answer to this question, as Mr. Lear, the vicar, is not now at Downton, for reasons assigned by him in a letter to the bishop; and do not think myself competent, as curate, to make out a new terrier, especially as I have been lame, by an accident, for more than three weeks and shall with great difficulty be able to attend his Lordship's visitation. But have no doubt that Mr. Lear will readily furnish the bishop's registry with everything required when he shall be able to return to Downton.

14. There is a free school at Downton, for twelve boys, founded by the Eyre family of Brickworth; present governors and trustees, John Eyre Esq. of Landford, Captain Eyre of Brickworth, and the steward of the lord of the manor. For the support of it are the profits of two fairs, a school house for

[3] Vicar, Thomas Lear. 1745–1828. New Coll. Oxford 1764.

the master rent free, and the interest of £130; amounting in all to £25 per annum.

15. The churchwardens are chosen every year, on Easter Monday, by the minister and parishioners together.

16. There is no public school or charity school in this parish but the free school before mentioned.

17. I do constantly reside on this cure, and in the vicarage house till within these three months, as the vicarage house was intended to be thoroughly repaired.

18. Part of the money is distributed among the poor communicants at the communion table. The rest I distribute to poor objects within the parish, as they occur.

19. I know not of any.

20. Downton, Salisbury.

   J. Williams, curate of Downton. Ord. D. by the bishop of Norwich, 25 Nov. 1770. Ord. P. 14 July 1771.

73 DRAYCOT CERNE f.613[4]   D. Malmesbury

1. Morning and evening.

2. Yes.

3. As incumbent.

4. [Blank]

5. Christmas, Easter, and Whitsuntide.

6. [a] About twenty. [c] More than usual.

7. None.

8. None.

9. The summer season.

10. [a] Yes. [b] Yes. [c] To the year 1691.

11. Yes.

12. None.

13. My living has not been augmented since I have been rector.

14. [a] Yes. A small endowment for a school and apprenticing boys, under the direction of trustees, viz. Sir James Tylney Long and the rector. [d] Mrs. Rachell Long, £100, for communion cloth new and beautifying the church, with an additional £30 by Sir James Tylney Long, under whose direction the legacy has been laid out.

15. Yes, one by the rector, the other by the parishioners.

16. Answered in the 14th question.

17. I reside chiefly on this living and divide my time between my two parishes, Draycot and Dauntsey.

18. To the sick and infirm, particularly those who attend the holy sacrament.

19. Happy in a patron that discountenances vice, encourages virtue, and sets an amiable example, I have no particular complaint to trouble your Lordship with.

---

[4] Letter missing.

20. Draycot near Chippenham, Wilts.

Ord. D. 1754. Ord. P. 1757. Presented by Sir James Tylney Long, and instituted 1779. LL.D. Oxford 1779.[5]

74 DRAYCOT FOLIAT f.619   D. Marlborough
[*The whole form is left blank; at the end, written across, under the address:*]
There is neither church, chapel, or place of residence, nor divine service performed in this parish, in the memory of man, save at the induction of the rector.

Edward Goddard,[6] rector

75 DURRINGTON f.627   D. Amesbury
1. Divine service is performed in the church at Durrington once every Lord's day, alternately at 11 o'clock in the morning and at 2 in the afternoon; it is not performed twice on account of the small value of the living.
2. Divine service is not usually performed on weekdays, except on the more solemn occasions.
3. I perform divine [service] as curate to the dean and chapter of Winchester, having been licensed to the cure in the year 1763.
4. With Durrington I serve the parish of Rowlston, 5 miles distant, to which I am duly instituted.
5. The holy sacrament of the Lord's Supper is administered at Christmas, Easter, Whitsuntide, and Michaelmas.
6. The number of communicants at Easter last was, as usual, about eighteen or twenty.
7. No reputed papists are in the parish.
8. I do not know of any dissenters in the parish, nor of any persons who profess to disregard religion; but it is to be wished that some were more constant in their attendance at the public worship of God.
9. The children are constantly catechized during Lent.
10. A register book of births and burials is duly kept, and returns thereof have been made into the registrar's office as often as called for. The register commenced in the year 1653.
11. A register book of marriages is duly kept.
12. There is no chapel of ease in the parish.
13. I am ignorant whether or not the dean and chapter of Winchester, who are possessed of the tithes of Durrington, have any terriers thereof. No augmentation hath been made of the living for many years past.
14. There is no free school, alms-house, or hospital in the parish, nor other charitable endowment.
15. The churchwardens are usually chosen about Easter, one by the minister and the other by the parishioners.
16. There is a public school, but no charity school in the parish.
17. I reside at Amesbury, a post town, two miles distant, there being no house belonging to the curacy of Durrington, except a cottage of very mean rank.

[5] No signature. Dr. Francis Marias West rector. See **64.**
[6] See **50.**

18. No money is usually given at the offertory.

19. I know of no other matter relating to the parish of which it may be proper to give your Lordship information.

20. Answered under Q.17.

R. Head M.A.,[7] curate of Durrington

76 EASTON GREY f.635   D. Malmesbury

1. Once every Sunday alternately at half past ten in the morning and half past one in the afternoon.

2. Upon Christmas day and Good Friday.

3. As curate.

4. One alternately, Westonbirt, about a mile distant.

5. Three times, Christmas, Easter, and Whitsuntide.

6. Eleven generally; at Easter last seven.

7. None.

8. Two Methodists. Six persons absent themselves from all public worship of God: Daniel Nicholson and Anne his wife, Thomas Kirby and Margaret his wife, John Vizer, and Thomas Cambridge.

9. The parishioners send their children to be catechized.

10. There is a register book duly kept and in good preservation; it goes back as far as the year 1725. Returns of births and burials are regularly made.

11. Yes.

12. None.

13. Did not procure the terrier, made out in the year 1698, till yesterday; and as it varies from the present state of things, must beg your Lordship's indulgence to have the glebe etc. measured and looked over.

14. [a] None. [d] Mr. John Ady has given 8s. to be distributed annually at Christmas among the poor by the minister and churchwardens, charged on lands lying in the parish of Sherston Pinckney.

15. Yes, one by the minister and the other by the parishioners.

16. Mrs. Elizabeth Hodges has given 40s. for teaching four children to read, charged on lands.

17. At Tetbury, three miles distant.

18. To the poor communicants.

19. [Blank]

20. Tetbury, a post town.

John Savage M.A.,[8] rector
John Richards M.A.,[9] curate

77 EBBESBOURNE WAKE f.643   D. Chalke

1. Once; according to the usual custom of the parish; and is now at half past ten every morning.

2. Ash Wednesday and Good Friday.

3. As curate.

[7] See 55.
[8] Queen's Coll. Oxford 1762.
[9] Perhaps John Richards who entered Oriel Coll. Oxford as Bible clerk or servitor 1776.

4. Swallowcliffe, two miles and an half distant. Under the dean of Salisbury.
5. At the great festivals and at Michaelmas.
6. The number of communicants is generally about fifteen; at Easter about sixteen or seventeen.
7. There are none.
8. There is a Methodists' meeting-house erected about two years since, attended constantly every Sunday and sometimes on weekdays too. The names of the teachers are unknown to me as also whether they are licensed or not. The number of the attendants increases.
9. [*Blank*]
10. There is a register book of births and burials, and regular returns of each have been made into the registrar's office. It commences in the year 1720.
11. There is.
12. There are none.
13. Of this William Coles Esq. of the Close, Sarum, can give the best information, who [is] the impropriator of the living.[1]
14. No free school, alms-house, nor hospital.
15. Two, chosen (at present) annually by the parishioners.
16. No public school or charity school.
17. I reside constantly in the parish but not in the parsonage house.
18. There are no offerings at the communion.
19. No.
20. Ebbesborne near Shaftesbury.
   William Waterman.[2] Ord. D. 15 July 1750. Ord. P. 19 Dec. 1756. A.M.

78 EDINGTON f.651   D. Potterne
1. The service alternately at eleven and three. The duty but once a day, the salary by no means being a proper support for more duty.
2. No duty on weekdays, holidays, or festivals.
3. As curate appointed by the lay rector.[3]
4. I serve the curacy of Stoke,[4] two miles distant.
5. Three or four times a year, namely Christmas, Easter, Whitsuntide, and Michaelmas.
6. The usual number communicated last Easter.
7. There are no reputed papists as to my knowledge nor is there any popish school.
8. There are no Presbyterians, nor any place of divine worship that is used by the above-mentioned sect.
9. The children are catechized on Sundays after church, and in the English language.
10. Yes, the register book is duly kept and in good preservation.
11. Yes, duly kept according to the directions of the Act of Parliament.

---

[1] He held the rectory on lease from the succentor of Salisbury, to whom it returned on the death of William Coles's daughter in 1829: Hoare, *Mod. Wilts.* iii, Chalke hundred, 166.
[2] Possibly Queen's Coll. Oxford 1738.
[3] Joshua and Drummond Smith of Erlestoke Park: *V.C.H. Wilts.* viii. 241.
[4] Erlestoke Chapel, Melksham, **139.**

12. They [*recte* there] are no chapels of ease and there is no fund, the salary for serving the church being paid by the lay rector.
13. As there are no lands etc. consequently there can be no terrier.
14. There is no free school nor any charitable endowment.
15. Every Easter, one by the rector, the other by the parish.
16. There is no school.
17. There is no house. I have till within this half year resided within four miles. The duty has not been once omitted for these two years.
18. Given to the poor by the churchwardens.
19. Not that I know of.
20. Charlton near the Devizes, Wilts.[5]
   Ord. D. by the bishop of Winchester 21 Sept. 1775.

John Baily LL.B.[6]

79 ST. EDMUND [SALISBURY] f.659   Sub-D. Salisbury
1. Prayers and sermon twice every Sunday unless there is a sacrament. In that case a sermon only in the afternoon.
2. Prayers every Wednesday, Friday, and Saturday, and likewise on all holidays and festivals. A sermon the first Friday in every month; one on 30 January and another on 7 September before the corporation.
3. As incumbent and have done so for twenty-nine years.
4. None.
5. The first Sunday in every month, on all the great festivals, and the following Sundays.
6. [*Blank*]
7. None that I know of.
8. Two Presbyterian meeting-houses, and one for Methodists.
9. The laudable custom is impracticable, unless the incumbent could afford to keep an assistant or two; but this the uncertainty and the smallness of the income will not permit of. I distribute many little tracts amongst my parishioners, principally *The Christian Monitor* and Gibson on profaning the Lord's day.[7]
10. A register book of births and burials is regularly kept.
11. Yes.
12. None.
13. There are no houses, lands, tithes, pensions, or profits belonging to the minister of this parish, but what arise from the charitable contributions of the parishioners, except Queen Anne's Bounty £8 18*s.* for preaching the Friday's sermon mentioned in the second answer, and the common surplice fees; which for so extensive and populous a parish are very inconsiderable.
14. There are 4 alms-houses. 1st Eyre's for 6 women, 3*s.* 6*d.* per week. 2d Mr. Christopher Eyre's for 6 men and their wives at 2*s.* 6*d.* per week.

---

[5] The curate is said to have acted as domestic chaplain to the lords of the manor during the
[6] 18th century; but in 1783 they were absentees: *V.C.H. Wilts.* viii. 247.
   Queen's Coll. Oxford 1767.
[7] Edmund Gibson, bishop of London, *The Sinfulness of neglecting and profaning the Lord's Day* (8th ed. 1749).

3d Froud's for 6 men and 6 women, 3s. 6d per week, built and endowed in 1750. 4th Taylor's for 6 men, 2s. 10d. per week, built in 1698.
15. The churchwardens are chosen every year in the Easter week, by the vestry.
16. No public school.
17. No house belonging to it.
18. To those that are thought the most proper objects, the bulk by the senior churchwarden, a small matter by myself.
19. [Blank]
20. Salisbury.

James Stirling Samber,[8] rector of St. Edmund's

80 WROUGHTON[9] [Ellingdon, als. Wroughton] f.667   D. Cricklade
1. Twice during the summer, and once during the winter season, at ten in the morning and 3 in the afternoon.
2. Divine service is performed on Christmas day and on Good Friday.
3. As curate.[1]
4. I serve the cure of Broad Hinton and the chapel of Berwick Bassett, three mile distant from each other. I have taken no licence.
5. Four times: at the festivals of Christmas, Easter, and Whitsunday and about Michaelmas.
6. From 20 to 35; at last Easter about 35, which I believe is more than the usual number.
7. We have no reputed papists, and of course no popish school or place of worship.
8. There are at present no dissenters of any denomination. At the time I engaged the cure I understood the Methodists held occasional meetings in the parish, but they have long since discontinued them. I do not know that there are any who *professedly* disregard religion; but there are many who commonly absent themselves from public worship.
9. The totally illiterate seldom are sent, or come, for private instruction. Those young persons in the parish who have had the advantage of being taught to read etc. are catechized at church on Sundays during Lent.
10. The register book is duly kept and in good preservation, and copies are annually taken. The register of births and burials extends back as far as 1588.
11. Yes.
12. There are no chapels of ease etc.
13. There is a terrier, bearing date 1671, signed by the registrar. I do not know that there has been any augmentation made to the living since that time.
14. There is a school for the instruction of poor children of the parish in

[8] St. John's Coll. Cambridge 1739. Sub-dean of Salisbury.
[9] A sinecure rectory in the gift of the bishop of Winchester. The rector was patron of the vicarage: *Wilts. Top. Coll.* ed. J. E. Jackson, p. 367; *Liber Regis* (1786).
[1] Rector, Edmund Ferrers. Christ Church Oxford 1768. Rector of Cheriton, Hants. Vicar, James Merest. 1752–1827. Oriel Coll. Oxford 1775. Curate in charge of Wortham, Suff., for many years. Vicar of Wroughton 1783. In 1812 he was keeping a school at Diss, Norf.: *W.A.M.* lxi. 459.

reading, writing, and accompts, founded by Thomas Benet Esq. of Salthrop in this parish. The endowment £20 per annum. The trustees are the owner of the land from which the endowment is paid and the incumbents of five neighbouring parishes. The salary is regularly paid to the master; and I believe the regulations concerning the school are duly observed. There is another charitable institution of £8 per annum formed from various benefactions formerly given, and applied annually to the purpose of apprenticing a child of some poor inhabitant of the parish. The trustees are A. Goddard Esq. and the vicar of Wroughton, and I believe W. Codrington Esq. and Mr. Bathe (one of the churchwardens) have been lately elected. There besides are some other benefactions, left for the benefit of the poor.

15. The churchwardens are chosen annually in the Easter week; one by the minister, and the other by the parishioners.

16. There is no other charitable institution of this kind but that mentioned under article 14. At the said school the children are instructed in the principles of the Christian religion, as explained in the Church catechism, and regularly brought to church.

17. I reside in the vicarage house.

18. By the minister, with the assistance of the churchwardens, to the most deserving among the poor; or to those in greatest distress, from illness, number of children, etc.

19. I do not recollect any.

20. The vicar's, Wortham, near Diss, Norfolk. The curate's, Wroughton near Swindon.

Date of admission into the order of deacons 1 Sept. 1771; priests 6 June 1773.

D. Williams[2]

81 ENFORD [Endford] f.675   D. Potterne

1. Twice at 11 a.m. and 3 p.m. Sermon morning and afternoon alternately.

2. On Christmas day, Good Friday, Easter Monday.

3. As curate.

4. I serve but one cure. I am not licensed.

5. Eight times, viz. on Good Friday, Easter Sunday, Whitsunday, Trinity Sunday, twice about Michaelmas, twice at Christmas.

6. About 20, but oftener under than over; at Easter usually a few more; to which the last festival afforded no exception.

7. There is neither papist, chapel, or school.

8. We have neither dissenter nor conventicle. Of those who seriously, staunchly, and openly profess to disregard religion I don't know that we have any, but of practical atheists we have our share, and many persons are more frequently absent from than present at divine service, though perhaps few only are so hardened as never to be seen there.

9. No. I have at different times read to them the greater part of Secker's lectures.

[2] See also **104**.

10. [a] Yes. [b] No: I believe it to be the business of the churchwardens. [c] To 29 May 1631.

11. Yes.

12. No. There is a tradition here that there were formerly two chapels in this parish; but their ruin has been so complete that no traces of them remain.

13. An improved terrier is now making out according to the bishop's recent direction.

14. There is no free school, alms-house, nor hospital; but the sum of £3 10s. is yearly at Easter distributed among such of the poor who receive no allowance from the parish. The dispensers of this are the overseers in vestry; but who was donor of the principal from which it arises I never could learn. No lands have ever been left for repairing the repair [sic] of the church or other pious uses.

15. Yes. One by the minister and one by the parishioners.

16. No.

17. Yes.

18. As the rubric directs.

19. I cannot recollect any.

20. I reside at Enford. The nearest post town is Pewsey.

Ord. D. 24 Sept. 1780. Ord. P. 23 Sept. 1781. No degree. I am, my Lord, with dutiful respect, your Lordship's very humble servant.

Caleb Carrington[3]

[Written from top to bottom of left hand margin:] By desire of Mr. James Boyer,[4] vicar of Enford, I am to inform your Lordship that he has the degree of A.B., was ord. D. 9 June 1759, ord. P. 17 May 1761, and was instituted to the vicarage of Enford 28 Dec. 1782.

82 EVERLEIGH f.683[5]   D. Marlborough

1. Prayers and preaching at eleven o'clock in the morning, prayers in the afternoon at 3 o'clock.

2. When a congregation can be raised.

3. As curate.[6]

4. [a] No. [c] No.

5. Four times in the year, at Christmas, Easter, Whitsuntide, and Michaelmas.

6. About twenty and to the best of my recollection at Easter last rather a greater number than usual, about thirty.

7. [a] None. [b] None. [c] None. [d] None. [e] None.

8. [a] No dissenter of any denomination. [e] None that I know of. [f] I fear

[3] Admitted sizar, Pembroke Coll. Cambridge 1788, aged 30.

[4] Balliol Coll. Oxford 1752.

[5] Letter missing.

[6] Clergy Books, 1783, give Basil Cane as rector (see **48**) but also have the following note on Everleigh: 'There is some management relative to this living, there being good reason to suppose that Dr. Starkey enjoys the profits. He does not appear to be the rector; as he holds a living in Cumberland from C.C.C. Oxford.' The living in Cumberland was Skelton: *Alum. Oxon.* s.v. his son John. Dr. Starkey was instituted to the rectory of Everleigh on the death of Basil Cane in 1791: *Wilts. Inst.* ii. 96.

that there are some who too frequently absent themselves from the public worship of God.

9. The children are duly catechized in the season of Lent; Lewis's exposition made use of. Bibles and Prayer Books are given to the children.

10. [a] Yes. [b] Yes. [c] The register goes back as far as 24 Dec. 1598.

11. Yes.

12. None.

13. A true terrier according to your Lordship's orders is sent and a copy inserted in the register.

14. [a] No. [d] No.

15. Yes. One by the minister and the other by the parishioners.

16. No public or charity school.

17. Yes. I have not been absent from my cure above six months since May 1770 when I first commenced curate; and then upon urgent business, and the church was properly taken care of in my absence.

18. The curate disposes of the money at his discretion, generally to the poor that attend the sacrament, and to the sick and needy.

19. No.

20. The parsonage house at Everley. Pewsey, distant about 5 miles.

Ord. D. by Thomas, lord bishop of Oxford, 1747. Ord. P. by the same bishop 1748.

Samuel Starkey D.D.,[7] curate

83 EISEY [Eysey] f.689   D. Cricklade

1. At one o'clock in the afternoon.

2. Never so accustomed.

3. Curate.[8]

4. With Cricklade.

5. The four usual feasts.

6. Usually six or eight.

7. None.

8. None.

9. Pretty constant.

10. Yes, but formerly very imperfect.

11. Yes.

12. None.

13. The vicar has it.

14. No school nearer than Cricklade.

15. Only one.

16. None.

17. The vicarage house down. The curate resides at Cricklade.

18. [*Blank*]

19. None.

20. [*Blank*]

[7] Brasenose Coll. Oxford 1740. B.A. from Corpus Christi Coll. Oxford 1743. His son was later owner of Spye Park: *V.C.H. Wilts.* vii. 186.
[8] Vicar, Richard Nicholas Goldsbrough. Magdalen Coll. Oxford 1767.

Ord. D. at the White Hall Chapel in London in the year 1771, by the bishop of Ely and ord. P. at the cathedral of Gloucester 1775.

E. Campbell[9]

84 FISHERTON ANGER f.697   D. Wilton
1. Prayers and sermon every Sunday between two and three o'clock in the afternoon. Have till very lately served a church five miles distant every Sunday morning.
2. Prayers on the 30 January, Ash Wednesday, and Good Friday.
3. Perform divine service as incumbent.
4. No other cure at present.
5. Three times in the year, viz. Christmas, Easter, and Whitsuntide.
6. Generally, about 20 communicants. At Easter last near 50, rather more than usual.
7. To the best of my knowledge, only one papist, and him rather of low rank.
8. A very few Presbyterians and two or three Quakers.
9. The children are catechized at church every Sunday afternoon during the season of Lent; and at that season have usually and frequently explained part of the catechism in a series of discourses.
10. The parish register book of births and burials is duly kept and regular returns made by the churchwardens into the registrar's office; the register goes as far back as the year 1663.
11. A marriage register book duly kept according to the Act of Parliament.
12. There is no chapel of ease in the parish.
13. Have no terrier.
14. A free school for 10 boys endowed with £20 per annum for clothing them and £10 per annum salary for a master to teach them to read and write and accompt. And £5 towards apprenticing them, when at the age of 13 years. Founded by one Mr. Nowes[1] late of Yeovil, Somerset. N.B. The money for clothing the boys and salary for the master is managed by the church-wardens in office, and the estates from whence it arises is by the trustees invested in the hands of an attorney at law, viz. one Mr. Richard Figes at Romsey, Hants.
15. Two churchwardens chose annually in the Easter week; the one by the rector, the other by the parishioners.
16. Answered in Q. 14.
17. Constantly reside as incumbent.
18. To such as attend sacrament and such as are ill and not able to come. N.B. given by the rector.
19. To the best of my knowledge, nothing else material.
20. The parsonage house. Sarum the nearest post town.
Ord. D. 3 March 1750. Ord. P. 24 Sept. 1752. Instituted 1 May 1758. Degree, A.M.

Richard Matthews,[2] rector of Fisherton Anger near Sarum

[9] See **60.**
[1] John Nowes: *V.C.H. Wilts.* vi. 166.
[2] St. John's Coll. Cambridge 1746.

85 FISHERTON DE LA MERE f.705   D. Wylye

1. Divine service is performed in this church but once every Sunday, it being a vicarage of small value, and never known to have double duty.

2. None observed, nor known to be observed by my predecessors, the parish being small and the inhabitants few in number.

3. As *curate*.[3]

4. I serve another cure within a mile of this parish,[4] but have no regular licence from the bishop.

5. The holy sacrament is administered in this church at three different times, viz. Easter, Whitsun, and Christmas.

6. The usual number of communicants in this parish is about sixteen, which was the number at Easter last.

7. We have no papists residing within this our parish of Fisherton, neither is there any place of resort for that purpose; nor any popish schools.

8. There are no Presbyterians, Independents, Anabaptists, or Quakers in this parish; no teachers of that profession, nor any that publicly profess to disregard religion as far as I know.

9. It hath not been customary to catechize the children of this parish publicly in the memory of any of the inhabitants, the number being few.

10. There is a regular register book of births and burials kept and due return of the same annually.

11. [We have no such book belonging to our parish, *crossed out*.] There is a register book of the same duly kept.

12. There are no chapels of ease or any such buildings, nor any ruinated chapels.

13. There is no terrier of houses, lands, tithes, pensions, etc. belonging to this parish, at present, but shall take care to have one properly drawn up and sent into the registrar's court.

14. None at all.

15. The churchwardens are always chosen in the Easter week, jointly.

16. No public school of any sort within this small parish.

17. I serve this church as curate, and constantly reside within a mile of the parish.

18. We have no such customs.

19. I believe, *none*.

20. My place of residence is Codford St. Mary, and the nearest post town is Heytesbury.

Henry Williams,[5] curate

86 FITTLETON f.713   D. Potterne

1. At the hour of 11 in the morning at [*recte* and] at 3 in the afternoon. Twice in general.

2. Yes.

---

[3] Vicar, Thomas Scotman. Perhaps Christ's Coll. Cambridge 1772.
[4] Codford St. Mary, **51.**
[5] See **51.**

3. As curate.[6]
4. None.
5. 4 times.
6. About 20 or 30.
7. None.
8. [a] None. [e, f] None.
9. [a] Yes. [c] At Lent according to the Form in the Common Prayer Book.
10. [a] Yes. [c] As far back as the year 1624.
11. Yes.
12. [a] None. [f] None.
13. [a] Yes. [b] Yes. [c] None. [d] None.
14. [a] One free school for ten boys, founded by Henry Clarke Esq. and Rev. Roger Kay, rector of Fittleton. Trustees, William Beach Esq. or his executors, — Gapper Esq. and his executors, the minister for the time being, and the churchwardens. [d] None; none.
15. Yes. One by the minister and one by the parish.
16. One free and public school supported by endowment for boys and girls. They are taught writing and reading and arithmetic. They are taught their catechism. They are not lodged, fed, or clothed. One boy annually is apprenticed, the others dispose of themselves. The school answers the end of the foundation.
17. Yes, in the parsonage house.
18. To the poor, and distributed by the churchwardens and by the minister.
19. None.
20. Fittleton, which is five miles from a post town called Amesbury.

J. Yeomans,[7] curate

The curate was ord. D. in the cathedral church at Oxford 14 June 1778 and was ord. P. at the same place 5 June 1783 and has taken the degree of M.A.

87 FONTHILL GIFFORD f.721 D. Chalke
1. Once, at half after ten in the morning, and at two in afternoon alternately. Divine service has been performed only once a day for some years past, probably owing to the smallness of the parish, and its vicinity to Fonthill Bishop.
2. Only on Good Friday, and one or two other days.
3. As curate.[8]
4. Two others, Fonthill Bishop and Berwick St. Leonard. The parishes adjoin each other, and the three churches are not more than a mile asunder. Not licensed by the bishop.
5. Four times; at Easter, Whitsuntide, Michaelmas, and Christmas.

[6] Rector, Stephen Jennor. 1732–97. Pembroke Coll. Oxford 1749. Vice-president of Magdalen Coll. Oxford (patrons of the living) 1771.
[7] Probably John Yeomans, Wadham Coll. Oxford 1772. Clergy Books, 1783, do not mention a curate.
[8] Rector, Dr. Charles Wake. Oriel Coll. Oxford 1739. Rector of East Knoyle, **115,** where he resided except when his duties as prebendary of Westminster required his residence there.

6. [a] From twenty to thirty. [b] I cannot particularly recollect, but believe nearly the same number as usual.
7. None.
8. [a] None. [e] I know of none.
9. I publicly catechize children in the church; and when I make use of a printed exposition it is generally Archbishop Wake's. I do it in the summer, and in the English language.
19. [a] I have. [b] I do. [c] The register of births goes back to the year 1749; that of burials to the same period.
11. There is.
12. None.
13. I have not; I must leave the question to the rector.
14. None.
15. They are; one by the minister and the other by the parishioners.
16. None.
17. [a] I do not. [b] At Chicklade, an adjoining parish. [c] Never absent longer than a few days.
18. As the communicants consist chiefly of the lower class of people it has not been customary to collect any money.
19. I know of no other matter.
20. Chicklade near Hindon.

                              John Thaine Frowd,[9] curate of Fonthill Gifford
        Ord. D. 25 Sept. 1774. Ord. P. 22 Sept. 1776.

88 FOVANT f.729   D. Chalke
1. Divine service is performed at half past ten o'clock in the morning and at two in the afternoon; prayers and preaching in the morning, prayers in the afternoon.
2. There is no duty on weekdays but on Good Friday, or when a festival falls on a weekday.
3. A curates.
4. I serve the curacy of Teffont Evias two miles from Fovant but I have no licence.
5. The sacrament is regularly administered at Christmas, Easter, and Whitsuntide and Michaelmas.
6. There are in general about 20 persons. The communicants are increased from about 5 or 6 to the number specified.
7. There are no papists in the parish.
8. There are no Presbyterians, Independents, Anabaptists, or Quakers in the parish, and the parishioners decently regular.
9. The children are catechized in Lent and at other times.
10. There is a register regularly kept, and due returns made.
11. There is a marriage register.
12. There is no chapel of ease.
13. There is a terrier of all lands etc. belonging to the rector, bearing the

[9] See **14.**

particular date.

14. There is no free school in this parish.

15. The churchwardens are chosen in the Easter week, the one by the minister, the other by the parish.

16. There is no charity school in the parish.

17. The rector is resident.

18. The minister always gives the money received at the offertory to the poor that communicate.

19. Nothing to the best of my knowledge.

20. Salisbury, having lately been elected master of the free grammar [school] in this city vacated by the Rev. Mr. Moore.[1]

James Evans,[2] E. Coll. Wad. Student in Civil Law. Ord. D. 24 Sept. 178- [blank]. Ord. P. 27 Feb. 1782.

[Written across under the address:] Rev. Mr. Earle [smudged out;] Rev. Dr. Eyre.[3]

89 FOXLEY f.737   D. Malmesbury

1. Divine service, both prayers and preaching, is performed once every Sunday either at ten o'clock in the morning or at two in the afternoon; and the reason it is performed no more than once is because it is a very small parish and there are very few inhabitants in it.

2. Only on Christmas day for the above reason.

3. As curate, because Mr. Thompson[4] the present rector has another living, namely the vicarage of Thatcham near Newbury, Berks., where he resides.

4. I serve my own church of Hullavington, which is distant about two miles from Foxley.

5. Three times a year, at Christmas, Easter, and Whitsuntide.

6. The number is generally about forty and I believe that was the number at Easter last.

7. There is no papist nor reputed papist in the parish of Foxley.

8. There is no Presbyterian, Independent, Anabaptist, or Quaker in the parish that I know of.

9. I have catechized the children and expounded the catechism to them; but not lately, because there are very few children in the parish.

10. There is a register book of births and burials belonging to the parish of Foxley, that is duly kept and in good condition, which begins with the year 1715.

[1] For Mr. Moore, see **108**.

[2] 1760–97. Goodridge exhibitioner, Wadham Coll. Oxford 1778: *Registers of Wadham College, Oxford* [ed. R. B. Gardiner, 1895], ii. 152. He was appointed, out of 17 candidates, to the mastership of the free grammar school and to the Eyre lectureship at St. Thomas's, Salisbury, which went with it, on 1 Jan. 1783: Benson and Hatcher, *Salisbury*, p. 535. He became a vicar choral in 1799 and master of the Choristers' School 1801–4, where he instituted a number of reforms: Dora H. Robertson, *Sarum Close*, p. 261.

[3] Dr. Thomas Eyre. See Chilmark, **41**, of which he was rector. He was fond of Fovant, making it his summer residence, and 'has spent a good deal of money to make it comfortable': *Pembroke Papers*, i. 365.

[4] Seth Thompson. Perhaps admitted sizar, Clare Coll. Cambridge 1751.

11. There is a register book likewise of marriages, that is duly kept.

12. There is no chapel nor the ruins of any chapel in the parish.

13. As I am only curate, I cannot answer this question.

14. There is no free school, alms-house, hospital, or other charitable endowment in the parish.

15. There is only one churchwarden and that churchwarden continues in the office many years for want of another proper person in the parish to serve that office.

16. There is no public school or charity school in the parish.

17. I constantly reside at the vicarage house of Hullavington, which is distant about two miles from Foxley.

18. To the poor communicants by me.

19. I cannot recollect anything else relating to the parish of Foxley with which it is proper to acquaint your Lordship.

20. Hullavington near Malmesbury, Wilts.

I am, my Lord, your Lordship's dutiful and obedient humble servant,

William Adlam B.A.,[5] curate of Foxley

90 FROXFIELD f.745　　　　　　　　　　　　　　　D. Marlborough

1 & 2. Service is performed alternately morning and afternoon; in the morning it begins at half past ten o'clock, in the afternoon at half past two o'clock; to have service performed twice every Lord's day is unusual, as well as to have it upon any holidays or festivals that happen on weekdays.

3. I perform divine service as curate.[6]

4. I serve the cure of Little Bedwin,[7] distant from Froxfield about a mile and a quarter; I have no licence for either of the two cures.

5. The holy sacrament of the Lord's Supper is administered four times in the year: at Christmas, at Easter, at Whitsuntide, and at the feast of St. Michael's.

6. Froxfield is a small parish. Our number of communicants generally amounts to six, never above eight. No difference at Easter last.

7. There are none of that persuasion in this parish.

8. There are none of that persuasion in this parish. I know of none that are particularly guilty of absenting themselves from all public worship of God.

9. Unusual.

10. The churchwardens make an annual return of births and burials at the visitation. There are three register books belonging to this parish, of the following dates, 1561, 1670, 1752, and in tolerable preservation.

11. There is a complete register book of marriages kept.

12. There is a chapel at the alms-house in this parish, where I read prayers every Wednesday and Friday, and holidays, and read prayers and preach once on a Sunday; my salary is paid out of the revenues of the alms-house as settled by the noble foundress's will.

13. There is no glebe, nor tithes of any sort which belong to the minister of this parish; an annual stipend of £28 made in quarterly payments by the

---

[5] See **107.**

[6] Vicar, Thomas Brown. See Stratford Tony, **233,** of which he was resident rector.

[7] No return, as it was a peculiar.

impropriator, with £8 Queen Anne's Bounty money,[8] make the whole of the vicar's income.

14. There is an alms-house in this parish, founded and endowed by the right noble Sarah late duchess dowager of Somerset, deceased, for 50 poor widows, 20 clergy and 30 lay. The trustees are twelve gentlemen of the first fortune and character in the neighbourhood; the revenue, and the statutes made for the regulation of it, are matters to me unknown. I have never heard of any lands or tenements left for the repair of this church.

15. The churchwardens are chosen every year in the Easter week; the right of choosing them is vested in the parishioners only.

16. There is no public school in this parish, nor can I learn there ever has been any: at present there are two women's schools for children, one kept in the village of Froxfield, the other in the alms-house.

17. I constantly reside at Froxfield vicarage house and may be absent a fortnight yearly, on a visit to my friends.

18. There is no money collected at the sacrament.

19. I know of none.

20. My residence is at Froxfield, and the nearest post town is Hungerford.

My deacon's orders bear date 22 Aug. 1760, my priest's orders 3 July 1763. No degree.

George Jenkins, curate of Froxfield

91 FUGGLESTONE ST. PETER f.753   D. Wilton

1. Divine service is performed twice on every Lord's day; at Fugglestone church at half past ten in the morning, and at Bemerton chapel at two in the afternoon.

2. Divine service is performed at each church severally on some weekdays, holidays, and festivals happening on weekdays.

3. As curate of the parish.

4. No other cure.

5. At Christmas, Easter, Whitsuntide, and on the Sundays next succeeding each quarter day.

6. [a] Generally about ten at the church, about twenty at the chapel. [b] Nearly the same.

7. [a] None. [b, c, d, e] No.

8. [a] Very few. [b] No. [c] No licensed teachers. [d] Nearly the same. [e, f] No.

9. The children are catechized by the curate in the vulgar tongue every Friday in Lent after prayers.

10. [a] Yes. [b] Yes. [c] To the year 1747 only, legible.

11. Yes.

12. [a] No chapels except the above mentioned, two miles from the mother church. [c] The income arising from the tithes of the parish as to the mother church to which it is a chapel of ease, the parish being large and the houses greatly dispersed. [f] No ruinated chapels.

13. The rector has.

---

[8] £200 in 1739: Hodgson, p. 416.

14. The alms-house founded by Adelais wife of Henry I, 1124, for two old widowers and two old widows of Wilton; the endowments are small, but equal to the expenses. They arise from the rent of lands appropriated to that use and preserved by the rector of the parish, who is the prior, and has the direction and management of the revenues, who carefully attends to the diligent observance of the statutes entrusted to his care.

15. On each Easter Monday, one by the minister, the other by the parishioners.

16. No school whatever.

17. Reside constantly on this cure, at the parsonage house.

18. No money ever collected at the offertory.

19. No.

20. Bemerton near Salisbury.

John Hawes A.M..[9] rector

Ord. D. 13 July 1740. Ord. P. 19 Sept. 1742. Collated June 1759.

Henry Hawes,[1] curate

Ord. D. 20 Dec. 1778. Ord. P. 29 Oct. 1780.

92 FONTHILL BISHOPS [Funthill Bishop] f.761   D. Chalke

1. Once: at half after ten in the morning, and at two in the afternoon alternately. Divine service has been performed only once a day for many years past, probably owing to the smallness of the parish and its vicinity to Fonthill Gifford and Berwick St. Leonard.

2. Only on Sundays.

3. As curate.[2]

4. Two others, Fonthill Gifford and Berwick St. Leonard; the latter parish adjoins to Fonthill Bishop and the churches are only half a mile asunder. Not licensed by the bishop.

5. Four times, at Easter, Whitsuntide, Michaelmas, and Christmas.

6. Generally from ten to fifteen. At Easter last near twenty communicated, a greater number than I ever remember.

7. None.

8. [a] There is only one Presbyterian family in the parish, consisting of a man and his wife, who sometimes attend the church, but generally frequent a meeting in the parish of Tisbury. [e, f] I believe there are none.

9. As there are very few children in this parish, and fewer in that of Berwick St. Leonard, and the church of Fonthill Gifford is so near, I have not catechized them separately in these two parishes.

---

[9] Exeter Coll. Oxford 1737. Rector of Wilton, **217,** served by a resident curate, and warden of St. Giles's Hospital, Wilton: *V.C.H. Wilts.* iii. 264. Rector and prebendary of North Newnton: *Wilts. Inst.* ii. 78. His name and particulars are in a different hand from the rest of the return.

[1] New Coll. Oxford 1775. Son of the rector. Vicar of North Newnton, **146,** served by the rector of Manningford Bruce; and of its appendant chapel, West Knoyle, **116,** served by the curate of Hill Deverill.

[2] Rector, Richard Mant. 1745–1817. Trinity Coll. Oxford 1761. Rector of All Saints, Southampton.

10. [a] I have. [b] I do. [c] The register of births and burials goes back to the year 1759, when the late register was by accident burnt.
11. There is.
12. None.
13. I have not, and must leave the question to the rector.
14. None.
15. They are, one by the minister, and the other by the parishioners.
16. None.
17. [a] I do not. [b] At Chicklade, an adjoining parish. [c] Never absent longer than a few days.
18. As the communicants consist chiefly of the lower class of people, it has not been customary to collect any money.
19. I know of no other matter.
20. Chicklade near Hindon.

John Thaine Frowd,[3] curate of Fonthill Bishop
Ord. D. 25 Sept. 1774 and ord. P. 22 Sept. 1776.

93 GARSDON f.769   D. Malmesbury
1. Divine service is performed at Garsdon from Michaelmas to Lady day at 10 o'clock in the morning and from Lady day to Michaelmas at 2 o'clock in the afternoon, and the service at Lea, which is a vicarage annexed to Garsdon, is at Lea in the afternoon for one half year, and in the morning for the other half year, according to ancient usage.
2. No.
3. Divine service was lately performed by Mr. Davies,[4] who hath lately resigned on account of ill health.
4. There was no other curacy served *by him* and he was licensed.
5. Three times in every year, viz. at Christmas, Easter, and Whitsuntide.
6. The stated number of communicants at both parishes is about ten, and their number for some years past has been upon the increase rather than the decline.
7 & 8. To all queries I answer in the negative, as there are no dissenters of any denomination whatsoever in either of the parishes. I wish I could add that all within their precincts live under the habits and influence of our most holy religion and attended upon the services of our excellent church more constantly with proper views and from right motives.
9. Such as used to send their children had them catechized in Lent, when the Church catechism was explained to them by plain questions suitable to their capacities; but it is to be lamented that parents and heads of families pay but little regard to this necessary duty, however they may be reminded of their obligation to it.
10. There is a register book duly kept in each parish, but neither goes further back than the year 1752 when the clerk's house was burned down and the books were consumed with it.

[3] See **14.**
[4] John Davies, rector of Shorncote, **174,** and formerly curate of Malmesbury. Possibly Jesus Coll. Oxford 1744.

11. There is a marriage register book kept in each parish according to the directions of the Act of Parliament against clandestine marriages.

12. To all these queries I answer in the negative.

13. A terrier is now made according to your Lordship's directions, a duplicate of which will be left with your Lordship's registrar. No augmentation hath been made to the living for time immemorial.

14. All these queries I answer in the negative.

15. The churchwardens in both parishes are chosen every year by the parishioners in the Easter week.

16. There is no school in either of the parishes.

17. The succeeding curate[5] is to reside in the parsonage house at Garsdon.

18. There is no money collected at the sacrament.

19. I know of no other matter respecting my parishes of which I can give your Lordship any further information.

20. I reside at Weyhill, Hants, and the nearest post town is Andover.

J. Simpson D.D.,[6] formerly fellow of Queen's College, Oxford

94 WEST GRIMSTEAD f.777   D. Amesbury

1. Divine service, both prayers and preaching, is performed every Lord's day morning and afternoon alternately at the mother church and chapel of ease, about the hours of 11 and 2.

2. No; for this reason, that no person will attend, the inhabitants wholly consisting of labouring people.

3. As incumbent.

4. No: but see Q. 17.

5. Three times in the year; at Easter, Whitsunday, and Christmas day.

6. Generally about 8 or 10, seldom more or less.

7. I answer in the negative to all these questions.

8. There is no dissenter of any denomination in the parish; nor are there any persons that profess an open disregard to religion, that I know of; there are some few that seldom come to the parish church.

9. None have been sent to me since the latter end of the summer 1782. When they come, I expound to them myself in the vulgar tongue.

10. There is a register book duly kept and preserved. The churchwardens will make the returns of what has been neglected. The register goes back to the year 1717.

11. There is.

12. There is one chapel of ease, of the name of Plaitford, distant about 6 miles from the mother church. It is served by Mr. Watkins,[7] who reads prayers and preaches there every Sunday, morning and afternoon alternately. It is maintained by the tithes of the parish.

13. I have the best account I could get, but no duplicate has been laid up in the registry, as some part of it has been doubted, and I fear will require a

---

[5] Clergy Books, 1783, give 'Mr. Blaise' as curate of Garsdon.

[6] Joseph Simpson, 1710–96. Queen's Coll. Oxford 1728. The signature, degree, etc. and the word 'Andover' under query 20 are in a different hand from the rest of the return.

[7] Possibly George Watkins, Oriel Coll. Oxford 1755.

contest at law, which I shall be unwilling to engage in. With respect to any augmentation *vide* Q. 17.

14. I must answer in the negative to all.

15. They are chosen every year in the Easter week, one by the minister and one by the parishioners.

16. I must answer in the negative to all.

17. My residence is in the adjoining parish of Farley in an hospital built by Mr. Stephen Fox in the year 1681 and annexed to the rectory; wherein I daily read divine service. Farley is a peculiar under the inspection of the treasurer of the cathedral church of Sarum.

18. No money is given but by me, and I dispose of it myself.

19. I think not.

20. Farley Hospital near Sarum.

My institution to the rectory of West Grimstead was on 10 Feb. 1768. Admitted to deacon's orders 1 Nov. 1749. Admitted into priest's orders 15 July 1750. My university degree is M.A.

Neville Wells[8]

95 GRITTLETON f.785   D. Malmesbury

1. Divine service is performed at eleven and two of the clock on Sundays. The sermon is always delivered in the afternoon except on sacrament days.

2. Divine service is performed on Christmas day and on Good Friday but on no other holidays or festivals.

3. The service is performed by the incumbent.

4. I serve no other cure except occasionally when I am requested so to do by my friends or neighbours.

5. The holy sacrament is administered four times in the year, viz. on Christmas day, Easter Sunday, Whitsunday or Trinity Sunday, and on the Sunday next after Michaelmas day.

6. The number of communicants is generally about ten or twelve. On Easter Sunday last I had only eight, which was owing to the absence from home of a most respectable gentleman and his family.

7. I believe no papist has resided in this parish within the memory of man.

8. There is in my parish a meeting-house for Anabaptists. It was built about twenty years ago and is endowed with the interest of some money and a dwelling house for the teacher. The present teacher's name is Mosely, who is licensed. Only one small farmer and some of the meaner persons of my parishioners are of this sect, their number about fifty. Of Quakers there are only one family which consists of three persons. I believe there are no persons who absent themselves from public worship.

9. Catechizing in the church has not been practised I believe during the incumbency of my two predecessors. Such as I catechize privately I use the Church catechism and give such comments as I judge necessary.

10. I have kept an exact account of births and burials during my incumbency

8 1725–1801. Exeter Coll. Oxford 1741. Vicar of Winterbourne Stoke, **223,** served by the curate of Orcheston St. George, **154.**

which commenced in 1763, and returned regularly a copy to the register. I have a very distinct old register book on vellum which commenced in 1653 and ends in 1719, from which time neither of my two predecessors kept a register book.

11. The register book is duly kept as the law requires.

12. There are no chapels nor any traces of such in my parish.

13. There are three terriers of the rectory of Grittleton in the registrar's office at Salisbury but all very imperfect ones. By a decree in the Court of Exchequer in 1770 the rector is in possession of all the tithes due of common right. He has built an entire new house with suitable offices. He has therefore delivered this day to the register a terrier conformable to the directions he received with this.

14. There is no free school, alms-house, or hospital. There is £1 a year charged on lands left for ever for the repair of part of the church which is railed off with iron rails, being the burying place of a Mr. Houlton and his family. His heir, the rector, and churchwardens are the trustees. The interest of £150 vested in the 3 per cent consol. left by divers persons is annually distributed by the rector and churchwardens to such persons who most want it and have no relief from the parish.

15. The churchwardens are annually appointed every Easter Monday. The present rector has, as the majority of the parishioners are his tenants, appointed all parish officers, but this he believes is only by courtesy and that the nomination of the churchwardens is one by the rector and the other by the parishioners.

16. The is no public school. The teacher of the Anabaptists receives, I believe, the interest of £100 for the teaching of some children of that sect but under what particular conditions I do not know.

17. My only place of residence is at my parsonage house at Grittleton. I am never absent except occasionally and this so seldom that I have only been from home one Sunday in the course of the last two years. I am sometimes by connections and business in London and by property in the north of England called from home. Whenever this has happened I have always had the cure regularly attend to by some of my respectable neighbours or by a curate.

18. I always distribute bread to the amount on the following Sunday, after divine service at church to the poor who are most regular in their attendance there.

19. I do not recollect at present any circumstance worth notice. If any matter hereafter occurs I will take the liberty to apprise your Lordship of it.

20. Grittleton near Chippenham, Wilts.

I am, my Lord, your Lordship's most obedient servant,

Thomas Pollok[9]

Thomas Pollok LL.D. Ord. D. by Dr. Secker 27 Feb. 1763. Admitted into priest's orders 24 April 1763 by Dr. Thomas, lord bishop of Sarum, and

---

[9] He 'endeavours to do credit to himself and to be useful to his parishioners . . . and performs his duty to the general satisfaction of all his parishioners in the most regular manner': Sarum Dioc. R.O., Churchwardens' presentments, 1783.

instituted by him the day following into the rectory of Grittleton in the county of Wilts.

96 HAM f.793   D. Marlborough

1. Divine service is performed at Ham twice every Lord's day. In the morning at eleven o'clock, the morning service according to the liturgy, and a sermon. In the afternoon at three, the evening service, and no sermon.
2. Divine service is performed in the church of Ham on no weekdays, holidays, or festivals that happen on weekdays.
3. As curate. [1]
4. The curate of Ham serves no other cure. He is not licensed to the cure which he serves.
5. The holy sacrament has been constantly administered at Ham four times a year, viz. on the great festivals and as near as may be before or after the feast of St. Michael the Archangel.
6. The present curate of Ham officiated there for the first time on the 4 May last. At Easter there were ten communicants; the curate is informed that the number of communicants was greater when alms were collected and distributed at the Lord's table.
7. None.
8. None of these descriptions are in the parish of Ham, to the best of the curate's knowledge and information.
9. The curate proposes to catechize such children and servants of the parishioners as shall attend, once in each month, in the English language, and occasionally to expound the catechism in his sermons according to his poor ability.
10. There is a register book of births and burials commencing 27 Nov. 1720 and none of earlier date. The only remaining book seems to have been carelessly kept and ill preserved. Of the returns the present curate can be no judge. The registrar's office will best answer that part of this question.
11. There is a marriage register but the curate presumes that the form in which the entries have been made are by no means conformable to the Act of Parliament against etc.
12. None.
13. The curate cannot find any terrier whatever. The rector of Ham proposes, with the assistance of the churchwardens and principal inhabitants, to make a true and perfect terrier and to transmit the same to my Lord Bishop.
14. None.
15. The curate is informed that the churchwardens are duly chosen every Easter week, one by the minister or his nominee, the other by the parishioners together.
16. None.
17. The present curate resides at Hungerford at the distance of near four miles. The principal reasons for his non-residence are the inconveniency of

[1] Rector, Israel Vanderplank. Procurator of the vicars choral for many years. Chaplain to the county gaol, 1774. Formerly vicar of Wilsford: *V.C.H. Wilts.* iii. 198; v. 185; *Wilts. Inst.* ii. 85.

furnishing the house and the conveniency of living near his friends. He proposes, however, to occupy part of the parsonage house before next winter.
18. The curate finds that the custom of collecting money at the offertory has been for some years discontinued. The small offertory made by the curate at Easter last was delivered to the parish clerk to be by him given to a needy person.
19. I do not recollect any other matter for your Lordship's attention.
20. Hungerford.

Thomas Walker,[2] curate

97 HANKERTON f.801[3]   D. Malmesbury
1. Once a day, morning and evening alternately; further explained under same article for Crudwell.
2. On great festivals and fasts.
3. As curate.[4]
4. I serve the church of Crudwell, distant one mile, where I reside and of which I am rector.
5. The holy sacrament is administered four times a year.
6. The number uncertain; not great.
7. No papist.
8. No dissenters.
9. Children attend with tolerable punctuality.
10. A register is duly kept and returns properly made into the registrar's office. Goes back from the year 1699.
11. A marriage register is duly kept.
12. No chapel of ease.
13. I believe there is no terrier in the parish but that there is an old [one] in the registry of Sarum.
14. No charitable endowments of house or land.
15. The churchwardens are chosen at Easter, one by the vicar, one by the parishioners.
16. No charity school.
17. Answered [in] article 4th.
18. The money is given to the poor by the vicar.
19. I do not recollect any other matter for your Lordship's attention.
20. The nearest post town is Malmesbury.

James Wiggett[5]

98 HANNINGTON [Hanningdon] f.807   D. Cricklade
1. Once at the church, the same at the chapel, the former at $\frac{1}{2}$ past 11 in the

[2] Perhaps Trinity Coll. Oxford 1772.
[3] Letter missing.
[4] Vicar, James Gyles. Probably Merton Coll. Oxford 1747. Curate of Powick 1785 and rector of Madresfield 1790: *State of the Bishopric of Worcester, 1782–1808* (Worcs. Hist. Soc. N.S. vi), 123, 127. His son, James F. Gyles (St. John's Coll. Cambridge, 1798), is described as 'of Wiltshire'.
[5] See **62.**

morning, the latter alternately at 10 in the morning and at ½ past one in the evening.

2. Never was a custom; if there was no one would attend, being chiefly farmers.

3. As curate.[6]

4. I serve Highworth every Sunday evening at ½ past 3 and Blunsdon[7] within 3 miles of it alternately with the chapel of Hannington. Not licensed.

5. At Easter, Whitsuntide, and Christmas I administer the sacrament at each.

6. At Hannington about 8 or 10 generally. At Blunsdon (a small place) about 12 or 14. No difference that I recollect at Easter.

7. Nothing of the sort in either Blunsdon or Hannington.

8. [a, b, c, d] The same answer as above will hold good respecting these enquiries. [e, f] None, but many that absent themselves.

9. In the present printed form of catechism once a year.

10. [a,b] The register book is properly kept, and the returns to visitations regularly made. [c] About 100 years at Hannington.

11. Yes.

12. [a, b] I mentioned above there is a chapel belonging to Hannington and how served. [c] By the will of one of the Frekes there was about £20 allowed but I rather think it was given chiefly to increase the value of the mother church. [f] None.

13. I can't with propriety answer these queries, as I don't know where the vicar is at present.

14. There is a kind of school designed for 8 poor children who are taught reading but not writing. The salary is very small, about £6 per annum, bequeathed by one of the Freke family.

15. Regularly in the Easter week they are chosen, one by the curate or vicar, the other by the inhabitants.

16. There is a sort of charity school, but I have heard the endowment (which is only £8 per annum for teaching about 8 children in reading) was improperly made, and the present owner of the estate may at pleasure overthrow it. However, at present it is kept on in its pristine fashion. They are clothed and apprenticed to different handicraft trades.

17. [a] I do not. [b] I live near at hand at Highworth, about a mile off.

18. No money is ever given.

19. None.

20. Highworth, a post town.

P. Jones M.A.[8]

Priest about 7 years, deacon 9.

99 HARDENHUISH f.815   D. Malmesbury

1. Divine service is performed once every Sunday, one Sunday in the morning, the next in the afternoon. I cannot serve it oftener, having another church in the neighbourhood.

[6] Vicar, Thomas Butler. Probably Queen's Coll. Oxford 1767.

[7] Blunsdon chapel, not to be confused with the rectory of Blunsdon St. Andrew.

[8] Probably Brasenose Coll. Oxford 1768.

2. No services but on Sundays except on Christmas day and any public occasion.

3. I perform divine service as incumbent.

4. I serve another church, of which I am incumbent, about four miles from this parish.[9]

5. The sacrament is administered at Christmas, Easter, and Whitsuntide.

6. Not more than six communicants in general; six communicated last Easter. It has sometimes happened that I have not had one.

7. No papist in the parish.

8. No Presbyterian, Independent, Anabaptist, or Quaker in the parish. My parishioners are attentive to their duty.

9. The parish is very small; no children to be catechized.

10. The register book is duly kept, and in good preservation, and regular returns made of births and burials as the canon requires. The register book goes back to the year 1739.

11. A [proper *crossed out*] register book is kept, according to the directions of the Act of Parliament.

12. No chapel of ease in the parish.

13. I have an account of the tithes and glebe lands belonging to the minister of the parish, but no regular terrier. The lands are so intermixed with other people's property that considerable time will be necessary to ascertain the boundaries. The moment it can be done, a terrier shall be made.

14. No free school, alms-house or any charitable endowment in the parish.

15. The churchwardens are chosen every year in the Easter week, by the minister and parishioners together.

16. No school in the parish.

17. I do not reside in the parish but at Stanton St. Quintin, four miles from it. The parsonage house is a poor cottage.

18. No money given at the offertory.

19. I know of nothing more relating to my parish necessary for your information.

20. I live at Stanton St. Quintin, my post town is Chippenham.

[*Written across the bottom of the page, opposite the address:*] Instituted to the rectory of Hardenhuish 29 March 1777. Ord. D. 22 Sept. 1771. Ord. P. 26 Sept. 1773. B.A., Trinity College Oxford.

Samuel Smith,[1] rector

100 HEDDINGTON [Headington] f.823   D. Avebury

1. This church is served alternately, divine service at 11 o'clock in the morning, and at 2 o'clock in the afternoon. The reason why the church is served but once a day is the lowness of the stipend which is but £20 a year. Another reason is the badness of the roads.

2. None.

3. As incumbent.

---

[9] Stanton St. Quintin, **184.**
[1] Trinity Coll. Oxford 1767.

4. I serve the cure of Stanton[2] only, about six miles distance. I took out a licence for this cure, when ordained deacon, and was allowed by the bishop £40 yearly and to be paid quarterly, whereas now I have no more than £20 yearly.[3]

5. The sacrament is administered four times in the year, viz. Easter, Whit-sunday, Michaelmas, and Christmas.

6. There are generally about thirteen communicants attends, there were at Easter last fewer than usual, by reason some went to visit their relations, who live out of the parish.

7. [a] I can with pleasure and satisfaction say there are none that go under that name. [b] None. [c] None. [e] None that I can find, from the strictest enquiry.

8. [a] There are none such that go by that appellation. None. None. None. There are one or two deluded people called Methodists. [f] There are a few that seldom or ever come to church, and I believe have not been at the house of prayer for years past.

9. Yes, I expound the Church catechism to them. I make use of Dr. Secker's, late Archbishop of Canterbury's, excellent lectures on the catechism of the Church of England. I catechize all the Lent, and that in the mother tongue.

10. Yes, and I make regular return of births and burials at every visitation. My register goes as far back as the year 1539.

11. Yes, Yes.

12. [a] None, none. [b] None. [c] None. [f] None.

13. [a] Yes. [b] Yes. [c] None.

14. [a] None, none. [d] None, none.

15. Yes. One by the minister, and the other by the parishioners.

16. None. None. None.

17. No, I reside at Stanton, about six miles distance. I have resided at Stanton 20 years and upward. The reason is because the house is in a ruinous condition, and all the buildings thereunto belonging, and therefore dangerous and unfit to be inhabited. Another reason is because my wife could not enjoy her health there, and for that reason was advised by her physician to seek a healthier situation, otherwise her life would be in danger.

18. There is none collected.

19. [*Blank*]

20. I reside at Stanton; the nearest post town is Devizes, about three miles distance.

I was ord. D. at Salisbury 21 July 1751, and took out a licence for the cure of Heddington at the same time. I subscribed the declaration to conform to the liturgy of the Church of England as it is now by law established 22 July

---

[2] Stanton St. Bernard, **182.**

[3] An Act for the better maintenance of curates . . . , 1713, 13 Anne, c. 11 (12 Anne, St. 2, c. 12 in Ruffhead), gave bishops the power to prescribe stipends for curates of £20-£50 a year, according to the value of the benefice, where the incumbent was non-resident, but the excess of curates over cures in the 18th century always made the Act difficult to enforce. The stipend of £20 was presumably paid him by the absentee vicar of Stanton St. Bernard.

1751. Ord. P. 21 June 1752. My institution commenced 15 Sept. 1752. I have taken no degree.

Francis Rogers,[4] rector of Heddington

101 HILMARTON f.831   D. Avebury

1. Once a day, in the morning at half after ten, and three in the afternoon alternately. I serve two other churches.

2. Christmas day and Good Friday; the other holidays, the people is busily employed in the husbandry business, and don't attend.

3. As curate.[5]

4. Two, Lyneham and Tockenham. The churches is in a line, about three quarters of a mile distance from each other. I be not licensed to neither of my cures.

5. Three times, at Christmas, Easter, and Whitsunday.

6. Ten in general, neither increase nor decrease.

7. No. A small meeting called Methodist doth assemble at Thomas Hand at Goatacre, in the hamlet of Hilmarton parish. No popish priest. No popish school.

8. I know but one Quaker and he is superannuated. As to the other sects, I know of none. Some do absent themselves from divine worship through profaneness and irreligion.

9. There are a few small children and I have catechized them several times in the vulgar tongue.

10. The register of births and burials is duly kept and in good preservation. The oldest book of births and burials go 90 years back.

11. Yes.

12. [a] [*Blank*] [f] None.

13. There will be a terrier returned at the visitation.

14. [a] There is a small endowment, £4 a year, 9 poor children, free. Mr. Jacob of Tockenham, or the Rocks, the founder. Mr. Jacob governor or trustee. [c] They are carefully preserved and employed. [d] No lands or tenements left besides for any pious use.[6]

15. Yes. One by the minister and the other by the parishioners.

16. See query 14. The children are taught plain English and instructed in the Christian religion, and are fed, etc. The school don't decrease.

17. Yes.

18. None given.

19. I don't know of none.

20. My residence is Hilmarton, and Calne my nearest post town.

J. D. Thomas,[7] curate of Hilmarton

My deacon's orders dated 23 Aug. 1772. My priest's orders 24 Sept. 1780. A literate [for . . .] years on ——.

[4] Perhaps Queen's Coll. Oxford 1742. He was patron as well as incumbent.

[5] Vicar, Thomas Heath. Queen's Coll. Oxford 1738. Also rector of Calstone, **34.**

[6] In this answer some of the lines run into the binding and appear in the margin of the first page of the return. 'The Rocks' was the estate where the Jacob family lived in Gloucestershire, just over the county boundary from Colerne: ex inf. Mr. R. E. Sandell.

[7] See also **201.** A very unformed hand to match his ungrammatical English.

102 HILPERTON f.839   D. Potterne
1. Divine service is performed once a day, viz. at eleven o'clock in the morning in the winter season, and at three in the afternoon during the summer. I never heard any reason given why divine service is not performed twice a day, only that it has not been usual, and probably on account of the few inhabitants.
2. It has not been the custom to have divine service on holidays.
3. As curate. [8]
4. I serve the cure of Whaddon, distance from Hilperton about a mile and a half, but am not as yet licensed.
5. The holy sacrament is administered four times in the year, viz. at Christmas, Easter, Whitsuntide, and Michaelmas.
6. There are seldom more than six or seven communicants. Easter last there were not so many.
7. There are no reputed papists in the parish, nor any place or chapelry in which they assemble for divine worship.
8. There are no dissenters in the parish, except Methodists, who have a house where they meet and which is licensed as the law directs. I don't know of any other persons in the parish who commonly absent themselves from church.
9. The children have been catechized this summer, which is the usual season.
10. A register book of births and burials is duly kept, and the returns into the registrar's office are regularly made. It goes back to 1694.
11. Yes.
12. There is not any chapel of ease in the parish.
13. The rector has a terrier of the glebe lands, tithes, and profits of the living of Hilperton which he will produce this visitation.
14. There is not any free school, alms-house, or hospital, or any other charitable endowment, in the parish. There are three houses left for beautifying the church, and the churchwardens are the trustees.
15. Two churchwardens are chosen every year in the Easter week, one by the minister, the other by the parishioners.
16. There is not any public school or charity school in the parish. There is only dame school.
17. I reside at Laycock, something more than six miles from the parish.
18. It has not been the custom to collect any offerings at the sacrament.
19. None that I know of.
20. The nearest post town to my place of residence is Chippenham. [9]

103 HINDON f.847   D. Chalke
1. Divine service is performed at half past eleven o'clock in the morning and at half past three in the afternoon. Prayers and preaching in the morning, prayers in the afternoon.
2. There are prayers every Wednesday and Friday throughout the year.

[8] Rector, John Montagu. See **56.**
[9] No signature. Clergy Books, 1783, give Mr. Brindley as curate. Probably Henry Brindley of Lacock, Christ's Coll. Cambridge 1754. See also **213.**

3. As curate.[1]

4. I serve the church of Pertwood once a fortnight, a mile from Hindon. In the intermediate space I serve Teffont Evias in the morning. I have no licence to this cure.

5. The sacrament is regularly administered, at Christmas, Easter, Whitsuntide, and Michaelmas.

6. There are in general about 20 communicants. They are increased from three or four to the number specified.

7. There is one family of reputed papists consisting of three persons, the master of which is a surgeon and apothecary. They have no public place of worship in this parish, nor is any popish priest resident in it, neither any popish school kept.

8. There are no Presbyterians, Independents, Anabaptists, or Quakers in this parish.

9. The children and servants are catechized in Lent and at other convenient times.

10. There is a register regularly kept of births and burials, in good preservation.

11. It has not been usual to marry in Hindon, the parishioners of which always are married at Knoyle.

12. This is a chapel of ease to East Knoyle.

13. There is no terrier belonging to this chapel to be found at Hindon, it being tithable to East Knoyle.

14. There is a free school endowed by William Beckford Esq. The master's name is *Thomas Ransom*.

15. [*Blank*]

16. There is no school but what is mentioned in the 14th article. It is supported by Mr. Beckford's contribution alone for poor boys and girls. They are instructed in the principles of the Christian religion.

17. I reside the major part of my time at Hindon [when the rector of T[2] is absent *crossed out*] but not in the parsonage house.

18. The minister distributes the money given at the offertory to the poor communicants.

19. Nothing to the best of my knowledge.

20. Partly at Hindon and partly at Fovant. The former the nearest post town. John Evans.[3] Ord. D. 23 Dec. 1781.

104 BROAD [Great] HINTON f.855   D. Avebury

1. Once, at half after eleven in the morning, and at half after two in the afternoon alternately. The smallness of the living may probably be one reason that it has not been usual to perform divine service twice on the Lord's day.

2. Divine service is performed on Christmas day and Good Friday.

[1] Hindon was a free chapel to East Knoyle, **115.**

[2] Teffont ? See note 3.

[3] Brother of James Evans, curate of Fovant, **88,** and Teffont Evias, **195.** For the complicated arrangements whereby the Evans brothers between them served Fovant, Teffont Evias. Hindon, and Pertwood see above, p. 9.

3. As curate.[4]

4. I serve the cure of Wroughton and the chapel of Barwick Bassett, each three mile distant from Broad Hinton.

5. Four times: at the festivals of Christmas, Easter, and Whitsunday, and about Michaelmas.

6. From 20 to 30; at last Easter the number might be about 25. I have known a greater number attend at that season.

7. There are no reputed papists, nor consequently is there any popish school or place of worship etc. in the parish.

8. There are no dissenters of any denomination in the parish, nor do I know that there are any who *professedly* disregard religion, but I fear there are several who commonly absent themselves from public worship.

9. The youth of the parish are catechized at church on Sundays during Lent. The totally illiterate are seldom sent, or come, for instruction.

10. The register book is duly kept and in good preservation, and copies are regularly sent to the visitation. The register of births and burials extends back as far as 1682.

11. Yes.

12. No chapel of ease.

13. There are copies of terriers of different dates, the originals of which are, I presume, in the bishop's registry. I do not know that any augmentation has been since made to the living.

14. There is a school for the instruction of the poor children of the parish in reading, writing, and accompts; founded by Thomas Benet Esq. of Salthrop Wilts., in the year 1743. The original endowment, £20 per annum. In 1751 the same benefactor gave, for the use of the master, a house and garden, and added 40s. per annum for their repairs. The trustees are the owner of the land from which the endowment is paid and the incumbents of five neighbouring parishes. The annual salary is regularly paid, and I believe the regulations made concerning the school are duly observed.

15. The churchwardens are annually chosen in the Easter week, one by the minister and the other by the parishioners; or both by the parishioners, in the absence of the minister.

16. In the school mentioned in A. 14 the children are instructed in the principles of the Christian religion as explained in the Church catechism; and regularly brought to the church.

17. [*Blank*]

18. By the minister to the most deserving or the most distressed among the poor of the parish.

19. I do not recollect any.

[4] Vicar, Richard Purdy. 1753–1808. Queen's Coll. Oxford 1763. Vicar of Gillingham, Dorset: Clergy Books, 1783.

20. The vicar's, Gillingham near Shaftesbury, Dorset.
The curate's, Wroughton near Swindon.[5]

105 LITTLE HINTON f.863   D. Cricklade

1. Divine service, both prayers and preaching, is performed every Sunday, unless prevented by illness, one Sunday in the morning at 11 o'clock, and one Sunday in the afternoon at two o'clock, as directed by late Bishop Hume.

2. Prayers are read on the festivals immediately following Christmas, Easter, and Whitsunday: Ash Wednesday, Good Friday, Ascension day, and the state holidays.

3. I perform divine service as curate.

4. I serve the cure of Bishopston, one mile distance, which cure belongs to the same incumbent, the Rev. Nowes Lloyd A.M.[6]

5. The holy sacrament is duly administered four times every year, viz. Christmas, Easter, Whitsuntide, and at Michaelmas.

6. The number of communicants in general, and at Easter last in particular, between 20 and 30.

7. There are no reputed papists nor any popish priest, or any popish school in this parish.

8. There are no dissenters of any sort or denomination, but there are several absenters, chiefly of the poorer sort.

9. The parishioners are very remiss in sending their children and servants to be instructed in the Church catechism, but, in hopes of bringing them to a better sense of their duty for the future, I have begun a familiar exposition of our Church catechism, which I purpose, please God, to go through with at all proper opportunities, particularly in the Lent season.

10. There is a register book of births and burials duly kept, and returns of them regularly made into the registrar's office, as the canon requires; and the said register is more than 200 years date.

11. A register book is duly kept, according to the directions of the Act of Parliament against clandestine marriages.

12. There are none.

13. To this, the Rev. Mr. Nowes Lloyd A.M. rector of Enbourn, Berks., who holds that rectory by dispensation with the rectory of this parish, who will attend your Lordship's visitation at Newbury, will answer.
[*In another hand:*] I know not of any terrier of the rectory of Hinton, and as there are only two acres of glebe land belonging to it (the income being paid in money) I presume there is no terrier. N. Lloyd, rector.

14. There is a charity school founded and endowed 7 Oct. 1777 by the Rev.

---

[5] No signature. Curate, D. Williams, curate of Wroughton, **80,** in which capacity he attended the visitation, and wrote to excuse himself from attending at Devizes, as the vicar of Broad Hinton was himself attending. 'Though had not a particular circumstance rendered it inconvenient, he would have been happy once more in hearing a charge to which he had already listened with much pleasure and satisfaction; and which, if the hope may be expressed without impertinence, he hopes soon to have an opportunity of perusing with equal satisfaction and advantage': Sarum Dioc. R.O., Misc. Vis. Papers, 8.

[6] Probably St. John's Coll. Oxford 1739. Vicar of Enbourne, Berks.

Mr. Thomas Coker A.M., rector of Doynton in the county of Gloucester, for the education of ten poor children, and the several deeds relating to the same are kept in a chest under three locks and keys, one of which is kept by the rector, one by the vicar of Bishopston, and one by the vicar of Shrivenham, Berks., who are appointed by the founders [*sic*] trustees of the said charity. Lands to the amount of £8 15*s*. per annum are properly settled.

15. The churchwardens are regularly chosen in the Easter week every year, one by the minister and one by the parishioners.

16. There is a charity school settled by endowment, as explained in my answer to Q. 14. The children, either boys or girls, are to be regularly brought to church, and are to be instructed in the principles of the Christian religion, but no provision made for them when they leave school.

17. My place of residence is at Bishopston, one measured mile only from this parish church, where I constantly reside all the year.

18. The money given at the offertory is generally divided amongst the poor communicants.

19. There is not.

20. Swindon is the nearest post town to Bishopston, my place of residence.
My deacon's orders bear date 23 Sept. 1722. My priest's orders 31 May 1724, both by the bishop of Oxford.

Cal. Colton A.M.,[7] curate of Hinton Parva

106 HUISH f.871   D. Marlborough
1. Once a day. At 11 o'clock in the morning or three in the afternoon.
2. Upon all festivals and holidays when I think there is any probability of having a congregation.
3. As incumbent.
4. I serve the cure of Bechingstoke, my own living, distant six miles from Huish.
5. Four times a year, at Christmas, Easter, Whitsunday, and Michaelmas.
6. From eight to twelve. At Easter last the number was nearly the same as usual.
7. There are none.
8. There are none.
9. [a] They do not. [c] In the summer season, in the English language.
10. [a] I have a register book regularly kept. [c] To the year 1603.
11. There is such a register as the Act requires.
12. There are none.
13. I have a terrier and have delivered a copy of it duly attested to the bishop's registrar. There has been an augmentation, an account of which I have delivered to the registry.
14. There is none.
15. There is but one qualified person in the parish; therefore he is continued

[7] Caleb Colton, Wadham Coll. Oxford 1716. According to the churchwardens he preached and read service every Sunday 'with a most excellent voice' and took 'great pains to instruct the people for confirmation': Sarum Dioc. R.O., Churchwardens' presentments, 1783.

from year to year.

16. There is none.

17. [a] I do not. [b] I reside upon my living of Bechingstoke, six miles distant from Huish.

18. There is no money given at the offertory.

19. There is none.

20. Bechingstoke near Devizes, Wilts.

Instituted 1 May 1775. Ord. D. 7 March 1773 and ord. P. 9 April 1775.

Charles Mayo[8]

107 HULLAVINGTON f.879   D. Malmesbury

1. Divine service, both prayers and preaching, is performed once every Lord's day, either at ten o'clock in the morning or at two in the afternoon. And the reason it is performed no more than once is because it has not been usual.

2. Prayers are read in my church upon the principal holidays throughout the year and there is a gift sermon preached in it on St. Thomas's day.

3. As incumbent.

4. I serve the cure of Foxley, and have served it many years, which is distant from me about 2 miles.

5. Three times in the year, namely at Christmas, Easter, and Whitsuntide.

6. The number of communicants generally is about 14 or 16; but last Easter I believe there were only 12, occasioned by the illness of some of the communicants.

7. There is not any papist nor reputed papist in my parish.

8. There is not any Presbyterian, Independent, or Anabaptist in my parish; but there are a few Quakers, who have a meeting-house here, which was built about the latter end of the last century, at which time, I have been informed, there were many more of this sect in this parish than at present. There are besides a few persons who commonly, though not always, absent themselves from the church.

9. I have catechized the children of my parish many times and expounded the catechism to them, which I have usually done soon after Whitsuntide, when the days are longest and the congregation is largest.

10. There is a register book of baptisms and burials belonging to my parish, which begins with the year 1694 and which is duly kept and in good condition. There is likewise another register of baptisms and burials more ancient than the former, beginning with the year 1559, but imperfect.

11. There is a register book of marriages belonging to my parish, which is duly kept.

12. There is no chapel nor the ruins of any chapel in my parish.

13. There was a terrier taken of my vicarage in the year 1704, and delivered to the bishop's registry, as appears by the churchwardens' account for that year; but there was no counterpart of it kept by the parish that I could ever find. About twenty years since that time, there was an augmentation made of my living by a purchase of lands with Queen Anne's Bounty;[9] but whether

[8] See **15.**

[9] In 1719: Hodgson, p. 417.

any account of such augmentation has been transmitted into the bishop's
registry I cannot say.

14. There is no free school, alms-house, etc. in my parish.

15. There are two churchwardens chosen every year in the Easter week, one
by the minister and the other by the parishioners.

16. There is a small charity school in my parish, for teaching six poor children
to read, which is supported by an annuity of £3 per annum, issuing out of an
estate at Clifton in the county of Glocester and given by Ayliffe Green,
gentleman, in the year 1690, who likewise gave 20s. for preaching a sermon
yearly on St. Thomas's day in the parish church of Hullavington and 20s.
more to be distributed yearly on the same day to the second poor persons.

17. I constantly reside at the vicarage house in the parish of Hullavington.

18. To the poor communicants by me.

19. I cannot recollect anything else relating to my parish of which it is
proper to inform your Lordship.

20. Hullavington near Malmesbury, Wilts.

I am, my Lord, your Lordship's dutiful and obedient humble servant.

William Adlam, A.B.,[1] vicar of Hullavington

P.S. The date of my deacon's orders is 22 Sept. 1745. Of my priest's orders
20 Sept. 1747 and of my institution 2 Aug. 1753.

108 IDMISTON f.887   D. Amesbury

1. Divine service is performed in my church of Idmiston and likewise in my
chapel of Porton once every Lord's day. Prayers at 11 in the morning; prayers
and preaching at 2 in the afternoon during the winter, and 3 in summer.

2. There is no divine service upon weekdays but when Christmas day falls on
a weekday; there being hardly any besides working people, they have not
been accustomed to attend the church oftener.

3. I perform divine service in the afternoon at Idmiston and Porton alternately
as incumbent;[2] the curate who did the whole duty for the late incumbent
serves them alternately in the morning.

4. I serve no other cure, but perform service at the cathedral most Sunday
mornings in order to be exempt from duty there in the afternoon, finding
no difficulty in providing for one of my parish churches constantly and
regularly every Sunday morning and not being able to provide for both once
a month only, when, according to the regular course, it is my duty to officiate
at the cathedral the whole day.

5. The holy sacrament of the Lord's Supper is administered both at Idmiston
and Porton at Christmas, Easter, and Whitsuntide.

6. The whole number of communicants at Idmiston is 30, and at Porton 16,
which are as many as can be remembered. Nearly the whole number of each
place communicated at Easter last.

7. None.

[1] Oriel Coll. Oxford 1741. See also **89.**
[2] Clergy Books, 1783, have the entry 'Porton Chap. Dr. —', but name no curate.

8. There are none of any sort who dissent from the doctrines or mode of worship of the established church. All regularly attend the church, and behave decently in the performance of their duty there.

9. The children and servants have been catechized by me, and an exposition read to them from Archbishop Wake, which in future will always be done during Lent. Owing to their not having been accustomed to it, I could not get them to attend so early as the last Lent.

10. There is a register book of births and burials duly kept and in good preservation. Returns have of late been regularly made. The register begins in the year 1577.

11. There is a marriage register duly kept according to the Act of Parliament.

12. There is no chapel besides the before-mentioned chapel of Porton which is within a mile of the church.

13. I have a perfect terrier of all things belonging to me as vicar of my parish, a duplicate whereof has been delivered to the bishop's registrar, since which no augmentation of my living has been made.

14. None.

15. There is a churchwarden at Idmiston, and a chapel-warden at Porton, chosen every year in the Easter week. There being very few capable of serving the office, they have generally by agreement served in rotation.

16. There are two schools for children in the parish; in one they are taught reading, in the other reading and writing. They are likewise instructed in the Church catechism in both. Their parents (who pay for their instructions, and under whose care they are out of school hours) bring them regularly to church.

17. I reside in the Close of Salisbury (being vicar of the Close), 6 miles from Idmiston.

18. It has never been customary to collect any money.

19. I have no other matter relating to my parish to lay before your Lordship.

20. The Close of Salisbury.

Edward Moore A.M. [3]

Collated to the vicarage of Idmiston cum Porton 14 Oct. 1782. Ord. D. 18 Dec. 1768, ord. P. 27 Jan. 1771.

109 IMBER f.895   D. Potterne

1. Divine service is performed at Imber at one o'clock. The reason divine service is not performed twice every Lord's day, I suppose, is its being a small parish.

2. It is performed on Christmas day, Good Friday, and Ascension day.

3. As curate. [4]

4. I serve the perpetual curacy of Heytesbury, about 4 miles distant from Imber, and am not licensed.

5. Four times a year, at Christmas, Easter, Whitsuntide, and Michaelmas.

6. [a] About twelve. [b] Nearly the usual number.

7. There are no papists at Imber.

[3] Wadham Coll. Oxford 1764. Master of the city grammar school 1772–82: Benson and Hatcher, *Salisbury*, 529 and 535. He was succeeded there by James Evans; see **88.**

[4] Clergy Books, 1783, give 'Mr. Colton' as perpetual curate.

8. There is one family of Anabaptists in the parish.
9. The children are catechized once a week in Lent.
10. A register of births and burials is duly kept at Imber and in good preservation; regular returns are also made. The register goes as far back as the year 1709.
11. Yes.
12. There are no chapels of ease belonging to Imber.
13. I do not know of any.
14. There is no free school or any other charitable endowment at Imber.
15. The churchwardens are chosen in the Easter week by the parishioners.
16. [*Blank*]
17. I reside at Heytesbury. There is no house belonging to the curacy of Imber.
18. The money given at the offertory is disposed of by a reputable, honest farmer, to the poorest and most deserving in the parish.
19. There is no other matter that I know of, of which it may be proper to give information.
20. The nearest post town is Heytesbury.

Lewis Jones M.A.,[5] curate of Imber

110 INGLESHAM f.903   D. Cricklade

[*Written across the top of the letter:*] For the lord bishop of Sarum.
1. Divine service, both prayers and preaching, is performed in the parish church every Lord's day, alternately at eleven in the morning and two in the afternoon by the parishioners' particular desire.
2. Divine service is performed on the holidays and festivals whenever any of the parishioners please to come.
3. As incumbent.
4. At present I serve no other church than my own.
5. The holy sacrament of the Lord's Supper is administered in the church four times in the year, viz. at Easter, Whitsuntide, Michaelmas, and Christmas.
6. About twenty. And last Easter there was about the same number as usual.
7. There are none of any condition whatever.
8. None that I know of.
9. I am always ready to catechize and instruct the young people of my parish whenever their parents please to send them, which I frequently exhort them to do. In particular I call upon them every Sunday in Lent, when I instruct them in the catechism, and expound it to them myself in English.
10. There is a register book duly kept and in good preservation. Copies of it are returned into the registrar's office every year at the visitation. The register goes as far back as the year of our Lord 1589.
11. There is.
12. There are no chapels in the parish of any kind whatsoever.

[5] Possibly Christ Church Oxford 1766. Heytesbury, of which he was perpetual curate, was a peculiar of the dean of Salisbury.

13. I have not such a one at present but will make one and deliver it to your Lordship's register. Since I had written the above I have made a terrier according to your Lordship's directions, and will deliver it into your register at your visitation.

14. There is no charity that I know of left to the parish or church, except a legacy (from Mrs. Jane Bray) of 20s. a year; which is taken every other year in cloth, and distributed amongst the poor, in proportion to their particular circumstances and the largeness of their families.

15. There is only one churchwarden in my parish, who is chosen yearly by the parishioners.

16. There is no school in the parish; neither has there been any formerly that I have ever heard of.

17. I reside on my living in the parsonage house.

18 & 19. No money is ever given at the offertory. I expressed my surprise at this circumstance when I first came to the parish and sent the plate for the purpose of gathering, but nobody except those of my own family chose to give, and I did not think proper to press them on this head too far lest by so doing I should prevent them from coming to the sacrament.

20. The place of my residence is the parsonage house. The nearest post town is Lechlade, in the county of Gloucester: and letters are always directed to me at Inglesham near Lechlade, Gloucestershire.

I was ord. D. by Dr. John Thomas, lord bishop of Peterborough, on Sunday 22 Sept. 1754 at the chapel of Kew in the county of Surrey. I was ord. P. by (another) Dr. John Thomas, lord bishop of Lincoln, on Sunday 14 March 1756, in Conduit Street chapel in the county of Middlesex. And I was collated to the vicarage of Inglesham by the same last-mentioned Dr. John Thomas, then bishop of Sarum, 7 Oct. 1763.

[*Written up the left hand margin:*] I took my M.A. degree at Cambridge in the year 1755.

Stanhope Bruce[6]

111 KINGTON [Keinton] ST. MICHAEL f.911   D. Malmesbury

1. Morning prayers and sermon at 11 o'clock. Evening prayers at 2 o'clock.

2. Wednesdays and Fridays and festivals.

3. As curate.[7]

4. I serve no other cure but Kington nor am I licensed.

5. The first Sunday in every month.

6. As I only entered on the cure in May, it cannot be expected I can speak with any degree of certainty.

7. Answered by the sixth question.

8. Answered by the sixth question.

9. Answered by the sixth question.

10. The register is duly kept, as far back as the year 1689.

11. There is.

---

[6] Peterhouse Cambridge 1748.

[7] Vicar, Edmund Garden. Reader to Gray's Inn, 1765 till his death, aged 92, in 1824: *W.A.M.* iv. 81; *Pension Book of Gray's Inn, 1669–1800*, pp. 302–3.

12. None.
13. Answered at the end of these questions.
14. A charity of £5, but being so late come to the cure it's out of my power to know particulars.
15. In Easter week, by minister and parishioners.
16. Not any but that mentioned in the 14th question.
17. I reside in the vicarage house as curate.
18. I as curate receive it, and propose in the winter to distribute what I may have to those who I think most want and deserve it.
19. Not any.
20. The first part answered by the 17th question. The nearest post town is Chippenham. [8]

[*Written at the bottom of the page and heavily crossed out:*] Mr. Garden vicar of Kington's most respectful compliments and duty I am desired to present to the Lord Bishop from him and hopes he can . . . in expectation of the death of . . . Garden in London. An official . . . your Lordship. [9]

112 WEST KINGTON [West Keinton] f.919[1]　　　　D. Malmesbury
1. Prayers and a sermon once every Lord's day, having two churches to serve.
2. Prayers and sermon on Christmas day, prayers on Good Friday.
3. As curate.
4. My own church at Nettleton, the adjoining parish, distant about a mile and half.
5. The 3 great festivals.
6. Generally 8 or 9; 8 last Easter.
7. None.
8. None.
9. The children are regularly catechized during Lent.
10. Yes.
11. Yes.
12. None.
13. This Q. I must leave to be answered by the rector, Mr. Hume, vicar of Bremhill. [2]
14. None.
15. Yes, one by the minister, one by the parishioners.
16. None.
17. I reside in my own parsonage house at Nettleton.
18. There is no collection made.
19. None.
20. Nettleton near Chippenham. Badminton post, Chippenham bag.
　　　　　　　　Daniel Mills, [3] curate of Kington and rector of Nettleton

[8] No signature. Clergy Books, 1783, give 'Mr. Kemble' as curate. Possibly Daniel Kemble, Balliol Coll. Oxford 1720.
[9] Some words are so heavily crossed out that they are undecipherable.
[1] Letter missing.
[2] See **26.**
[3] See **145.**

113 KEEVIL [Keivil] f.925   D. Potterne

1. Twice, prayers in the morning at half past ten, in the evening at half past two, sermon alternately morning and evening.
2. On Easter Monday and Tuesday, Whitsun Monday and Tuesday, and Christmas day.
3. As curate.
4. I serve no other cure. I am not licensed.
5. Four times, viz. at Easter, Whitsunday, Michaelmas, and Christmas.
6. The number of communicants I am told have been generally six. Last Easter nine, three more than usual.
7. None.
8. [a] No Presbyterians, Independents, Anabaptists, or Quakers. There is a Methodist meeting at the house of one John Hill, a labouring man, the preacher or teacher is one Rainer, a barber from Bradford. The house is not licensed. I believe the preacher is not licensed. The meeting till within the last quarter was once a fortnight, now once a month. [e] None to my knowledge.
9. When I came into the parish three months ago, I made enquiry concerning the customs of the place, and could find no other than the children's being catechized in Lent.
10. [a] Yes. [b] Yes. [c] Births 1559. Burials 1562.
11. Yes.
12. None.
13. I have a true and perfect account and terrier of all houses, lands, tithes, etc. which belong to the vicar of the parish. No duplicate thereof hath ever been laid up in the bishop's registry since the year 1704.
14. There is no free school, alms-house, hospital, or other charitable endowment in our parish. There is a school for teaching children English and arithmetic.
15. On every Easter Monday, one by the minister, and other by the parishioners.
16. None.
17. [a] I do, but not in the house. [b] I reside at Steeple Ashton, one short mile from the church. [c] Not at all.
18. By the minister and churchwardens.
19. The communion table is not railed in. The communion cloth, pulpit cloth, sounding board, and covering to the font are all in a bad state.
20. Steeple Ashton near Trowbridge, Wilts.

L. Docker B.A.,[4] vicar of Keevil. Instituted 15 Jan. 1783. Ord. D. 2 June 1751. Ord. P. 23 Sept. 1753.

James Fothergill B.A.,[5] curate of Keevil. Ord. D. 26 May 1782.

114 KEMBLE[6] f.933   D. Malmesbury

1. Twice every other Sunday, 11 and 3. My age is 70 and upwards, and for

---

[4] Lancelot Docker, Queen's Coll. Oxford 1744. He was non-resident: *V.C.H. Wilts.* viii. 261
[5] Probably Queen's Coll. Oxford 1777.
[6] In Gloucestershire since 1897.

many years past I have had a bad state of health.[7]

2. My parish consists of labourers and farmers, and no one comes, unless Mr. Coxe's family[8] are there.

3. As incumbent.

4. No.

5. Four times, at Easter, Whitsuntide, Michaelmas, and Christmas.

6. About 20. Last Easter rather more.

7. None.

8. [a] None. [f] Several, I fear, who absent themselves from all public worship.

9. I cannot say they do. I expound to them myself. In the summer part of the year, in English. In winter I hear them say it at my own house.

10. [a] Yes. [c] To the year 1582.

11. I never heard of any clandestine marriages at Kemble.

12. None.

13. Yes. But the parish has been lately inclosed; and the particulars, by order of Parliament,[9] are deposited with the patron of the church, and the clerk of the peace.

14. [a] None. [d] A small setate for the benefit of the second poor; which is constantly distributed the day after Christmas every year by the minister and officers of the parish.

15. One and one.

16. None.

17. Yes.

18. A collection has been attempted but without success.

19. I know of none.

20. Cirencester in Gloucestershire is the nearest post town.

John Copson A.M.[1] was ord. D. 20 May 1733; ord. P. 19 Dec. 1736. Instituted to Malmsbury 17 Jan. 1749. Kemble 21 Feb. 1765. He was also presented by Thomas Long Esq. to the living of Kelways near Chippenham, which is worth between £6 and £7 a year, served by some neighbouring clergy; and at the desire of the late Sir Robert Long held by me for the benefit of the widow, who receives £4 per annum from the Queen's Bounty. The presentation bears date 11 Nov. 1754 and is held under sequestration.[2]

115 EAST [Bishop's] KNOYLE f.941   D. Chalke

1. Divine service, both prayers and preaching, is performed in the church of Bishop's Knoyle. Divine service begins every Lord's day at half hour after ten in the morning, when there is always a sermon except on sacrament

---

[7] He was assisted by the curate of Minety, **143.**

[8] Charles Westley Coxe, M.P. for Cricklade 1784–5 and patron of the living.

[9] Kemble and Poole Keynes Inclosure Act, 12 Geo. III, c. 70 (Priv. Act).

[1] Queen's Coll. Oxford 1729. Vicar of Malmesbury, **133,** served by a resident curate.

[2] There is no return for Kellaways. The church was destroyed before 1760 and rebuilt in a different situation in the later 18th century: *Wilts. Top. Coll.* 116; Pevsner, *Buildings of England, Wilts.* (1963), p. 249. Served by Dr. West, rector of Dauntsey, **64,** and Draycot Cerne, **73:** Clergy Books, 1783.

Sundays, when the sermon is in the afternoon. Divine service begins each Sunday afternoon at half hour after two.

2. No divine service is performed upon any weekdays or holidays.

3. Dr. Wake as incumbent occasionally performs divine service. Mr. Russ is his curate.

4. Mr. Russ serves no other cure and resides in this parish upon his own estate.

5. The holy sacrament of the Lord's Supper is administered in the church of Bishop's Knoyle four times every year, viz. at Christmas, Easter, Whitsuntide, and the Sunday after Michaelmas.

6. Commonly about 30. Last Easter there were near 40 communicants.

7. There are no reputed papists in this parish, nor have any persons been lately perverted to popery, nor is any popish school kept in my parish.

8. There are no Presbyterians, Independents, Anabaptists, or Quakers in my parish. I know of no persons in my parish who profess to disregard religion or who commonly absent themselves from all public worship of God.

9. The children and servants of this parish are always catechized in Lent. Mr. Russ expounds the catechism to them from an exposition of his own which he compiled for their use.

10. There is a register book of births and burials duly kept and in good preservation; and returns, I believe, have been regularly made of births and burials into the registrar's office. The register of births and burials goes as far back as the year 1538, the 30th of Henry VIII.

11. A register book is duly kept according to the directions of the Act of Parliament against clandestine marriages.

12. No chapel of ease in my parish or any ruinated chapel. The chapel of Hindon in this parish is a free government chapel. The chaplain is maintained from lands in Hindon on which buildings have been erected and the Lord Chancellor presents. All great and small tithes from Hindon are paid to the rector of Bishop's Knoyle.

13. I am informed there are 3 terriers in the bishop's registry. Two of them I have had copies of. No terrier has been delivered in since I came to the rectory, and no augmentation has been made of the living.

14. There is no free school, alms-house, hospital, or other charitable endowment in this parish. No lands or tenements have been left for the repair of my church, or for any other pious use.

15. The churchwardens in my parish are chosen every year in the Easter week, one by me and the other by the parish.

16. Mr. Trippet, formerly rector of this parish, left by his will £100, the interest of it to be applied for the maintenance of a schoolmistress to teach 6 boys and 6 girls to read, and to learn them their catechism. Mrs. Shaw, widow of Dr. Shaw, formerly rector of this parish, left likewise £100, the interest of it to be applied to the same purpose, and for the same number of children.

17. I have constantly resided upon this cure, and in the parsonage house ever since the year 1746, and always myself performed divine service in this parish until I was a prebendary of Westminster; am now never absent for any length

of time, except when I am called upon to reside at Westminster. I was ordained deacon 1 Dec. 1744 and priest 8 May 1746 and was instituted to this rectory 14 May 1746. I took my Doctor of Laws degree 22 Nov. 1758. C. Wake.
18. The money given at the offertory is disposed of by the officiating minister among the poor communicants and other poor of the parish.
19. I know of none.
20. At Bishop's Knoyle near Shaftesbury.

Charles Wake,[3] rector
John Russ,[4] curate, who took the degree of M.A. 21 July 1749.

116 WEST [Little] KNOYLE f.949   D. Chalke

1. Divine service is performed once each Sabbath day at half an hour past ten. Divine service is performed once only on account of the smallness of the parish and living. [*Footnote at the bottom of the page:*] It would be an act of injustice not to inform your Lordship that from the attention and munificence of Henry Hoare Esq.,[5] who has some lands in the parish of Little Knoyle, the church is not only in exceeding good repair, but may vie in point of neatness and decent ornaments with any in your Lordship's diocese. H.H., vicar.
2. On Christmas day and on Ash Wednesday.
3. As curate.
4. I serve also Hill Deverill, five miles from Knoyle. I am not licensed to serve this cure.
5. The holy sacrament is administered on Christmas day, Easter Sunday, Whitsunday, and the Sunday nearest to Michaelmas day.
6. Usually about ten or twelve. At Easter last nearly that number.
7. No papists. Consequently no place of devotion or any priests of that persuasion.
8. No dissenters whatever. The parishioners regularly attend on Sundays the public worship of God in the parish church.
9. I catechize the children on Sundays during the summer months after the second lesson, in the vulgar tongue.
10. The register book which is in good preservation goes back to the year 1718, the register to that time having been unfortunately destroyed by fire.
11. There is.
12. [a] None. [f] None.
13. [a] Yes. [c] No.
14. The only endowment to the parish of Little Knoyle was given by Christopher Willoughby Esq. who by will left £16 per annum for the support of the aged poor of that parish, under the direction of the vicar and church-wardens. This income arises from certain lands held under the corporation of the city of Salisbury.
15. The churchwardens are chosen on Easter Monday, one by the vicar, the other by the parishioners.

[3] See Fonthill Gifford, **87,** of which he was rector.
[4] Probably Oriel Coll. Oxford 1740.
[5] Henry Hoare of Stourhead. This note, and the vicar's name etc. at the end of the return, are both in the curate's handwriting.

16. There is no school whatever in the parish of West Knoyle. Nor has there ever been any within the remembrance of any of the inhabitants.

17. I reside constantly at Horningsham, one mile from my other cure, (viz.) Hill Deverill.

18. There is no money given at the offertory.

19. None whatever.

20. Horningsham near Warminster.

Rev. Samuel Clarke,[6] curate of Little Knoyle. Was ord. D. at Sarum 23 Sept. 1770. Ord. P. at Sarum 22 Sept. 1771.

Henry Hawes A.M.,[7] vicar of Little Knoyle. Ord. D. 20 Dec. 1778. Ord. P. 29 Oct. 1780.

117 LACOCK f.957   D. Malmesbury

1. Prayers and preaching in the morning at 11 o'clock, prayers at 3 o'clock in the afternoon.

2. On Wednesdays and Fridays during Lent, every day in Passion week, and on such holidays and festivals as a congregation can be assembled.

3. As incumbent, viz., vicar.

4. The incumbent does no duty out of his own parish.

5. On every first Sunday of the month and on Christmas, Easter, and Whitsunday.

6. About thirty at the monthly sacrament; on the great festivals upwards of fifty.

7. There are no papists or chapels in this parish.

8. There is one person of the sect called Quakers, Mr. Ezekiel Dickinson, a gentleman of considerable landed property in this parish, a quiet man and a good neighbour.

9. Parents in general in this parish are strict in sending their children to be instructed in the catechism, which I expound to them myself during the season of Lent.

10. The register book is kept in good preservation and goes back as far as the year 1559.

11. Yes.

12. There are no chapels of ease in this parish.

13. The vicar has a terrier of all houses, tithes, profits, etc. belonging to this vicarage. [*Four lines have been rubbed out.*]

14. There is no free school, alms-house, hospital, or other charitable endowment in this parish.

15. One by the minister, the other by the parishioners, annually in the Easter week.

16. There is no charity school in this parish.

17. Constant residence as vicar in the vicarage house, and seldom absent above a day or two, and then on business.

---

[6] See Chirton, **44,** of which he was vicar.

[7] Vicar of North Newnton, **146,** to which West Knoyle was appendant. See Fugglestone, **91,** where he was resident curate.

18. Given by the vicar, in general to such ancient people as do not receive alms of the parish.

19. I do not recollect any.

20. Lacock near Chippenham.

E. Popham,[8] vicar of Lacock, was admitted into the holy order of priests at Oxford in the month of May 1763. Was instituted to the vicarage of Lacock in the month of August 1765, and admitted (at Oxford) to the degree of D.D. in the month of May 1774.

118 LANDFORD f.965   D. Amesbury

1. Morning service, both prayers and a sermon every Lord's day at eleven o'clock throughout the year; and evening prayers at half past two o'clock from Lady day to Michaelmas; according to custom.

2. Yes, on several.

3. As incumbent.

4. I serve no other cure.

5. Four times, viz., at Easter, Whitsuntide, Michaelmas, and Christmas.

6. The number of communicants generally speaking is from 25 to 30. At Easter last I think the number was much as usual.

7. There are not any such people.

8. I do not know of one under any such denominations; neither are there any who profess to disregard religion; and very few who commonly absent themselves from the public worship of God.

9. The children of the parish are taught their catechism every year during Lent, in the mother tongue.

10. [a, b] Yes. [c] The one at present in use commences in the year 1755. There is an old one which goes as far back as the year 1583/4.

11. Yes.

12. There are not any such.

13. [a, b] Yes. [c] There has been no augmentation

14. There is none.

15. The churchwardens are elected every year in the Easter week; one by the minister, the other by the parish.

16. There is a small day-school in the parish, for sixteen poor children, who are taught to read and work; supported by voluntary subscription.

17. I constantly reside upon the cure, mostly in the house belonging to it.

18. It is disposed of by the rector of the parish, to the poor at his discretion.

19. I do not know of any.

20. My place of residence is Landford; the post town is Sarum.

Henry Eyre A.M.[9] Instituted to the rectory of Landford 3 Nov. 1778. Ord. D. 20 Sept. 1778. Ord. P. 1 Nov. 1778.

[8] Edward Popham, St. Mary's Hall Oxford 1755. Rector of Chilton Foliat, **42.**

[9] Queen's Coll. Oxford 1770.

119 LITTLE LANGFORD[1] f.973　　　　　　　　　　D. Wylye

1. Service is performed every Sunday once in the day, when there is a sermon; there not being more than seven or eight inhabitants of the parish, once in the day is as often as a congregation can be formed.
2. There are not inhabitants sufficient to make a congregation on weekdays.
3. As curate.[2]
4. I serve my own church of Steeple Langford, distance one mile.
5. Four times in the year.
6. Seldom more than 3 or 4 communicants on account of the very few inhabitants.
7. None.
8. None.
9. At present there are no children to be instructed.
10. There is no register except of marriages; and in the three years I have served this church there has neither been wedding, christening, or burial.
11. Yes.
12. [a-e] [*Blank*] [f] None.
13. As curate it is not in my power to give an answer to this question.
14. None.
15. There are only two farmers in the parish and they serve the office of churchwarden in rotation.
16. None.
17. I reside at Steeple Langford but serve this cure regularly every Sunday.
18. There never is any collected.
19. None that I know of.
20. Steeple Langford near Sarum.

Samuel Weller,[3] curate

120 LANGLEY BURRELL f.981　　　　　　　　　　D. Malmesbury

1. Twice a day every Sunday, prayers and sermon at 11 in the morning, prayers at 4 in the afternoon.
2. On Christmas day, St. Stephen's, Easter, and Whitsun weeks.
3. As incumbent.
4. None. Licensed by the late bishop.
5. Thrice, viz. at Christmas, Easter day, and Whitsunday.
6. [a] Generally 7 or 8. [c] Less.
7. None.
8. [a] None. [f] A few.
9. There being no schoolmaster or mistress properly qualified to instruct them, they are rather defective in this point.
10. [a] I have. [b] I do. [c] To the year 1702.
11. There is.
12. [a] None. [f] None.

---

[1] One of Lord Pembroke's livings, it was described by Dr. Eyre as 'a very pretty rectory of £100 per annum': *Pembroke Papers*, ii. 353.
[2] Rector, Henry Hawes. See Box, **21**, of which he was resident curate.
[3] Rector of Steeple Langford, **187**.

13. [*Blank*]
14. None.
15. They are; by the minister and parishioners.
16. None.
17. I do.
18. By myself and to those who constantly attend public service.
19. None that I know of.
20. Langley Burrel, Chippenham.
   Samuel Ashe A.B.,[4] rector. Instituted 6 March 1777. Admitted to deacon's orders 11 June 1775, priest's orders 23 Feb. 1777 by the present bishop of Worcester.

121 LATTON f.989   D. Cricklade
1. [a] Once a day. [b] I serve also another church.
2. On some particular holidays.
3. As incumbent.
4. One cure,[5] the church of which and that of my own parish are within half a mile of each other.
5. Four times: Christmas, Easter, Whitsunday, and Michaelmas.
6. [a] Between twenty and thirty. [b] About the usual number.
7 & 8.   Thank God, not a dissenter in my parish.
9. Every Sunday.
10. [a] Yes. [c] Near 200 years.
11. There is.
12. [a] None. [f] None.
13. There is at present no such thing that I know of, but directions are given to the churchwardens to prepare one, being myself out of order.
14. Nothing of the kind.
15. Yes. The minister may name one.
16. Nothing of the kind.
17. I reside on my cure. My vicarage house is only a hovel, and has not been inhabited by a clergyman these many years.
18. None given.
19. None.
20. J. Lyne,[6] Down Ampney House near Cricklade, Wilts.
   Ord. D. in 1779, ord. P. in 1780, instituted the same year. Degree A.B.

122 LAVERSTOCK f.997   D. Amesbury
1. Once, sometimes at 10 in the morning and sometimes about 2 in the afternoon. The reason why not twice is custom and the narrowness of the stipend.
2. It is not.
3. As curate.[7]

[4] Lincoln Coll. Oxford 1771.
[5] Down Ampney, Glos.
[6] John Lyne, Exeter Coll. Oxford 1775.
[7] Laverstock was a perpetual curacy; patrons, the vicars choral of Salisbury: Sarum. Dioc. R.O., Diocese Book.

4. I do, viz. Winterbourn Earls and Winterbourn Dansey, at the distance of two miles and a half.

5. On the three grand festivals of Easter, Whitsuntide, and Christmas.

6. About 15. The number at Easter, I believe, was 8, less than usual.

7. There are none, neither is there any place for papists to assemble, or any popish priest or school in the parish.

8. There is a family of Presbyterians, 4 persons of mean rank all of one family. There is no place of divine service for any sects whatsoever. I believe there are no persons who disregard religion or commonly absent themselves from all public worship.

9. They do not, notwithstanding notice has been given for catechetical instruction.

10. There is, and returns usually though not regularly made. We have registers that go back to 9 May 1567. The last book goes back to 26 Oct. 1727.

11. There is.

12. There are none. There is no ruinated chapel.

13. The parsonage is impropriate.

14. [a] There are none. [d] No lands or tenements have been left for the repair of the church or for any other pious use, but there is a silver chalice with this inscription, 'Given by George Welch 1697. 1: 10: 0' and a handsome flagon with this inscription, 'The gift of Ann Winchcomb.' There are 2 bells in the church.

15. They are, by the minister and churchwardens [*recte* ? parishioners] together.

16. There is no public or charity school.

17. I reside in the Close of Sarum, one mile distant from the parish.

18. There is none given.

19. There is not.

20. At Salisbury.

I was ord. D. 24 Sept. 1749 and admitted priest 17 June 1753.

Richard Trickey A.B.,[8] curate of Laverstock

123 WEST [Bishop's] **LAVINGTON** f.1005   D. Potterne

1. Divine service is performed in this church once every Lord's day at a quarter of an hour after two o'clock in the evening, excepting on Sundays when the holy sacrament of the Lord's Supper is administered; then it begins at a half of an hour after ten in the morning. The reason that divine service is not performed *twice here* each Lord's day is that the congregation who attend prayers in the afternoon [*added in the margin* I mean this when divine service did use to be *twice*, every Sunday, when prayers and sermon in the morning and prayers in the afternoon] are but *few* in number, generally go to hear a sermon and prayers across the field to Market Lavington.

2. Yes, on Christmas day, Good Friday, and a few other holidays.

[8] Balliol Coll. Oxford 1748. Vicar of Wilsford, **216,** and perpetual curate of Winterbourne Earls, **220.**

3. As curate.[9]

4. I serve the curacy of Market Lavington with this, at the distance of *one mile* from hence; but am licensed to neither of my cures.

5. 4 times in the year, (viz.) at *Christmas, Easter,* Whitsuntide, and Michaelmas.

6. About 45. Rather more than the usual number, last Easter.

7. [a] We have in this parish *one* professed Roman Catholic *only* and the same is an old woman in the workhouse. [b] No. [c] No. [d] No. [e] No.

8. None of any sect except the Church of England. A few also who profess a *disregard* to religion, by absenting themselves from the public worship of the church, but *none avowedly.*

9. Some do and some do not. I both expound to them myself and every Saturday at my school make use of a printed exposition the editor of which is Dr. Stonhouse.[1] The children of this parish are also publicly catechized at church in Lent. They all say it in English.

10. [a, b] Yes. [c] As far as the year 1598.

11. Yes.

12. There are no chapels of ease belonging to this parish.

13. I have an account of all the lands, tithes, and profits which at present belong to this living; but whether a duplicate thereof hath at any time been laid up in the bishop's registry is what I am totally ignorant of. This living also some years past has been augmented, an account of which augmentation shall be transmitted to the bishop's registrar at this visitation.

14. There is a free school in this parish[2] of which I am the deputy master. There is also in this parish an alms-house for 10 poor people, (viz.) 7 old widowers and 3 old widows. The founders, it is said, were some of the *Danvers* or *Dantsey* family. The trustees are the duke of Marlborough and the company of the Mercers, London. The former nominates, the latter appoint. The whole revenue of the school at present is £40 per annum (formerly it is said to be more), £20 of which with the house and garden I have for teaching or acting as sub-master or usher. The headmaster who lives in Dorsetshire has the other £20. 7 of the poor people have 13*s.* 4*d* per quarter regularly paid them through my hands; they have also a house each to live in. The other 3 are paid 13*s.* per quarter each by the duke of Marlborough's steward. We have no statutes to be observed; nor have any lands or tenements that I know of been left for the repair of our church, or for any other pious use.

15. The churchwardens of this parish are chosen every year in the Easter week, *one* by the minister, the *other* by the *parishioners.*

16. The charity school in this parish is supported by a settled endowment of £40 per annum. It is for *boys,* and *all* of the parish are admitted to its benefit as soon as they are able to read tolerably in their Testaments. They are taught English, Latin, *writing*, and accompts, and instructed in the principles of the

[9] Vicar, Edward Emily. Trinity Coll. Cambridge 1758. Master of St. Nicholas Hospital, Salisbury.
[1] Dr. James Stonhouse, rector of Great and Little Cheverell, **38** and **39.**
[2] Now Dauntsey's School.

Christian religion, and on Sundays come regularly to church spontaneously. They are neither lodged, fed, or clothed at the school-house and when they go from school are left to the care of their parents. The school at present flourishes. I have been more than 3 years the deputy master of it and had at different times more than 40 together. The present number is 30, but in the winter there are generally more.

17. I constantly reside upon *this* cure, and at the school-house, and am *never* absent from my cures.

18. There is no collection made here.

19. No other matter than what has already been related.

20. My place of residence is West Lavington grammar school and the nearest post town is Market Lavington.

I am an unbeneficed clergyman and no graduate. I was ord. D. on Sunday 4 Aug. 1776, by *James*, then bishop of St. David's, now bishop of Ely, and ord. P. on Trinity Sunday 14 June A.D. 1778, by Richard, then bishop of Litchfield and Coventry, *now* bishop of Worcester. Have been in this diocese ever since I was ordained a deacon A.D. 1776. And Market Lavington which I also serve at present was my first cure.

J. Williams,[3] clerk. Bishop's Lavington, 28 July 1783

124 MARKET LAVINGTON f.1013   D. Potterne

1. Divine service is performed in this church *twice* every Lord's day. The *morning* service begins at half an hour after 10 o'clock, the *evening* service at half after three. There are also *two* sermons preached here, during the summer half year, and *one* during the winter.

2. Yes, every *Friday* and *holiday*, throughout the year.

3. As curate.[4]

4. I serve another cure, which is Bishop's Lavington, at the distance of *one mile* from this; but am licensed to neither of my cures.

5. The holy sacrament of the Lord's Supper is administered in this church four times in the year, (viz.) at *Christmas, Easter, Whitsuntide*, and *Michaelmas*.

6. Nearly about forty, and the *usual* number.

7. [a] No. [b] No. [c] No. [d] No. [e] No.

8. No Presbyterians, Independents, or Anabaptists, but *one family* of *Quakers* consisting of 3 persons, (viz.) two brothers and a sister. There is a Quakers' meeting-house also in the parish but the number resorting thither on Sundays etc. are only the 3 persons above mentioned. Their number in this place has of late years considerably decreased. We have no other sect excepting Quakers.

9. Some do and some do not. I both expound to them myself, and occasionally use a printed exposition, the editor of which is Dr. Stonhouse. The

---

[3] Said by tradition to be 'a Welshman of drunken habits'. In 1785 he violently assaulted one Axford, an overseer of the poor of a neighbouring parish, with whom he had quarrelled over a burial fee, who later sued him for injuries sustained in the brawl. According to Axford, Williams was very poor when he came to Wiltshire, 'but has since married an old maid just going into the grave, with 8 or £10,000': *W.A.M.* xxxv. 448–9.

[4] Vicar, John Dobson. See **65.**

children of this parish are commonly catechized at my school every Saturday and *publicly* at church in *Lent*. They say it in English.

10. [a] Yes. [b] Yes. [c] It goes back to the year A.D. 1673.

11. Yes.

12. There are no chapels of ease belonging to this parish.

13. My worthy vicar will answer this question himself.

14. There is no free school in this parish.

15. The churchwardens of this parish are chosen every year in the Easter week, *one* by the minister and the *other* by the parishioners.

16. There neither *is*, nor *has been*, any public or charity school founded in this parish.

17. I do not reside upon *this* cure, nor in the house belonging thereto, but on my other cure at the distance of one mile from this, where also the curates of this church have resided for 30 years past and upwards. I never am absent from my cures.

18. The money given at the offertory is by the minister disposed of to such poor people of the parish as he thinks to be real objects of such a charity.

19. No.

20. My place of residence is at West Lavington grammar school. The nearest post town is Market Lavington.

I am an unbeneficed clergyman and no graduate. I was ord. D. on Sunday 4 Aug. 1776, by *James*, then bishop of St. David's, now bishop of Ely, and ord. P. on Trinity Sunday 14 June A.D. 1778, by Richard, then bishop of Litchfield and Coventry, *now* bishop of Worcester. Have been in this diocese ever since I was ordained deacon A.D. 1776. And *this* was my first cure.

J. Williams,[5] clerk. 28 July 1783

125 LITTLETON DREW f.1021   D. Malmesbury

1. At eleven o'clock and one alternately. It used to be at one only.

2. Only on the greater festivals and that since my own incumbency. The inhabitants consisting but of two or three working farmers at rack rents and labourers barely enough to assist them in the cultivation of their lands.

3. As incumbent.

4. I serve another small cure, my own, viz. Bidstone, about 4 miles distant.

5. At Easter, Whitsuntide, and Christmas.

6. [a] About six. [c] Rather increased.

7. No.

8. William Jones, by trade a weaver of Castle Comb, a Methodist teacher, has been used to attend in a private house belonging to Mr. Wallis (a Moravian of considerable property in the parish but resident in Devonshire) or his tenant, Chappell, but the meeting has been declining for some time and is now nearly dissolved.

9. In general they do. I expound to them myself in the mother tongue yearly between Easter and Whitsuntide.

---

[5] See **123**.

10. The register books are regularly kept and the returns regularly made by myself. The oldest register I can find goes back to the year 1706.

11. There is.

12. No chapel of ease or ruinated chapel.

13. I have from an actual survey taken as correct a terrier as possible adjusted to the present possession of lands, which is herewith sent.

14. None.

15. Yearly at Easter. One by the minister, the other by the parishioners.

16. No.

17. I reside at Corsham alms-house as mentioned in my other answers.

18. These offerings were introduced here by the present incumbent who distributes them in bread at Christmas.

19. Not that I now recollect.

20. Corsham near Chippenham, Wilts.

Charles Page[6]

126 LUCKINGTON f.1029   D. Malmesbury

1. Divine service is performed in this church twice on every Lord's day, viz. prayers in the forenoon at 11 o'clock and prayers and preaching about two in the evening.

2. There is no divine service here on weekdays, nor at any other times besides the Lord's day, except Christmas day, Good Friday, and Easter and Whitsun holidays.

3. I perform divine service as incumbent.

4. I serve no other cure.

5. The holy sacrament of the Lord's Supper is administered in this church four times a year, viz. at Christmas, Easter, on Whitsunday, and the Sunday after Michaelmas.

6. There are generally in this parish about 25 or 26 communicants, and at Easter last there were 18 at that festival which was less than usual.

7. There are no papists, nor popish priests in this parish.

8. There are no dissenters of any denomination in this parish, nor any other place made use of for divine worship but the church, and in general it is very well attended, though I confess with concern some few persons do too commonly absent themselves from public worship of God.

9. The servants and children are constantly catechized in this church, at the Lent season, and I expound the catechism to them at the same time.

10. There is a register book of births and burials, duly kept and in good preservation, and a transcript returned into the registrar's office every year at the visitation. The register goes back as far as the year 1644.

11. There is a register book duly kept, according to the directions of the Act of Parliament against clandestine marriages.

12. There is no chapel of ease, nor ruinated chapel, belonging to this parish.

13. I have a copy of a true terrier, kept in the register, and made since the inclosure, of all the houses, lands, pensions, etc. belonging to the minister of

[6] See **16.**

this parish, a duplicate whereof has been laid up in the bishop's registry, and as there has been no augmentation made since, I hope your Lordship will not require me to make a new terrier.

14. There is no free school, alms-house, hospital, or other charitable endowment, in this parish, only a small portion of land, let for the yearly rent of £1 12s. 6d., left for the repairs of the church, which is received by the churchwardens, and constantly accounted for at the Easter vestry.

15. There is but one churchwarden in this small parish, chosen in the Easter week by the minister every year.

16. There is no public or charity school founded in this parish. There is a dame's school, kept for the children, some paid for by the parents, and some of the poorer sort by the minister.

17. I constantly reside in the house belonging to my cure, and have been scarcely ever absent for a month at a time during my incumbency.

18. There are no offerings in this parish at the holy communion, not being, it seems, customary.

19. I have no other matter, at present, necessary or proper to inform your Lordship of.

20. Luckington is my place of residence, and Tetbury the nearest post town.

My institution bears date 16 Dec. 1758. Deacon's orders ditto 22 March 1735/6. Priest's ditto 24 May 1736. M.A. in the two universities of Dublin and Oxford.

John Woodroffe,[7] rector of Luckington, Wilts.

127 LUDGERSHALL f.1037[8]   D. Amesbury

1. Divine service is performed twice every Lord's day, prayers and a sermon at eleven in the morning and prayers at three in the afternoon.

2. Divine service has occasionally been performed in the church upon festivals and holidays that happen on weekdays but for want of a congregation has of late been discontinued.

3. I perform divine service as *rector* of the parish.

4. I serve no other cure.

5. The holy sacrament is administered four times in every year, viz. on Easter day, Whitsunday, the Sunday nearest to the feast of St. Michael, and on Christmas day.

6. I have kept an exact account of the number of communicants since my residence which commenced at Christmas 1777, in which time I find the greatest number of communicants on Easter day 1779, viz. 23, and the least number, on the last Easter day, was 15.

7. There are not that ever I could discover any papists or any reputed such in my parish, neither is there any Romish chapel or popish school.

8. There are no Presbyterians, nor any other sectary of any description whatever in my parish, neither is there any other place made use of for divine worship except the parish church.

[7] Jesus Coll. Oxford 1758.
[8] Letter missing.

9. I catechize the children and younger part of my parishioners, and expound the catechism to them in the English language after the 2nd lesson on Sunday afternoons in the summer.

10. I have a register book in tolerable preservation in which I always enter the births and burials myself and have regularly transmitted a transcript of it to the registrar's office every year at the visitation. It consists of four volumes. The 1st, of parchment, begins *anno* 1609. The 2nd, of parchment also, begins *anno* 1653. The 3rd, of paper, begins *anno* 1697 and the 4th, of paper, *anno* 1756.

11. There is a register book duly kept according to the directions of the Act of Parliament against clandestine marriages.

12. There are no chapels of ease in the parish nor any ruinated chapels, though I have been informed that some years since there was to be seen at Biddesden, a hamlet of Ludgarshall about 2 miles distant consisting of only 2 houses, the site of a chapel situated in one of the chapel closes of which there are two, and likewise a close called Church close adjoining, all of which now constitute a part of the Biddesden estate.

13. I have no terrier of houses, lands, tithes, etc. nor could I ever hear of one, either in this place or in the bishop's registry, where I searched in the year 1778 for that purpose. Of the two former, viz. parsonage house or glebe land, there is neither, nor can I find the least traces of there ever having been any belonging to the living. Of the latter, viz. tithes, as rector I am entitled to every species, and to every species *in kind*, there being no modus or exemption from payment of tithes in kind in any part of the parish. I never heard of any augmentation of the living, but there is a pension or fee-farm rent payable to the king of £4 every Michaelmas out of the profits arising therefrom.

14. There is neither free school, alms-house, or other charitable endowment in the parish.

15. The churchwardens in my parish are chosen every year in the Easter week, one by the minister and the other by the parishioners.

16. There is not, nor ever was that I can learn, any public school or charity school founded in the parish.

17. I constantly reside upon this cure in a house belonging to the right honourable Lord Sydney[9] of which he gives me the use, there being as I before observed in answer to the 13th query neither parsonage house nor glebe.

18. The money given at the offertory is disposed of by myself as minister to the poor of the parish when sick or otherwise disabled from maintaining themselves, of which distribution I keep an exact account.

19. There is no other circumstance relating to the parish worthy of your Lordship's notice except that I think its boundaries not sufficiently ascertained on the side next Chute Forest.

20. I reside at Ludgarshall; the nearest post town is Andover, Hants, 7½ miles distant.

I was ord. D. by the late bishop of Oxford at Oxford 2 June 1776. Ord. P. by the present bishop of Oxford at Oxford 15 June 1777. Instituted to the

[9] Thomas Townshend, created Baron Sydney 1783, nephew of George Selwyn, the famous wit, M.P. for Ludgershall and patron of the living.

rectory of Ludgarshall by the late bishop of Salisbury at Bath 17 June 1777. Admitted to the degree of B.C.L. of Pembroke College Oxford 18 June 1783.

John Selwyn,[1] rector of Ludgarshall

128 LIDDINGTON [Lydington] f.1043   D. Cricklade

1. Half hour after ten in the morning, two in the afternoon alternately; twice not customary for a long time past; another church at the distance of one mile and a half only, served with it.
2. On all holidays; and on Wednesday and Friday throughout Lent in one or other of the parishes alternately.
3. As incumbent.
4. Chisleden as incumbent likewise, the distance at about one mile and a half.
5. At the four customary or most usual seasons.
6. Generally about a dozen.
7. No papist or dissenter in the parish.
8. The congregation in general commendably numerous.
9. The children are catechized on Sundays, and on Wednesdays or Fridays throughout Lent. A course of sermons on the catechism is preached on the Lent Sundays once in two years.
10. The register pretty duly kept from the year 1692 inclusive, and an extract now returned annually into the registrar's office.
11. There is.
12. Nothing to be said on any of the items of this query.
13. An exact and decisive one, entered in your Lordship's registry. An inclosure in 1776; and the Queen's Bounty within these ten years[2] hath augmented the living above £50 per annum; neither of these augmentations as yet returned to the registry.
14. No concern with any article of this query.
15. The churchwardens very regularly chosen at Easter, one by the minister, the other by the parishioners.
16. Nothing to this parish.
17. Residence at my other benefice of Chisleden, distant about one mile and a half.
18. No collection.
19. Nothing at present occurs.
20. Chisleden near Swindon, Wilts.[3]

Instituted 15 April 1771. Ord. D. 24 Dec. 1749, and ord. P. 23 Dec. 1750 by Dr. Benson bishop of Gloster. Was admitted to the degree of A.M. 22 June 1748.

129 LYDIARD MILLICENT f.1051   D. Cricklade

1. Divine service, both prayers and preaching, are performed upon the Lord's day about ten o'clock in the morning, and prayers begin in the afternoon between three and four.

[1] Pembroke Coll. Oxford 1774.
[2] 1773, £200 to meet a benefaction: Hodgson, p. 417.
[3] No signature. Vicar, William Richard Stock: see **45.**

2. Upon some holidays and festivals that happen on weekdays.

3. As curate. [4]

4. I serve no other cure. As the rector is upward of eighty, I hope I shall not be required to apply for a licence.

5. The holy sacrament is administered in my church four times in the year, viz. at Christmas, Easter, Whitsuntide, and Michaelmas.

6. About ten in general, and that number not exceeded at Easter last.

7. No.

8. No.

9. The children are catechized in Lent.

10. We have a register book of births and burials which goes as far back as the year 1600.

11. Yes.

12. No. No ruinated chapels.

13. We have no terrier in our parish. As I officiate as curate I am not sufficiently informed to give a proper account of these matters.

14. There is an sum of 10s. arising from a little ground in this parish given to the second poor.

15. The churchwardens are chosen every year in the Easter week, one by the minister and the other by the parishioners.

16. No.

17. I reside in the parish, about a quarter of a mile from the church, but not in the house belonging to this cure. I am seldom or ever absent.

18. No money given at the offertory.

19. No.

20. Wootton Bassett is the nearest post town.

I was ord. D. in the year 1777. Ord. P. in 1778.

William Evans, curate of Lydiard Millicent

130 LYDIARD TREGOZE f.1059   D. Cricklade

1. Divine service is performed every Sunday morning at eleven o'clock. It never was remembered to be performed twice a day. The people of the parish are principally dairy men, and in the afternoon are employed in their country business, which cannot be neglected.

2. On Christmas day and Good Friday only.

3. As incumbent.

4. I serve no other cure.

5. Four times in the year, at Easter, Whitsuntide, Michaelmas, and Christmas.

6. We have generally about 16 or 18 communicants. I cannot say exactly how many there were at Easter last, but the number never varies much.

7. We have none.

8. We have none.

9. We have the misfortune to have no school in the parish where the poorer sort might be taught their catechism, and was I to call on them to send their

[4] Rector, Timothy Burrell. Probably St. John's Coll. Cambridge 1717.

children to church on Sundays to be catechized, I fear it would be in vain. I never could learn that any of my predecessors had succeeded.

10. Our register book of births and burials is duly kept and in good preservation; returns of births and burials have been regularly made into the registrar's office. The register books go as far back as the year 1605, but I believe they are not all perfect.

11. There is a register book, duly kept.

12. We have none.

13. I have nothing more than copies of such terriers as are to be found in your Lordship's registry at Salisbury, since which there has been no augmentation made to the living.

14. We have neither free school, alms-house, or other charitable endowment in our parish; nor have any lands or tenements been left for the repair of the church or for any other pious use.

15. Our churchwardens are chosen every year in the Easter week, one by the rector, the other by the parishioners.

16. We have no school whatever in the parish.

17. I reside at Wootton Bassett, the parish adjoining. On coming to the living I found but an indifferent house, and being a single man and having very near relations at Wootton Bassett, I found it most convenient to board with them.

18. The money given at the offertory is distributed among the poor communicants and, if any surplus, to the poor of the parish.

19. I know of none.

20. I reside at Wootton Bassett, a post town.

Institution dated 31 March 1780. Ord. D. 23 Sept. 1770. Ord. P. 14 June 1772. Degree, B.A.

R. Miles,[5] rector of Lydiard Tregoz

131 MADDINGTON f.1067   D. Wylye

1. Divine service is performed alternately at ten and three in the afternoon. Divine service is never performed in this church but once, owing I imagine to the smallness of the parish etc.

2. It has not been customary to perform any service on weekdays.

3. I perform divine service as curate.[6]

4. I serve also the curacy of Orcheston St. Mary together with Shrewton. Neither of the cures are distant a mile from each other. The late bishop of Salisbury did not require me to take licences to my cures; therefore have none.

5 [recte 6]. The number of communicants are about thirty, and on last Easter day did not appear to vary from the former years. This fifth question (owing to a mistake) answers to the sixth. Q.5. How etc. The holy sacrament is administered at Christmas, Easter, and Whitsuntide.

6. This question is answered opposite Q. the 5th in the third page.[7]

[5] Richard Miles, 1738–1839. Balliol Coll. Oxford 1766.
[6] Perpetual curate, the Hon. Mr. — Digby. Probably Hon. Charles Digby, Christ Church Oxford 1761. Nephew to Lord Ilchester, patron of the living: Complete Peerage, s.vv. Digby, Ilchester.
[7] This same mistake is made in his returns for Orcheston St. Mary, 155, and Shrewton, 177.

7. There are no reputed papists, no priest, school, or chapel where they assemble.

8. There are no Presbyterians, Independents, etc., neither are there any (according to my knowledge) who absent themselves from public worship.

9. It has not been customary to catechize children at this small parish church; neither will time properly admit of it; because one or more churches are incumbent on the curate to serve.

10. I have a register book of births and burials duly kept, the register goes about so far back as 1670 both for births and burials.

11. There is a register book kept to prevent clandestine marriages.

12. There are no chapels of ease in the parish.

13. There is no terrier. Maddington is a donative and the minister's income is from small tithes (viz.) wool, etc., etc. It is about £40 per annum.

14. There is no free school neither has there been left any lands etc. for repairing the church.

15. In every Easter week the churchwardens are chosen by the minister and parishioners together.

16. There is no public school.

17. I reside in one of my parishes, and within a mile of the others; I do not reside in the parsonage house as it being too small for a family.

18. There is none given.

19. None.

20. Orcheston St. Mary is my residence and Market Lavington is the nearest post town.

I entered commoner at Queen College in Oxford where I resided about three years, and was ord. D. at Salisbury at Michaelmas in the year 1777 and ord. P. at London at Christmas by the bishop of Glocester in the year 1781.

[*On a separate sheet of paper:*] I have unfortunately lost the directions for describing the parsonage house etc. for the parish of Maddington; therefore have here mentioned the answers. [8]

Q.1. The parsonage house is built of stone and brick and covered with tile, it has about *six* rooms in it. There is no out-houses.

Q.2. No land. There is a small garden surrounded by a wall. There are no trees in the churchyard.

Q.3. Small tithes only are due to the minister.

Q.4. The donative is about £40 per annum.

Q.5. There are no tithes due to the curate and £20 per annum is paid to him for serving the church.

Q.6. There are only three bells. The communion plate is a flagon, small cup, and plate, all silver. There [are] no books besides of Common Prayer, and Bible etc.

Q.7. There is no land etc. for repairing the church.

Q.8. The churchwardens.

Q.9. The clerk's wages is by custom; he is paid by the parish and appointed by the minister.

J. Legg, [9] curate of Maddington

[8] See above, p. 3, n. 2.
[9] Joseph Legg, 1754–1833. Queen's Coll. Oxford 1775.

132 MAIDEN BRADLEY f.1075 D. Wylye

1. Divine service is performed twice every Lord's day. Prayers and preaching in the morning, service beginning at half an hour after ten and prayers in the afternoon beginning at two o'clock.

2. No services on weekdays or holidays.

3. I perform divine service as perpetual curate nominated by the dean and chapter of Christ's Church, Oxford.

4. I serve no other cure.

5. The holy sacrament of the Lord's Supper is constantly administered four times in the year, viz. on Easter day, Whitsunday, the first Sunday after Michaelmas, and on Christmas day.

6. The number of communicants are generally about thirty, which was nearly the number on Easter Sunday last.

7. There are no reputed papists in my parish nor is there any place where they assemble for divine worship nor any popish school kept.

8. There are no Presbyterians, Independents, Anabaptists, or Quakers to my knowledge in my parish, nor is there any place made use of for divine worship but the parish church. There are some who commonly I believe absent themselves from all public worship of God.

9. My parishioners duly send their children and servants to be catechized in the church, which is generally done for seven or eight Sundays in the summer, immediately after the second lesson at evening prayers, and in the English language; and in the course of my sermons I take care to explain to my parishioners the essential parts of the Church catechism.

10. There is a register book of births and burials duly kept and in good preservation, and returns of births and burials have been regularly made into the registrar's office for more and [*recte* than] thirty years past [to my knowledge *crossed out*] (i.e.) during the time I have served the cure of Maiden Bradley.

11. There is a register book duly kept against clandestine marriages according to the directions of the Act of Parliament made for that purpose.

12. No chapels of ease in my parish. No ruinated chapels to my knowledge.

13. I know of no terrier of houses, lands, tithes, pensions, or profits that belong to me as minister of my parish. I have only £40 a year paid by the duke of Somerset as tenant to the dean and chapter of Christchurch. No augmentation has [been] made thereto during the time that I have served the cure of Maiden Bradley, which is now more than thirty years; during which time the dean and chapter have acted as visitors of my cure.

14. There is no free school, alms-house, or other charitable endowment in my parish to my knowledge. Nor any benefactions left for the repair of the church.

15. The churchwardens of my parish are chosen every year in the Easter week solely by the parishioners. But I have been informed that it was the custom formerly for the minister to choose one. But how or when this custom was altered I know not.

16. There are schools in my parish to teach children to read, who are instructed in the Church catechism, and regularly brought to church to be examined in it.

But there is no public school endowed or supported by any charity by voluntary subscriptions that I know of.

17. I do not reside upon the cure of Maiden Bradley, there being no house belonging to it, and though I reside at four miles distance yet I am never absent, but in case of sickness.

18. It is not usual for any money to be given at the offertory.

19. There is no other matter relating to my parish that I know of, of which it may be proper to give information.

20. My place of residence is Tisbury near Hindon.[1]

133 MALMESBURY f.1083   D. Malmesbury

1. At one o'clock in the afternoon in one of the chapels, at three o'clock in the church.

2. Upon every holiday but not on any weekday except in Lent.

3. As curate.[2]

4. [a, b] I serve the cure of Ashley about four miles distant from the other. [c] I am.

5. Four, viz. Christmas, Easter, Whitsuntide, and Michaelmas.

6. [a] In general fifty. [b] About forty. At Michaelmas more than fifty.

7. None, nor any popish priest, nor popish school kept in the parish.

8. There are many dissenters of various denominations, but the exact number I cannot tell. I know of no other place made use of for divine worship. Their teachers do not reside in this parish. Their number since I have resided here I think is much the same. [e, f] None.

9. I read catechetical lectures every Lent. The children are brought upon weekdays in Lent to be catechized.

10. The register of births and burials is in good preservation. Proper returns are made every visitation. The register books go back to the year 1660.

11. I have not seen any.

12. [a] Two. Rodbourn and Corston. [b] They are served once every Lord's day alternately. [c] There are no estates or funds that I know of. [d] Two miles. [e] By me, H. Strong. [f] None.

13. There is a terrier lodged in the registrar's court. I don't know that there has been any augmentation.

14. [a] There are two free schools and a charitable endowment of £20 which is distributed every New Year's day. [b] Robert Cullurn. Twelve gentlemen of the parish, I believe. [d] None.

15. They are. One by the minister and the other by the parishioners.

16. [a] Yes. Two. [b] By a settled endowment. For boys only. The one confined to fifteen, the other free for everyone. [c] Writing and accounts. [d] Yes. [e] They are not. [f] I know not. [g] Yes.

17. I constantly reside upon this cure.

18. The money is always distributed to the poor communicants.

19. None.

---

[1] No signature. Perpetual curate, John Gray.

[2] Vicar, John Copson. See Kemble, **114,** of which he was resident vicar.

20. Malmsbury, which is a post town.[3]

134 MANNINGFORD ABBOTS [Manningford Abbas] f.1091

D. Marlborough

1. Twice every Lord's day, viz. at ½ past 10 o'clock and at ½ past 2 o'clock; preaching only once in the day, and that alternately in the morning and evening unless prevented by occasionally assisting my neighbours.
2. On weekdays at the principal festivals only, and on Good Friday.
3. As incumbent.
4. No.
5. Four times in the year, viz. at Christmas, Easter, Whitsuntide, and Michaelmas.
6. From twenty to thirty; at Easter last fourteen, which is about the usual number.
7. None.
8. None.
9. They do not. Indeed in so small a parish (for it contains but twenty-two dwelling-houses) a sufficient number can seldom be procured to catechize in public, and few of the children have been so educated as to be able to repeat the Church catechism even in private. (Books of Common Prayer have been distributed gratis.)
10. The register of births and burials is duly kept, and in good preservation, and the returns regularly made into the registrar's office. The old register goes back to the year 1559. That now in use begins 13 Nov. 1732.
11. A register book is duly kept according to the directions of the Act.
12. None.
13. I apprehend there is one in the office at Sarum, but none here. A new terrier is now prepared and signed, and a duplicate kept. No augmentation.
14. None.
15. Usually in the Easter week; one chosen by the minister, the other by the parishioners.
16. None.
17. I reside in the house belonging to this cure, and am very seldom absent.
18. None given.
19. No other matter that I at present recollect.
20. Manningford Abbots near Pewsey, Wilts.
   Deacon's orders dated 2 June 1765. Priest's orders dated 22 June 1766. B.A.[4]

135 MARLBOROUGH, ST. MARY f.1107   D. Marlborough
1. Divine service is performed twice on the Lord's day, both prayers and preaching, at ½ past ten in the morning and at three o'clock in the afternoon, excepting those mornings on which the sacrament of the Lord's Supper is administered, when the sermon is omitted.

---

[3] No signature. Curate, H. Strong. See also **7**.
[4] No signature. Rector, John Fletcher. Probably All Souls' Coll. Oxford 1761.

2. Divine service is performed on Mondays and Wednesdays in the morning, and on Saturdays in the evening, but on no festivals which fall on the intermediate days, as service is on those days performed at the other church.

3. I officiate as curate of the parish of St. Mary.[5]

4. I do not serve any other cure, nor am I licensed to the cure of St. Mary, as the late bishop of Salisbury did not deliver licences to those who were ordained by him.

5. The sacrament of the Lord's Supper is administered on Christmas day, Easter day, Whitsunday, Trinity Sunday, and on the first Sunday in every month.

6. In general between 20 and 30 persons communicate, at Easter last the number of communicants amounted to about 60 as usual.

7. There are no reputed papists in this parish.

8. There are about 30 Presbyterians and as many Quakers in this parish. There are no other places of divine worship than such as are used by those sects. As I have but very lately undertaken the cure of this parish I cannot affirm anything concerning the increase or decrease of the number of such sectaries from observation. I know of no persons who profess to disregard religion, or who commonly absent themselves from all public worship of God.

9. The children and servants have been generally catechized in the last quarter of the year, in English, when Lewis's catechism has been used as an exposition.

10. A register book of births and burials is duly kept, and well preserved, extending as far back as the year 1623, returns of which have, I believe, been regularly made.

11. A register book is duly kept according to the directions of the said Act.

12. There are no chapels of ease nor ruinated chapels in this parish.

13. I have an attested copy of a terrier deposited in the registry of the diocese, made in the year 1698, since which time this living has been augmented by Queen Anne's Bounty.[6]

14. There is a free school in this parish, designed for the education of any male children born in this town; founded by King Edward VI, and governed by the corporation of this town; the master has a salary of £30 per annum besides an house. Since this school was founded, some scholarships have been appropriated to it of £15 per annum each, at Brazen-nose College Oxford and St. John's College Cambridge by a duchess of Somerset. The revenue of that part of the Green called Church Land, and also the sums arising from the renewals of the leases of a dwelling-house, and meeting-house situated on the Green, are appropriated to the repairs of the church under the direction of the churchwardens. No lands nor tenements have been left for any other pious use.

15. The churchwardens are chosen annually in the Easter week, one by the minister, the other by the parishioners.

16. No public school has been founded, nor is there any charity school in this parish.

---

[5] Vicar, Henry Whinfield. Probably Peterhouse Cambridge 1744, and father of the curate.
[6] In 1733: Hodgson, p. 417.

17. I reside in the town of Marlborough though not in the parish of St. Mary, nor in the house belonging to it. I do not intend to be absent for any considerable time in the course of the year.

18. The money collected at the offertory is distributed among the poor of the parish under the direction of the minister.

19. I know of no matter of which it is proper to give information.

20. I reside in Marlborough, a post town.

I was admitted to the degree of B.A. in the university of Cambridge in January 1778. Was ord. D. in May 1780, and ord. P. in December 1780.

E. H. Whinfield[7]

136 MARLBOROUGH, ST. PETER f.1115   D. Marlborough

1. Twice on every Sunday, at half an hour past ten o'clock in the morning and at three in the afternoon, but the sermon is omitted on sacrament days in the morning, agreeable to the wishes of the most constant communicants, the aged and the infirm.

2. Morning prayers are read therein on Tuesdays, Thursdays, and Fridays weekly, and also on holidays.

3. As incumbent.

4. By the help of a constant assistant,[8] I serve my other church of Preshute—not half a mile distant from my church in Marlborough.

5. On the last Sunday in every month, and on Christmas day, Easter day, and Whitsunday.

6. At the monthly sacraments about 30 on an average. At the great festivals many more and at Easter last about 70, a number rather greater than less than usual.

7. There is a gentleman's family (of the name of Hyde) professing the popish religion. His servants are partly of the same persuasion, but the greater part of them are permitted and exhorted to resort to the church. Four or five more people of little account frequent the gentleman's house on Sundays and other days, as he keeps a reputed popish priest constantly therein.[9] The name of the present is Butler—who seems not very zealous to pervert the servants and neighbours—of consequence no popish school is kept in the parish.

8. There are 5 or 6 Presbyterian families, including their minister, resident in this parish, but their place of worship is not in it. One of them is a gentleman professing the law, but his wife and daughter constantly resort to our communion. Two other families are in trade. One of them comes to church when there is no meeting, but his wife and children constantly. The children of the other and of the minister come to church when there is no meeting—which happens either morning or evening every Sunday. The other Presbyterians are elderly maidens. This sect is greatly reduced of late years, as by marrying wives of the Church of England, so by many of them turning Methodists, who

[7] Edward Henry Whinfield, Peterhouse Cambridge 1775: 'Doubtless son of Henry, 1744.'

[8] Clergy Books, 1783, give 'Mr. Meyler junior' as curate. Probably John Meyler (son of the vicar), Jesus Coll. Oxford 1776.

[9] The Hyde family provided a mass centre, with a succession of Benedictine chaplains, from about 1753 to 1794: V.C.H. Wilts. iii. 91.

assemble in a former Presbyterian meeting-house in this parish, by the name of Independents, and licensed as such. This sect is supported, as I am informed, by Lady Huntingdon and an opulent tradesman of this parish, who is owner of the meeting-house. Their teacher's name is Cornelius Winter,[1] who seems to have had a liberal education, and who complains of the decrease of his hearers—I know several who used to resort to the meeting who are returned to our communion. There are 4 or 5 families of Quakers, which sect is also declining apace. I thank God I know not one in the parish who professes to disregard religion, but must lament that too many absent themselves from the public worship of God.

9. The parishioners in general duly send their children and servants to say, and be instructed in, their catechism according to my appointment, the junior part at prayer-time on Thursday mornings, and such as are of age to be confirmed, and servants, on Sunday evenings, from the first notice I receive of a confirmation to be held, to the time thereof. I examine them in the catechism according to a small tract entitled 'The Church Catechism broke into short questions', and further explain the whole to them in English, and in notes of my own compiling—when my health permits.

10. The register books have been badly kept for several years before I became incumbent, but I now pay particular attention to their correctness, and true copies thereof are returned to the registrar's office yearly according to the canon. The oldest register book I have seen belonging to this parish begins in the year 1611.

11. Yes, but rather imperfectly in my predecessor's time.

12. None.

13. I lately procured the copy of a short and imperfect terrier of the parish from the bishop's registry, but a perfect and complete one has now been drawn up, and a duplicate thereof will be delivered to the bishop's registrar at the visitation to be holden for and at this church.

14. None that I ever heard of.

15. The churchwardens are chosen every year in the Easter week, one by the minister, and the other by the parishioners.

16. None that I know or have heard of.

17. I constantly reside in the parsonage house.

18. By the minister at his discretion and on the recommendation of the communicants, to the sick, needy, and prisoners in Bridewell.

19. None.

20. At Marlborough, a post town.

[*Written across, under the address:*] I, Thomas Meyler M.A.[2], was ord. D. 20 Sept. 1741. Ord. P. 13 June 1742. Collated to the rectory 21 Jan. 1774.

137 ST. MARTIN [SALISBURY] f.1123   Sub-D. Salisbury

1. Prayers at ten in the morning, and prayers and preaching at a quarter of an hour before three in the afternoon.

---

[1] See **9** n. 2.

[2] 1718–86. Jesus Coll. Oxford 1738. Master of Marlborough grammar school, 1750–74: *V.C.H. Wilts.* v. 359. Vicar of Preshute, **164.**

2. Divine service is performed on Wednesdays, Fridays, and Saturdays and on all holidays and festivals.

3. I perform service as incumbent.

4. I serve no other cure.

5. The sacrament is administered four times in the year viz. at Christmas, Easter, Whitsuntide, and Michaelmas.

6. The number of communicants are in general about seventy and did not appear last Easter to vary from former years.

7. There are no reputed papists in my parish, nor chapel for such to assemble in, no popish priest, nor popish school.

8. There is an Anabaptist meeting-house in my parish but those who resort to it chiefly if not altogether come from other parishes. The preacher's name is Phillips.[3] There is also a Quaker meeting-house under the same predicament.

9. It hath not been usual for the city clergy to catechize children; in my parish there is a school under the patronage of the bishop where children are constantly taught their catechism and instructed in the principles of the Christian religion and thereby the end of the minister's catechizing is in a great measure answered.

10. I have a register book for births and burials duly kept and the returns are regularly made. The register both of births and burials goes back as far as the year 1559.

11. There is a register book according to the Act of Parliament against clandestine marriages.

12. There are no chapels of ease.

13. There is a terrier dated 1705 and a duplicate thereof in the bishop's registry. There hath been no augmentation made of my living and the minister hath no glebe except the churchyard.

14. There is no free school but that referred to in the ninth article. There are two alms-houses endowed, one founded by Mr. Bricket, sometime mayor of this city, for six poor women. Another called the Trinity for twelve poor men, the founder's name is [blank].[4] The alms-houses endowed are under the direction of the mayor and corporation for the time being. There are some small donations in my parish and some lands have been given, the produce of which is to be applied to apprenticing orphans and some dwelling-houses for paupers all under the direction of the minister and vestry.

15. The churchwardens are chosen every year in the Easter week, by the minister and parishioners together.

16. There is no school but that referred to in the ninth article.

17. There is no parsonage house. I reside within about a third of a mile of my church, and in the course of the year am absent about ten Sundays. The reason of such absence is on account of business or health.

18. The money collected at the offertory is disposed of by the minister and

[3] Henry Philips, Brown Street Baptist church. He also kept a school: *V.C.H. Wilts.* iii. 123 n.; ibid. vi. 158, where it is stated that he ceased to be pastor at the Brown Street church in 1779.

[4] There is some conflicting evidence regarding the name of the founder—probably Agnes Bottenham, in the 14th century: *V.C.H. Wilts.* iii. 357.

churchwardens to the sick poor and other necessitous persons.

19. There is nothing farther necessary to communicate.

20. My place of residence is in the parish of St. Edmund, Sarum.

I was ord. D. on 25 Sept. 1763 and ord. P. on 13 Dec. 1767. I was instituted to St. Martin's rectory 30 Dec. 1767.[5]

138 MARDEN f.1131 D. Potterne

1. Divine service is performed once only in the day, at 10 o'clock in the morning and 2 in the afternoon alternately and regularly. This from the smallness of the living and fewness of inhabitants has been always the customary duty.

2. No, for want of a congregation.

3. As curate.[6]

4. No.

5. 3 times in the year at the 3 great festivals.

6. About ten one time with the other.

7. None.

8. None of any sect, and but few absenters.

9. Sometimes, when they are catechized in Lent, without any exposition.

10. Yes, and returns from it duly made. The register of births and burials from the year 1685 and 1687.

11. Yes.

12. None.

13. There is one preparing, which from the vicar's absence could not be completed in time.

14. None at all.

15. Yes, one by the minister and one by the parishioners in the Easter week.

16. None at all.

17. The vicar is not resident, being master of the free grammar school on Blackheath; the curate lives in a neighbouring parish at a small distance from the cure.

18. No money is given at the offertory.

19. None.

20. Erchfont near Devizes, Wilts.

Signed by me, Charles Gibbes,[7] curate of Mardon

139 MELKSHAM f.1139 D. Potterne

1. As there is a chapel of ease, as well as the church, it is the custom to have only single duty at each of them every Sabbath day, which is performed alternately, at eleven o'clock in the morning and half an hour past two in the afternoon. I know of no other reason why divine service is not performed twice a day.

---

[5] No signature. Rector, Dr. John Baker. Wadham Coll. Oxford 1757. He was said to have a good private fortune and was a protegé of Lord Pembroke: *Pembroke Papers*, ii. 308, 353, 366.

[6] Vicar, William Williams.

[7] See Chitterne All Saints, **46,** of which he was vicar.

2. There is divine service every Wednesday during the Lent season and on the other weekdays as directed by the rubric, at Christmas, Easter, and Whitsuntide.

3. I perform divine service as *curate*.[8]

4. I serve no other cure, nor am I yet licensed.

5. There are three sacraments in the year administered at Christmas, Easter, and Whitsuntide.

6. There are commonly about a dozen or fourteen communicants, and much the same number last Easter.

7. There are no reputed papists that I know of in the parish.

8. There are some Anabaptists and Quakers; and of late years several Methodists have sprung up, and built a tabernacle in the parish. The teacher's name is *John Honeywill*,[9] and licensed as the law directs. I know of no other persons but the above mentioned who commonly absent themselves from church.

9. It has been usual to catechize the children annually during the summer season, which duty I am now performing, and likewise do expound to them the catechism.

10. A register book of births and burials is duly kept and the returns into the register office are regularly made. It goes back to 1568.

11. There is.

12. The chapel of ease is at Seend, about three miles from the mother church, and duty is performed, as mentioned in the first quere, by the minister belonging to the church. There are not any estates or funds particularly appropriated to its maintenance, but [it] is supported by the mother church.[1]

13. There is a terrier of all houses, lands, tithes, pensions, and profits belonging to the living of Melksham, a duplicate of which is, I suppose, deposited in the bishop's registry; but I do not know of any augmentation that hath been made to [the] living.

14. There is nothing of this sort in the parish of Melksham.

15. There are two churchwardens chosen every year in the Easter week, one by the minister, the other by the parishioners.

16. There is a school in the parish where boys are taught English and writing, but no charity school.

17. I constantly reside upon my cure, but not in the house belonging to it.

18. The collection made at the administration of the sacrament is disposed of by the minister to the poor.

19. I do not know of any.

20. Melksham is my place of residence, which is a post town.

William Stone,[2] curate, Melksham

---

[8] Vicar, Joseph Newton. Probably Lincoln Coll. Oxford 1722. 'This parish populous, and ill taken care of. The incumbent old and lives at Gloster': Clergy Books, 1783.

[9] John Honeywell, from the countess of Huntingdon's college and first pastor of the Melksham Congregational church: *V.C.H. Wilts.* iii. 132.

[1] Erlestoke was also a chapelry of Melksham, served by John Baily, perpetual curate of Edington, **78**: Clergy Books, 1783; *V.C.H. Wilts.* vii. 84, 104.

[2] Perhaps Brasenose Coll. Oxford 1769.

140 MILDENHALL f.1147   D. Marlborough

1. Prayers and preaching every Sunday at eleven o'clock morning. Prayers afternoon at three.
2. Prayers Easter week, Whitsuntide, and Christmas.
3. A curate kept.
4. No other church.
5. Easter Sunday, Whitsunday, and Christmas day.
6. Between twenty and thirty.
7. No papists.
8. No Presbyterians or any other sect.
9. The children are catechized in Lent.
10. A proper register book is kept.
11. A proper register book.
12. Only one church.
13. A terrier of houses etc. is delivered. No augmentation.
14. No school or endowment.
15. Churchwardens are chosen Easter Monday, one by rector, the other by parishioners.
16. No school.
17. The rector resides in the parsonage.
18. The money is given to some of the poorest who attend the sacrament.
19. [*Blank*]
20. Mildenhall near Marlborough.

                                        Richard Pococke A.M.,[3] rector

141 MILSTON f.1155   D. Amesbury

1. Prayers twice, preaching once, constantly.
2. On some of the principal holidays.
3. As incumbent.
4. None in your Lordship's jurisdiction.
5. Four times.
6. About ten.
7. None.
8. None.
9. I used to catechize, as long as any appeared for that purpose, of late none have been sent. I shall be always ready to do my duty in this and I hope all other respects.
10. Yes.
11. Yes.
12. No.
13. A true and perfect account of everything belonging to the rectory is contained in the award which is confirmed by Act of Parliament.[4]
14. None.
15. Yes.

[3] Perhaps Brasenose Coll. Oxford 1740. Member of the Committee of Correspondence of 1780: see above, p. 8, n. 25.
[4] Milston and Brigmerston Inclosure Act, 19 Geo. III, c. 8 (Priv. Act).

16. No.
17. I live wholly in the parish, though not in the parsonage house.
18. None given.
19. None.
20. Near Amesbury.

Ed. Polhill,[5] rector of Milston

142 MILTON LILBORNE f.1166   D. Marlborough
1. Divine service is performed in my church every Sunday alternately in the morning and afternoon. Divine service for many years past has not been performed twice on account of the smallness of the living.
2. Divine service has not been performed in this church upon any weekdays holidays or festivals (Good Friday and Christmas day excepted) for many years past because, I presume, the greatest part of the inhabitants being farmers and labourers it would be a great inconvenience for them to attend.
3. I perform divine service as incumbent.
4. I serve two other cures, viz. Collingbourn Kingston and Easton, a donative belonging to the right honourable the earl of Ailesbury; service at one o'clock in the afternoon. Collingbourn is distant three miles from Easton, and Easton one mile from Milton. I am not licensed to the cure of Collingbourn Kingston.
5. The holy sacrament is administered four times a year at Collingbourn and Milton, viz. Christmas, Easter, and Michaelmas.
6. I have generally in my parish of Milton about seventeen communicants, the number at Easter was nearly about that which I have mentioned.
7. There are no reputed papists in my parish, neither doth any popish priest reside, nor is there any popish school kept in the parish.
8. There are no Presbyterians, Independents, Anabaptists, or Quakers in my parish, consequently no teachers. There are none who profess to disregard religion. I am happy to inform your Lordship that I have no complaint to make against any of my parishioners.
9. I am sorry to observe that my parishioners have not duly sent their children and servants since I have been vicar to be instructed by me. I mean to enjoin all persons to send their children and servants to be catechized by me every Sunday in the Lent season in the English language and according to my own exposition.
10. There is a register book duly kept and in good preservation; returns are regularly made of births and burials into the registrar's office; goes back to the year 1686.
11. There is a register book duly kept against clandestine marriages.
12. There are no chapels of any kind whatever in my parish either in a perfect or ruinous condition.
13. There is no terrier in the parish of Milton. I have heard there are three in your Lordship's registry. I have, however, taken care to have one drawn as

[5] Edward Polhill, Trinity Coll. Oxford 1754. Member of the Committee of Correspondence of 1780: see above, p. 8, n. 25.

accurately as circumstances will admit of according to your Lordship's directions.

14. There is no free school, alms-house, hospital, or other charitable endowment in my parish, consequently no governors etc. There has not any lands or tenements been left for the repair of the church, or for any other pious use in the parish.

15. Churchwardens are chosen every year in the Easter week, one by the vicar, the other by the parishioners.

16. There is not nor has there been (in my parish) founded any public or charity school.

17. I do not reside in the vicarage house, my place of residence is Heathy Close about two miles from Milton. I constantly serve the church myself.

18. There has not since I have been vicar, and I believe for a great many years before, [been] any alms collected at the sacrament.

19. There is nothing relating to my parish that I could wish to inform your Lordship of.

20. My place of residence is Heathy Close and the nearest post town Pewsey.

Instituted 20 Aug. *1777*. Ord. D. 20 Dec. *1767*. Ord. P. 25 Sept. *1768*. Degree B.A.

John Swain[6]

143 MINETY [Minty] f.1174　　　　　　　　　D. Malmesbury

1. Service is performed once every Lord's day at ten in the morning and at two in the afternoon alternately. The latter part answered in query the fourth.

2. Upon particular festivals.

3. As curate.

4. Mr. Copson being infirm, I have for some time past assisted him in the cure of Kemble, distant from Mintye about three miles. I am not licensed to the cure of Myntye.

5. The sacrament is administered four times in the year, at Christmas, Easter, Whitsuntide, and the first Sunday after Michaelmas.

6. The number of communicants at Easter last were four or five, nearly the usual number.

7. No.

8. No.

9. Yes, between Easter and Whitsuntide. I make use of no printed exposition, but expound to them myself.

10. Yes. The register goes as far back as the year 1663.

11. Yes.

12. No.

13. I am entirely ignorant of that particular.

14. No.

15. Two churchwardens are every year chosen in the Easter week, one by the minister and the other by the parishioners.

16. No.

---

[6] See **58.**

17. I constantly reside in the parish, but not in the vicarage house at present. I shall remove to it at Michaelmas.
18. There is none given.
19. No.
20. My place of residence is Myntye near Malmesbury.
  Ord. D. 30 May 1779.

Thomas Jones,[7] curate of Myntye

[*Written across under the address, in another hand:*] 10 Oct. 1762 deacon. 30 Nov. 1763 priest. 6 Aug. 1776 institution.

W. J. Brickenden,[8] vicar of Myntye

144 MONKTON FARLEIGH f.1182　　　　　　D. Potterne

1. Once as usual upon the Lord's day and that alternately, morning and evening: in the former at 10 o'clock, in the latter at 3 o'clock.
2. No.
3. As incumbent once in a month, at other times by my curate the Rev. Mr. Elderton.[9]
4. Yes. Two. Langridge and Dointon.[1] The former at the distance of six, the latter of ten miles.
5. Three times. On Easter day, Whitsunday, and Christmas day.
6. Generally fourteen. At Easter last sixteen.
7 & 8. There is not a dissenter in my parish.
9. [*Blank*]
10. [a] Yes, and it is in good preservation. [b] Yes. [c] So far as the year 1570.
11. Yes.
12. Not any.
13. [a] Yes, a duplicate of which is laid up in the bishop's registry. [c, d] There has, an account of which has been transmitted thither also.
14. Not any.
15. Yes. One by the minister and the other by the parishioners.
16. Not any.
17. No. I reside in the parsonage house at Langridge.
18. There is not any given.
19. There is not.
20. Langridge, about 3 miles distant from Bath.
  Peter Gunning M.A.[2] was ord. D. at Wells 24 Sept. 1769, and ord. P. 1 July 1770, and collated to the rectory of Monkton Farley 17 May 1780.

145 NETTLETON f.1190[3]　　　　　　D. Malmesbury

1. Divine service, both prayers and preaching, is performed in my church

---

[7] Perhaps Jesus Coll. Oxford 1761.
[8] Probably William John Brickenden, Magdalen Coll. Oxford 1756. Vicar of Appleton, Berks.: Clergy Books, 1783.
[9] See **1.**
[1] Langridge, diocese of Bath and Wells; Doynton, diocese of Gloucester.
[2] Oriel Coll. Oxford 1762.
[3] Letter missing.

once on the Lord's day, at ten o'clock in the morning or at two in the afternoon alternately. Divine service is not performed twice every Lord's day because I serve two churches.

2. Prayers and a sermon on Good Friday and prayers on Easter Monday, and prayers and sermon on Christmas day.

3. As incumbent.

4. Yes, the cure of West Kington, at the distance of a mile and half.

5. Three times in the year, at Easter, Whitsuntide, and Christmas.

6. Ten or twelve. Twelve communicated last Easter which was as great a number as any we have had.

7. No papists in my parish, nor does any popish priest reside in my parish or resort to it. No popish school in my parish.

8. No Presbyterian, nor Independent, nor Quaker, but two Anabaptists of the lower rank. No place of divine worship for them in my parish. Too many persons absent themselves from the public worship of God.

9. Yes, and I expound to them myself. Young persons are catechized by me in Lent and in the English language.

10. Yes, and our register of births and burials go as far back as the year 1695.

11. Yes.

12. [a] No chapels of ease in my parish. [f] None.

13. I have no terrier.

14. [a] No free school, nor alms-house, nor hospital, nor charitable endowments in my parish. [d] None.

15. Yes, one by the minister and the other by the parishioners.

16. No public school in my parish.

17. [a] Yes, and in the parsonage house. [c] About not more than a week at a time and that not often.

18. The money collected is given to the poor.

19. None.

20. In the parsonage house at Nettleton—Nettleton near Chippenham, Badminton post, Chippenham bag.

Ord. D. 21 Dec. 1740. Ord. P. 20 Sept. 1741. Instituted to Nettleton 16 May 1753. Degree B.A.

Daniel Mills,[4] rector of Nettleton

146 NORTH NEWNTON [Newington als. Newnton] f.1196   D. Avebury

The following queries are answered by me in the double capacity of rector of Manningford Crucis and curate of North Newnton. George Wells LL.D.,[5] rector of Manningford Crucis; ord. D. 6 June 1762. Ord. P. 25 Sept. 1763. Instituted 26 Sept. 1763.

1. Only once a day at each church, viz. at half past ten and at half past two alternately. And only once because of the number of churches in the neighbourhood to which the inhabitants may resort and hear both prayers and a sermon.

[4] Perhaps Merton Coll. Oxford, B.A. 1740. Curate of West Kington, **112.**
[5] 1740–1815. Oriel Coll. Oxford 1757.

2. Prayers are read at Manningford C. on Good Friday and on the day after each of the grand festivals. Prayers used to be read at North Newnton as above but omitted on account of their not being attended.

3. As rector of M.C. and as curate of N.N.[6]

4. Answered above as to the first part. N. Newnton is somewhat less than half a mile distant from M.C. The stipend, the whole sum, is for vicarial tithes amounting to £20 7s. per annum and collected with difficulty.[7] I am not licensed to this lucrative cure.

5. At Christmas, Easter, and Whitsunday and the Sunday following each of these festivals at N.N. and in addition to these at M.C. on or about Michael-mas.

6. The communion is remarkably and uniformly well attended at M.C. and very indifferently at N.N.

7. No.

8. No.

9. In the present dearth of bread and of provisions in general few of the children of the labouring poor are sent to school or instructed to read. In consequence I do not catechize them. When I have done it has been, as is most reasonable to imagine, in the English tongue.

10. Register books are provided and regularly kept. Copies are duly made out but whether returned or not I cannot confirm. This quere would be put with greater propriety perhaps to the keeper of the office.

11. Certainly; I do not imagine there is a single parish in England without such.[8]

12. No as to M.C. It has been said that Knoyle is a chapel to N. Newnton[9] but whether it be so or not, not having the means of information in my custody and it being moreover a matter of the utmost indifference to me, I have not inquired.

13. No. As to M.C. the want of it may very well be dispensed with, there being only a single acre of land belonging to the rectory exclusive of the Homestall. No right of common. The parsonage house and all the premises, which are very convenient, have been new built since the institution of the present incumbent. The church and chancel likewise, the first repaired at the expense of the parish, the last at that of the rector, are in such a condition as may possibly be equalled but cannot be exceeded by any parish church in the county.

---

[6] Vicar, Henry Hawes; also vicar of West Knoyle. See below, query 12 and n. 9. For Hawes see Fugglestone, **91**, of which he was resident curate.

[7] Although he served as curate, he was getting the whole vicarial tithes as stipend, presumably by arrangement with the vicar. Clergy Books, 1783, give Hawes as vicar but do not mention a curate.

[8] But see **7, 25, 96, 114, 133, 157,** and **195,** where there was either no marriage register or one in which the entries were not 'conformable to the Act of Parliament.'

[9] West Knoyle, **116,** was appendant to North Newnton, the patron being the holder of the prebend of North Newnton. In 1783 this was John Hawes (rector of Fugglestone and Wilton), the vicar's father, presented by Lord Pembroke in 1759. In his capacity of prebendary, Hawes had also presented his son to the vicarage of North Newnton in 1780: Clergy Books, 1783; *Liber Regis; Wilts. Inst.* ii. 78, 91; see also above, p.13 n. 43.

14. No.

15. No. The churchwarden, for there is but one at M.C. who was originally
nominated by the rector, having continued in office several years.

16. No.

17. I reside at the parsonage house of M.C. I am seldom, I had almost said
never, absent. The parochial clergy are in a manner tied down to a single spot
by a multitude of restraints, some of them very irksome and disagreeable to
say the least of them. They are precluded from almost every possibility of
bettering their condition; being out of the sight of those men who have it in
their power to do something for them and with whom some of them have
possibly formed connections, they are in consequence out of their minds; and
a constant attendance on the duties of their profession like the impotence of
the man in the Gospel usually puts it in the power of some other person to
step before them.

18. No money is offered.

19. Not that I know of.

20. Answered above. [Post town] Pewsey, Wilts.

   [*Written across under the address in a different hand:*] This and Manningford
Bruce (called Manningford Crucis, as within) answered by Dr. Wells as
curate of Newnton and rector of Manningford Bruce in Marlborough
deanery.

147 LONG NEWNTON [Newnton] f.1204   D. Malmesbury

1. Divine service is performed at eleven o'clock in the forenoon in the winter,
and two o'clock in the afternoon in the summer.

2. On none, holidays excepted.

3. As incumbent.

4. I serve no other cure.

5. At Christmas, Easter, and on Whitsunday.

6. Near 19 (which is about the usual number) communicated at Easter last.

7. No.

8. [a] No. [f] No.

9. The children that are sent are catechized in the English language at any
time of the year.

10. The register book (which is duly kept) goes back to the year 1685.

11. Yes.

12. There are no chapels.

13. No.

14. There is a school of about £3 10s. a year where children learn to read.

15. One by the minister and one by the parishioners.

16. The children of the above school are not fed or clothed.

17. I reside on my cure.

18. By the minister in charitable purposes.

19. There is none.

0. Place of residence, Newnton. Post town, Tetbury.

Date of institution 2 July 1779. Deacon's orders 29 May 1774. Priest's
rders 18 Dec. 1774. Degree Doctor of Laws.[1]

48 SOUTH NEWTON f.1212   D. Wilton

. Divine service is performed once a day in my church. It has not been
ustomary oftener.

. Divine service is performed in my church on Good Friday and on Christ-
nas day.

. I perform divine service as incumbent.

. I serve no other cure.

. The holy sacrament is administered at four times of the year, on the three
reat festivals, and on the Sunday after Michaelmas.

. The number of communicants not more than ten at my church. The parish
s very widely extended, and some of the hamlets are much nearer the neigh-
ouring churches, where, I understand, many of the parishioners regularly go.

. There is not a reputed papist in my parish.

. There are a few Presbyterians in my parish (no other sect that I know of)
vho usually go to a meeting in the neighbourhood, there being no place made
se of by them for divine worship. I know of no persons who openly profess
o disregard religion or who commonly absent themselves from all public
vorship of God.

. The parishioners, and more particularly the young persons, will be carefully
nstructed by me in the next Lent season.

0. The register book of births and burials is duly kept and in good preserva-
ion. The register of births and burials goes back as far as 1695.

1. A register book is duly kept, according to the directions of the Act of
Parliament against clandestine marriages.

2. There are no chapels of ease in my parish.

3. I have lately taken out of the registry a true and perfect account and
errier of all houses, tithes, and profits which belong to me. No augmentation
as been made of my living.

4. There is no school, alms-house, hospital, or other charitable endowment
n my parish. There are no lands or tenements left for the repair of my
hurch, or for any other pious use.

5. The churchwarden, there being but one, has usually been chosen in
aster week by the minister and parishioners together.

6. There is not, nor has there been founded, any public school or charity
chool in my parish.

7. I now reside constantly at Salisbury within three miles of my parish.

8. It is not usual to collect any money at the sacrament in my parish.

9. There is no other matter relating to my parish about which it is necessary
o trouble your Lordship.

No signature. Rector, Edward Estcourt. St. John's Coll. Oxford 1768.

20. At Salisbury.

Henry Hetley[2] was instituted to the vicarage of South Newton 21 Jan
1773. Ord. D. 14 June 1767. Ord. P. 24 Sept. 1769. B.D. 24 June 1778.

149 NEWTON TONY f.1220   D. Amesbury

1. Morning prayers and sermon at eleven. Evening prayers at half hour
after two.
2. On Ash Wednesday, Good Friday, Easter Monday and Tuesday.
3. As incumbent.
4. I serve no other cure.
5. The sacrament is administered on Christmas day, Easter day, Whitsunday
and Michaelmas.
6. Number of communicants is generally about twenty. The number at
Easter last was the same as usual.
7. There is one gentleman a reputed papist and two servants in his house.
None perverted to popery. No place of worship in the parish and no popish
priest resident.
8. [a] There are none. [e, f] There are none.
9. My parishioners send their children to whom I expound the catechism
every year soon after Whitsuntide, in the English language.
10. I have a register book in which I duly enter the births and burials. The
register goes back to 1556.
11. Yes.
12. [a] There are none. [f] No.
13. I have a terrier of all lands, tithes, etc., a duplicate of which is in the
bishop's registry. Since that was done, an augmentation hath been made of
the living, which hath not been transmitted to the registry.
14. There is no free school, alms-house, hospital, or other endowment.
15. The churchwardens are chosen every year, in the Easter week, by the
minister and parishioners.
16. There is not (nor has there been founded) any public or charity school in
our parish.
17. I do constantly reside upon this cure, and in the parsonage house.
18. The money is given by me to the poor who are best attendants on the
church.
19. There is none.
20. Newton Tony near Amesbury.

Instituted to Newton Tony 3 June 1776. Ord. D. 2 Dec. 1764. Ord. P.
17 Feb. 1765. Degree M.A.

John Ekins,[4] rector

[2] 1743–1832. St. John's Coll. Cambridge 1762. Vicar of Aldworth, Berks.: Clergy Books,
1783. 'A decent, well-behaved man,' tutor to Lord Herbert in 1771, and a protegé of
Lord Pembroke (patron of South Newton) who presented him to Wilton in 1788. A
member of Wilton corporation: *Pembroke Papers*, i. 353 n.; ii. 366, 434.
[3] Presumably Thomas Bradshaw of Wilbury House, where a room was registered as a
Catholic chapel in 1797: *V.C.H. Wilts*. iii. 91.
[4] King's Coll. Cambridge 1751. Vicar of Trowbridge, **203,** served by a resident curate
He became dean of Salisbury in 1786.

150 NORTON f.1228   D. Malmesbury

1. Divine service is performed in our church at half hour after nine in the morning once a fortnight. I can give no other reason but that of prescription why it is not performed every Lord's day.

2. This I must answer in the negative and from prescription too. Such is the circumstance of the parish that I believe a congregation could not be formed.

3. As incumbent.

4. I serve no other cure in this diocese. [5]

5. The sacrament is administered four times in each year at the three great festivals and Michaelmas.

6. We have but few inhabitants and the number therefore of communicants cannot be very great. I never knew more than seven or eight, but through sickness or death last Easter they were reduced one half.

7. No papist of any denomination.

8. No dissenter of any kind. No dissenting teacher or meeting-house. I know of none that profess to disregard religion, and the generality of the people are pretty constant attenders upon God's public worship.

9. Children are sent, but it is very seldom that you can prevail for the attendance of servants. The season is some time or other in the summer, and all are catechized in the English language. I have not hitherto either expounded the catechism, or made use of any printed exposition, but in future shall be very assiduous, under the guidance, if any one, of Archbishop Secker.

10. We have a register book for births and burials, of which there is a regular return made every year into the registrar's office. They go back to 1663.

11. We have a register book for marriages agreeable to the Act of Parliament.

12. There is no chapel standing or in ruins.

13. I know of no terrier, nor of any augmentation.

14. There is no school that properly comes under this description.

15. I believe they are chosen at that season, but always by the parishioners.

16. There is a little school endowed with £4 per annum issuing from some estate in Bristol. All the poorer children are admissable to be taught to read; I have often had experience that a proper care is taken of them.

17. I cannot, as the house would not contain my family; I reside at Beverstone near Tedbury in Glostershire, the distance from Norton is about six miles.

18. There is, nor ever was, I am told, no offertory.

19. Nothing that I can think of at present.

20. Beverstone near Tedbury, Glostershire.

Thomas Hornidge, [6] vicar

[*Written vertically in left hand margin:*] Thomas Hornidge B.A. Ord. D. 15 Aug. 1742. Ord. P. 23 Dec. 1744. Instituted to Norton 6 April 1752.

151 NORTON BAVANT f.1236   D. Wylye

1. Divine service is, as it always have been, performed once on every Lord's day. The time, generally at one o'clock as the most convenient for the parish.

---

[5] Probably incumbent of Beverstone, Glos., where he resided.
[6] Probably Pembroke Coll. Oxford 1738.

The clear yearly value of the living, not exceeding £63 or £64, has always been the reason why divine service is not performed twice every Lord's day.

2. Divine service is performed only on Good Friday and Christmas day, on which days there is a sermon.

3. My church is, and has been, served by a neighbouring clergyman at about one mile distant for four of five years, my health not permitting me during that time to serve it myself; I answer these queries myself, my residence not being more than one measured mile from this church, consequently can, and do, pay a proper attention to the service of it.

4. Mr. Thring, the clergyman who officiates here, serves his own church likewise, distant only one mile. The name of Mr. Thring's own parish is Sutton Veney.

5. The holy sacrament is administered four times every year, viz. Easter, Whitsuntide, Sunday after St. Michael, and at Christmas.

6. Not more than seven or eight. This I can safely answer for as I frequently attend myself on sacrament days.

7. Not one reputed papist in my parish. No place in my parish in which they assemble for divine worship. No popish priest resides in my parish, nor resorts to it, neither is there any popish school kept in my parish.

8. There are three Presbyterians, a farmer and his wife and a miller. No Independents, Anabaptists, or Quakers. No teacher. The number of Presbyterians less, as part of the above mentioned family have left the parish. Here are none that I know of who profess to disregard religion; but here are some who do not frequent the public worship so frequently as could be wished.

9. They do not, but have desired them for the future duly to send them to me, which request if they comply with it, shall be my endeavour privately to instruct them, that they may be able to make a good appearance in the public church in Lent, the usual time of catechizing; at which time I will recommend it to my curate, if I am not able myself diligently to attend on them. I did not while I served the church myself make use of any particular exposition, but frequently in my sermons explained parts of the catechism.

10. The register books of births and burials are duly kept, and in good preservation; and the returns of births and burials are regularly made into the registrar's office. The register for births goes back to the year 1653. The register for burials to the year 1684.

11. There is a register book duly kept according to the direction of the Act of Parliament against clandestine marriages.

12. [a] There is no chapel in my parish. [f] We have only one church.

13. Have no account of any houses, lands, tithes, pensions, or profits. Have endeavoured to procure a perfect account of everything belonging to me as minister of this parish, and will deliver it to be laid up in the bishop's registry.

14. There is no free school or any other charitable endowment in my parish. There are no lands or tenements left for the repair of the church, or for any other pious use.

15. The churchwardens are chosen every year in the Easter week by the minister and parishioners together if they agree; if not, one by the minister, the other by the parishioners.

16. There is no public school founded in my parish, or any charity school.
17. I do not reside on the cure; I reside at Bishopstrow (scarce one measured mile distant from this place), of which parish I am the rector as will appear from my answers to your Lordship's queries directed to the officiating minister of Bishopstrow.
18. There is no collection; the communicants are generally very poor people, and rather objects of charity.
19. I do not know of any other matter relating to my parish of which it is necessary to give your Lordship information.
20. I reside at my living in Bishopstrow, one measured mile from Warminster, a post town.

Instituted to this living 24 Sept. 1765. Ord. D. by the bishop of Bristol in the cathedral church of Christ in Oxford 2 Feb. 1753. Ord. P. by the bishop of Oxford in the cathedral church of Christ in Oxford 9 June 1754. Took my M.A. degree in the university of Oxford 13 Nov. 1754.

Thomas Fisher,[7] vicar of Norton Bavant in the county of Wilts.

28 July 1783

152 OAKSEY f.1244 D. Malmesbury

1. At ½ after ten o'clock in the morning and ½ after one in the afternoon during the summer; and ½ after one during the winter. The latter part answered in the answers to 2nd, 4th, and 17th.
2. On some of the principal festivals.
3. As incumbent.
4. For some years I served the cure of Mynty. At present I serve, and more than two years last past have served, no cure but my own.
5. Four times, viz. Christmas day, Easter Sunday, Whitsunday, and the first Sunday after Michaelmas.
6. Owing to sudden illness the sacrament was not administered at Easter last. But on the Sunday when it was afterwards administered the number of communicants were about ten, nearly the usual number.
7. No.
8. No.
9. My parishioners never send their children and servants to be instructed *publicly* in their catechism. I have been obliged therefore to instruct the few that will attend privately in my own house. I make use of no printed exposition, but expound to them myself in the manner which I think best adapted to their respective capacities.
10. [a] Yes. [c] So far back as the year 1670.
11. Yes.
12. No.
13. [a] Yes. [c] There has been no augmentation.
14. No.
15. Two churchwardens are chosen every year, one by the minister, the other by the parishioners.

7 See **17.**

16. No.

17. I constantly resided in my parsonage house from the time when I was inducted to Michaelmas 1781, when I removed for the benefit of my health, and by the advice of my physician, to a neighbouring town, viz. Cirencester, distant from Oaksey about seven miles, where I resided that and the following winters. The intermediate summer I resided in my parsonage house. I am now returned to the same place, where I propose, if my health permits, to reside constantly for the future.

18. There is none given.

19. I know of none.

20. Oaksey, Cirencester, Glocestershire.

Ralph Smith LL.B.[8] Ord. P. by the bishop of Salisbury 29 June 1759. Instituted to the rectory of Oaksey 3 Oct. 1770.

153 ODSTOCK f.1252   D. Chalke

1. Divine service is performed in my church upon every Lord's day, both prayers and preaching in the morning at eleven o'clock and prayers in the afternoon at three o'clock, except on the first Lord's day of every month, when divine service, both prayers and preaching, is performed in a neighbouring church, at the distance of near half a mile, in the afternoon.

2. Divine service is performed in my church on Ash Wednesday and Good Friday.

3. I perform divine service as incumbent of my parish.

4. I serve no other cure.

5. The holy sacrament of the Lord's Supper is administered in my church four times in the year, at Christmas, Easter, Whitsuntide, and Michaelmas.

6. I have generally six or seven communicants in my parish. At Easter last I had five and at Whitsuntide six communicants.

7. There are eight reputed papists in my parish, one man, four women, and three children. The lord of the manor, his priest, and servants gave me a great deal of trouble for many years. They left the parish about twelve years ago.[9] Since that time there has not been any popish priest resident in or resorting to it. There has not been any popish school kept in it. The reputed papists in my parish are all poor people.

8. There is not one Presbyterian, Independent, Anabaptist, or Quaker in my parish, nor any person who professes to disregard religion. There are three persons who commonly absent themselves from the public worship of God in my church, and I believe they do not go to any other place of public worship. I have admonished them privately many times, but without effect.

9. They do not. When there was a school in my parish for children who were old enough to learn their catechism, I used to attend it; but now there is no school for such children. The farmers have no children, and the poor people cannot afford to send their children to school when they are able to earn anything towards their maintenance.

---

[8] 1734–1808. Merton Coll. Oxford 1752.
[9] The Webbs of Odstock House: *V.C.H. Wilts.* iii. 88.

10. I have a register book of births and burials duly kept, and in good preservation; but the churchwardens do not apply to me for a copy of it. My register of births and burials, with some defects, goes as far back as the year of our Lord 1541.

11. I enter all marriages according to the directions of the Act of Parliament against clandestine marriages, but in my small parish, in which there cannot be any clandestine marriages, I did not think it necessary to have a separate register book for that purpose. A copy will be delivered in this year.

12. Nothing under this article.

13. I have a terrier, but I am not certain that it is perfect, the authenticity of it depending upon the information I received from an old labourer when I first came into the parish. Before the inclosure of the parish takes place, I shall compare it with the terrier in the bishop's registry.

14. Nothing under this article.

15. The churchwardens in my parish are chosen one by the minister and the other by the parishioners. There is at present but one churchwarden, chosen by the minister, and sworn into his office with difficulty and at an extraordinary expense, which was owing to one of the churchwardens, leaving the parish, not delivering up the church book, and not making a presentment. It will be set right at the ensuing visitation.

16. Nothing under this article.

17. I constantly reside upon this cure, and in the house belonging to it. I am absent about a month or five weeks once in two or three years, when I visit my relations in Gloucestershire.

18. There is not any money given at the offertory.

19. Lord Radnor, the present lord of the manor, is going to inclose it. The rector to have every fifth acre of arable land, and every ninth acre of meadow and pasture. When the inclosure is completed I shall make a new terrier, and lay a duplicate thereof in the bishop's registry.

20. Odstock near Sarum.

John Bedwell[1]

The date of my deacon's orders is 5 June 1737. Of my priest's orders 17 June 1739. I was instituted to the rectory of Odstock 28 April 1741. I was instituted to the rectory of Teffont Evias 15 Feb. 1769.

John Bedwell M.A. in the university of Oxford

154 ORCHESTON ST. GEORGE f.1260   D. Wylye

1. At eleven in the morning and 2 in the afternoon alternately, once a day as has been usual.

2. None have been usual.

3. As incumbent.

4. Stoke[2] is served with the above, 3 miles distant. Not licensed.

5. Four times in the year, Christmas, Easter, Whitsun, and Michaelmas.

6. One time with another about ten communicate.

[1] Brasenose Coll. Oxford 1731. Rector of Teffont Evias, **195,** served by a non-resident curate.

[2] Winterbourne Stoke, **223.**

7. No papists in the parish nor any popish school.

8. No Presbyterians, Independents, Anabaptists, or Quakers in the parish.

9. They have most of them learned their catechism; they are catechized in English.

10. [a] Yes. [b] Yes. [c] To the year 1656.

11. There is.

12. [a] None. [f] None.

13. [a] Yes. [b] Yes. [c] None.

14. None.

15. They are chosen in the Easter week by minister and parishioners together.

16. None.

17. Yes.

18. None collected.

19. None.

20. Orcheston St. George near Amesbury, Wilts.

Instituted 29 June 1772. Ord. D. 5 July 1767. Ord. P. 25 Sept. 1768.

T. Grove A.M.[3]

155 ORCHESTON ST. MARY f.1263   D. Wylye

1. Divine service is generally performed at a quarter before two in the afternoon and on sacrament days at eleven. It never was customary to have service here twice, owing I suppose to the smallness of the parish.

2. It has not been customary to perform any service on weekdays.

3. I perform service as curate.[4]

4. I serve also the curacy of Shrewton together with Maddington. Neither of my cures are distant a mile from each other. The late bishop of Sarum did not require me to take licences to my cures; therefore have none.

5. [recte 6]. The number of communicants are about twelve, and on last Easter day about the same number. This number (owing to a mistake) answer to no. 6. Q.5. How etc. The holy sacrament is administered at this church at Christmas, Easter, and Whitsuntide.

6. This question is answered Q. the fifth in the third page.

7. There are no reputed papists, no priest, school, or chapel where they assemble.

8. There are no Presbyterians, Independents, etc., etc. neither are there any (according to my knowledge) who absent themselves from public worship.

9. It has not been ever usual to catechize children at this small parish church; neither will time properly admit of it, because one or more churches are incumbent on the curate to serve.

10. I have a register book of births and burials duly kept, the register goes about so far back as 1688 both for births and burials.

11. There is a register book kept to prevent clandestine marriages.

12. There are no chapels of ease in the parish.

13. There is no terrier. The rector's income is from great and small tithes

---

[3] Thomas Grove, St. John's Coll. Cambridge 1761.

[4] Rector, John Freeman. Sidney Sussex Coll. Cambridge 1760, migrated to Clare Coll., patrons of the living.

viz. from corn, hay, wool, etc., etc. The rector's annual income is about £160.

14. There is no free school, neither has there been left any lands etc. for repairing the church.

15. In every Easter week the churchwardens are chosen by the minister and parishioners together.

16. There is no public school.

17. I constantly reside upon this cure and am not a mile distant from either of my other cures. I do not reside in the parsonage house as it being too small for a family.

18. There is none given.

19. None.

20. This is my place of residence, and Market Lavington is the nearest post town.

I entered as commoner at Queen's College in Oxford where I resided about three years and was ord. D. at Salisbury at Michaelmas in the year 1777, and ord. P. at London at Christmas by the bishop of Glocester in the year 1781.[5]

156 PATNEY f.1280   D. Potterne

1. Divine service with a sermon is regularly performed every Sunday morning and evening alternately.

2. It has not been usual for many years to have prayers on weekdays.

3. As curate.[6]

4. I serve my own church likewise at Woodborough where I reside, at about three miles distant from Patney.

5. Three times in the year, viz. Christmas, Easter, and Whitsuntide.

6. About six.

7. None.

8. [a-d] None. [e, f] I am sorry to say too many.

9. Children that learn to read learn their catechism.

10. [a, b] Yes. [c] 1592.

11. Yes.

12. None.

13. [*Blank*]

14. None.

15. Yes, one by the minister and the other by the parishioners.

16. None.

17. Answered at Q.4.

18. No offertory.

19. Nothing at present.

20. Woodborough near Devizes, Wilts.

George Gibbes D.D.,[7] curate

[5] No signature. Curate, Joseph Legg: see **131.**

[6] Rector, James Foster. Magdalen Hall Oxford 1723. Vicar of Britford, a peculiar of the dean and chapter: Clergy Books, 1783.

[7] See **226.**

157 PERTWOOD f.1288   D. Wylye

1. The parish of Pertwood being so small as to consist but of one family it has been usual to perform service there but once a fortnight, which is done at one o'clock.

2. There is no duty on weekdays, holidays, or festivals.

3. As curate.[8]

4. Hindon, which is a chapel of ease to East Knoyle. Have no licence to this cure.

5. The parish is so small as not to admit a canonical number to communicate.

6. The parish consisting but of one family, they usually attend at Hindon.

7. There are no papists in this parish.

8. There are no Presbyterians, Independents, Anabaptists, or Quakers in the parish and the parishioners are decent and regular.

9. The parish is so small that it affords no catechists.

10. There is a register duly kept in good preservation and returns properly made.

11. There is a register of marriages but not according to the Act, the parish being so small as to remove all apprehensions of clandestine marriages.

12. There is no chapel of ease in this parish.

13. There is a terrier the duplicate whereof is laid up in the bishop's registry.

14. There is no free school of any sort in this parish.

15. There is but one churchwarden in the parish, who is perpetually so, as he is the only person that can take the office in the parish.

16. There is no school of any kind in this parish.

17. The major part of my time I reside at Hindon, which is but a mile from Pertwood.

18. [*Blank*]

19. Nothing that I know of.

20. Hindon, which is a post town.

   Ord. D. 23 Dec. 1781[9]

158 PEWSEY f.1296   D. Marlborough

1. Prayers and sermon at 11 o'clock in the morning and 4 o'clock in the afternoon.

2. On the great festivals but not on common holidays.

3. As incumbent.

4. None.

5. Four times in the year, viz. Easter, Whitsunday, Michaelmas, and Christmas.

6. Generally from sixty to four score.

7. [a] None that I know of. [b] No. [c] No. [d] No. [e] No.

8. [a] No. [b] No. [e] No. [f] Yes.

9. No. I explain and labour to enforce the catechism in my discourses on Sunday afternoons; guiding myself chiefly by Pearson on the creed and

---

[8] Rector, John Nairn. See Boscombe, **19,** of which he was absentee vicar.

[9] No signature. Curate, John Evans. See **103.**

Bishop Burnet on the 39 articles with Dr. Beveridge's *Thesaurus Theologicus*.[1]
10. [a] Yes. [b] Yes. [c] To 1568.
11. Yes.
12. None.
13. [a] Yes. [b] Yes. [c] No.
14. None.
15. Yes, one by the parishioners and one by the minister.
16. None.
17. [a] Yes, yes. [c, d] Absent only occasionally, in cases of illness, or other necessary occasions.
18. None collected.
19. None.
20. Pewsey is a post town.[2]

159 POULSHOT [Polshott] f.1304   D. Potterne
1. Once a day between ten and eleven in the morning. The parishioners cannot conveniently attend afternoon service, being chiefly employed in dairy business.
2. No.
3. As curate.[3]
4. I serve no other cure, but am rector of Leigh Dalamere in this diocese, which I do serve in person.[4]
5. Four times a year, on the three great festivals of Christmas, Easter, and Whitsuntide, and at Michaelmas.
6. About five or six persons.
7. No.
8. No dissenters of any kind.
9. No. I do not find that any come to be catechized.
10. Yes.
11. Yes.
12. No.
13. None perfect. The rector will procure one as soon as possible.
14. Nothing of the kind.
15. Yes, one by the minister and one by the parishioners.
16. There is no such school whatever.
17. No. At Devizes, about two miles from the parish. I am only a temporary curate since the last incumbent died, and officiate till the present rector comes to reside.

---

[1] John Pearson, bishop of Chester, *An Exposition of the Creed* (1659); Gilbert Burnet, bishop of Salisbury, *An Exposition of the 39 Articles of the Church of England* (1699); William Beveridge, bishop of St. Asaph, *Thesaurus Theologicus* (1710).
[2] No signature. Rector, Joseph Townsend. Clare Coll. Cambridge 1758. A popular preacher and author of theological, medical, and travel books. Son of the patron of the living. Member of the Committee of Correspondence of 1780: see above, p. 8.
[3] Rector, Benjamin Blaney. See **160**.
[4] There is no return for Leigh Delamere. Clergy Books, 1783, give Henry Jaques as rector and Mr. Still as curate. For Still see **229**.

18. Seldom any collected, but what is, is given to the poor.

19. No.

20. At Devizes.

Henry Jacques,[5] curate of Polshott, A.B., was ord. D. in the year 1732 and was ord. P. in the year 1736. Likewise was instituted to the rectory of Leigh Dalamere in the diocese of Sarum in the year 1752.

160 POULSHOT[6] [unfoliated]   D. Potterne

1. Divine service is performed once every Sunday at eleven o'clock in the morning, except every fourth Sunday, when it begins between one and two in the afternoon. This has always been customary. And the parish consisting of dairy farms, the occupations of the inhabitants, it is said, will not admit of a double attendance. The afternoon service on the 4th Sunday is calculated to facilitate holding a vestry for parish business afterwards.

2. I do not find that divine service has ever been performed on a weekday, except on Christmas day, Good Friday, and on fast and thanksgiving days appointed by special proclamation.

3. I am rector of the parish.

4. I serve no other cure.

5. Four times in the year, on Christmas day, Easter day, Whitsunday, and on the Sunday before or next after Michaelmas day.

6. The number of communicants on Whitsunday last was eight or nine. I never administered the sacrament in the church before, but am told that this was about the usual number.

7. There are no papists in my parish that I know of.

8. There are no dissenters of any kind in my parish, nor any that profess upon principle to disregard religion; although there are some who seldom, if ever, attend the public service of the church. I do, and shall as often as occasion serves, admonish such of their duty in this particular.

9. I do not find that the children or servants in the parish have been publicly instructed in the Church catechism of late. But it is my design as soon as possible to revive this salutary practice, and to expound the catechism publicly in the church at some convenient season of the year for the general benefit according to the best of my judgement.

10. The register of births and burials has been, and is, duly kept, and returns regularly made into the registrar's office. It goes as far back as the year 1627.

11. There is a register book duly kept according to the directions of the Act commonly called the *Marriage Act*.

12. There are no chapels of ease in the parish, nor do I know of any that ever have been.

13. I have no perfect terrier at present, but am endeavouring to make out one, and as soon as it is completed, a duplicate thereof shall be sent to be laid up in your Lordship's registry.

---

[5] Christ Church Oxford 1728.

[6] A second return for Poulshot, made by the newly-appointed rector. This form has no address across the last page and the sheets are not bound into the volume. Presumably it was sent in late. See **233**, also loose.

14. I know of no charitable endowment in the parish, except a gift of £20 left by the will of one Mr. Daniel Mayo, the interest of it to be applied to the instruction of poor children of the parish, under the direction of the minister, churchwardens, and overseers of the poor. The parish have taken this money, and applied it to the repair of a parochial house, paying 20s. a year as the interest of it; but having given no security for it, I have called upon them to do so, and am taking measures for that purpose, as also for a better application of the money than has hitherto been made of it.

15. The churchwardens are chosen every year in the Easter week, one by the minister and the other by the parishioners.

16. There is at present no public school in the parish. But there is now on foot a plan for establishing one by voluntary subscription, in addition to the 20s. a year, the interest of Mr. Mayo's legacy. All the children of the poor are designed to be taught in it *gratis*, if the funds will admit, and care will be taken to have them instructed in the principles of the Christian religion, and brought regularly to church. How far this charity may be extended, or what success it will meet with, is for time to discover.[7]

17. I mean to reside (as I do at present) upon this cure, and in the house belonging to it as long as ever I can. If the situation, which is said to be a damp one, should oblige me to reside elsewhere in the winter months, I shall endeavour to fix my residence somewhere near at hand, where I may attend to the care of the parish as much as [may] be and shall make my absences as short as possible.

18. There has not usually been any money given at the offertory till Whitsunday last, when a small collection was made, and the sums given, and which shall be hereafter given, will be faithfully applied by me to charitable uses, for which I shall be always ready to give account.

19. To Q. 19 I reply in the negative.

20. Devizes is the nearest post town to Poulshot, the place of my residence.

Benjamin Blayney B.D.[8] was collated to the rectory of Poulshot in the year 1783. Was ord. D. by the bishop of Worcester 22 Dec. 1751, and ord. P. by the same 20 Dec. 1752.

161 POOLE KEYNES[9] [Poole] f.1312   D. Malmesbury

1. Once every Lord's day, morning and evening alternately; in the morning at eleven o'clock, in the evening at half hour after two; oftener than which it has not been performed time out of mind. The rectory when I came to the possession of it did not exceed £70 per annum clear.

2. On Christmas day only.

3. As incumbent.

4. Yes; the cure of Somerford Keynes, distant from Poole one mile and quarter, which I have served 18 or 19 years without being licensed.

---

[7] The school was attended by 20 children in 1819. On his death in 1801 the rector left £12 a year towards its maintenance: *V.C.H. Wilts.* vii. 123.

[8] 1728–1801. Worcester Coll. Oxford 1746. A distinguished scholar who became Regius Professor of Hebrew at Oxford in 1787: *D.N.B.*

[9] In Gloucestershire since 1897.

5. Three times, Easter, Whitsuntide, and Christmas. At Whitsuntide last the sacrament was not administered, there not being a sufficient number of persons to administer it to.

6. Four or five; at Easter last, four.

7. Neither papist nor reputed papist in the parish.

8. No sectaries of any denomination; but too many, as is the case of most places, who but too commonly absent themselves from the public worship of God.

9. No children have been catechized for some years past, there being no school in the parish where poor children may be taught to read, nor anybody capable of teaching. While there was a little private school, the children were usually catechized in Lent. There are but two families in the parish that have children, besides those of the poor.

10. There are two register books, the old one in bad preservation and in some places illegible; that in present use is duly kept and in tolerable good preservation, and the returns of births and burials regularly made into the registrar's office. The register of births and burials goes back to the year 1660.

11. Yes.

12. There is no chapel of ease at Poole. The parish is but very small.

13. There is at present no perfect account and terrier of all the houses, lands, etc. which belong to the minister of Poole, an inclosure having lately taken place in the parish, which has caused a great alteration. But I am now making one according to your Lordship's directions, which will be delivered to your Lordship's registrar at the ensuing visitation.

14. No free school or charitable endowment of any kind, or lands or tenements left for the repair of the church. The church and chancel have lately been rebuilt from the foundations, the church by the parish, and the chancel by myself.

15. The churchwardens are chosen every year at Easter, one by the minister and the other by the parishioners.

16. No school of any kind either public or private.

17. I reside constantly upon this cure and in the house belonging to it.

18. There is no money to be disposed of, none being given.

19. None.

20. Poole near Cirencester.

George Green A.M.,[1] rector of Poole. Ord. D. 23 Sept. 1744, ord. P. 22 Sept. 1745, at Wells. Instituted to the rectory of Poole 6 Dec. 1760.

162 POTTERNE f.1320   D. Potterne

1. Prayers and sermon every Sunday morning at eleven. Prayers in the afternoon, $\frac{1}{2}$ after three in summer, sooner in winter.

2. Only in Lent or near the great festivals.

3. As incumbent.

4. Not any.

5. At the three great festivals and at Michaelmas.

---

[1] Probably Queen's Coll. Oxford 1739. Vicar of Little Shefford, Berks.: Clergy Books 1783. See also **179**.

. Very decent, sometimes near one hundred. Was not here at Easter.
. None.
. [a] One farmer a Quaker removed out of the parish. [b] Some Methodists
assemble on Sundays for whom a low fellow preaches, but not numerous.
e, f] I found too many of these [and none more obstinate than Mr. Sutton's
bailiff, a large farmer, *crossed out*].
. This I found totally neglected but intend to revive it.
10. [a] Very regular. [c] From the year 1556. [b] Yes.
11. Yes.
12. None.
13. I find an old terrier of tithes only but shall send one complete for both my
livings as soon as I can do it with precision.
14. No school.
15. Yes, one by the vicar and the other by the parishioners.
16. None.
17. I divide my residence between my livings but constantly upon one or the
other.
18. To the poor who receive.
19. If anything occurs I will faithfully acquaint your Lordship.
20. Residence at Potterne near Devizes.

Arthur Coham M.A.,[2] vicar of Potterne
Ord. D. 29 May 1743, ord. P. 23 Dec. 1744 by Edmund lord bishop of
London. Collated to Potterne and Brixton Deverell 26 March 1781.

163 POULTON[3] f.1328   D. Cricklade
1. Divine service is regularly performed once on every Sunday, alternately
in the morning a little before eleven and in the afternoon a little before two.
More frequent duty is incompatible with the service of my church at Coln
St. Aldwin's, Gloucestershire, which is almost four miles distant from
Poulton.
2. Divine service is never omitted upon Christmas day, Good Friday, or any
public fast or thanksgiving day.
3. As perpetual curate.
4. I am vicar of Coln St. Aldwin's,[4] and serve the church there. Its distance
from Poulton is mentioned above. I am duly licensed as curate of Poulton.
5. The sacrament of the Lord's Supper is administered at Christmas, Easter,
Whitsuntide, and Michaelmas.
6. The number of communicants rarely exceeds ten or twelve, which was, I
believe, the number at Easter last.
7. There is no papist in the parish, nor have any attempts been lately made,
so far as I know and believe, to pervert any of the inhabitants of the place to
popery.
8. There is one, and only one, family of Protestant dissenters. I am acquainted

[2] Exeter Coll. Oxford 1739. Archdeacon of Wilts. and rector of Brixton Deverill (for which
there is no return), served by a curate: Clergy Books, 1783.
[3] In Gloucestershire since 1897.
[4] In the diocese of Gloucester.

with none who openly profess to disregard religion; but there are some, I fear who seldom attend the public worship of God, notwithstanding that they have occasionally been admonished in private.

9. The young persons of the parish are examined in the catechism publicly on several Sundays in the course of the summer. I cannot say that I have hitherto delivered to them any formal exposition of the catechism. But it is my constant endeavour in my sermons to explain the doctrines and the duties of the Christian religion, as set forth in the Church catechism.

10. There is a register book duly kept, and returns are annually made into the registrar's office. It goes back so far as to the year 1695.

11. There is also a register book of marriages duly kept.

12. There is no chapel in the parish.

13. There is no terrier, for—alas!—there is no house, land, or tithe belonging to the curacy. The whole stipend is the sum of £20 10s. paid by the impropriator. Perhaps at some future time an augmentation may be hoped for from the governors of Queen Anne's Bounty.

14. There is no free school in the parish, or charitable endowment of any kind, except a small legacy of money to be given to the poor annually upon old Christmas day.

15. The churchwardens are chosen annually, in the Easter week, one by the minister and the other by the parishioners.

16. There is no charity school.

17. There is no house belonging to the incumbent.

18. The communicants being for the greater part persons in indigent circumstances, it hath not been customary to collect any money at the offertory.

19. If anything more relating to the parish of Poulton should occur worthy of your Lordship's notice, I will take the liberty to communicate it; I have the honour to be, my Lord, your Lordship's most obliged and dutiful servant, John Keble.

20. Fairford, Gloucestershire.

John Keble M.A.[5] Ord. D. 11 March 1770. Ord. P. 26 May 1771. Licensed as curate of Poulton 7 June 1782.

164 PRESHUTE f.1326 [misfoliated]   D. Marlborough

1. Divine service, both prayers and preaching, is performed once only every Lord's day, alternately in the morning at half an hour past ten o'clock and in the afternoon at three; and were prayers only to be read there the other part of the day, a congregation would seldom be mustered here, as the church stands so near to Marlborough St. Peter's, where they may hear a sermon also, together with the music of an organ erected there of late years.

2. On Christmas day and Good Friday there are performed herein both prayers and preaching.

3. As incumbent.

4. I serve also my church of Marlborough St. Peter's, not half a mile distant herefrom.

---

[5] 1746–1835. Corpus Christi Coll. Oxford 1763. Father of John Keble the Tractarian.

5. Four times, on, or near, Christmas day, Easter day, Whitsunday, and Michaelmas day.

6. The number of communicants continue about twelve, sometimes more, sometimes fewer.

7. One reputed papist, landlord of the Castle inn, lives in this parish, whose family are all members of the Church of England; consequently there is no place of papists assembling for divine worship, no popish priest, no popish school kept in the parish.

8. I know of no dissenters of any denomination in the parish, but am informed that some of the poorer inhabitants steal now and then into the Methodist, or Independent meeting-house at Marlborough.

9. I am sorry to accuse my parishioners of great remissness, in this part of their duty. Some plead their poverty, others their distance from the church, as their excuse; I hear those that come say their catechism in English on 6 or 7 Sundays in the summer season and explain the catechism to them from notes of my own compiling, when able to attend myself.

10. Yes. The earliest register of births and burials begins in the year 1607, those prior to that year having been burnt in vicarage house, which then stood in a part of the present churchyard.

11. Yes.

12. None.

13. I have received from the bishop's registry at Sarum copies of different terriers of different dates, as also of an instrument of augmenting the vicarage of Preshute, and of a composition respecting some of the tithes mentioned in the instrument of augmentation, from all which I hope to be able to draw up a true and perfect terrier of all lands, tithes, pensions, and profits which belong to me as minister thereof, whereof a duplicate will be delivered to the registrar at the visitation to be holden at Marlborough St. Peter's 28 July 1783.

14. A cottage, garden, and four acres and two roods of land (called Mosses) lying and being in the hamlet of Manton in this parish (formerly occupied by one Hitchcock) now by John Braithwaite Esq. at £6 per annum is left for the repairs of the church for ever. Which rent is received and accounted for yearly by the churchwardens. Twenty marks, the gift of Mr. John Coleman of Dinton (the interest whereof was to be laid out in apprenticing poor children of the parish) on 20 April 1750, were put at interest in the hands of Mr. John Neate senior then renter of Barton farm in the parish, who by the parish book appears to have paid the interest thereof up to the 20 April 1762. But he, as appears, dying insolvent in the year 1782, both the principal and interest are likely to be lost and sunk for ever; when in good credit, he left off his business to an only son.

15. Yes, one by the minister when he chooses to interfere, and the other by the parishioners.

16. None.

17. The house belonging to the vicar of Preshute having been destroyed by fire in, or shortly before, the year 1607, and never since rebuilt, I constantly reside at the parsonage house of Marlborough St. Peter's, not half a mile from Preshute church; and as the last and present incumbents have enjoyed both

benefices, it is to be wished that all future bishops will confer them on one and the same person,[6] as one will furnish him with bread and cheese, and the other with a place to eat and sleep.

18. By the minister to the poor and needy, at the discretion of the minister and the recommendation of the communicants.

19. None, unless it be whether John Neate junior can be compelled to make up the loss of the charitable donation before specified, ans. 14th.

20. At Marlborough, a post town.

[*Written under the address:*] Thomas Meyler M.A.,[7] was ord. D. 20 Sept. 1741. Ord. P. 13 June 1742. Instituted to the vicarage 17 Nov. 1773.

165 PURTON f.1334   D. Cricklade

1. Twice a day, prayers and sermon at 11 o'clock in the morning, and prayers only at half after 3 in the afternoon.

2. Good Friday and Christmas day, and Easter Monday.

3. As incumbent.

4. None.

5. Four times. Easter day, Whitsunday, Christmas day, and the Sunday after New Michaelmas.

6. Generally between thirty and forty. Easter last, number 34.

7. None.

8. [a] None. [f] There are some few of this latter class, i.e. who seldom appear at divine service.

9. I catechize the children during Lent, and make use of Archbishop Secker's lectures on the subject.

10. [a] Duly. [c] Near 400 years.

11. Duly.

12. None.

13. The last terrier was taken in the year 1711.

14. This question answered on the opposite side [*i.e. under no.* 16].

15. One of the churchwardens is chosen by the vicar, and the other by the parishioners, on Easter Monday, annually.

16. There is a charity school, for teaching reading and writing to twenty poor children, founded by Mrs. Miriam Stevens; took place about four years since, the stipend, £17 10s. per annum, charged on a freehold estate in this parish. The trustees are the vicar of Purton and the rectors of the two Lydiards, adjoining parishes.

17. Constantly resident.

18. By the minister to such of the poor inhabitants as are occasionally in the greatest distress.

19. [*Blank*]

[6] A proposal by Bishop Barrington to unite the two benefices of Preshute (in the gift of the Choristers' School) and Marlborough St. Peter (in the gift of the bishop) was approved by legal advisers to the school in 1786, but nothing seems to have come of the proposal: Dora H. Robertson, *Sarum Close*, p. 248.

[7] See **136.**

20. At Purton near Swindon, Wilts.

J. Prower,[8] ord. D. 1771. Ord. P. Dec. 1771 and collated to Purton vicarage at the same time. Took the degree of A.M. 1773.

166 RODBOURNE CHENEY f.1350 D. Cricklade

1. [a] Once, alternately at eleven and three; i.e. both prayers and preaching are once each Lord's Day. [b] Because it has been no oftener of ancient use.
2. No; for no one attends; and it is very difficult, in a parish consisting chiefly of farmers and labourers and farmers, to assemble a congregation even on Ash Wednesday or Good Friday.
3. As incumbent.
4. At Little Bluntesdon,[9] about two miles distant. Never imagined a licence was necessary for so small a cure.
5. Easter, Whitsuntide, Michaelmas, and Christmas.
6. Eight or nine generally. Last Easter, eight; last Whitsuntide, ten.
7. Certainly no.
8. No. Some few perhaps are absent through age or infirmities.
9. The children are sent, and I have expounded to them myself. Lent is the usual time. The young people understand no language but English.
10. Yes. The register professes to begin according to an Act of Parliament bearing date 24 Aug. 1653,[1] in which year one birth and one burial are mentioned prior to the Act.
11. Yes.
12. No.
13. There are three terriers in your Lordship's registry, the last is dated about 100 years past: I had copies of them from your Lordship's registrar this present year, but they are at present under examination, and I can give no further account of them. There is likewise an endowment which I have not yet seen, but I believe it will be necessary. There has been no augmentation.
14. No.
15. The churchwardens are chosen one by the minister, the other by the parishioners, yearly at Easter.
16. An attempt was made to found a charity school by one of the late incumbents, but failed through the invalidity of his will by which the support of it was bequeathed, and I believe partly through the inability of his heirs.
17. Constantly.
18. Nothing is ever given at the offertory.
19. None that I know of.
20. Rodbourne Cheney near Swindon.

J. Nelson B.A.,[2] vicar

Ord. D. 23 Feb. 1766. Ord. P. 28 June 1767. Instituted 2 April, inducted 8 April 1779.

[8] John Prower, 1748–1826. Wadham Coll. Oxford 1766.
[9] Blunsdon St. Andrew, **18.**
[1] *Acts and Ordinances of the Interregnum*, ed. Firth and Rait, ii. 715–18.
[2] John Nelson. Perhaps Christ Church Oxford 1761.

If the answers are not sufficiently explicit, or if the questions have been misunderstood, the incumbent would wish to wait upon the proper officers, to communicate such information as is within his power.

167 ROLLESTON [Rolston] f.1358   D. Wylye

1. Divine service is performed in the church at Rowlston once every Lord's day, alternately at 11 o'clock in the morning and at 2 in the afternoon; it is not performed twice on account of the small value of the living.

2. Divine service is not usually performed on weekdays, except on more solemn occasions.

3. I perform divine service as incumbent, having been instituted in the year 1758.

4. With Rowlston I serve the cure of Durrington, 5 miles distant, to which I am duly licensed.

5. The holy sacrament of the Lord's Supper is administered at Christmas, Easter, Whitsuntide, and Michaelmas.

6. The number of communicants at Easter last was, as has been usual, about eight or ten.

7. No reputed papists are in the parish.

8. I do not know of any dissenters in the parish, nor of any persons who profess to disregard religion, but it is to be wished that some were more constant in their attendance at the public worship of God.

9. The children have been called upon to be catechized, but none have attended.

10. A register book of births and burials is duly kept, and returns have been made into the registrar's office as often as called for. The register commenced in the year 1653.

11. A register book of marriages is duly kept.

12. There is no chapel of ease in the parish, nor any ruinated chapel.

13. There is what appears to be a true terrier of the parish; but I do not know whether a duplicate thereof is in the bishop's registry nor do I know of any augmentation being made of the living.

14. There is no free school, alms-house, or hospital in the parish. In the year 1704 £10 per annum were given by Mrs. Anne Estcourt to put out poor boys to be bound apprentices, which benefaction is under the direction of the minister and churchwardens.

15. The churchwardens are usually chosen about Easter, one by the minister and the other by the parishioners.

16. There is no school in the parish.

17. I do not reside at Rowlston, but at Amesbury, a post town, five miles distant, where I am very near to Durrington, which is by far the most extensive cure.

18. No money is usually given at the offertory.

19. I know of no other matter relating to the parish of which it may be proper to give your Lordship information.

20. Answered under Q. 17.

R. Head M.A.,[3] rector of Rowlston
Ord. D. 21 Sept. 1746. Ord. P. 20 Sept. 1747.

168 ROWDE f.1366   D. Avebury
Roude near Devizes,[4] Wilts. William Higginson *vicar*.

1. Prayers and a sermon are duly performed once every Sunday, sometimes in the morning and sometimes in the afternoon. It has never been usual to have service twice, nor is the salary adequate.

2. Service is only performed on Sundays, excepting Christmas day and Whit Monday and Easter Monday.

3. As incumbent.

4. I serve no other cure.

5. The sacrament is administered four times every year, Christmas, Whitsun, Easter, and Michaelmas.

6. There are about ten or twelve communicants in general.

7. I do not know of any papists in my parish nor is there any school or popish priest.

8. There are a few dissenters.

9. No.

10. [a] Yes. [b] Yes.

11. Yes.

12. No chapels.

13. [a] Yes. [b] Yes. [c] No.

14. No.[5]

15. Yes. One is chosen by the minister and the other by the parishioners.

16. No.

17. I reside, but not in the vicarage house. I live about a mile from the church. I am not often absent nor for any long time.

18. To the poor people.

19. No.

20. Devizes.

W. Higginson M.A.[6]
Admitted to the degree of M.A. of University College 26 June 1762. Ord. D. by the bishop of Oxford on Sunday 1 June 1760. Ord. P. by the bishop of Chester in Whitehall chapel Sunday 7 March 1762. Instituted to Roude 18 Sept. 1764.

---

[3] See Compton Chamberlayne, **55,** of which he was absentee vicar; served by a non-resident curate. See also **75.**

[4] The letter is misplaced and bound *after* the queries and answers. It has been addressed to the rector etc. of Corsham, crossed out and Rowde substituted. William Higginson was incumbent of both benefices.

[5] Several charities were in fact in existence in 1783: *V.C.H. Wilts.* vii. 222.

[6] University Coll. Oxford 1756. Vicar of Corsham, **169.**

169 CORSHAM f.1374[7]   D. Malmesbury

Corsham near Chippenham, *Wilts*. William Higginson[8] vicar. William Lewis curate.

1. Prayers and a sermon in the morning and prayers in the afternoon.
2. Most holidays.
3. As curate.
4. No other cure.
5. Four times in the year.
6. Generally forty or fifty.
7. I do not know of any papists.
8. I do not know of any dissenters excepting some few reputed Quakers.
9. Yes.
10. Yes.
11. Yes.
12. No.
13. Yes.
14. There is an alms-house for poor women endowed by a Lady Hungerford, the particulars of which I am unacquainted with.
15. At Easter, one by the minister and the other by the parishioners.
16. There is an endowment I believe on the alms-house for instructing a few poor boys. I believe Lord Radnor is patron of it.
17. I reside about three miles from the church. I am seldom absent, nor for any long time.
18. To the poor.
19. The vicarage of Corsham is a peculiar and has from time immemorial had the privilege of proving wills and granting licence to marry.[9]
20. At Chippenham.

170 RUSHALL [Russall] f.1386   D. Potterne

1. Twice, at ten, and two in the afternoon. Sermon once every Sunday in the afternoon.
2. No.
3. As curate.[1]
4. [a, b] Yes, Upheven, distant about half a mile. [c] No.
5. Four, at Michaelmas, Christmas, Easter, and Whitsuntide.
6. About six or eight; at Easter, six.
7. [a] None. [b] None. [c] Yes, in the village. [d] No. [e] No.

[7] Letter missing. The form has been addressed to the rector etc. of Rowde, crossed out and Corsham substituted. Although the wording of the return suggests that it was made by the curate, the handwriting is the same as the return for Rowde and is presumably that of the vicar of both parishes. Perhaps he sent in both returns together, and Corsham was thus bound up in the wrong alphabetical order.

[8] See **168**.

[9] Corsham was one of the very few places on which the privilege of a peculiar or consistory had been conferred, giving the vicar certain episcopal privileges within the parish. The peculiar was abolished in 1857: *W.A.M.* xliii. 526.

[1] Curate, Rees Deer. See also **204**.

8. [a] A few Anabaptists. [b] No. [c] Freeman. [d] Being but lately come, I cannot positively say, but from what I have gleaned, rather decreasing. Why or by what means I am not able to declare. [e, f] I know of none who profess to disregard religion; but there may be some who are not as attentive as they should.
9. The children are sent, but having not been catechized for some years, I am under the necessity of teaching them in my house.
10. [a] Yes. [b] As far as I know. [c] The oldest register commences at 1651.
11. Yes.
12. [a] None. [f] None.
13. Yes; a terrier some time since laid up in the bishop's registry and a copy thereof in the possession of the lord of the manor.
14. [a] None. [d] None.
15. They are chosen every year, occasionally by the minister, in general by the parishioners.
16. [a] None. [b] No.
17. Yes.
18. There is nothing offered.
19. Nothing to my knowledge.
20. Rushall, Pewsey.

Henry Whitfield D.D.[2] [rector]. Deacon 1754. Priest 1756. Instituted to Russal 7 Jan. 1778.

171 SEAGRY f.1394   D. Malmesbury
1. But once a day, at two o'clock, on account of the smallness of the living.
2. Only on Good Friday and Ash Wednesday.
3. As incumbent, having at present no curate.
4. None at present.
5. On Easter Sunday, Whitsunday, and Christmas day.
6. Generally ten or twelve. Easter last, ten.
7. None that I know of.
8. None that I know of.
9. Yes, in Lent. I make use of no printed exposition.
10. [a, c] Yes, three. 1st 1610. 2d. 1762. 3d. 1782. [b] Yes.
11. Yes.
12. None that I know of.
13. [a] None that I ever saw, but am lately informed that Mrs. Pulsford the late vicar's widow, now in your college,[3] has or had one in her possession. If it proves that she has not, I will make as I can, and that as soon as possible. [c] Yes. £400 from the Bounty of Queen Anne augmentation, £200 by myself and friends.[4] [d] None, unless from the governors or trustees of the Bounty of the Queen.
14. None that I know of.
15. Yes; two, one by the minister and one by the parishioners.

[2] New Hall Oxford 1749. M.A. from Merton Coll., one of the patrons of the living.
[3] The College of Matrons, founded by Bishop Seth Ward, in the Close, Salisbury.
[4] 1771 and 1775: Hodgson, p. 417.

16. None that I know of.

17. Not constantly, on account of my daughter's health. When absent Dr. West, rector of Draycott the adjoining parish, does the duty.[5]

18. To the poor by myself or churchwardens.

19. None that I know of.

20. At my family house at Rainscombe near Marlborough.

   Instituted to Seagry 3 Aug. 1762. Ord. D. 8 Feb. 1756. Ord. P. 17 May 1761. Oxon. commenced A.B. about 1745.[6]

172 SEMLEY f.1402   D. Chalke

1. Morning prayers and sermon every Sunday at 11 o'clock. Evening prayers at 3 in the afternoon.

2. At the principal festival seasons of the year, Good Friday, etc.

3. As incumbent.

4. [a] No other. [c] Instituted and inducted.

5. Four times in the year, viz. at Christmas, Easter, Whitsuntide, and Michaelmas.

6. [a] From twenty to thirty. [b] Much as usual.

7. [a] A few, chiefly labourers employed at Wardour Castle. [c] None. [d] None. [e] None.

8. [a] Two Presbyterians only, farmers. None of any other sect. [b] None in the parish of any sect. [e, f] None that I know of.

9. [a] Duly. [b] Myself. [c] In the summer. The English language.

10. [a] A register book is duly kept. [b] At every visitation. [c] To 1657.

11. A marriage register book is duly kept.

12. [a] None in the parish. [f] None.

13. [a] A terrier is now made, and a duplicate delivered to the registrar. [c] None.

14. [a] None of any sort. [d] Two acres, let at £1 15s. per annum given for repairing the church; managed by the churchwardens.

15. Every year at Easter, one by the rector, the other by the parishioners.

16. [a] None. [b] None.

17. For the greatest part of the year, and in the parsonage house.

18. By myself, to the sick poor.

19. Nothing more.

20. Semley near Shaftesbury.

   Lewis Stephens M.A.,[7] rector of Semley. Ord. D. 25 May 1755. Ord. P. 13 June 1756. Instituted 1 July 1778.

173 SEDGEHILL f.1410   D. Chalke

1. Being a chapel of ease[8] it never has been served but once in the day.

2. Never.

---

[5] See **64**.

[6] No signature. Vicar, Benjamin Rogers. 1720–1802. Queen's Coll. Oxford 1738.

[7] 1731–1803. Christ Church Oxford 1749. Clergy Books, 1783, also give Mr. Brickley as curate. See **173**.

[8] Annexed to Berwick St. Leonard, **14**.

3. As curate.
4. I occasionally serve Semley,[9] distant 3 miles from Sedgehill.
5. Upon the 3 grand festivals, Easter, Whitsuntide, and Christmas, and at the feast of St. Michael.
6. [a] From twenty to thirty. [b] Much as usual.
7. [a] None. [b] None. [c] None. [d] None. [e] None.
8. [a] None of any sect. [f] Few if any.
9. [a] Never. [b] I always expound myself. [c] The English.
10. [a] A register book is duly kept. [b] At every visitation. [c] To 1760.
11. A marriage register book is duly kept.
12. [a] None. [f] None.
13. [a] Cannot say anything to this question. [c, d] Can make no reply to this.
14. [a] None of any sort. [d] None at all.
15. Every year at Easter, by the parish only.
16. [a] None. [b] None. There neither is or has ever been anything of the sort, the reason why I cannot say, unless it be the smallness of the parish, which suppose to be the case.
17. [a] Never. [b] At Shaston, distant 3 miles.
18. Myself. The sick and poor.
19. Nothing more.
20. Shaston.

Thomas Brickle,[1] curate of Sedgehill

174 SHORNCOTE[2] [Sherncot] f.1436   D. Cricklade
1. Once on every Lord's day, at 2 o'clock in the afternoon; and as the inhabitants are so few in number, divine service never was performed there but once on every Lord's day for time immemorial.
2. No.
3. The church is at present served by Mr. Eddy, curate of South Cerney, but should my health be restored I intend to serve it myself, at least occasionally.
4. I lately served the curacies of Malmsbury and Garsden, to the former of which I was licensed by the late Dr. Thomas of Winchester, when he was bishop of Salisbury, but I have now quitted both on account of ill health.
5. Three times in every year, viz. at Christmas, Easter, and Whitsuntide.
6. As the parish is small, the number of communicants is consequently small and incapable of much increase. At Easter last there were only three, and much the same as usual.
7 & 8. To all these queries I answer in the negative, as there are no dissenters of any denomination whatsoever in my little parish. I wish I could add that all within it lived under the habitual influence of our most holy religion, and attended upon the service of our excellent church constantly with proper views and from right principles.
9. Such as send their children have them, I believe, catechized in Lent, when the Church catechism is properly explained to them; but it is to be lamented

[9] Clergy Books, 1783, spell his name 'Brickley' under Semley and 'Brickhill' under Sedgehill.
[1] Probably Balliol Coll. Oxford 1743.
[2] In Gloucestershire since 1897, having been amalgamated with Somerford Keynes in 1894.

that parents and heads of families pay but very little regard to this necessary duty, however they may be reminded of their obligation to it.

10. There is a register book for births and burials in pretty good preservation. It goes as far back as the year 1633.

11. There is a separate marriage register book according to the directions of the Act of Parliament against clandestine marriages.

12. To all these queries I answer in the negative.

13. There is a true and perfect terrier bound up with the old register book, a duplicate whereof will be left with your Lordship's registrar. There has been no augmentation to the living; but a late Act of Parliament[3] respecting the inclosure of Ashton Keynes common has assigned lands in lieu of the tithes, which were due to me from some part of that parish.

14. All these queries I answer in the negative.

15. The churchwarden is chosen every year by the parishioners in the Easter week.

16. I never heard of any school in the parish, and therefore I must answer all these queries in the negative.

17. I do not reside upon this cure as the living is so small, and the house is so very inconvenient for my bad state of health; but I reside at Malmsbury which is about seven or eight miles distant from it, where I have a house of my own and can be much better attended in my affliction.

18. There is no money collected at the sacrament.

19. I know of no other matter respecting my parish of which I can give your Lordship any further information.

20. I reside at Malmsbury, which is a post town.

I was instituted to this living on the 3 Jan. 1765. I was ord. D. on the 13 Aug. 1758, and ord. P. on the 15 June 1760. I was bred at Oxford but have taken no degree.

John Davies,[4] rector of Sharncote, Wilts.

175 SHERRINGTON f.1444   D. Wylye

1. My lord, twice a day, morning and evening, at the hours of half after ten in the morning, and of two in the afternoon; prayers and preaching.

2. Yes, constantly, upon holidays and upon the yearly festivals. Constantly also, upon the eves before the sacrament.

3. As incumbent.

4. None.

4. None.

5. Four times. At Christmas, Easter, Whitsuntide, and at Michaelmas.

6. Not many, my parish being but small. *Easter* last, we made seven; sometimes more, sometimes less. Not so many at any time as we ought.

7. We have no papist, reputed or real. And therefore have no place here where they assemble for divine worship, nor any popish school kept in the parish.

8. Presbyterians, Independents, Anabaptists, Quakers, there are none of

---

3 17 Geo. III, c. 139.
4 Perhaps Jesus Coll. Oxford 1744.

them here. Neither, I thank God!, any profane persons. Few as we are, absenters are too common, and too many. Not without care on my part to make them otherwise. The plea is children and want of clothing.

9. I catechize every year, in Lent. At the same time I make a present to them of some well approved exposition, *Lewis etc.*, as well to the servants as to the children. Parents and masters, neither of them as they are bound in duty to be, are not so exact nor careful here.

10. Yes, duly kept, and in good preservation. I deliver out a copy of it yearly at the time of the visitation. Our register contains the present century to this present year '83, and goes as far back in the former as to the year '77,—1677.

11. Yes my Lord.

12. None. Neither are there any ruinated chapels, nor chapels in the parish of Sherrington.

13. My terrier is in the bishop's registry. There hath been no augmentation made to my living since it was there deposited. For my own part, I found no terrier left behind for me by the former rector, nor that he had any to succeed to when he was made incumbent himself. No doubt there is a fault. And we are thankful to your Lordship for your paternal care as to this matter.

14. The parish of Sherrington hath no such thing of any kind in it. We have not, neither, any lands nor tenements left for the repair of our church, nor for any other pious uses, except only a gift of charity to the poor of Sherrington, to the amount of £67, now deposited in the hands of Edmund Lambert Esq. of Boyton, at the yearly interest of £4 for an hundred, under bond. I distribute it yearly myself to the poor at *Christmas.*

15. Every year in the Easter week. The parish being small, and but few principal inhabitants, we content ourselves with one; and with him, as quite sufficient for his office. He is chosen at *Easter*, by myself and the vestry together.

16. We neither have, nor have had, any public or charity school in this parish.

17. I reside constantly upon my cure, and in the house belonging to it. Having no dignity myself, I have no title to the allowed absence for such as have.[5]

18. The offertory money is disposed of by myself, to the widow and aged poor. Especially if they make one at the altar.

19. None.

20. My place of residence is Sherrington. My nearest post town Heytesbury.

I was instituted to the rectory of the parish church of Sherrington 3 Jan. in the year of our Lord 1778. I was ord. D. at Oxford in year 1738, 14 Jan. I was ord. P. at Oxford 17 June 1739. My degree is M.A.

Thomas Wilmot Case,[6] rector of Sherrington

176 SHERSTON [Great Sherston] f.1452   D. Malmesbury

1. I have the care of two churches, and the duty at each is alternate. I read

---

[5] Presumably he had in mind Canon XLIV of the Canons of 1604, which allowed prebendaries and canons to be absent from their benefices with cure for not more than one month in the year.

[6] Oriel Coll. Oxford 1733.

prayers and preach at both of them once every Sunday; the hours at the former are ten, or between ten and eleven in the morning, and two or half an hour after two in the afternoon; at the latter, half an hour after ten in the morning, and between one and two in the afternoon.

2. I generally read prayers Monday and Tuesday in the Easter and Whitsun weeks, and would gladly do it on other festivals or fasts if my parishioners could be prevailed on to attend them; it is a constant rule with me to preach upon Christmas day and Good Friday at both my churches.

3. As incumbent.

4. [*Blank*]

5. The sacrament is regularly administered, at each church, on the three great festivals of Easter day, Whitsunday, and Christmas day, or the Sundays following, and on the two Sundays immediately after Michaelmas.

6. The communicants at each church are in general from 14 to 18, the number that communicated last Easter, viz. 18 at Sherston, 14 at Alderton. I have endeavoured both by private and public exhortation to increase that number, but not with the desired success.

7. [*Blank*]

8. We have no dissenters. It is with concern I acknowledge there are some persons under my care who, if they do not profess to disregard religion, evidently discover by their practice a total neglect of its important duties. I should with pleasure adopt any means which might have a tendency to bring them to a sense of their unhappy condition; it is not to be wondered at if such persons wholly absent themselves from the public worship of God; but besides these, I have several in my parish who, though not so dissolute as the former, are far from being constant in their attendance on the service of the church; I will continue my endeavours to bring them to a more regular discharge of this great duty.

9. My parishioners have not sent their children and others in a regular manner to be instructed by me; but I have already given directions for that purpose and intend, in future, to catechize them every summer; after they are perfect in their catechism, I design putting into their hands a short, familiar exposition.

10. The register books of baptisms and burials, in each parish, are in good preservation; the entries are properly made, and returns regularly transmitted at the respective visitations. The register for Sherston commences the 23 Jan. 1653, for Alderton the 25 March 1653.

11. The marriages are constantly registered in a book for that purpose agreeable to Act of Parliament.

12. The chapel of ease annexed to this parish is Alderton, at the distance of two miles: I receive £30 yearly for the care of it from the dean and chapter of Glocester who are the patrons of this living.

13. In the bishop's registry are three terriers which belong to this parish; the last contains a particular statement of the glebe, tithes, etc., and bears date the 5 of Jan. 1704; of this I have a duplicate. As no augmentation has taken place since that time, I apprehend a new terrier is unnecessary.

14. [d] The present annual rent of the lands and tenements which belong to

the church of Sherston-magna is somewhat more than £12; this is regularly paid to the churchwarden appointed by the parish, who delivers in his account of receipts and disbursements every Easter to be inspected, approved, and signed by the minister and parishioners then present.

15. The churchwardens are appointed every year on Monday in the Easter week, the one by the minister, the other by the principal parishioners.

16. In the parish of Sherston are two small day-schools, for instructing young children of both sexes in reading, spelling, and the Church catechism; they are each of them supported by a settled endowment; the one belongs to the parish in general, the other to a particular hamlet; in the former the number instructed at a time is five, in the latter six. When the children can read with ease and are perfected in their catechism they are discharged, and others admitted in their room.

17. I have been constantly resident since the time of my institution, reside at present in the vicarage house, and am never absent, unless on occasional visits to my friends. I beg leave to inform your Lordship that when I first entered upon my living I found the house and the other buildings in so ruinous a state it was impossible to repair them in such a manner as to make them in any degree comfortable and convenient; and my predecessor having died insolvent, no sum could be recovered for dilapidations. Under these disadvantages I at last came to a determination to rebuild the whole, and for that purpose solicited some assistance from the dean and chapter of Glocester, who granted me a benefaction of £80. In the execution of my design I have, exclusive of this sum, expended not less than £420. My vicarage (including the chapel annexed), after deduction of taxes etc., does not clear me more than £80 per annum. This is principally occasioned by a modus for milk, which custom has established in the parish; with the view of setting aside this modus, I once took the opinion of the present Lord Chief Baron of the Exchequer who, after a mature consideration of the circumstances, recommended it to me not to proceed.

18. It has never been usual, at either of my churches, to receive offerings at the celebration of the Eucharist; and as the communicants are in general poor, I have not thought it prudent to introduce the custom.

19. I hope to be forgiven by your Lordship, if I mention that with the income arising from my living as above-stated, and a small addition to it, I am obliged to support a very large family.

20. Sherston near Tetbury.

My institution is dated the 19 Jan. 1770. Deacon's orders 23 Feb. 1766, priest's orders 28 June 1767.

Thomas Turner A.B.[7]

177 SHREWTON f.1464   D. Wylye

1. Divine service is performed alternately at ten, and three in the afternoon. It never was customary to have service here twice, owing I suppose to the smallness of the parish.

2. It has not been customary to perform any service on weekdays.

[7] Probably Pembroke Coll. Oxford 1763.

3. I perform service as curate. [8]

4. I serve also the curacy of Maddington together with Orcheston St. Mary. Neither of my cures are distant a mile from each other. The late bishop of Salisbury did not require me to take any licence to my cure, therefore have none.

5 [*recte* 6]. The number of communicants are about six and thirty, and on last Easter day did not appear to vary from the former years. This fifth Q. owing to mistake answers to the sixth. Q. 5. The holy sacrament is administered at Christmas, Easter, and Whitsuntide.

6. This question is answered opposite Q. the fifth in the third page.

7. There are no reputed papists, no priest, school, or chapel where they assemble.

8. There are no Presbyterians, Independents, etc., etc., neither are there any (according to my knowledge) who absent themselves from public worship.

9. It has not been customary to catechize children at this small parish church; neither will time properly admit of it, because one or more churches are incumbent on the curate to serve.

10. I have a register book of births and burials duly kept; the register goes about so far back as 1640 both for births and burials.

11. There is a register book kept to prevent clandestine marriages.

12. There are no chapels of ease in the parish etc.

13. There is no terrier. The vicar's income is from small tithes (viz.) hay, wool, etc. The vicar's annual income is £47.

14. There was £10 per annum left by Ann Estcourt in 1706 for apprenticing poor boys and is now under the direction of the minister and churchwardens, but at present some difficulties have been made in regard to the payment. [9] Some land has been left let at £3 4s. per annum for repairing the north aisle of the church; the person who left it is unknown.

15. In every Easter week the churchwardens are chosen by the minister and parishioners together.

16. There is no public school.

17. I reside in one of my parishes, and within a mile of the others. I do not reside in the parsonage house as it being too small for a family.

18. There is none given.

19. None.

20. Orcheston St. Mary is my residence, and Market Lavington is the nearest post town.

I entered as commoner at Queen's College in Oxford, where I resided about three years and was ord. D. at Salisbury at Michaelmas in the year 1777 and priest at London at Christmas by the bishop of Glocester in the year 1781. [1]

[8] Vicar, John Skinner. 1750–1823. Trinity Coll. Oxford 1768. A vicar of Salisbury Cathedral and master of the Choristers School, 1780–1801: Dora H. Robertson, *Sarum Close*, pp. 245, 258.

[9] Thomas Cripps, churchwarden, presented 'William Smith my partner and Robert Jennings, late churchwarden of the said parish, for embezzling £20, being charity money left to the said parish by Mrs. Ann Estcourt': Sarum Dioc. R.O., Churchwardens' presentments, 1783.

[1] No signature. Curate, Joseph Legg: see **131**.

178 GREAT SOMERFORD f.1472   D. Malmesbury

1. Divine service is performed twice in my church on the Lord's day, prayers and preaching in the morning, and prayers (and sometimes preaching) in the afternoon; it begins about eleven o'clock in the morning and about three o'clock in the afternoon.

2. Divine service is performed in my church on some of the principal holidays or festivals that happen on weekdays, though the congregation is very small in the morning, but is considerably increased in the evening by having prayers and preaching after their daily work is done.

3. I perform divine service as incumbent of my parish.

4. I serve no other cure.

5. The holy sacrament of the Lord's Supper is administered in my church four times in the year, viz. on the nativity of Christ, Easter day, Whitsunday, and the first Sunday after St. Michael's day.

6. I have generally about thirty communicants in my parish.

7. There is nothing of that kind in my parish.

8. There is nothing of that kind in my parish, except two men of no consequence who are called Quakers. There are some persons in my parish who commonly absent themselves from the public worship of the church, who pretend, when I have talked to them upon that subject, that they go to the Methodist meeting or some other place of public worship in some of the neighbouring parishes.

9. Some of the parishioners send their children to be catechized, and some do not. I expound to them myself in such a way as I think most suitable to their capacities, but I endeavour to follow, as well as I can, the expositions of Archbishop Wake and Archbishop Secker. I have done it at different times of the year, sometimes in Lent, sometimes between Easter and Whitsuntide, and sometimes after Whitsuntide; I find by experience the last to be the most convenient and best attended.

10. I have such a register book duly kept and in good preservation, and regularly make such returns; it goes back as far as 11 May 1707.

11. There is such a register book duly kept.

12. There is nothing of that kind in my parish.

13. I have a terrier which was left with me by the executrix of my last predecessor; it is properly drawn up and attested, and I believe there is a duplicate of it in the bishop's registry. There has been no augmentation of my living since that was done.

14. [a] There is nothing of that kind in my parish. [d] There are some lands and tenements left for the repair of the church. The rector and some of the principal inhabitants have the direction and management of them.

15. The churchwardens in my parish are chosen in the Easter week, one by the minister and the other by the parishioners.

16. There is nothing of that kind in my parish.

17. I do constantly reside upon this cure, and in the house belonging to it.

18. It is disposed of by the rector to some of the poor people who attend the holy sacrament.

19. Nothing more at present.

20. Somerford Magna, commonly called Broad Somerford near Malmsbury.
Institution 7 Aug. 1777. Ord. D. 18 Sept. 1763. Ord. P. 17 June 1764.
Degree B.D. 13 April 1749.

My Lord, I hope I have answered all your Lordship's queries to your
satisfaction. I am, my Lord, your Lordship's most obedient humble servant,

William Tonkin[2]

179 SOMERFORD KEYNES[3] f.1480   D. Cricklade

1. Divine service, both prayers and preaching, is performed once every Lord's
day, morning and evening alternately; in the morning at a quarter before
eleven o'clock; in the evening at a quarter after two; oftener than which it has
not been performed since I have known the parish. The vicarage upon the
present footing is not more than £50 per annum clear.
2. Upon Christmas day only.
3. As curate[4] these eighteen or nineteen years, but without being licensed.
4. Yes; the cure of Poole of which I am rector, distant from Somerford
Keynes one mile and quarter.
5. Four times, Easter, Whitsuntide, Michaelmas, and Christmas.
6. Eight or nine; at Easter last, nine.
7. There is neither papist nor reputed papist at Somerford.
8. No sectaries of any denomination; but too many, as is the case in most
places, who but too commonly absent themselves from the public worship of
God.
9. No children or servants have been catechized for some years past, neither
have any been sent for that purpose. There is no school in the parish but a
little private one, where those few who are taught to read learn the catechism.
10. The register book of births and burials is duly kept, and in tolerable
preservation; and the returns of births and burials into the registrar's office
are regularly made. The register extends back to the year 1560.
11. Yes.
12. There is no chapel of ease in this parish.
13. There is no terrier to be found in the parish; but there is a duplicate laid
up in the bishop's registry at Salisbury, delivered in by the late vicar, Mr.
Turner, a copy of which is in the hands of the present vicar, Mr. Dry, since
which there has been no augmentation or alteration, I believe, made in the
vicarage.
14. There is no free school or charitable endowment of any kind; nor lands or
tenements for the repair of the church.
15. The churchwardens are chosen yearly in the Easter week, one by the
minister and the other by the parishioners.
16. There is neither public nor charity school in this parish; only a little
private school kept by a poor old woman, where a few children are taught to
read and instructed in the Church catechism.
17. No; I reside at Poole, one mile and quarter distant from this place.

[2] Exeter Coll. Oxford (patrons of the living) 1735.
[3] In Gloucestershire since 1897.
[4] Vicar, Dr. John Dry. Perhaps Merton Coll. Oxford 1743.

18. There is no money to be disposed of, none being given.
19. None.
20. Poole near Cirencester.
    George Green A.M.,[5] curate of Somerford Keynes, ord. D. 23 Sept. 1744. Ord. P. 22 Sept. 1745, both at Wells.

180 LITTLE SOMERFORD f.1488   D. Malmesbury

1. Once a day, between ten and eleven in the forenoon. Divine service is performed but once a day as the parish is small.
2. Divine service is not performed here on weekdays etc.
3. As curate.[6]
4. I serve Sutton Benger together with this church of Little Somerford. They are four miles distant from each other.
5. Four times, Christmas, Easter, Whitsuntide, and Michaelmas.
6. Generally about half a dozen. Last Easter there were seven communicants, which is nearly the usual number.
7. I know of no papists in this parish etc.
8. I know of none in this parish who totally absent themselves from church; there are amongst us some of the people called Methodists, but they have no places set apart for divine service.
9. I have not *yet* been able to procure a *regular* attendance of the younger part of the parish for the purpose of catechizing, but I hope soon to be able to do it.
10. A register book is duly kept; returns of births and burials are regularly made.
11. There is.
12. There are no chapels of ease in this parish.
13. We have no terrier, but I have drawn one out, agreeable to the best information I could procure.
14. We have no free school etc. in this parish.
15. The churchwardens are chosen in the Easter week. They are chosen by the minister.
16. We have no charity school etc. in this parish.
17. I reside here, as curate of the parish.
18. Distributed by me amongst the poor of the parish.
19. I know of none.
20. I reside here at Little Somerford. The nearest post town is Malmsbury.
    The incumbent of the parish serves the church of Swindon. I received deacon's orders at midsummer 1780, and priest's orders midsummer 1782, having previous to my entering into orders taken a bachelor's degree at Oxford, where I was also ordained; the date of my degree is in Lent 1780.

John Morgan[7]

[5] See **161.**
[6] Rector, William Jones. Resident in Swindon, **194,** as curate assisting the vicar.
[7] Probably Pembroke Coll. Oxford 1776. See also **192.**

181 SOPWORTH f.1496   D. Malmesbury

1. My church is served for the most part twice every Lord's day throughout the year; generally there are prayers only for morning service, prayers and preaching for the evening.

2. Divine service is performed only on Christmas day, Good Friday, public fast days, or other days appointed by proclamation that may happen on weekdays; the parish consisting of 3 or 4 farmers, day labourers, and poor people, who have their bread to get daily, I cannot on other days raise a congregation.

3. I perform it as incumbent.

4. I serve no other church, unless it be sometimes to assist the neighbouring clergy in cases of emergency.

5. It is administered 3 times in the year, viz. on Christmas day, Easter Sunday, and Whitsunday.

6. I have generally seven or eight communicants inclusive of my own family. I had about the said number last Easter Sunday.

7. There are no such reputed persons in this parish; there have none, that I know of, been perverted to popery; there is no such place of worship, no such priests resort hither, nor any such school kept.

8. There are no persons of either of these denominations that I know of, in this parish [nor have been for many years, *crossed out*] (2 Anabaptist women about 5 or 6 years ago in this place) nor is there any place used here for divine worship besides my church. I know of no persons in this parish who profess to disregard religion or who absent themselves from all public worship of God; but this I must say, that a great part of the persons who dwell in the parish scandalously and very frequently absent themselves from the public worship here, notwithstanding my frequently admonishing them both publicly and privately.

9. I frequently expound the catechism publicly in the church in the time of Lent, in the mother tongue. The exposition is partly my own, and partly that of Dr. Wake.

10. There is a register book of baptisms and burials and marriages duly kept; and I regularly make returns of all baptisms and burials and marriages once yearly at the clergy visitation. The register goes back only to the 26 Feb. 1697/8. The register before that time is long since lost.

11. There is such a register book duly kept here against clandestine marriages.

12. There is no chapel of ease belonging to this parish, nor any ruinated chapel in it; no further reply therefore to this Q. necessary.

13. There is no terrier here of any kind to prove what belongs to the minister, nor can I say when there was any such instrument in being; but think it proper here to inform your Lordship that in the year 1728 the lands, which before lay in common fields, were by the joint consent of the proprietors inclosed, and the parsonage lands, which before were interspersed in small parcels, were changed and almost all laid together, whereby afterwards the living was considerably augmented, and let for £100 per annum, which before, I believe, was scarcely of half that value. I hope your Lordship will not think me

impertinent in saying here that the living has all along been highly rated, and that the outgoings are very considerable.

14. There is not any one thing mentioned in this Q. in or belonging to this parish.

15. This being a small place, there is only one churchwarden thought necessary, and is yearly chosen in the Easter week by the minister.

16. There is a small charity school in this parish for teaching seven poor boys or girls to read, supported by the duchess of Beaufort during her pleasure; which is all that is to be replied to this Q.

17. I customarily reside upon this cure, and dwell in a house belonging to the duke of Beaufort,[8] where I have lived ever since, and before I had the living. The parsonage house is let. I seldom sleep out of my dwelling house one night throughout the year.

18. I always dispose of the money given at the offertory to the poor, at my own discretion.

19. I know of no other matter relating to this parish proper to inform your Lordship of.

20. For answer to this Q., see that to Q. 17.

29 July 1783. John Perfect B.A.[9] was ord. D. 6 March 1757, ord. P. 13 March 1757, and instituted rector of Sopworth 14 March 1757.

182 STANTON ST. BERNARD [Stanton Bernard] f.1512   D. Avebury

1. This church is served alternately, divine service begins at 10 o'clock in the morning and 3 o'clock in the afternoon. The reason is the lowness of pay, being no more than £20 a year. Another reason is the badness of the roads.

2. There is divine service performed on all holidays and festivals throughout the year.

3. As curate.[1]

4. I serve the cure of Heddington only, about six miles distance. I took a licence out for Heddington when I was ordained deacon.

5. Four times in the year, at Easter, Whitsunday, Michaelmas, and Christmas.

6. There are generally twenty-seven communicants attends. I can observe no difference at Easter from any other time of the year.

7. [a] I have the pleasure and satisfaction to affirm there are none that go under that name. [b] None. [c] None, none. [d] None. [e] None.

8. [a] There are no such persons in this parish that go by that name. [b] None. [c] None. [d] *Blank*]. [e] There are two or three deluded people called Methodists. [f] There are a few that seldom or ever come to the house of prayer, and I believe hath not been at church for years past.

9. No. I do often exhort the parishioners to send their children and servants to be instructed in the catechism, but my exhortations to that end are all slighted and disregarded.

[8] Patron of the living.

[9] Probably Christ Church Oxford 1734.

[1] Vicar, Thomas Bromley. St. John's Coll. Cambridge 1767. Assistant master at Harrow 1771–1808, where he was housemaster of Lord Herbert, son of Lord Pembroke, patron of the living: *Pembroke Papers*, i. 38.

10. Yes. I make regular returns of births and burials. My register goes as far back as the year 1568.

11. Yes.

12. [a-d] None, none, none, none. [e] [*Blank*]. [f] There are none.

13. [a] Yes. [b] Yes. [c] None.

14. [a, b, c] None. [d] None.

15. Yes. One by the minister, and the other by the parishioners.

16. [a] None. [b] None. [e] None.

17. Yes, and constantly in the vicarage house.

18. There is none collected.

19. [*Blank*]

20. I reside at Stanton. The nearest post town is Devizes, about five miles distance.

I have answered this [*i.e. the postscript*] from Heddington.

Francis Rogers,[2] curate of Stanton

183 STANTON FITZWARREN f.1520   D. Cricklade

1. [a] At half hour after one and half hour after eleven alternately. [b] The parishioners are few and do not wish it, and the curate's salary is not adequate.

2. No.

3. J. Hippesley[3] of Stow in Glostershire is incumbent. Edward Clarke of Highworth is the present temporary curate.

4. [a] Edward Clarke vicar of Highworth[4] serves the parish church of Highworth, two miles distant. [c] No, nor wish to be.

5. Four times, viz. at Christmas, Easter, Whitsunday, and St. Michael.

6. Three or four.

7. No.

8. No.

9. None are catechized in church.

10. Yes, commencing 1542.

11. Yes.

12. No.

13. Neither rector nor curate know anything of it.

14. No.

15. One by the minister and one by the parishioners.

16. No.

17. J. Hippesley, the incumbent, lives 20 miles distant. Edward Clarke, the curate, lives two miles distant.

18. None is collected.

19. No.

20. Highworth.[5]

[2] See **100.**

[3] John Hippesley, 1736–1822. Balliol Coll. Oxford 1752. Rector of Stow-on-the-Wold. Members of his family were patrons of both livings: *Liber Regis.*

[4] Highworth was a peculiar of the dean of Salisbury.

[5] No signature. The return was presumably made by Edward Clarke, the temporary curate.

184 STANTON ST. QUINTIN [Stanton Quinton] f.1528

D. Malmesbury

1. Divine service is performed only once upon the Lord's day, one Sunday in the morning about eleven o'clock, and the next Sunday at half past one in the afternoon. I serve another church.
2. No divine service performed but on Sundays, except Christmas day, Good Friday, and Easter Monday and Tuesday.
3. I officiate as incumbent.
4. I serve another church of which I am incumbent,[6] about four miles from this parish.
5. The sacrament is administered in my church at Christmas, Easter, and Whitsuntide.
6. In general eight communicants.
7. No papists in my parish.
8. No Presbyterian, Independent, Anabaptist, or Quaker in my parish.
9. Having no school in the parish, the children are not sufficiently prepared to say their catechism in public.
10. The register book is duly kept and in good preservation, and regular returns made of births and burials as the canon requires. The register book commences from the year 1679.
11. The register book is kept according to the direction of Parliament.
12. No chapel of ease in my parish.
13. I have no terrier of the lands etc. belonging to me as minister of this parish. An Act[7] passed the sessions to inclose part of this parish and to give lands in lieu of tithes; as soon as the business is completed I will take care that a proper terrier shall be sent to the bishop's registry.
14. No free school, alms-house, hospital, or any charitable endowment whatever in my parish.
15. The churchwardens are chosen every year in the Easter week, one by the minister, the other by the parishioners.
16. No school of any kind in the parish.
17. I reside in the parsonage house.
18. No money given at the offertory.
19. I know of nothing more relating to my parish necessary for your Lordship's information.
20. I live at Stanton St. Quinton, my post town is Chippenham.

[*Written opposite the address:*] Instituted to the rectory of Stanton St. Quinton 29 March 1780. Ord. D. 22 Sept. 1771. Ord. P. 26 Sept. 1773. B.A. Trinity College Oxford.[8]

185 STAPLEFORD f.1536

D. Wylye

1. Divine service is performed once every Lord's day, both prayers and preaching at 11 in the morning and 2 in the afternoon alternately. It has never been customary to perform service oftener.

[6] Hardenhuish, **99.**

[7] 22 Geo. III, c. 26

[8] No signature. Rector, Samuel Smith: see **99.**

2. It has never been customary to perform divine service on any weekday except on Christmas day when it falls on a weekday.

3. As curate.[9]

4. I serve Berwick [St. James] about a mile from Stapleford. I have no licence.

5. The sacrament is administered at Christmas, Easter, and Whitsuntide.

6. The number of communicants about 20. Always more at Easter than at any other time.

7. None.

8. None.

9. I have catechized and prepared the children and servants for confirmation. It has not been customary for the parishioners to send them to me at any particular season for that purpose.

10. There is a register of marriages kept according to the Act of Parliament.

11. [Blank]

12. None.

13. None.

14. None.

15. There is two churchwardens chose at Easter, one by the rector and the other by the parishioners.

16. None.

17. I reside in Salisbury, 7 miles from Stapleford.

18. None collected.

19. None.

20. Salisbury, 7 miles from Stapleford.

George Trenchard,[1] curate

186 STEEPLE ASHTON f.1544   D. Potterne

1. Prayers and sermon at Steeple Ashton beginning at half past ten in the morning. Ditto at Semington chapel beginning at half past one. Prayers in the evening at Steeple Ashton at half past three.

2. On saints' and red letter days, throughout the year, and on Fridays in Lent.

3. As curate.[2]

4. I serve no other cure. I had letters dismissory for priest's orders from the late bishop of Sarum at which time it was not required of me to be licensed.

5. Four times at Steeple Ashton, and the same at Semington, viz. Easter, Whitsuntide, Michaelmas, and Christmas.

6. From 30 to 50. The number of late greater than usual.

7. Not any.

8. None but Methodists, a few of whom meet at a labourer's house, not licensed; preachers, one Newborn, a weaver, and one Sly, a tailor. Their number less by some hundreds than of late years. They are of the Huntingtonian sect.

---

[9] Vicar, James Lloyd. Clergy Books, 1783, have the note 'in Wales' against his name.

[1] See 12.

[2] Vicar, Lawrence Elliott or Eliot. Magdalene Coll. Cambridge 1743. The college owned the advowson and the vicar had to be unmarried: V.C.H. Wilts. viii. 213.

9. Those who have learned their catechism are instructed by me every Friday in Lent. I expound to them myself in the *English* language.

10. Yes, both at the church and the chapel. The church register goes as far back as the year 1558, that of the chapel as the year 1604.

11. Yes.

12. The chapel of Semington has prayers and a sermon every Sunday; also a sermon on Good Friday, for which the preacher receives 20s., being the legacy of Mrs. Joan Bisse. There are lands appropriated for its maintenance, of which an account will be given in the terrier. Distant from Steeple Ashton 2 miles, and served by the curate of Steeple Ashton.

13. Mr. Eliot, the vicar, is at present at Hambledon in Surrey, in a very indifferent state of health.[3] He has desired me to mention that the terrier shall be exhibited as soon as he can attend to make it out.

14. No free school, alms-house, or hospital. Thomas Somner of Wellowe in county Somerset left 40s. annually for the schooling of two poor boys of the tithing of Semington, payable by his executors out of his estates in the said tithing to the overseers of the poor for the time being, who nominate the boys. A copy of the will, and also an account of the lands etc., will be given in the terrier.

15. Church and chapel wardens appointed every year on Easter Tuesday, two by the minister, and two by the parish.

16. No charity or public school. The schoolmaster of the private school, a very ingenious and diligent man, instructs the children under his care in the principles of the Christian religion. Teaches reading, writing, arithmetic, and the mathematics; which he has acquired merely by his own industry and application. It is reported that Mr. Flicks, who died in January last, left a legacy of £5 per annum to this school, but I believe the will is not proved.

17. I *constantly* reside upon this cure, but not in the house belonging to it, that being occupied by two of the vicar's servants.

18. It is distributed by the minister directly after divine service at the rate of one shilling to every poor person present at the sacrament. The overplus accounted for in a book, and reserved to buy bread, coals, or other necessaries for the poor in the winter.

19. [*Blank*]

20. Steeple Ashton near Trowbridge, Wilts.

F. Gough

Admitted into deacon's orders 24 Sept. 1780. Priest's 17 March 1782.

187 STEEPLE LANGFORD f.1552   D. Wylye

1. Service is regularly performed twice every Lord's day in my church; in the morning prayers begin at 11 o'clock, after which there is a sermon, and at 3 o'clock in the afternoon prayers only.

2. On all the great festivals and on many other days.

3. As incumbent.

4. Little Langford, 1 mile distant from my own church.

---

[3] He died in 1784. His brother was vicar of Hambledon: *Alum. Cantab.*

5. Five times in the year.
6. From 30 to 40.
7. None.
8. None.
9. Regularly for 3 months.
10. The register book is duly kept and in good preservation. The returns of births and burials regularly made. The register goes back to the year 1674.
11. Yes.
12. None.
13. The terrier is delivered in according to order.
14. None.
15. In the Easter week, one churchwarden by the parish, the other by the rector.
16. None.
17. I constantly reside in the parsonage house.
18. I dispose of it to the sick and ancient.
19. None.
20. Steeple Langford near Sarum.
   Instituted to the rectory of Steeple Langford 4 Aug. 1779. Admitted deacon 1 June 1760. Priest 17 May 1761. My degree B.D.

Samuel Weller,[4] rector

188 STOCKTON f.1560   D. Wylye

1. Divine service is regularly performed in this church twice every Lord's day. Prayers at half after eleven o'clock in the morning, with sermon and prayers at half past two in the afternoon.
2. No weekly duties performed, except on holidays, which are always observed.
3. As curate.[5]
4. I serve another curacy adjoining this parish, but have no regular licence.
5. The sacrament is always administered in this church on four different times, i.e. at Easter, Whitsun, the feast of St. Michael, and Christmas.
6. The number of communicants in general are about thirty, which was the number at Easter last.
7. We have [no] popery whatever in this parish.
8. One Anabaptist only, no meeting-house of any sort whatever in this parish, neither popish priests nor any teacher of such schools, of none of the within-mentioned sects. None that publicly profess to disregard religion, but orderly attend divine worship.
9. The children of the parish are always catechized in Lent time, and they constantly attend. I expound to them myself always in English.
10. There is a register book of births and burials duly kept, and a copy of the same sent to the registrar's court.
11. There is, and properly observed.

---

[4] 1736–95. Corpus Christi Coll. Oxford 1751. See also **119.**

[5] Rector, Edward Innes. See Devizes St. John, **66,** of which he was resident rector.

12. We have no chapels of ease nor any such building within our parish.

13. There is a true and correct terrier herewith delivered.

14. We have an alms-house in this parish founded by John Top Esq. late of Stockton; the endowment is about £70 a year, the number of people eight. Their allowance is 2s. per week, a garment annually, with garden, orchard, and firewood. Trustees, Edmund Lambert Esq., Mr. Windham, Dr. Smyth, Mr. Penruddock, and Mr. Lansdown.

15. The churchwardens are always chosen in the Easter week, one by the minister, the other by the parishioners.

16. No public schools whatever, nor any such endowment, in this parish.

17. I constantly reside in the adjoining parish, and my house within a hundred yards of this parish.

18. [Blank]

19. [Blank]

20. [Blank][6]

189 STOURTON f.1568   D. Wylye

1. Twice, viz. at $\frac{1}{2}$ past 10 in the morning and $\frac{1}{2}$ past two in the evening.

2. Every day in Passion week, Monday and Tuesday in Easter and Whitsun week, and on Ascension day, St. Stephen's, St. John Evangelist, and Innocents.

3. As incumbent.

4. None.

5. On Christmas day, Easter Sunday, and Whitsunday, and on two Sundays after Trinity.

6. Usually forty.

7. [a] At least a hundred. [b] None. [c] A chapel.[7] [d] One died lately who had resided 15 or 16 years, but hitherto no successor. [e] A woman's school for children.

8. [a] Only two Presbyterians. [f] None.

9. [a] Constantly in Lent and sometimes on four or five Sundays after Trinity. [b] I do neither. [c] In their mother tongue.

10. [a] I have. [b] I do. [c] To 1574.

11. There is.

12. None.

13. [a] I have. [b] There has. [c] £16 per annum by the late Mrs. Hoare. [d] I believe by my predecessor.

14. None.

15. They are appointed in Easter week by the rector.

16. None.

17. I do constantly, and have done more than 28 years.

18. By the rector alone at his discretion.

[6] No signature. Curate, Mr. Williams. Probably Henry Williams, curate of Codford St. Mary, **51,** and Fisherton de la Mere, **85,** and resident at the former: see above, queries 4 and 17.

[7] The Catholic Lord Stourton had a chapel and a priest at Bonham House in the parish: V.C.H. Wilts. iii. 91.

19. None.
20. Stourton near Mere, Wilts.

Instituted to the living of Stourton in Feb. 1755; ord. D. and P. in May 1742; took my degree of M.A. July 1749.

Montagu Barton A.M.,[8] rector of Stourton

190 STRATFORD-SUB-CASTLE [Stratford] f.1576 SubD. Salisbury

1. Divine service is performed at ten o'clock in the morning and at two o'clock in the afternoon. Prayers only in the morning, prayers and a sermon in the afternoon.
2. There is no duty on weekdays but on Good Friday or when a festival falls on a weekday.
3. As curate under the dean and chapter.[9]
4. The curacy of Woodford,[1] two miles from Stratford.
5. The sacrament is administered at Christmas, Easter, and Whitsuntide.
6. Above 40; at my first administering, only 4.
7. No dissenter of any denomination.
8. The parishioners decently regular.
9. The children are catechized during Lent, and the parishioners have at the time the catechism expounded to them.
10. A register is regularly kept and due returns made; it goes back to the year 1689.
11. There is a register book of marriages duly kept.
12. No chapel of ease.
13. It is a curacy held under the church of Salisbury.
14. There is no charitable endowment whatever.
15. The churchwardens are chosen annually on Easter Monday by the parish.
16. There is no charity school.
17. I reside in Salisbury, two miles from my cure on which there is no house for residence.
18. None collected.
19. No other matter.
20. Salisbury.

J. Harington[2]

191 STRATTON ST. MARGARET f.1584 D. Cricklade

1. Once, at half an hour after one at the request of the parishioners. The reason is not only custom but necessity; the vicarage not being a sufficient

[8] 1717–90. King's Coll. Cambridge 1737.

[9] Clergy Books, 1783, give Canon William Bowles as curate and Dr. John Harington as sub-curate. William Bowles, 1736–1788. St. John's Coll. Oxford 1734. He inherited Heale House, Woodford in 1759 and entertained Dr. Johnson there in 1783: V.C.H. Wilts. vi. 224.

[1] A peculiar of the dean and chapter.

[2] 1732–95. Exeter Coll. Oxford 1749. Bishop's surrogate at the visitation: Sarum Dioc. R.O., Misc. Vis. Papers, 8. Member of the Committee of Correspondence of 1780: see above, p. 8, n. 25.

maintenance for a minister, the vicars have been obliged to serve a neighbouring church.

2. On Ash Wednesday and Good Friday; the parishioners being engaged in the business of husbandry do not attend the service of the church at other times.

3. As incumbent.

4. I do not at present.

5. Thrice, viz. Christmas day, Easter, and Whitsunday.

6. [a] Between twenty and thirty. [b] To the best of my remembrance about eighteen. [c] Less than usual.

7. I have the pleasure to inform your Lordship that we have none residing in the parish. There is no school for the education of papists, or popish priest residing in our parish according to the best of my knowledge. I make no doubt but that they have itinerant teachers, who are popish missionaries, who hold forth in their conventicle; having had accounts of strangers very fine teachers to perform amongst them.

8. [a] There are Anabaptists. [c] They have no settled teacher. [d] Their number is considerably less than formerly. They are (I am informed) deserted by their teachers. [e, f] Too many.

9. I have taken particular care of the catechizing our children. They are catechized two or three times every week. They are catechized in the vulgar tongue.

10. We have register books of baptisms and burials in good preservation. A copy of baptisms and burials are regularly transmitted yearly to the register's office. Our registers of burials and baptisms go back to the year 1653.

11. There is a register book duly kept according to the Act of Parliament against clandestine marriages.

12. We have no chapels of ease in our parish.

13. [a] I have a terrier of the houses, lands, tithes, and profits which belong to me as minister of the parish. [b] I cannot tell. [c] I am not informed.

14. Lands have been left for the repair of our church, about two or three acres in the common fields. I cannot learn the name of the benefactor.

15. One churchwarden by the minister and the other by the parishioners.

16. Out of a settled endowment of £3 a year charged on lands by a John Hering's last will and testament, whereof £2 10s. is appointed for the teaching of six children of either sex, and 10s. being part of the said £3 to be equally divided between four poor women if so many poor women attend to receive the sacrament, or poor men if so many on failure of the said women; what is very remarkable in the affair is the [? recte that] John Herring was a professed Anabaptist,[3] and the said children are to be instructed according to the forms of the Church of England. And is further seemingly a paradox, the poor women are to receive the holy sacrament on Christmas day at the parish church of Stratton St. Margaret.

17. I constantly reside upon this cure and in the house belonging to it.

18. There is no collection.

[3] John Herring's house in Stratton Green was licensed as a Baptist meeting house in 1709: V.C.H. Wilts. iii. 115.

19. I know not of any.

20. In the vicarage house of Stratton St. Margaret as aforesaid. The nearest post town is Swindon.

My Lord, may it please your Lordship, I hope that my answers to the above interrogations may give your Lordship satisfaction, they are according to the best of my knowledge and belief. I am in perfect sincerity and truth your Lordship's most obedient servant,

W. Goodinge.[4] Stratton St. Margaret, 25 July 1783

192 SUTTON BENGER f.1606   D. Malmesbury

1. Once a day, at the hour of *two* by *request of the parishioners* as being most convenient to them. Attempts have been made since I came to the living to bring them to church in the morning but without effect.

2. On Christmas day and Good Friday only.

3. By my curate[5] except at the festivals of Christmas, Easter, and Whitsuntide, when I attend in person for a fortnight each, and for some time in the long vacation.

4. I serve no other cure. My curate serves the cure of Little Summerford in the morning. The curate was ordained on my curacy and title.

5. At Christmas, Easter, Whitsuntide, and at Michaelmas regularly.

6. Generally not more than twelve. There is a disinclination or rather misgrounded apprehension of the danger of attending communion which I have not been able to remove.

7. Not a papist.

8. A few Quakers only, about seven in two families of low degree. No meeting in the parish nor is there any other meeting-house. Three or four of the families attend the Methodists at Christian Malford church etc. occasionally. [f] No complaint on the last head. [*Written across the foot of the page:*] The number of Methodists I believe are rather increased owing to a meeting-house established at Christian Malford by the Rev. Rowland Hill[6] and others where they have a variety of illiterate preachers, but the meeting seems greatly on the decline. Many of their followers seem to be regular well-meaning but mistaken people.

9. The season for catechizing is in Lent; few children attend but the girls of a little day-school.

10. The registers are tolerably regular to the [year] 1694. Very regular of late years.

11. There is.

12. No chapel of ease.

13. [a] There are two terriers but neither of them of any use as material alterations have since taken place in the parish. [c] There has, of a small estate at Brinkworth called Windmill farm of 12 acres.

14. [a] None. [d] A small plot called Church piece let annually by the vestry,

[4] Walinger Goodinge. University Coll. Oxford 1721.

[5] John Morgan: see **180.**

[6] The well known preacher and follower of Whitefield. For his work in Wiltshire see *V.C.H. Wilts.* iii. 131–4.

since I came to the living advanced thereby from 12s. to 23, and last year to 35s.; the money disposed of by the churchwardens, intended for ornamenting the church and which much wants it.

15. Regularly by the minister one and one by the parishioners.

16. No school but a small day-school for girls.

17. I reside at Pembroke College Oxford during term time as senior fellow, divinity reader, and tutor. [*Across the foot of the page:*] N.B. My curate was constantly resident in my parish till last March in lodging adjoining to the church, my own house being lately rebuilt and not yet finished. He was obliged to quit his lodging, the rooms he occupied being wanted by the family, nor was he able to procure others at that time. He now resides in the parsonage house of his other cure, 4 miles distant.

18. No collection.

19. A written account of the boundary of the parish; rural deans to inspect the state of the church.

20. Pembroke College Oxford. The curate at Little Sommerford.

Charles Davies A.M.,[7] fellow of Pembroke College Oxford. Ord. D. at London 3 March 1765. Ord. P. ditto 26 Dec. 1766. Instituted to Sutton 26 March 1774.

193 SUTTON MANDEVILLE f.1614   D. Chalke

1. Divine service twice every Lord's day, prayers and sermon at ten in the morning, prayers at three afternoon.

2. Divine service never known to be performed on any holiday or weekday except Easter and Whit Mondays and the day after Christmas.

3. As rector.

4. For some years have served the cure of Swallowcliffe at about two miles distance. The dean's peculiar, no curate ever known to have a licence.

5. Three times in the year only, at Christmas, Easter, and Whitsuntide.

6. The parish is but small, none but elderly people usually communicate, about ten last Easter. Medium number about eight.

7. No papist in the parish.

8. No Presbyterian, Independent, Anabaptist, or Quaker. Two or three reputed Methodists, but no place of worship. The very poorest sort are too apt to be absent from public worship.

9. Do catechize and expound to young persons, chiefly in Lent; have made some use of Dr. Clark's exposition.

10. Have a register book of births and burials duly kept; do regularly make returns; it goes back to the year 1658.

11. There is such a register duly kept.

12. No chapel of ease.

13. Have such a terrier. There are three or four in the bishop's registry of different dates; have a copy of one taken in Queen Ann's reign. No augmentation, nor diminution, in any respect; have not had health or time to take a new terrier; will make one, if necessary, as soon as possible.

[7] 1743–1827. Jesus Coll. Oxford 1762.

14. No free school, alms-house, or other charitable endowment. No lands or tenements left for the repair of the church.
15. Churchwardens chosen every year in the Easter week, by minister and parishioners together.
16. No public nor charity school.
17. Have constantly resided in the parish for upwards of forty-three years, in a house belonging to a small freehold estate of my own. Found a tenant at first in the parsonage house, and it has always been occupied by the several tenants since.
18. No money is ever given at the offertory.
19. I know of none.
20. Place of residence, Sutton Mandeville; nearest post town Hindon.

Henry Fricker[8]

Collated December 1738. Instituted January 1739. Ord. D. 1736. Ord. P. 1737. Degree, M.A. Formerly fellow of Wadham College Oxford.

194 SWINDON f.1622   D. Cricklade

1. Prayers and sermon at half hour after ten in the morning, and prayers at ½ hour after three o'clock in the afternoon.
2. Prayers on holidays or festivals on weekdays.
3. As assistant to the vicar.
4. The cure of Marston in the parish of Highworth[9] at the distance of three miles from Swindon. Not licensed to the cure.
5. Seven times, viz. on Christmas day and the Sunday following, on Easter day and Sunday following, on Whitsunday and Trinity Sunday, on the Sunday after Michaelmas.
6. Generally between 40 and 50 at Easter and at other times.
7. No papist in the parish.
8. No dissenters but many who commonly absent themselves from the public worship.
9. Catechized in the summer.
10. [a] Answer in the affirmative. [c] To the year 1640 inclusive.
11. There is.
12. No chapel of ease.
13. No proper terrier, but it is hoped that the terrier now preparing is such as desired.
14. A free school[1] of which the bishop of Sarum is visitor; and of which a full account is preparing for his Lordship.
15. Churchwardens regularly chosen one by the vicar, the other by the parishioners.
16. *Vide* the answer to query the 14th.
17. The vicar resides constantly upon the cure, and in the vicarage house.
18. Given by the vicar to the poor who do not receive payments from the parish, when the churchwardens are not qualified by the rubric to be consulted.

[8] Wadham Coll. Oxford 1729. Clergy Books, 1783, have the note '73 years of age'.
[9] A peculiar of the dean of Salisbury.
[1] Founded in 1764 in Newport Street: *V.C.H. Wilts.* ix. 160–1.

19. None recollected at present; when any shall occur your Lordship's assistance and authority shall be requested.
20. The vicar's assistant[2] resides in the parish of Swindon which is a post town.

Thomas Smyth D.D.[3]

[Inducted after institution by the bishop, 10 June 1758, *crossed out*.]
Instituted vicar of Swindon 2 June 1758. Ord. D. 5 June 1726, ord. P. 24 Sept. 1727.

195 TEFFONT EVIAS f.1630   D. Chalke
1. Divine service (i.e. prayers and preaching) is performed at ten by my brother.[4] And prayers are read by me in the afternoon at a quarter past three. Alternately I preach in the afternoon.
2. It has not been usual to perform service on the weekdays but on festivals.
3. As curate.[5]
4. I serve the cure of Fovant two miles distant, but have no licence.
5. The sacrament is administered at Easter, Whitsuntide, Michaelmas, and Christmas.
6. There are in general about a dozen, the number rather increased than not.
7. There are no papists in the parish.
8. There are no Presbyterians, Independents, Anabaptists, or Quakers in this parish.
9. I purpose catechizing the children etc. in Lent.
10. There is a register duly kept and proper returns made.
11. There is a register for marriages but not according to the Act, the parish being so small as to remove all apprehensions of clandestine marriages.
12. There is no chapel of ease in the parish.
13. There is a terrier of all houses, land, etc., bearing date 28 July 1703, a duplicate whereof is laid up in the bishop's registry.
14. There is no free school in the parish.
15. There is but one churchwarden who is chosen in Easter week by the minister and parish *jointly*.
16. There is no charity school in the parish.
17. My brother, the Rev. J. Evans, resides part of his time about two miles from it.
18. It has not been usual to give any money at the offertory.
19. Nothing to the best of my knowledge.
20. Salisbury.

James Evans.[6] E College Wadham Oxford. Student in Civil Law. Ord. D. 24 Sept. 1780. Ord. P. 27 Feb. 1782.

[2] William Jones, rector of Little Somerford, **180.**
[3] Probably St. John's Coll. Oxford 1722. Also rector of Codford St. Mary, **51,** served by a resident curate.
[4] John Evans, see **103.**
[5] Rector, John Bedwell. See Odstock, **153,** of which he was resident vicar.
[6] See **88.**

196 TILSHEAD [Tidulside] f.1638   D. Wylye

1. [a] Once a day, about one o'clock. [b] It being customary for time immemorial, owing to the fewness of inhabitants.
2. No, there being no hearers.
3. As curate. [7]
4. Yes, Chittern All Saints and Chittern St. Mary, 3 miles distance.
5. Four times, viz. on the three great festivals and Michaelmas.
6. About twenty-three in general.
7. None at all.
8. None of any denomination whatever.
9. No.
10. Yes, and regular returns made thereof into the registrar's office.
11. Yes.
12. No.
13. There is one preparing by the vicar.
14. None at all.
15. Yes, one by the parishioners and the other by the minister.
16. No.
17. No, but three miles off at Chittern All Saints.
18. None given.
19. Nothing at all.
20. Chittern All Saints. The nearest post town Heytesbury.

Thomas Davies, [8] clerk

197 NORTH TIDWORTH f.1646   D. Amesbury

1. Twice every other Sunday and once every other Sunday alternately; the sermon at 11 in the morning, and 3 in the afternoon in alternate orders as above.
2. None excepting Christmas day and the public festivals and fasts.
3. As curate. [9]
4. I serve Fyfield[1] near Weyhill, Hants, which rectory I reside on; it is 4 miles distant from North Tidworth.
5. At the 3 great festivals, Christmas, Easter, and Whitsuntide.
6. About 10. And the same number I believe last Easter.
7. [a] None. [d] None. [e] None.
8. [a] None of any sect in or near the parish! [b] None. [c] None. [e, f] None, but a very regular decent congregation.
9. The catechism is duly attended to; and there are several small schools where they are regularly instructed.
10. There is a register book regularly kept of births and burials. The oldest register remaining commences in the year 1700. A former one was lost, and destroyed about 30 years since by the parish clerk's children.

[7] Vicar, Lewis Jones.
[8] See **46.**
[9] Rector, Thomas Fountaine. (Wrongly given as John in Clergy Books, 1783). Trinity Coll. Cambridge 1757. Chaplain to George III and vicar of Old Windsor.
[1] Diocese of Winchester.

11. The marriage register prescribed by the Act of Parliament is duly kept.
12. [a] None. [f] None.
13. The terrier is sent in; there has been no alteration in the lands since the terriers were delivered in. The alterations in the buildings are specified.
14. There is an alms-house founded by Dr. Thomas Pierce, dean of Sarum in the year 1689, for 4 inhabitants in succession for ever.
15. Two churchwardens are chosen every year by the minister and parishioners jointly.
16. None.
17. I reside in the rectory of Fyfield aforesaid.
18. None given.
19. None.
20. Fyfield near Andover, Hants.

Henry White A.M.,[2] curate. Who constantly has served the cure since midsummer 1760, and resided there 3 years till he came to reside on his own rectory of Fyfield above mentioned.

Rev. Mr. Thomas Fountaine, the rector, attended the late visitation at Reading.

198 TISBURY f.1654   D. Chalke
1. Prayers and sermon between the hours of 10 and 12 o'clock in the morning, and prayers and sermon between 3 and 5 o'clock in the evening.
2. Prayers are read twice in the week during Lent, every day in Passion week, Easter Monday and Tuesday, Ascension day, Whit Monday and Tuesday, and also during the Christmas holidays.
3. As incumbent.
4. None.
5. Seven times, viz. on Christmas day and Sunday following, Easter Sunday and Sunday following, Whitsunday and Trinity Sunday, and at Michaelmas.
6. Between forty and fifty communicants. On Easter Sunday and Sunday following rather more than usual.
7. I believe there are upwards of two hundred papists in the parish. The only papist of consequence is Lord Arundell. There is a chapel in Lord Arundell's house where they assemble for divine worship.[3] Three popish priests, viz. Wheble, Forester, and Lewis. One popish school.
8. There are about forty Presbyterians in the parish, but none of any consequence. Their teacher's name is Morgan. There is also a Methodist chapel but no teacher in the parish. Both these meetings, I believe, are decreasing. Some of the lower class are remiss attendants on the public worship of God.
9. The children are catechized during Lent in the English language. I have made use of Wake's exposition of the catechism.

[2] 1734–88. Oriel Coll. Oxford 1749. Brother of the naturalist, Gilbert White of Selborne. Vicar of Upavon, **204,** served by the curate of Rushall, **170.**
[3] Wardour House, seat of Lord Arundell, was the biggest Catholic centre in Wiltshire. The chapel was built in 1776 and there was a regular succession of Jesuit chaplains: *V.C.H. Wilts.* iii. 92–3.

10. The register book of births and burials in good preservation. The church-wardens make a return of births and burials annually at the visitation. The register of births goes back to 1566, and of burials to 1689.
11. The register kept as the Act directs.
12. No chapel.
13. I believe it to be as good a terrier as can be made. It has been laid up in the bishop's registry. There has been no augmentation since.
14. No free school, alms-house, or hospital. No lands left for the repair of the church.
15. The churchwardens are chosen at Easter, the one by the vicar and the other by the parishioners.
16. Mrs. Coombes left £400 to the parish, the interest of which is to be applied for the instruction of poor children. There are now thirty poor boys and girls taught to read and instructed in the principles of the Christian religion.
17. Constant residence in the house belonging to the vicarage.
18. It has not been usual to collect any.
19. Nothing that I know of.
20. Tisbury, about 3 miles from Hindon.[4]

199 TIDCOMBE [Titcombe] f.1662   D. Marlborough
1. Once; at ten o'clock, morning, and at three, afternoon, alternately.
2. No.
3. As curate.[5]
4. Yes, Chute,[6] about four miles distant from Tidcombe. I am not licensed.
5. Four times, viz. Easter, Whitsunday, the Sunday after St. Michael, and Christmas.
6. About eight. There are generally more communicants at Easter than at other times. About twelve communicated last Easter.
7. None.
8. None.
9. Yes, of late they have, after being exhorted. I read lectures on the Church catechism and make use of Wake's exposition to those who are catechized. [c] During summer, and in the English language.
10. [a] Yes. [c] As far back as 1639.
11. Yes.
12. No.
13. [*Blank*]
14. No.
15. There is only one churchwarden, who is chosen annually by the parishioners.
16. No.
17. [*Blank*]
18. There is none given.

[4] No signature. Vicar, William Nicholson. Perhaps Queen's Coll. Oxford 1734.
[5] Perpetual curate, Thomas Baker. See Buttermere, **33,** of which he was rector.
[6] A peculiar of the dean of Salisbury.

19. I know of none.
20. Chute. Andover the nearest town.

John Gillmore,[7] curate

200 ST. THOMAS [SALISBURY][8] f.1670   SubD. Salisbury
1. Prayers at ten o'clock in the morning. Prayers and sermon at three in the afternoon.
2. Every Wednesday, Friday, and Saturday, and on all holidays.
3. As incumbent.
4. No other cure.
5. Every first Sunday in the month, and on Christmas day, Easter day, and Whitsunday.
6. One hundred upwards, and no variety in numbers has been observed for years past.
7. There are sixteen reputed papists in my parish, but no place where they assemble for public worship. No persons have been lately converted to popery as far as I know and believe. A popish priest does reside in my parish, his name is Turner.[9] No popish school in the parish.
8. There are twenty-one Quakers, forty-three Presbyterians. No other places made use of for divine worship, nor is there any other places where the above mentioned dissenters assemble. Their numbers have not increased according to my observation. The dissenting minister residing in my parish is Mr. Benjamin Williams.
9. It hath not been usual for the city clergy to catechize.
10. Yes.
11. Yes.
12. There are no chapels of ease.
13. There is no terrier.
14. None.
15. By the minster and vestry.
16. None.
17. I constantly reside, but there is no house for the minister.
18. By the minister and vestry unitedly.
19. No other matter.
20. Salisbury.

Arthur Dodwell M.A.[1] was nominated to the curacy of St. Thomas church by the dean and chapter on 21 Jan. 1774. Ord. D. 1 April 1767. Ord. P. 28 March 1769.

[7] Perhaps Brasenose Coll. Oxford 1773.
[8] This return has been bound in the wrong order, the page containing queries 15–20 before the pages containing queries 1–14.
[9] Richard Turner, S.J., chaplain to Mrs. Mary Arundell, widow of a son of Lord Arundell of Wardour, whose house in Rosemary Lane, off the Close, seems to have been the mass centre for Salisbury at the time: *V.C.H. Wilts.* vi. 156.
[1] Probably Magdalen Coll. Oxford 1760, and son of William Dodwell, archdeacon of Berks. 1763–85.

201 TOCKENHAM [Tokenham] f.1678[2]   D. Avebury

1. Whilst I was able to perform duty myself I regularly did my duty at Tokenham on Sunday mornings about eleven o'clock and for many years back at Lyneham about half an hour after one. I must refer your Lordship to my letter herewith sent.

2. None in either of the two churches, as I am well persuaded none would attend in either parish.

3. At Tokenham as rector, at Lyneham[3] as curate, being employed by the churchwardens, who have a sequestration.

4. I served Lyneham. The parish comes to my garden at Tokenham. The church is about a mile from me. I have no licence as it was not safe to take one when I last undertook the cure of Lyneham, occasioned by a lawsuit against the minister by one of the impropriators.

5. Three times a year in both parishes, at or near Easter, Whitsuntide, and Christmas.

6. At Tokenham I have but seven now that ever received the sacrament, at Lyneham ten or twelve. They are decreased at Tokenham but rather increased at Lyneham.

7. None in either parish.

8. In Tokenham none. In Lyneham a set whom we call Methodists.[4] They have lately built at Clack, in the parish of Lyneham, a neat chapel and a small neat house for their minister. His name was Young, but having lately failed in his trade in some branch of clothing he has now left it, and I do not hear that any other has yet succeeded him. He was occasionally assisted by others, particularly Mr. Hill. I think their number rather decreases and consist chiefly of the lowest class of people. They both baptize and bury. I believe the house is licensed.

9. I do not catechize the children at Tokenham, there not being six in the parish who can read of a proper age for that duty. At Lyneham there are more, but I think they are very well served by having service every Sunday and their children baptized and the dead buried for the trifling pay the minister receives for the duty.

10. Yes. The old register goes back as far as the year 1653, in Tokenham.

11. Yes, in both parishes.

12. None in either parish.

13. I refer your Lordship to my letter.

14. Answered in Q. 16.

15. The churchwardens in both parishes are annually chosen in Easter week. At Tokenham we have seldom more than one who is chosen by me. At Lyneham, one by the minister and the other by the parishioners.

16. At Tokenham none. At Lyneham a school was founded about 60 years ago by a Mr. Ralph Brome to teach not exceeding 30 poor children gratis of

---

[2] Letter missing.

[3] For the complicated history of Lyneham see *V.C.H. Wilts.* ix. 90–104.

[4] It seems likely that this in fact refers to the Providence Chapel of the Baptists, built in 1777: *V.C.H. Wilts.* ix. 103. A society of Whitefield's followers was founded at Lyneham in the 1740s, and the Mr. Hill referred to in the return is presumably Rowland Hill: ibid.

that parish, in reading, writing, and arithmetic and to instruct them in the principles of the Christian religion according to the Church of England. The sum given was £450. Great part of which was laid out in the purchase of lands by the then trustees. The remainder I lately paid to the earl of Radnor who is now the only trustee. The parish finds an house.

17. I have constantly resided at Tokenham in the house belonging to the living.

18. None ever given.

19. I refer your Lordship to my letter.

20. Tokenham near Wotton-Bassett, Wilts.

[*Letter on a separate sheet:*] My Lord, In answer to your Lordship's queries I have rather informed you how the duty of the parishes was done before my illness than how it is now done. But as your Lordship has a right to know that, I beg leave to acquaint you with the following particulars. In the month of June 1781 I was seized with a violent fit of illness which rendered me quite incapable of doing any duty. I applied to the Rev. Mr. Thomas, who lives at and serves the church of Hillmarten, and agreed with him to serve Lyneham for me till Michaelmas following. My church at Tokenham was supplied by my neighbouring clergymen. In the month of September I attempted to do my duty at Tokenham but found myself quite unable to the task, and then agreed with Mr. Thomas to serve both the churches which he has continued to do ever since, by serving Hillmarten and Tokenham alternately in the morning and afternoon and Lyneham which lays directly between the other two at about half after one, the hour I used to serve it as being most convenient for the parishioners. But I frequently do occasional duty in both parishes.

As to a terrier of Tokenham I have none, there are some in your Lordship's registry, though none of late date and by what I remember of them not explicit enough to be of any great use to the rector and I fear it is impossible to return a new one as my parishioners and myself could never agree on one. For in the year 1699 the owners of the lands thought proper to make an inclosure of the fields, which before were corn, without Act of Parliament, without faculty, and contrary to the consent of the then rector, took possession of the rector's lands in the common fields, and gave him what they thought proper in lieu thereof. The fields were soon laid down in grass and they pleaded a modus of 4*d.* a cow. So that the living by this means was very considerably reduced. Before the inclosure it was worth £160 per annum, when I came to it in 1744 it was let at £85, viz. glebe £40 and tithes £45. I made some little alteration in my tithes and so continued till about 12 years ago. I then considering the nature of the modus was determined to try its validity and gave notice to the tenants that I would take my tithes in kind. They applied to their landlord who lived in the parish and was possessed of full two-thirds of my little parish but he would not stand the contest, the tenants therefore agreed with me at an advance in tithes of about £20 per annum. This will explain to your Lordship why I think it impossible to make a new terrier as I will never consent to the validity of the inclosure, and the owners and occupiers of the lands will never do it without.

I have a copy of the terrier of the parish of Lyneham which was delivered in January 1704 from your Lordship's registry, which says the rights of the minister are founded by a decree of Chancery in Charles II's reign and are a salary of £13 per annum payable at Michaelmas by different sums from six different impropriators, the vicarage house, churchyard, and Easter offerings. And this is all the minister now receives or has received for 40 years past, the time I first did my duty there, though the rents of the parish are nearly £3,000 a year, and it contains about eight hundred souls. I am your Lordship's most obedient and very humble servant,

Algernon Frampton,[5] rector of Tokenham and minister of Lyneham.
13 Dec. 1783

202 TOLLARD ROYAL f.1684 D. Chalke

1. Divine service is performed twice every Lord's day and a sermon preached every morning of it. The hours eleven and three, sometimes sooner or later according to the season of the year.

2. Of custom no such thing hath been done, but preceding and subsequent to the great festivals I have done it.

3. As incumbent.

4. I do not.

5. Four times every year, Christmas, Easter, Whitsunday, and the first Sunday after Michaelmas.

6. This parish is but very small as to number of inhabitants and (excepting a distant small tithing of it which is very near to a neighbouring parish where they usually go to worship) contains but 42 dwellings or nearly so. They are regular people at communion and the number seldom varies very much; last Easter near 50 communicated.

7. [a] Not any. [c] Not any. [d] Not any. [e] Not any.

8. [a] Not any. [b, c, d] There is a small house which I am informed is licensed from the bishop's court at Sarum where a few meet to worship. They have no one appointed teacher but sometimes one person sometimes another comes once a week, whether licensed or not I do not know. They call themselves Methodists, appear to me to be peaceable well-disposed people, but few in number and near the same number as usual.

9. The parishioners, I flatter myself, teach their children their catechism and I have reason to think are in general careful in that respect. I take occasion sometimes after evening service in the summer months to expound to them myself.

10. There is a register book of births and burials kept. How far due returns have been made by the officers heretofore I do not know, but have directed the churchwardens to make regular returns yearly at the visitation to the registrar.

11. There is.

12. There are none.

[5] 1720–88. St. John's Coll. Cambridge 1737.

13. There is a terrier which was laid up in the bishop's registry about one hundred years since. Another will be made and sent to the registrar according to the directions given.

14. Not any.

15. The churchwardens are chosen every year on Easter Monday, one by the rector and the other by the parishioners.

16. There is not nor hath there been that I can learn any school founded in my parish.

17. I reside constantly in my parsonage house, occasional visits to my friends and relations only excepted.

18. It is customary in this parish for the communicants to dispose of their own money.

19. I know not of any.

20. I reside in the parsonage house in Tollard and the nearest post town is Shaftesbury. My address is: Tollard to be left at the Cashmore turnpike near Salisbury.

Henry Churly Manley LL.B.[6]

Ord. D. on 21 Sept. 1766. Ord. P. 25 Sept. 1768 and instituted to the rectory of Tollard Royal 12 Nov. 1770.

203 TROWBRIDGE f.1692   D. Potterne

1. At Trowbridge prayers and preaching at half past ten in the morning. The same at 2 o'clock in the afternoon, excepting once a fortnight when only morning service prayers at 4 o'clock, there being prayers and sermons at Staverton chapel that evening at 2 o'clock.

2. Prayers every Wednesday, Friday, and holidays [at Trowbridge *crossed out*].

3. As curate.[7]

4. The cure of Trowbridge only, to which licensed. [c] Yes.

5. Once in every month and also at Christmas, Easter, and Whitsuntide.

6. The usual number of communicants is between forty and fifty, as at Easter last.

7. None.

8. Many of various sects and ranks, viz. a Presbyterian meeting, Mr. Stephenson teacher; two Anabaptist meetings, Messrs. Waldron, Twining, and Rawlins teachers;[8] two Methodist meetings, Messrs. Clark and Raynor teachers; a Sandemanian meeting,[9] Mr. Spalden teacher; I cannot say whether or not these persons are licensed; the Methodists are rather increased according to my observation.

[6] St. John's Coll. Cambridge 1762. Bought the patronage with a Mr. Andrews of Gower Street, London, in 1787: Sarum Dioc. R.O., Diocese Book.

[7] Rector, John Ekins. See Newton Tony, **149**, of which he was resident rector.

[8] William Waldron, a clothier, and Thomas Twining of the Conigre chapel; Nathaniel Rawlings of Particular Baptist Back Street chapel: *V.C.H. Wilts.* vii. 157–9.

[9] The Sandemanians were a small Scottish sect, with few communities outside Scotland. They laid great stress on the sole efficiency of faith: *Oxford Dictionary of the Christian Church.*

9. No. The children of the free school are catechized on prayer days during Lent.

10. The charge and also the profits of the registers are given to the clerk by the rector and churchwardens.

11. Yes.

12. A chapel of ease at Staverton 2 miles from Trowbridge, where there is prayers and sermon once a fortnight in the evening, and the sacrament at Christmas, Easter, and Whitsuntide. No fund or estate is appropriated to it. [e] By the curate of Trowbridge. [f] None.

13. [*Blank*]

14. Two alms-houses; one (supported by endowment) for six widows who have no relief from the parish, and of which Richard Long Esq. of Steeple Ashton and Dr. Long are trustees. The other alms-house is supported by the parishioners for the relief of the parish poor and under the management of the churchwardens and overseers.

15. The churchwardens are chosen every year in the Easter week by the parishioners.

16. There is a free school supported by settled endowment for twenty boys and girls who are taught to write and read, and regularly instructed in the principles of the Christian religion according to the church liturgy.

17. I am constantly resident in the parsonage house and [seldom, *crossed out*] never absent from my curacy unless on particular business.

18. By the churchwardens for the use of the free school.

19. [*Blank*]

20. Trowbridge is both a market and post town.

Deacon's orders 3 May 1772. Priest's orders 25 Sept. 1774. M.A. degree 1 Aug. 1770.

Charles Hodgkin,[1] curate of Trowbridge

204 UPAVON [Uphaven] f.1700   D. Potterne

1. Once every Sunday as has been customary time immemorial.

2. Never but on Christmas day or public fasts or thanksgivings.

3. As curate.

4. Rushall church is served by the present minister, where he resides within $\frac{1}{2}$ a mile.

5. At the principal festivals, viz. Christmas, Easter, and Whitsuntide, and at Michaelmas.

6. In general about 20, only 17 at Easter.

7. None or any dissenting meeting within the parish.

8. Very few; one [or two or perhaps three at most, which, *crossed out*] did attend the meeting at Rushall aforesaid, but who now goes to church. A very decent and full congregation.

9. The catechism is duly attended to.

10. The register is duly kept, and begins from the year 1607.

11. There is a proper marriage register duly kept.

---

[1] Clergy Books, 1783, say he is 'about to remove'.

12. [a] None. [f] None.
13. There is a copy of terrier taken in the year 1704 from the bishop's registry in Sarum. No augmentation.
14. A small donation or charitable endowment for the poor; the writings are kept in the parish chest, 2 guineas per annum.
15. The churchwardens are chosen every year at a vestry by the parishioners.
16. None.
17. The present curate resides in the parsonage house of Rushall aforesaid.[2]
18. The money given to the offertory is distributed to the poor by the churchwardens.
19. None.
20. Answered above. Pewsey is the post town.

Henry White,[3] the vicar, resides on his rectory at Fyfield near Andover, Hants. Institution to Uphaven 2 Jan. 1760. Ord. D. 1759. Ord. P. 1760. By the then bishop of Sarum.

205 UPTON LOVELL f.1708   D. Wylye
1. My Lord, prayers and sermon in the morning at ten o'clock, and prayers at two in the afternoon.
2. Prayers constantly Monday and Tuesday after Christmas, Easter and Whitsunday, Ash Wednesday and Good Friday, and other festivals if a congregation assembles.
3. As incumbent.
4. No other.
5. Four times, Easter, Whitsuntide, Michaelmas, and Christmas.
6. My parish being small not many; sometimes eight, nine, or ten; Easter last, eight.
7. No reputed papist, none lately converted to popery, no place in which they assemble for divine worship but the Church of England; no popish priest in the parish, nor popish school.
8. Not any, my Lord. Absenters too common and too many, notwithstanding my endeavours to make them otherwise.
9. Children sent to be catechized during the Lent season, and I make a present to them of Dr. Synge's exposition of the Church catechism.[4]
10. Yes, a register of births and burials duly kept and in good preservation; a copy delivered out and sent to the registers office every visitation; goes as far back as to the year 1712.
11. Yes, my Lord.
12. None at all, my Lord.
13. My terrier is in the bishop's registry. I found no terrier nor have there been any augmentation made.
14. None at all, my Lord.
15. Every year in the Easter week, one by the minister and one by the parish.

[2] Rees Deer, curate of Rushall, **170.**
[3] See North Tidworth, **197,** of which he was curate. Both returns are in the same hand.
[4] Probably Edward Synge (1659–1741), archbishop of Tuam, who published a large number of religious tracts.

16. None at all, my Lord.
17. I reside constantly and in the parsonage house.
18. None given but what I give myself.
19. None, my Lord.
20. Upton Lovell near Heitesbury.

I was ord. D. in the chapel within the palace of Sarum the 23 Sept. 1753.
I was ord. P. in the chapel within the palace of Sarum 22 Sept. 1754. I was
instituted to the rectory of the parish church of Upton Lovell the 3 Oct. in the
year of our Lord 1755. My degree is M.A.

John Crouch,[5] rector of Upton Lovell, Wilts.

206 UPTON SCUDAMORE [Upton Skidmore] f.1716   D. Wylye
1. At half of an hour after ten in the morning, and at two o'clock in the
afternoon. A sermon in the morning.
2. No.
3. As incumbent.
4. No.
5. Four times in the year: at Christmas, Easter, Whitsuntide, and Michaelmas.
6. [a] Forty two. [b] About the number that usually communicate.
7. No papists. No chapelry. No popish priest or school.
8. One family that is Presbyterian. No Quaker. No meeting-house. No
persons who profess to disregard religion. No persons who commonly absent
themselves from all public worship of almighty God.
9. They do send their children. I make use of Wake's catechism. I catechize
in Lent.
10. [a] I have. [b] I do. [c] To the beginning of the reign of Charles I.
11. There is.
12. [a] No. [f] There was formerly a chapel in the parish. No remains of the
ruins.
13. I have a terrier of all lands. No augmentation.
14. [a] No. [d] There are about four acres of land which were left to the
church for repairing it before the Reformation. The churchwardens have the
management of it.
15. Yes, one by the minister, the other by the parishioners.
16. No.
17. Yes.
18. To the poor by the rector.
19. I do not know that there is.
20. Upton Scudamore near Warminster.

T. Owen M.A.[6]

I was instituted into the living of Upton Scudamore last November three
years. T. Owen.

[5] Wadham Coll. Oxford 1748.
[6] Thomas Owen, 1749–1812. Jesus Coll. Oxford 1767.

207 URCHFONT f.1724 D. Potterne

1. On every Lord's day prayers and sermon once at the church and once at the chapel at the hours of ten and three in the morning and afternoon, when the congregations are very full.

2. On the great holidays, such as Ash Wednesday, Good Friday, the Ascension, etc.

3. As incumbent sometimes but mostly by a curate,[7] my health being too weak and precarious to enable me to undertake the care of the parish without an assistant.

4. No.

5. At the three great festivals and the Sunday after Michaelmas, or as near as possible to those days, at the church and chapel.

6. Upwards of an hundred, and at Easter last many more.

7. No papists, but a very small meeting of Lady Huntingdon's Methodists, which I hear is licensed, and served by a preacher of the name of Sloper[8] from Devizes.

8. No dissenters that I know of, but too many I fear who wilfully and habitually absent themselves from the church and its ordinances.

9. They do not, I presume because there is yet no regular endowment or subscription for the education of poor children which I will immediately recommend and promote effectually, if it be possible in the parish.

10. There is a register of births and burials as far back as 1563, a copy of which is regularly returned to the registrar's office.

11. Yes.

12. There is a chapel at Stirt, about three miles from the mother church, to the minister of which there was a benefaction of £200 given by John Curll of Turleigh Esq. 1713; for one hundred nothing has been paid for many years, but I will endeavour to get it again if it be possible.

13. There is a terrier in the registry in which there is no account of the above benefaction; and there will be another made, according to your directions, as soon as some matters relative to the tithes, now in litigation, are thoroughly settled.

14. None.

15. Two chosen at Easter, the one by the vicar and the other by the inhabitants.

16. None.

17. Not in the parish but in the very next village, owing to the kind indulgence of the bishop, who was very well acquainted with particular situation and the convenience I had for a much more comfortable residence at Pottern before I was instituted to the vicarage of Urchfont.

18. There is no collection made.

19. None at present that I know of, but if any should happen you shall be properly acquainted with it by, my Lord, your most dutiful and obedient humble servant,

[7] Mr. Lewis.

[8] Probably Robert Sloper, one of the founders in 1777 of St. Mary's chapel, Devizes: *V.C.H. Wilts.* iii. 131 n. Note that the vicar includes the Methodists in his answer to the query about Catholics.

Henry Kent D.D.[9] and vicar of Urchfont near Devizes, Wilts.

20. [Blank]

The date of my deacon's orders 23 Feb. 1745. The date of my priest's orders 21 Dec. 1746. Institution to the vicarage of Urchfont 19 July 1780.

Pottern, 31 July 1783

208 SUTTON VENY [Veny Sutton] f.1732[1]   D. Wylye

1. Divine service is always performed twice every Lord's day; at half an hour after ten o'clock in the morning prayers begin, and at three o'clock prayers and a sermon, when there is always a full congregation.

2. Divine service is never performed in my church upon any weekday, except Good Friday when there is prayers and a sermon and Mondays in the Easter and Whitsun weeks.

3. I perform divine service as incumbent.

4. I serve the cure of Norton Bavant, which is distant one mile from my house. I never had a licence.

5. The holy sacrament of the Lord's Supper is administered in my church four times in the year, Easter day, Whitsunday, the first Sunday after the 29 September and Christmas day.

6. The number of communicants are about twenty which is as nearly the number that communicated at Easter last, and was neither greater nor less than usual.

7. There are no reputed papists, chapel, popish priest, nor school in my parish.

8. There are no Presbyterians, Independents, or Quakers in my parish. There are six Anabaptists and an Anabaptist chapel; it is distant two miles from my church and on that part of the parish which joins Longbridge Deverel. I know of none who profess to disregard religion, though there are some who very seldom come to church.

9. I always catechized the children and servants weekly in Lent ever since I had this living. I never made use of any printed exposition.

10. The register book of births and burials is duly kept, and in good preservation, and there is regularly made a return of births and burials into the registrar's office, as the canon requires. The register of births and burials goes back to 1653.

11. The register book is duly kept, according to the directions of the Act of Parliament against clandestine marriages.

12. There is no chapel of ease in my parish. There is no ruinated chapel in my parish.

13. I never had a perfect account or terrier of the houses, lands, tithes, and profits, which belong to me as minister of the parish, except what I have lately made and delivered to the registrar.

14. There is no free school, alms-house, hospital, or any other charitable endowment in my parish. There are three acres and one rood of lands for the

[9] Merton Coll. Oxford 1737. Member of the Committee of Correspondence of 1780: see above, p. 8, n. 25,
[1] Letter missing.

repair of the church; the churchwardens have the direction and management of them.

15. The churchwardens are chosen every year on Monday in the Easter week, one by the minister and the other by the parisioners.

16. There is no public or charity school in my parish.

17. I do constantly reside upon this cure and in the house belonging to it.

18. There is no money given at the offertory; the inhabitants of the parish are farmers at rack-rent.

19. I know of no other matter relating to my parish worthy of your Lordship's information.

20. Sutton Veny is the place of my residence, and Heytesbury is the nearest post town.

My deacon's orders are dated 18 Dec. 1774. My priest's orders are dated 22 Dec. 1776. Instituted to the rectory of Sutton Veny 12 April 1780.

Brouncker Thring B.A.[2]

209 WANBOROUGH f.1738   D. Cricklade

1. Divine service is performed twice a day, prayers and preaching in the morning and prayers only in the afternoon.

2. I generally read prayers on Wednesdays and Fridays preceding the sacrament Sundays.

3. As curate.

4. I serve no other curacy, nor am I licensed to the cure I do serve.

5. Five times, viz. on Christmas day, the Sunday before Lent, on Easter Sunday, on Whitsunday, and on the Sunday nearest to the 29 September.

6. Generally between twenty and thirty.

7. I neither know nor have heard of any papist in the parish and believe there are none.

8. Nor is there, that I can find out, a dissenter of any denomination in the parish.

9. Very seldom, although I have not failed frequently to remind them of their duty in this respect and have offered them every assistance in my power.

10. There is a register book of births and burials as far back as 1584; but the entries of both are so imperfectly made, except for these last fifteen years, that I much doubt whether they could be admitted as evidence in any court.

11. There is one, and duly kept as the statute directs.

12. Not any.

13. It does not appear there ever was one in this place.

14. Not any.[3]

15. The churchwardens are regularly chosen on the Tuesday in Easter week, one by the parishioners and the other by the vicar or his curate.

16. Not any.

[2] All Souls' Coll. Oxford 1771. M.A. from St. John's Coll. Cambridge 1792. See also Norton Bavant, **151,** where he acted as curate.

[3] But see *V.C.H. Wilts.* ix. 185–6.

17. I do not reside here at all but at Swindon about four miles distant. I am curate only. The Rev. Christopher Fox,[4] vicar, resides at Chiddeston near Basingstoke, Hampshire.
18. It is not customary to give any money at the offertory.
19. I do not recollect any.
20. Swindon, a post town.

J. Benet, curate, Wanborough

210 WARMINSTER f.1746 D. Wylye

1. Divine service is performed twice every Lord's day, both prayers and preaching in the forenoon at half an hour after ten, and in the afternoon at three o'clock at church.
2. Divine service is performed at the chapel, standing in the middle of the town, on Wednesday and Friday and all holidays during the week.
3. As curate.[5]
4. I serve no other cure but Warminster. I have no licence for the cure I serve.
5. The holy sacrament is administered on Christmas day, Easter, and Whitsunday, and usually the first Sunday in every month, at the church.
6. According to my observation, I cannot say particularly, from forty to sixty. I imagine nearly the latter number at Easter last; about as many as usual.
7. There is one papist, an apothecary. There have no persons I know of been converted to popery. The rest of these questions are answered in the negative.
8. There are two meeting-houses, one for Presbyterians, the other for Independents. There are some few Anabaptists, but I know not how many. One or two Quakers. There are no other places made use of for divine worship, except the two above-mentioned, by any sect. The names of their teachers are Fry and Andrews.[6] Whether their number is increased I am not able to certify, as I have been but five months in the parish. I have heard they rather decrease. I know of and hope there are none of my parishioners who disregard religion or absent themselves from the worship of God. Whether the teachers of the Presbyterians and Independents are duly licensed I cannot say.
9. The children come themselves, and are catechized during Lent, according to the custom of the parish, in English. I have as yet made use of no exposition, as I have not been through this service.
10. The two first questions are answered in the affirmative. Our register goes back as far as the year 1556.
11. Yes.
12. We have no chapel of ease,[7] neither any ruinated chapel.

[4] Perhaps Brasenose Coll. Oxford 1742.
[5] Vicar, Millington Massey. Also vicar of Kingston Deverill, for which there is no return: Clergy Books, 1783. St. John's Coll. Cambridge 1755. Chaplain to Lord Weymouth. Answers 13 and 15, in a different hand from the rest of the return, are perhaps in his handwriting.
[6] Nathaniel Andrews was minister of the Old or Presbyterian meeting; Fry presumably of the Independents: *V.C.H. Wilts.* viii. 125–6.
[7] The former chantry chapel of St. Lawrence was used as a chapel of ease: *V.C.H. Wilts.* viii. 117.

13. [a] None. [b] Ditto. [c] Ditto.
14. [a] A free school for 20 poor boys. Another for 20 poor girls. [b] The
1st founded by — Eyre Esq. the other by Mrs. Elisabeth and Mrs. Anne
Hiscock. [Trustees] proprietors of the Brickworth New Town estates and the
vicar for the time being. [c] Revenue of one £12 a year in land, and the interest
of £200, carefully preserved and employed. [Statutes] well observed. [d] None
lately.
15. Yes, one by the minister and the other by the parish.
16. None.
17. I reside at Romsey but a resident clergyman does the occasional duty. I
am engaged in a school at Romsey.
18. By the minister and churchwardens to charitable uses.
19. None that I know.
20. The vicar's, Ipswich, Suffolk. The curate's, Romsey, Hants.
    William Watson A.B., curate.[8] Ord. D. 21 Dec. 1759, and ord. P. 21 Dec.
1760.

215 WILCOT f.1794   D. Marlborough
1. Divine service, both prayers and preaching, is performed once on the
Lord's day, and evening prayers are read every other Lord's day from Easter
to Michaelmas. Morning service begins at half hour after ten o'clock and
evening service at two or three o'clock when there is a sermon, but between
five and six when there has been service in the morning. This has been the
accustomed duty.
2. Yes, Christmas day, and the day after, Good Friday, Easter Monday, and
Whit Monday.
3. As incumbent.
4. I serve the cures of Wilsford and Cheriton. The former is four miles, the
latter five miles, from hence. I am not licensed to either cure.
5. Four times, viz. Christmas, Easter, Whitsuntide, and Michaelmas.
6. The communicants are generally between twenty and thirty. There were at
Easter last about twenty.
7. There is no reputed papist living in this parish, nor do I know or believe
that any resort to it.
8. There are no Presbyterians, Independents, or Quakers in this parish.
There are six Anabaptists (including children) of the lower class. There is no
place, at this time, made use of for public worship except the church, from
which several of the parish commonly absent themselves.
9. My parishioners send their children and servants to be instructed, and
I catechize them in the English language once a fortnight in summer in time
of evening service, when there is no sermon, and expound to them with the
assistance of Lewis's catechism.
10. We have a *paper* register wherein I duly enter the baptisms and burials.
I have desired the churchwardens to provide one with *parchment* leaves.

[8] Perhaps Queen's Coll. Oxford 1755.

Returns of baptisms and burials into the registrar's office are regularly made. Our oldest register goes back as far as the year 1564.

11. Yes.

12. There is no chapel of ease nor ruinated chapel in this parish.

13. There is in the bishop's registry a terrier of the vicarage of Wilcot bearing date the 22 December 1704. The vicarage hath since been augmented by an estate purchased for £400, of which £200 was given by the governors of Queen Anne's Bounty, and £200 by Francis Wroughton Esq.[9] I believe no account of such augmentation hath been transmitted to the registry.

14. There is no charitable endowment in this parish. Nor have any lands been left for the repair of the church or for any other pious use.

15. The churchwardens are chosen every year by the parishioners, but I am informed that my predecessor, who was vicar upwards of sixteen years, did once choose a churchwarden during his incumbency.

16. There is no public or charity school in this parish. There is a little day school for boys and girls.

17. I reside constantly in the vicarage house.

18. This money is disposed of by myself to poor objects, oftentimes when they are sick and in the greatest distress.

19. I do not know of any.

20. Wilcot is my place of residence. Pewsey is the nearest post town.

T. Markes,[1] vicar

I have been admitted to the degree of M.A. in the university of Oxford. My deacon's orders are dated 23 Sept. 1764. My priest's orders are dated 22 June 1766. My institution to the vicarage of Wilcot is dated 21 May 1779.

216 WILSFORD [Willasford] f.1802   D. Potterne

1. Divine service is performed once on a Lord's day, and begins at one o'clock in the afternoon or half hour after, excepting sacrament days, when it begins at ten o'clock in the morning. Mr. Trickey's[2] answer to the latter part of this query is, 'custom and the smallness of the income'.

2. Only on Christmas day.

3. As curate.

4. I serve my own parish of Wilcot and the cure of Cheriton. Wilcot is 4 miles and Cheriton about two miles from Wilsford. The distance from Wilcot to Cheriton is 5 miles.

5. Four times, viz. at or near Christmas, Easter, and Whitsuntide, and Michaelmas.

6. The communicants generally are about 14 or 16. About 12 persons communicated last Easter.

7. There is no reputed papist in this parish, nor do I believe that any resort to it.

---

9 In 1722: Hodgson, p. 418.

1 Thomas Markes, 1741–1810. Christ Church Oxford 1758. See also **44, 216**.

2 Vicar, Richard Trickey. See Laverstock, **122,** of which he was perpetual curate; also of Winterbourne Earls, **220**.

8. There are no dissenters in this parish, nor is there any place made use of for public worship besides the church, from which several commonly absent themselves.

9. I have but lately *begun* to catechize the young persons of this parish in the English language.

10. [a] We have. [b] We do. [c] To 1588.

11. Yes.

12. There is no chapel of ease nor ruinated chapel in this parish.

13. Mr. Trickey informs me that no terrier can be found.

14. [a] No. [d] No.

15. The churchwardens are chosen yearly, in the Easter week by the parishioners.

16. There is no public or charity school in the parish. There is a day-school, kept by the clerk, who teaches boys and girls in the aisle of the church.

17. I reside on my living at Wilcot, which place is distant four miles from Wilsford.

18. It is not usual to collect any money at the offertory.

19. I do not know of any.

20. Wilcot is my place of residence. Pewsey is the nearest post town.

T. Markes,[3] curate

I was admitted to the degree of M.A. in Oxford 6 July 1770. My deacon's orders are dated 23 Sept. 1764. My priest's orders are dated 22 June 1766.

217 WILTON f.1810   D. Wilton

1. Twice a day; at eleven o'clock in the forenoon, prayers and a sermon; and at three o'clock in the afternoon, only prayers.

2. Divine service is performed in the church on holidays and festivals that happen on weekdays.

3. Only as curate of the parish.[4]

4. There is another church belonging to Wilton, about a mile and half distance.[5] Service betwixt twelve and one o'clock, prayers and a sermon. I have a licence.

5. Four times in the year, the Sunday before Christmas, Christmas day, Easter Sunday, and Whitsunday.

6. In general about forty, and about the same number last Easter.

7. There are two reputed papists in the parish, who are carpet-weavers. There are no persons lately perverted to popery. No place in the parish, or chapelry for them to assemble for divine worship. No popish priest resides in the parish or resorts to it. No popish school kept in the parish.

8. There are a great many Presbyterians and a few Quakers. There is a Presbyterian meeting. There is also a Methodist meeting of which sect there are a great number. I am unacquainted with the teachers of each sect, as they are not resident. The number, especially of the Methodists, increases. I believe

---

[3] See **215.**

[4] Rector, John Hawes. See Fugglestone, **91,** of which he was rector.

[5] Netherhampton chapel: Clergy Books, 1783.

there are none who openly profess to disregard religion, or absent themselves from all public worship of God.

9. The parishioners do not send their children or servants to be catechized. There are children from the free school who come in Lent, and they are catechized in the English language.

10. There is a register book of births and burials duly kept in good preservation and I believe returns are made of births and burials into the registrar's office. The register of births and burials goes as far back as the year 1578.

11. There is a register book duly kept, according to the directions of the Act of Parliament against clandestine marriages.

12. There are no chapels of ease in the parish.

13. As curate I am totally unacquainted with the terrier and tithes, nor can I give your Lordship any account of the living.

14. There is a free school in the parish for twenty boys; the founders were Walter Dyer and Richard Uphill. The governors or trustees are the mayor and corporation. The revenues about £100 per annum. They are carefully preserved and employed as they ought to be. The statutes and orders are well observed. I don't know of any lands or tenements left for the repairs of the church.

15. The churchwardens are chosen every year in the Easter week. One is chosen by the rector, the other by the parishioners.

16. There is a free school which is a charity school for twenty boys. It is supported by a settled endowment. The children are taught reading, writing, and arithmetic. There is great care taken to instruct them in the principles of the Christian religion, and to bring them regularly to church. They have a new coat, waistcoat, breeches, stockings and shoes, and a hat every year at Easter. When they leave school they have £5 to apprentice them. The school flourishes.

17. I reside constantly on my cure and in the parsonage house.

18. The money at the offertory is disposed of by the clerk of the parish to the sick and poor.

19. I know of no other matters relating to the parish of which I can give your Lordship any information.

20. Wilton is my place of residence, where we have letters from Salisbury three times a week.

J. Hewit,[6] curate of Wilton

I was ord. D. in the year 1757 and ord. P. 1758 and am M.A.

218 WINKFIELD [Wingfield] f.1818   D. Potterne

1. Divine service is performed in Winkfield church *once* every Lord's day, either in the morning or afternoon (at the usual hours of ten and three) alternately as has been the custom time immemorial, nor would it be practicable in so small a parish to assemble a competent number of inhabitants both parts of the day. The parish contains 35 houses and these widely dispersed.

[6] Possibly John Hewit, Pembroke Coll. Cambridge 1752.

2. Divine service is performed on Christmas day and Good Friday.

3. As incumbent.

4. The curacy of North Bradley, distant about two miles.

5. Four times, on the three great festivals and on some Lord's day about Michaelmas.

6. The number of communicants is usually about twenty. It was so last Easter.

7. There is no reputed papist etc. in my parish.

8. One of the churchwardens (William Couch, chosen by the parishioners) and his family are reputed dissenters. But it is not known that they attend any place of divine worship. The wife of the other churchwarden (John Rose) is reputed a dissenter but she regularly attends the public worship at church and has of late received the holy sacrament there according to the form by the Church prescribed. The number of persons who disregard religion and commonly absent themselves from all public worship of God bears too large a proportion to the whole parish. We have no separate meeting of any description.

9. It is not practicable in the present state of ignorance and irreligion to prevail upon parishioners to send their children and servants to be catechized and instructed by their minister, nor will those children or servants (very few excepted) who are of an age capable of receiving instruction attend their minister for that purpose. Attempts have been made to this end but without success.

10. The register book is duly kept and in good preservation. The register of births and marriages commences in the year 1654 and proceeds with great regularity from that time. That for burials commences in the year 1744. Returns are duly made as the canon requires.

11. The register book of marriages is kept as the Act of Parliament requires.

12. No chapel of ease in the parish of Winkfield.

13. I have a terrier handed down to me from my predecessors which I take to be a copy of one laid up in the bishop's registry. But I have not yet been able to obtain any certain information on that head. The transcript I have contains an account of the glebe lands belonging to the rectory of Winkfield.

14. No free school, alms-houses, etc. in the parish of Winkfield. [7]

15. The churchwardens are chosen every year in Easter week, one by the minister and the other by the parishioners.

16. There is no public school in the parish of Winkfield.

17. I reside constantly upon my cure, but not in the parsonage house, the same being (though in good repair) much too small and incommodious for the accommodation of my family; nor has it been the residence of an incumbent for sixty years last past.

18. The money given at the offertory is disposed of by the rector towards teaching 4 or 5 poor children to read and instructing them in the catechism.

19. Nothing of moment.

---

[7] Several charitable bequests are mentioned in *V.C.H. Wilts.* vii. 76.

20. The nearest post towns are Bradford and Trowbridge, distant each of them about 2 miles from Winkfield.

Edward Spencer[8]

Ordained by the bishop of Salisbury, deacon 19 Sept. 1762, priest 25 Sept. 1763. Instituted to the rectory of Winkfield 15 Aug. 1775.

219 WINTERBOURNE BASSETT f.1826   D. Avebury

1. Once every Sunday, between ten and eleven and two and three alternately, having the care of another church.
2. Very seldom.
3. As curate.[9]
4. Serve my vicarage of Clyffe-Pypard.
5. Three times, viz. Easter, Whitsuntide, and Christmas.
6. About 6; three at Easter last, sometimes a few more.
7. None, as I have heard of.
8. None, as I have heard of.
9. There never was any catechism.
10. We have one duly kept and in good preservation. Births and burials are regularly returned, and go as far back as 1661.
11. There is one.
12. There are none.
13. None as I know of.
14. None as I know of.
15. They are chosen one by the minister and the other by the parishioners.
16. None as I know of.
17. No, reside at Clyffe Pypard, adjoining parish, about two miles from church to church.
18. To the poor.
19. None as I can recollect at present.
20. Clyffe Pypard near Wotton Bassett.

Edward Goddard,[1] curate

220 WINTERBOURNE EARLS f.1834   D. Amesbury

1. Once every other Sunday sometimes at 11 o'clock in the morning and sometimes at 3 in the afternoon. The reason is custom and the stipend, it being only £10 per annum. Winterbourn Earls and Winterbourn Dansey are served alternate Sundays.
2. It is not.
3. As curate.[2]
4. I do, viz. Winterbourn Dansey, a quarter of a mile distant, and Laverstock, about two miles and a [quarter, *crossed out*] half.

---

[8] 1740–1819. St. Edmund Hall Oxford 1768. He bought the advowson when he became rector in 1775: *V.C.H. Wilts.* vii. 74. See also **24.**

[9] Rector, Dr. Joseph Chester. Magdalen Coll. Oxford 1759.

[1] See Clyffe Pypard, **50,** of which he was rector.

[2] i.e. perpetual curate.

5. Three times, viz. on Easter day, Whitsunday, and Christmas.
6. From ten to sixteen. I believe ten, and it was a less number than usual, at Easter.
7. There are none, neither is there any place for papists to assemble or any popish priest or school in the parish.
8. There are none of either denomination nor is there any place of divine worship for any sectaries whatsoever. I know of no persons who disregard religion or commonly absent themselves from public worship and I believe there are none of that character.
9. They do not, notwithstanding notice has occasionally been given for catechetical instruction.
10. There is, and the returns have been regularly made when called for. There are registers of baptisms and burials that go back to 1557. The last register goes back to 13 Jan. 1691.
11. There is.
12. [a] There are none. [f] We have none.
13. It is an impropriate parsonage.
14. There is none of either sort.
15. They are, by the minister and churchwardens [recte parishioners] together.
16. There is no public school or charity school.
17. I reside in the Close of Sarum, three miles and a half distant from the parish.
18. There is none given.
19. I know of none.
20. At Salisbury.
   I was ord. D. 24 Sept. 1749 and admitted a priest 17 June 1753.
                    Richard Trickey A.B.,[3] curate of Winterbourn Earls

221 WINTERBOURNE GUNNER f.1842   D. Amesbury
1. At half past ten in the morning and half past two or three in the afternoon.
2. On saints' and holidays.
3. As rector.
4. No.
5. At Easter, Whitsuntide, Michaelmas, and Christmas.
6. Nine, or ten.
7. None that I know of.
8. There are no dissenters from the church, but a few Methodists.
9. Yes, in Lent, they are catechized in English.
10. Yes.
11. Yes.
12. No.
13. Yes.
14. No.
15. Yes according to law.

[3] See **122, 216.**

16. There is a school for children but not endowed.
17. I reside.
18. There is none given.
19. Nothing wanting but a pair of stocks, or a pillory, and a table of the clerk and sexton's fees, and the trees which darken the church to be felled.
20. Winterbourn Cherborough,[4] Wilts. Salisbury.

Collated 8 Oct. inducted 23, 1768. Ord. D. by Thomas Cantuar 24 Sept. 1758. Ord. P. by Richard Peterborough 2 March 1760.

Charles Coleman A.M.[5] or by diploma LL.D. in both universities. Obtained by Dr. Lowth, then lord bishop of Oxford.

222 WINTERBOURNE MONKTON f.1852   D. Avebury

1. The answer to this question the same as that which respects the performance of divine service in the church of Avebury to which it is united, viz. once every Lord's day alternately with the other united church.
2. Prayers on weekdays after the three principal festivals, as also on some other holidays.
3. I perform divine service as incumbent of this and the other united church of Avebury.
4. I serve no other church but the united church of Avebury above mentioned.
5. The holy sacrament is administered in this church 4 times in the year, viz. Christmas, Easter, Whitsuntide, or the Sunday next after those festivals, according to the alternate service with Avebury happens, as also on the nearest Sunday to the feast of St. Michael, either before or after.
6. This parish being very small, and the number of inhabitants few, the number of communicants is consequently few, not often exceeding ten, which was nearly the number at Easter last, and has been nearly the same for some years past; though I am sorry to say that there ought to be many more, who are deterred from communicating under a notion that they thereby bind themselves to lead a better and more Christian life than they are otherwise obliged to do, under a heavier and more severe punishment hereafter.
7. There are no reputed papists in this parish, none lately perverted to popery, no place where papists assemble for divine worship, no popish priest, no popish school in this parish.
8. There are no Presbyterians, Independents, Anabaptists, Quakers, or any other sectarists in this parish, none who profess to disregard religion, yet too many who absent themselves from the public worship of God under a pretence that they have no clothes in which they can appear with decency or that they have trifling avocations, which are far from being justifiable.
9. There being no school in this parish, and the number of children so few— as they are at the same time so poor, so badly clothed, and obliged to work for their bread so young—I have not been able of late to cause any of them to come before me for instruction, but hope soon to put some of them under the care of the schoolmaster at Avebury.

[4] *Alias* Winterbourne Gunner.
[5] Perhaps Trinity Coll. Oxford 1754.

10. A register book of births and burials is regularly kept, and returns duly made at the visitation, but the copy not always signed as it ought to be; to guard against which inattention in churchwardens the bishop's register should reject them unless properly authenticated, though I conceive that church-wardens in general entertain a notion that such copies never reach the registry.
11. A register book according to the directions of the Act of Parliament against clandestine marriages is duly kept.
12. There are no chapels of ease in this parish.
13. As one churchwarden only was chosen by me in this parish, and as he died in his office, no terrier of house, land, etc. belonging to me as minister of this parish can be at this time exhibited, but will be transmitted to your Lordship's registry as soon as the same can be properly authenticated.
14. There is no free school, no alms-house, no hospital, or any other endow-ment of that sort in this parish; no lands or tenements left for the repair of the church or any other pious use.
15. One churchwarden only was chosen in this parish last year, by the minister, who dying in the year, the office devolved on his successor in the principal farm, the rest of the owners and occupiers thinking themselves so far beneath him that they presume not to act with him; his word being in all points a law, must alone take the oath at the ensuing visitation.
16. There is no public school or charity school of any sort in this parish.
17. I have, by the indulgence of my diocesans (which indulgence I now humbly pray for a continuance of from your Lordship), resided for some years past in the town of Calne, distant 7 measured miles from Avebury, for the reasons given your Lordship in answer to your Lordship's queries respecting my residence there.
18. The money given at the offertory, the greatest part of which must come out of the poor incumbent's pocket, disposed of by me to the aged poor and needy, particular regard being had to those who frequent the communion, not absolutely excluding the sick, at the same time, who appear to be in great distress though perhaps they may not have been communicants, especially if they are disposed to become such during their illness.
19. If any other matter relating to this parish should hereafter occur, of which it may be proper to give your Lordship information, the opportunity and encouragement intimated to me in this quere, of communicating the same to your Lordship from time to time, and in due time, will be thought an honour by, my Lord, your Lordship's most dutiful and most faithful servant, James Mayo,[6] vicar of the united churches of Winterbourne Monckton and Avebury.
20. Calne, a post town between Marlborough and Chippenham, Wilts.

223 WINTERBOURNE STOKE f.1860   D. Wylye
1. At eleven in the morning and one in the afternoon alternately, as has been usual.
2. None have been usual.

---

6 See **9.**

3. As curate. [7]
4. Orcheston St. George is served with this cure, about 3 miles distant.
5. Four times, Christmas, Easter, Whitsuntide, and Michaelmas.
6. One time with another about 20 communicate.
7. No papists or chapelry.
8. No Presbyterians, Independents, Anabaptists, nor Quakers.
9. All that can read can say their catechism.
10. Yes.
11. Yes.
12. None.
13. Am only curate.
14. None.
15. I believe so.
16. None.
17. Reside about three miles from it.
18. None collected.
19. None.
20. Orcheston St. George, near Amesbury. [8]

224 WINTERSLOW f.1868   D. Amesbury
1. Twice, viz. at eleven in the forenoon and at $\frac{1}{2}$ past two in the afternoon.
2. On Good Friday only, when a few poor people attend to share among them 4 shillings' worth of bread, which was bequeathed for the sacrament that day.
3. As incumbent.
4. I serve no other cure.
5. Five times, viz. on Christmas day, Good Friday, Easter day, Whitsunday (if it be not the monthly meeting of the parish, and in that case the H.S. is deferred to Trinity Sunday), and on some Sunday near about Michaelmas.
6. [a] From twenty to thirty. [b] Six or seven and twenty.
7. No.
8. [a] There is one family of Anabaptists. But the young folks of it come to church. I have no other dissenters, and no meeting-house. [e, f] Upon the whole my church is very well attended; and it has been observed by strangers that no congregation ever behaved with greater decency.
9. There is a bequest of 6s. 8d. to the clerk yearly for teaching the children their catechism and of 5s. for him to divide among those who come to learn. This has made the parishioners less attentive to this duty. There are however a good many children attend. I hear them myself. I have formerly read lectures of my own compiling, but I have used Archbishop Secker's ever since they have been published. Sometimes I have used them as lectures, and sometimes preached them as sermons. Our season for catechizing is some weeks in the summer months.
10. [a, b] I have been always very attentive to my register book. I believe the returns have always been regularly made. [c] To the year 1598.

---

[7] Vicar, Neville Wells. See West Grimstead, **94**, of which he was rector.
[8] No signature. Curate, Thomas Grove. See Orcheston St. George, **154**, of which he was rector.

11. Yes.
12. No.
13. I have the copy of a terrier dated 27 Dec. 1677 from the bishop's registry. There hath been no augmentation (properly so called) of the living since, but it has been much improved as to the glebe, and is still improving at my expense. I hope it will be completed within these 12 months. As soon as it is I shall be happy to deliver in a new terrier, if it can be done without subjecting me to disputes with the parish.
14. Our charities etc. are, 50s. a year issuing from an estate (of which as rector of W. I have the letting) at Alderbury given in 1715 by the then rector for the following purposes, to the clerk 6s. 8d for catechizing the children, 5s. for him to divide among the children, and 3s. 4d. for him to buy bread on Good Friday, and £1 15s. for the rector to divide among the widows and fatherless. 8d. per annum is paid out of an estate, to be added to the 3s. 4d. I have in my hands £100 at 5 per cent, which £5 the overseers dispose of as they think fit. In 1724 £20 per annum was left to be divided between a poor man and a poor woman of Middle Winterslow. The lord of the manor of West Winterslow and St. John's Oxford are trustees for the estates: and the president of that college etc. with the rector of Winterslow appoint the man and woman. There is land to the yearly value of £8 in the parish. It was allotted to the poor in lieu of common. They receive the rent, divide it among them, and of course no one is the better for it, for it does not amount to 1s. 6d. to a family.
15. Yes.
16. There is no foundation school. There is a decent man gets a small livelihood by teaching to read and write.
17. I think myself justified in saying *constantly*. I have been rector 16 years. I had no house. I bought one (the nearest to the church) where I spent most of my time. I built a new house. I have lived in it these 8 years. I have never been absent more than a month at a time, and that was but once, and for the benefit of sea bathing. I have business which calls me to London sometimes, but I am seldom absent a fortnight together.
18. There is no money ever given at the offertory.
19. I do not recollect any.
20. Winterslow. Salisbury on the west and Andover on the east.

I was ord. D. at Oxford, by the bishop of that see on 18 Jan. 1767. The bishop of Salisbury gave me priest's orders on the 21 June following, and instituted me to the living the 22, and I was inducted the 24.

Peter Bellinger Brodie A.M.,[9] rector of Winterslow and chaplain to Lord Holland and Holland.[1]

225 WISHFORD f.1876   D. Wylye
1. Divine service is performed twice every Lord's day at the hours of eleven and three.

[9] 1743–1804. Worcester Coll. Oxford 1765.
[1] Of Winterslow House; grandson of Caroline Fox, created Baroness Holland 1762, and of Henry Fox, created Baron Holland of Foxley 1763.

2. Divine service is performed Christmas day, Good Friday, Easter Monday and Tuesday, and on Whit Monday.

3. As incumbent.

4. Burcombe chapel is served by me every other Sunday at one o'clock. The distance is about three miles.

5. The holy sacrament is administered four times in the year, at Easter, Whitsuntide, Michaelmas, and Christmas.

6. About twenty communicants.

7. No papists.

8. None.

9. The children are catechized in the English language.

10. The register book of births and burials is duly kept, and returns regularly made. The register goes back to 1653.

11. A register book is duly kept.

12. No chapel of ease.

13. There is a true and perfect terrier and a duplicate thereof laid up in the bishop's registry. No augmentation since.

14. There is a free school for twenty boys and twenty girls. Sir Richard Howe was the founder, but I do not know that there are any governors or trustees. Lord Chedworth[2] presides over it. There is an alms-house for four persons and a tender. There is two or three estates left for the support of it, amounting yearly to about £37. Lord Chedworth at present is the only trustee and nominates persons to the alms-house. Sir Richard Grobham of Great Wishford was the founder in 1628 and his will is in the Pregogative Court of Canterbury. [*Continues at the top of the next page and down the left hand margin:*] The alms-house is properly filled, and Lord Chedworth appoints to it as heir to the manor of Great Wishford. But it may be proper to remark that there were six or more trustees, and was the manor to be sold at any time and improper people put into the alms-house, it might be worth enquiry whether more trustees ought not to be appointed. Unfortunately there is in Sir Grobham's will no rules laid down for the appointment of persons to the alms-house. [*Continues in left hand margin of previous page:*] There was a charitable endowment left by Mr. Daniel Hand about the year 1735 for placing out boys. The revenue about £12 per annum. For the proper disposal of this charity we have his will, and the revenue is employed as it ought to be. [*Continues in the left hand margin of next page:*] There is also land, called Midsummer, and £10 per annum paid out of an estate at Stapleford for the repairs of the church. There is in hand £80.

15. Churchwardens are chosen every year, one by the minister, the other by the parishioners.

16. The children are instructed in the principles of the Christian religion.

17. Constantly resident.

18. No money collected.

---

[2] The Wishford estates of Sir Richard Grubham Howe Bt. (d. 1730) passed to his cousin, the 1st Lord Chedworth. The baronetcy passed to another cousin. John Howe, the first baronet (created 1660) was the son of John Howe and Jane, sister of Sir Richard Grubham of Wishford, who died *c*. 1675: *Complete Peerage;* and G.E.C. *Baronetage*, iii. 123.

19. There is no matter relating to the parish which it is necessary to give your Lordship information of.
20. Wishford, Sarum.

James Birch,[3] rector of Wishford
Instituted to Wishford 1774. Ord. D. 1764. Ord. P. 1770. Degree B.D.

226 WOODBOROUGH f.1884 D. Avebury
1. Divine service with a sermon is regularly performed every Sunday, morning and evening alternately, and during the summer months when service is in the morning, prayers are then read in the afternoon.
2. On some of the holidays at the time of the great festivals.
3. As rector.
4. The curacy of Patney at about three miles distant.
5. Four times, viz. Christmas, Easter, Whitsuntide, and about Michaelmas.
6. About thirty.
7. None.
8. [a] None. [e, f] Am sorry to say too many.
9. Those children that are ever taught to read are always taught their catechism.
10. [a, b] Yes. [c] To the year 1567.
11. Yes.
12. None.
13. No.
14. [a] None. [d] Some lands the rents of which are applied by the church-wardens to the repairs of the church.
15. Yes, one by the rector and the other by the parishioners.
16. None.
17. Have been constantly resident in the parsonage house ever since my institution in the year 1764.
18. No offertory.
19. Nothing at present.
20. Woodborough near Devizes, Wilts.

George Gibbes D.D.[4]
Ord. D. in the year 1763. Ord. P. in the year 1764 and in the same year instituted into the rectory of Woodborough.

227 WOOTTON BASSETT f.1900 D. Avebury
1. Divine service is performed twice every Lord's day, at 11 in the morning and between 3 and 4 in the afternoon, in winter soon after 3, in summer about 4 o'clock.
2. Yes, on Wednesdays and Fridays and holidays the year through.
3. As vicar.
4. No.
5. Eight times, twice at Christmas, once on the 1st Sunday in Lent, twice at

[3] See **32.**
[4] 1741–1813. Trinity Coll. Oxford 1757. Son of Charles Gibbes, vicar of the Chitternes, **46** and **47,** and curate of Marden, **138.** See also **156.**

Easter, twice at Whitsuntide, and once on the 1st Sunday after Michaelmas.
6. Between 60 and 70; and not less than usual.
7. A popish family, four in number, live in this parish on an estate of near
£100 per annum. I do not know that they use any endeavours to make
converts. They have no chapel unless within their own house. No popish
priest resides within this parish. A Mr. Smith who lives with a Mr. Arundel
near Chippenham, Wilts., visits occasionally the said family. No popish
school is kept in my parish.
8. [a-d] There are no persons in my parish who profess themselves Presbyterians, Independents, Anabaptists, or Quakers. A Rev. Mr. Hill has some years
since built a meeting-house here, where he and some others, have done duty
in their way; the followers are few. I have been lately told that the meeting-
house is to be let for a cottage, the preachers' attendance having been
discontinued for some time. [e, f] Yes. The body corporate seldom come to
church unless to *qualify* themselves for their respective offices in the corporation. The present mayor indeed is an exception to their general behaviour.
He and 3 or 4 others are not ashamed to be seen at church and behave with
decency suitable to their station.
9. Yes, in Lent or later in the year when the days are longer, and I make use
of Archbishop Secker's or some other exposition for the occasion.
10. Yes, and regularly make returns of births and burials into the registrar's
office. The register (with a few breaks) goes back to the year 1592.
11. Yes.
12. No.
13. In 1704 a terrier of all the houses, lands, and tithes which belong to this
vicarage has been laid up in the bishop's registry. No augmentation hath been
made to this vicarage.
14. There is a free school for teaching 18 poor boys of the borough of
Wootton Bassett. Richard Jones Esq. of Stowey juxta Chew Magna in the
county of Somerset was the founder. Lewis Long Esq., alderman of this
borough, and the Rev. Algernon Frampton, rector of Tockenham, are the
trustees. The lands belonging to the said school lie at Haydon and Haydon
Wick in the parish of Rodbourn Cheney in the county of Wilts. and are let
for £—. [1696 *is written in the margin, more or less level with the name of the
founder.*]
15. The churchwardens are chosen every year in the Easter week, one by the
minister, the other by the parishioners.
16. 18 poor girls are taught the principles of the Christian religion, writing,
and the 4 first rules of arithmetic, and to work with the needle by a voluntary
benefaction of £12 annually, given by the earl and countess of Clarendon.
17. I constantly reside upon this cure and in the house belonging to it.
18. To the poor at the discretion of the vicar.
19. In 1774 Humphrey Stanley married Mary Selwood; soon after, the said
Humphrey was transported for 14 years. No intelligence whatever having
been received of or from the said Humphrey for upwards of seven years the
said Mary wishes to know if she is at liberty to marry another. Your Lordship's directions shall be obeyed by your Lordship's most dutiful,

Timothy Meredith A.M.[5] Admitted deacon 1751. Priest 1752. Instituted 1772.
20. Wootton Bassett, Wilts.

228 WOOTTON RIVERS f.1906   D. Marlborough

1. I perform divine service on the Lord's day, morning and afternoon at half past ten and half hour past three.
2. I perform divine service on weekdays on the day immediately following the great festivals and on fast days only, and always to a very small congregation.
3. As rector.
4. I serve no other cure.
5. I administer the holy sacrament four times in the year, viz. on the three great festivals and on the Sunday after Michaelmas.
6. There are generally near thirty communicants and at Easter about forty; as well as I can recollect there was upwards of that number last Easter. The number seems to have increased since religious tracts have been distributed amongst my parishioners.
7. There is not a reputed papist in my parish.
8. Or dissenter. There are a few persons amongst the poorest sort who very seldom come to church. The reason they commonly allege is the want of decent apparel.
9. No children ever catechized before I came to reside. I generally catechize in Lent when a few children only attend and those by encouragement from me. I have not hitherto made use of any exposition but intend to do it in future.
10. There is a register book in vellum where I enter births and burials but I have made no returns of them into the registrar's office nor has the custom been observed for many years, but I purpose doing in future.
11. There is a register book duly kept, according to the directions of the Act of Parliament against clandestine marriages.
12. There is no chapel of ease in my parish.
13. I have at present no terrier of the lands etc. belonging to the rectory but I will endeavour to get one made with all convenient speed and will remit a copy to the registry according to the directions. No augmentation hath been made of the living except a pension of £20 per annum for my life only from Brasenose College.
14. There is no free school, alms-house, hospital, or charitable endowment except £10 for apprenticing of boys belonging to this and several other manors which were left by Sarah, duchess of Somerset, for charitable uses. She was foundress of Froxfield alms-house for fifty widows. She likewise endowed Brasen-nose College Oxford and St. John's Cambridge with scholarships and left the rectory of Wootton Rivers to be presented to alternately by those colleges to one of her scholars.[6]
15. The churchwardens are chosen every year in the Easter week, one by the minister, the other by the parishioners.

[5] 1727–93. Christ Church Oxford 1748.
[6] Mr. Mayo was presented by Brasenose: Sarum Dioc. R.O., Diocese Book.

16. There is no public or charity school in my parish, only a few children are put to school by myself and some by Mrs. Ernle, sister to Sir Edward Ernle who resides at Brimslade Park (now disparked) which is extra-parochial and adjoining to my parish. Besides Brimslade Park there is a tract of ground called the Great Park, containing about ten farms belonging to Lord Ayles-bury. It is divided into two districts each of which takes care of its own poor. Those belonging to the north district generally to the Marlborough churches, and those of the south to Wootton Rivers.

17. I was presented to my living in the year 1768, came to reside in 1770, have not been absent from it for a fortnight together ever since except once for a month on a visit to my relations, and reside in the parsonage house.

18. No collection was made till I came to reside. What is now collected I distribute to the poor present and to others whom I deem proper objects.

19. Nothing that I know of.

20. Wootton Rivers near Pewsey, Wilts.

I, William Mayo M.A.,[7] was ord. D. on 21 May 1749 and ord. P. on 10 June 1750. Was instituted into the rectory of Wootton Rivers on 11 May 1768.

229 NORTH WRAXALL f.1914   D. Malmesbury

1. The parish of North Wraxall very extensive and the inhabitants at least a mile and three quarters from the church, they cannot conveniently come to church but once a day. Consequently the service is one Sunday in the morning and the other in the afternoon.

2. On Good Friday and Ash Wednesday.

3. As incumbent.

4. Leighdalamere, about four miles distant.

5. Four times, Christmas, Easter, Midsummer, and Michaelmas.

6. Five generally.

7. None.

8. None.

9. The inhabitants are mostly farmers and send their servants as often as they can conveniently. I instruct them in the catechism during Lent.

10. Our register book is regularly kept.

11. The marriage register book is according to the Act of Parliament.

12. No chapel of ease.

13. Some years since there were some lands exchanged which are set forth in the terrier which is now delivered in. A copy of which is deposited in the church chest.

14. There is no charitable endowment whatever, nor lands left for the repair of the church.

15. The churchwardens are chosen every Easter week, one by the rector, the other by the parish.

16. There is no school in the parish.

17. I constantly reside in the parsonage house.

18. To the second poor.

[7] 1726–1800. Brasenose Coll. Oxford 1742.

19. None.
20. North Wraxall in the county of Wilts. Marshfield is the nearest post town. I was instituted to the above rectory 20 April 1761. My degree is A.M. [8]

230 WYLYE f.1922 D. Wylye
1. Prayers in the morning at ½ an hour after ten, and in afternoon prayers and sermon at 3 o'clock and at ½ an hour after 2 for three or four months when the days are short.
2. On Wednesdays and Fridays and on all holidays and on some twice with the addition of an homily.
3. As curate. [9]
4. No. I have a licence from Bishop Gilbert to Tidworth. [1]
5. Six times, at the beginning of Lent, Easter, Whitsuntide, first Sunday in August, Michaelmas, and Christmas.
6. Too, too variable. At Easter last, somewhat more than 40; at Whitsuntide more than 50. I have had near or quite 60.
7. I know of none such.
8. [a] I know of none such. [e, f] Many by no means regard religion as they ought, nor come to church by any means as they ought.
9. Tolerably, but room for amendment, I suppose. I did for years expound Lewis's catechism, and some of the children learnt it, till my health forced me to leave it off. And I have in my time twice preached a course of sermons on the catechism. [c] In English, every Wednesdays and Fridays and holidays in general, when any number of children to say the catechism, but I was forced some time back on account of my health to omit catechizing on Sundays, but have lately revived it and hope under God to keep on with it.
10. [b] I believe I never omitted giving or tendering one every year to a churchwarden for the almost three and twenty years last past. [c] To 1653.
11. Yes.
12. [a] None at all. [f] None.
13. This belongs, I apprehend, to the rector; but I have been aiding herein with the minister's churchwarden, Christopher Fricker, since I received your Lordship's queries.
14. There is but one charitable endowment in this parish and is as follows: Mr. Willoughby left £8 a year payable by the mayor and corporation of Marlborough, £6 equally to two aged persons, £1 to the minister for a yearly sermon etc., and 10s. to the churchwardens and the same to the clerk. The deed of gift is kept by me with the book respecting the payments and elections. Upon the decay of the old one there has been a new frame hung up in the church setting forth the heads of the charity. And all things with respect to it have been regularly performed during my care of the parish except that I find a difficulty to make the poor wear the badge on their [*continues down the left hand margin*] sleeve, as ordered, though I often reprove them for not doing it,

[8] No signature. Rector, Henry Still, 1731–1804. Oriel Coll. Oxford 1749. See also **159**.
[9] Rector, John Dampier. Merton Coll. Oxford 1769: see above, p. 13.
[1] Presumably he was curate of North Tidworth, **197**, before Henry White, who became curate there in 1760, the date when Eyre became curate of Wylye: see below, query 17.

and tell them that they are liable according to the deed to lose the gift by not wearing it, and I have had a thought sometimes of depriving them of it and electing others to receive it; but as the gift is so small that they who enjoy it would have as much from the parish, if they had not that, perhaps there would be nothing got by so doing; the new elected ones would perhaps be as negligent in wearing it as the old ones.

15. Yes, one by the minister, the other by the parishioners.

16. None at all.

17. Yes, never absent, only one Sunday in almost three and twenty years.

18. By myself and according to the present needs and wants of the poor, observing in general a rotation.

19. [*On a separate piece of paper:*] The mother of James Hinwood and Mary Perrot had two mothers and one father, unless, as is said, Mary was by another man.[2] I should not, I am well persuaded, have ventured to marry them had the report reached me time enough, as the certainty of the report is very difficult to come at, if possible to be obtained. I endeavoured to convince James and Mary that they ought not to marry and absolutely refused to do it. They got a licence and were married at Pertwood about 7 or 8 miles off. James, as I hear at least, to prevent my putting him into the court, got somebody else to do it. I tried to have them punished, but difficulties and the report, lest I should hurt the guiltless, stopped me hitherto and they now live together and have two children. There wants more care in granting licences. I have 2 instances in my parish. The soul-hurting printing, publishing, and vending the Salisbury Journal on Sundays to the profanation of the Lord's day even in my parish and sundry others calls for exertion of authority; I have tried to get evidence against the deliverer in my parish.

20. Wylye near Heitsbury.

John Eyre,[3] curate of Wylye. Deacon 1753. Priest 1755. D.D.

The terrier, my Lord, is not quite finished but I will endeavour to have it delivered to your register in a little time.

231 YATESBURY f.1930   D. Avebury

1. At half past two in the afternoon.

2. Only on Good Friday.

3. As curate.[4]

4. Yes, Compton Bassett at two miles distance.

5. Three times, at Christmas, Easter, and Whitsuntide.

6. Generally about fourteen; at Easter last, sixteen.

7. [a] No. [c] No. [d] No.

8. No.

9. Usually in Lent.

10. [a] Yes. [c] To the year 1563, beginning in July that year.

11. Yes.

12. No.

---

[2] Presumably he means that Mary may be half-sister to James's mother.
[3] Hertford Coll. Oxford 1745.
[4] Rector, John Rolt. See Bromham, **29**, of which he was resident rector.

13. For an answer to this I must beg leave to refer your Lordship to the rector, the Rev. Mr. Rolt.
14. No.
15. In the Easter week, one by the minister, the other by the parishioners.
16. No.
17. No. At Calne, about 4 miles distant.
18. To the poor communicants.
19. No.
20. Answered above.
Ord. D. in June 1767 and ord. P. the year following. M.A.

Thomas Greenwood[5]

232 YATTON KEYNELL [Yatton Kemmell] f.1938   D. Malmesbury

1. There are prayers one part of the day, and prayers and sermon the other, in my church, alternately. The morning service beginning at $10\frac{1}{2}$, the afternoon at $2\frac{1}{2}$.
2. On Christmas day and Good Friday, the same service as on Sundays; prayers on Ash Wednesday, and on Monday and Tuesday in Easter and Whitsun weeks. On these latter occasions I have had so few as 2 this year.
3. As incumbent.
4. I read prayers on saints' days, and perform the surplice duty on weekdays for Dr. Scrope at Castle Combe (not 2 miles from me). In his illness or occasional absence, I serve his church on Sundays.
5. Seven times, viz. Christmas day, on one of the introductory Sundays to Lent, Easter day, Whitsunday, and 3 of the Sundays after Trinity, at equal distances.
6. About 12. Last Easter there happened to be but 8. One of the number is since dead, and one is bed-ridden.
7. [a] There are none. [b] No.
8. I know of no regular dissenters in my parish of any denomination, though too many absenters from the public worship of God; and some may at times visit the meeting-house at Castle-Combe.
9. The children are sent, but not the servants. Of late I have given extempore explanations of my own. I catechize between Easter and Michaelmas, in the afternoons, when there is no sermon nor any extraordinary duty.
10. [a] Yes. [b] Yes. [c] There is one that commences Oct. 1653 and ends March 1742, from which time that in present use goes on.
11. Yes.
12. [a] No. [f] No.
13. I have only one, dated in the year 1704, not signed by the minister. There is a person in the parish that has 2 others by him, who refuses me a sight of them, pretending that one of them was made by the minister and signed by his particular friends and as to occasion a lawsuit with the parish, in which he was cast, but that what I have is the truest. The truth of which I somewhat doubt.
14. [a] No. [d] No.

[5] Perhaps Brasenose Coll. Oxford 1763. See also **54.**

15. Yes, one by the minister and the other by the parishioners.
16. There is only a dame's school for children to learn to read.
17. Yes.
18. By myself, towards paying for poor people's children learning to read. What is wanting more in that way I make up myself.
19. Not that I know of.
20. Yatton-Keynell near Chippenham, Wilts.

James Pidding A.B.[6]

Ord. D. 5 Nov. 1758 at Wells. Ord. P. 25 March 1764. Instituted to the rectory of Yatton-Keynell 26 March 1764.

233 STRATFORD TONY[7] f.1946   D. Chalke

1. Divine service is performed, both preaching and praying, at half past ten in the morning, and prayers again at two in the afternoon.
2. On none except the great festivals.
3. As rector.
4. None.
5. On each great festival.
6. Very few, but I hope their numbers will increase.
7. No dissenters of any kind that I know of.
8. Ditto.
9. I am sorry to find that it has not been the custom, but shall pay particular attention to it.
10. Yes.
11. There is a register book of marriages.
12. None of any kind.
13. No terrier has yet been delivered in to me.
14. None, of any kind.
15. Yes, one by the minister, the other by the parish.
16. No school or any charitable endowment.
17. I reside constantly in the parsonage house.
18. [Blank]
19. None that I know of.
20. Stratford Tony is four miles from Sarum.

Instituted 23 Oct. 1783 to the rectory of Stratford by his Lordship, at Mongewell. Ord. D. 21 Oct. 1764. Ord. P. 22 June 1766.

T. Brown[8]

---

[6] 1736–1821. Balliol Coll. Oxford 1754. See also **35.**
[7] This return is loose at the end of the volume and has no address on the last page. As the rector was not instituted until 23 Oct. 1783, it was evidently sent in late. See Poulshot, **160,** also loose.
[8] Thomas Brown B.D. Corpus Christi Coll. Oxford (patrons of the living) 1757. See also **90.**

INDEX

References other than those preceded by 'p.' are to the parish numbers. A reference under a parish name to the return for that parish is given in bold type. Places other than major towns may be presumed to be in Wiltshire unless otherwise identified. Variant forms of place-names are indexed only where it helps the reader to find the right entry. The names of Oxford and Cambridge colleges in the footnotes are not indexed. Apart from bishops, peers, Roman Catholic priests, and nonconformist preachers, people are identified, by office, rank, or occupation, only (a) when their forenames or initials are unknown, or (b) when there are two people of the same surname and forename.

WILTSHIRE RECORD SOCIETY

(As at 31 December 1971)
President: PROFESSOR RALPH B. PUGH, M.A., F.S.A.
Honorary Editor: CHRISTOPHER R. ELRINGTON, M.A., F.S.A.
Honorary Treasurer: MICHAEL J. LANSDOWN
Honorary Secretary: MRS. NANCY D. STEELE, B.A.

Committee:
E. J. M. BUXTON, M.A., F.S.A.
I. GEOFFREY MOORE, Ph.D., F.I.C.E., F.I.Mech.E.
K. G. PONTING
MAURICE G. RATHBONE, A.L.A.
MISS ELIZABETH CRITTALL, M.A., F.S.A. (*co-opted*)
PHILIP STYLES, M.A., F.S.A. (*co-opted*)
RICHARD E. SANDELL, M.A., F.S.A., F.L.S., representing the Wiltshire Archaeological
and Natural History Society

BRIGADIER A. R. FORBES, as Secretary and Treasurer of the Wiltshire Archaeological and
Natural History Society

Honorary Auditor: G. HYLTON EVANS, F.C.A.

PRIVATE MEMBERS

AILESBURY, The Marquess of, D.L., J.P., Sturmy House, Savernake Forest, Marlborough

ALLEN, N., 46 Westland Road, Faringdon, Berks.

ANDERSON, D. M., 64 Winsley Road, Bradford on Avon

APPLEBY, E. C., 1 Jacks Lane, Frome, Som.

APPLEGATE, Miss Jean M., 55 Holbrook Lane, Trowbridge

ARCHER, P. J., Cotswold View, 9 Station Road, Highworth

AUSTIN, Mrs. D. M., Woolcombe Farm, Toller Porcorum, Dorchester, Dorset

AVERY, Mrs. Susan, 24 Old Hertford Road, Hatfield, Herts.

AWDRY, Mrs. R. W., M.B.E., Haven Court, Cary Park, Babbacombe, Devon

BADENI, The Countess, Norton Manor, Malmesbury

BARNES, C. Egbert, J.P., Hungerdown House, Seagry, Chippenham

BEATTIE, J. M., Dept. of History, University of Toronto, Canada

BERRETT, A. M., 65 Mandeville Road, Southgate, London N.14

BIDDULPH, G. M. R., c/o Personnel Records, British Council, 65 Davies Street, London W.1

BIRLEY, N. P., D.S.O., M.C., Hyde Leaze, Hyde Lane, Marlborough

BLAKE, T. N., 16 West Hill Road, London S.W.18

BLUNT, C. E., O.B.E., F.B.A., Ramsbury Hill, Ramsbury, Marlborough

BONNEY, Mrs. H. M., Flint Cottage, Netton, Salisbury

BRICE, G. R., Branchways, Willett Way, Petts Wood, Kent

BRIGHT, Sq.-Ldr. Bruce, c/o 1 Westlecot Road, Swindon

BROOKE-LITTLE, J. P., M.V.O., Richmond Herald of Arms, College of Arms, Queen Victoria Street, London E.C.4

BROWN, W. E., The Firs, Beckhampton, Marlborough

BRUGES, Major W. E., 1 Bower Gardens, Salisbury

BUCKERIDGE, J. M., 104 Beacon Road, Loughborough, Leics.

BUCKLAND, L. J., Twelvetrees, Amesbury, Salisbury

BURGE, Miss H. M., The Old Rectory, Huish, Marlborough

BURGE, S. F. M., The Old Rectory, Huish, Marlborough

BURNETT BROWN, Miss Janet M., Lacock Abbey, Chippenham

BUXTON, E. J. M., Cole Park, Malmesbury

CAREW-HUNT, Miss P. H., Cowleaze, Edington, Westbury

CARTER, Miss N. M. G., Gatehouse, Cricklade

CLANCHY, M. T., Dept. of History, The University, Glasgow W.2

CLARK, J. W., Manor Farm, Etchilhampton, Devizes

CODRINGTON, Miss N. E., Wroughton House, Swindon

CRITTALL, Miss Elizabeth, 16 Downside Crescent, London N.W.3

CROWLEY, D. A., 333 Cranbrook Road, Ilford, Essex

DANIELS, C. G., 81 Goffenton Drive, Old-bury Court, Fishponds, Bristol

DIBBEN, A. A., 222 King Street, Hammer-smith, London W.6

DOYLE, Leslie, Cheviot, Clay Lane, Wythen-shawe, Manchester 23

DUGDALE, H. J., Apple Tree Cottage, Wilton, Grafton, Marlborough

DYKE, P. J., 35 Buckleigh Avenue, Merton Park, London S.W.20

ECCLES, The Viscount, K.C.V.O., P.C., Dean Farm, Chute, Andover, Hants

EDWARDS, W. A., Long Acres, Everleigh, Marlborough

ELLIS, R. L., 5 Avebury Park, Lovelace Gardens, Surbiton, Surrey

ELRINGTON, C. R., Institute of Historical Research, University of London, Senate House, London W.C.1

FANE, Mrs. Edmund, Boyton Manor, Warminster

FILBY, P. W., Librarian, Maryland Histori-cal Society, 201 West Monument Street, Baltimore, Md. 21201, U.S.A.

FORBES, Miss K. G., Bury House, Codford, Warminster

FOY, J. D., 28 Penn Lea Road, Bath, Som.

FRY, Mrs. P. M., 18 Pulteney Street, Bath, Som.

FULLER, Major Sir Gerard, Bt., Neston Park, Corsham

GIBBON, Canon Geoffrey, 1 North Grove, London N.6

GIMSON, H. M., Grey Wethers, Stanton St. Bernard, Marlborough

GODDARD, Mrs. G. H., The Boot, Scholard's Lane, Ramsbury, Marlborough

GOULD, C. P., 1200 Old Mill Road, San Marino, California, U.S.A.

HALL, G. D., President, Corpus Christi College, Oxford

HALLWORTH, Frederick, Northcote, West-bury Road, Bratton, Westbury

HAM, Chester W., Jr., 187 Rounds Avenue, Providence, Rhode Island, 02907, U.S.A.

HARFIELD, Capt. A. G., 244 Signal Squadron (Air Support), R.A.F. Benson, Oxford

HARFIELD, Mrs. A. G., 244 Signal Squadron (Air Support), R.A.F. Benson, Oxford

HATCHWELL, R. C., The Old Rectory, Little Somerford, Chippenham

HAWKINS, M. J., 121 High Street, Lewes, Sussex

HAYMAN, The Rev. P. E. C., The Vicarage, Rogate, Petersfield, Hants

HEDGES, R. K., Charlton House, Shaftes-bury, Dorset

HOARE, H. P. R., Gasper House, Stourton, Warminster

HOBBS, Miss N., 140 Western Road, Sompting, Lancing, Sussex

HODGETT, G. A. J., King's College, London W.C.2

HUMPHREYS, Cdr. L. A., R.N. (Rtd.), Elm Lodge, Biddestone, Chippenham

HURSTFIELD, Prof. Joel, 7 Glenilla Road, London N.W.3

JACKSON, R. H., 17 Queens Road, Tisbury, Salisbury

JENNINGS, R. A. U., Newlands, 46 London Road, Salisbury

JEREMY, D. J., Curator, Merrimack Valley Textile Museum, North Andover, Mass. 01845, U.S.A.

JOHN, D. Murray, O.B.E., Town Clerk, Borough of Swindon, Civic Offices, Swindon

JONES, The Rev. Kingsley C., 22 Brookside Road, Fulwood, Preston, Lancs.

KEATINGE, Lady, Teffont, Salisbury
KEMPSON, E. G. H., Sun Cottage, Hyde Lane, Marlborough
KNIGHT, E. R., 5 Linley Close, Swindon
KOMATSU, Prof. Y., Institute of European Economic History, Waseda University, Tokyo 160, Japan

LANGTON, Sir Henry, D.S.O., D.F.C., D.L., Overtown House, Wroughton, Swindon
LANSDOWN, M. J., 37 Hilperton Road, Trowbridge
LATHAM, Mrs. W. J., Dark Lane House, Marlborough
LAURENCE, Miss Anne, 29 Sydney Street, Chelsea, London S.W.3
LAURENCE, G. F., 1 Monks Orchard, Petersfield, Hants
LEVER, R. E., Reads Close, Teffont Magna, Salisbury
LITTLE, J. E., The Pantiles, Chapel Lane, Uffington, Berks.
LONDON, Miss V. C. M., Underholt, Westwood Road, Bidston, Birkenhead

MCCULLOUGH, Prof. Edward, Sir George Williams University, 1435 Drummond Street, Montreal 25, Quebec, Canada
MACKINTOSH, Duncan, C.B.E., Woodfolds, Oaksey, Malmesbury
MANN, Miss J. de L., The Cottage, Bowerhill, Melksham
MARGADALE of Islay, The Lord, Fonthill House, Tisbury
MASTERS, H. A. C., Hossil Lane, Stanton Fitzwarren, Swindon
METHUEN, The Lord, Corsham Court
METHUEN, The Hon. Mrs. Anthony, Ivy House, Corsham
MILLBOURN, Sir Eric, C.M.G., Conkwell Grange, Limpley Stoke, Bath, Som.
MITTON, A. W. D., The Dungeon, 239 Earl's Court Road, London S.W.5
MOODY, G. C., Montrose, Shaftesbury Road, Wilton, Salisbury
MOORE, I. G., Raycroft, Lacock, Chippenham
MORRIS, Miss Bronwen, 9 Cleveland Gardens, Trowbridge
MORRISON, The Hon. Charles, M.P., Fyfield Manor, Marlborough
MOULTON, A. E., The Hall, Bradford on Avon

NAN KIVELL, R. de C., 20 Cork Street, London W.1
NEWALL, R. S., Avon Cottage, Lower Woodford, Salisbury

NORTHAMPTON, Emma, Marchioness of, O.B.E., The Curatage, Horningsham, Warminster

OSBORNE, Major Robert, c/o Lloyds Bank Ltd., Westbury-on-Trym, Bristol

PAFFORD, J. H. P., Hillside, Allington Park, Bridport, Dorset
PASKIN, Lady, Wishford, Salisbury
PERRY, S. H., 117 London Road, Kettering, Northants.
PETO, Brig. C. H. M., D.S.O., D.L., Lockeridge House, Marlborough
PONTING, K. G., Becketts House, Edington, Westbury
POTHECARY, S. G., 41 Australian Avenue, Salisbury
POWELL, W. R., 2 Glenmead, Shenfield, Romford
PUGH, Prof. R. B., 67 Southwood Park, London N.6

RAMSAY, G. D., St. Edmund Hall, Oxford
RATHBONE, M. G., Craigleith, Snarlton Lane, Melksham Forest
RAYBOULD, Miss Frances, 20 Radnor Road, Salisbury
REEVES, Dr. Marjorie E., 38 Norham Road, Oxford
REYNOLDS, A., The White House, Riverfield Road, Staines, Middlesex
ROGERS, K. H., Silverthorne Cottage, Erlestoke, Devizes
ROOKE, Mrs. R. E. P., The Ivy, Chippenham
ROOKE, Miss S. F., The Ivy, Chippenham
ROSS, Harry, Leighton Villa, Wellhead Lane, Westbury
ROWE, Mrs. H. M., 85 Charnhill Drive, Mangotsfield, Bristol
RUNDLE, Miss Penelope, 11 West Street, Wilton, Salisbury

SANDELL, R. E., Hillside, 64 Devizes Road, Potterne
SANDQUIST, T. A., Dept. of History, University of Toronto, 5, Canada
SAWYER, L. F. T., 51 Sandridge Road, Melksham
SHADBOLT, Mrs. L. G., Birkhall House, High Kelling, Holt, Norfolk
SHEWRING, D. G., 4 Clifton Street, Treorchy, Rhondda, Glam.
SOMERSET, The Duke of, D. L., Bradley House, Maiden Bradley, Warminster
STEDMAN, A. R., 9 The Green, Aldbourne, Marlborough

STEELE, Mrs. N. D., Milestones, Hatchet Close, Hale, Fordingbridge, Hants

STEVENSON, Miss J. H., Institute of Historical Research, University of London, Senate House, London W.C.1

STEWART, Miss K. P., Moxham Villa, 57 Lower Road, Bemerton, Salisbury

STRATTON, J. M., Manor House Farm, Stockton, Warminster

STYLES, Philip, 21 Castle Lane, Warwick

TANNER, Miss J. M., 155 Shrivenham Road, Swindon

TAYLOR, C. C., Royal Commission on Historical Monuments (England), 13 West End, Whittlesford, Cambridge

THOMPSON, Mrs. M. W., Box Cottage, Wilcot, Pewsey

TURNER, Miss M., 4 Elm Grove Road, Salisbury

TWINE, S. W., 2 Elgin Road, Wood Green, London N.22

VERNON, Mrs. B., Keevil Manor, Trowbridge

VERNON, Miss T. E., Dyer's Leaze, Lacock, Chippenham

WADE, Miss Elmira M., O.B.E., Bridge Cottage, Lacock, Chippenham

WALKER, Rev. J. G., Buttermere Hill, Churt, Farnham, Surrey

WATKINS, W. T., Carn Ingli, 16 Westbury Road, Warminster

WEINSTOCK, Sir Arnold, Bowden Park, Lacock, Chippenham

WIGAN, Mrs. D., Fifteenth Century Cottage, Etchilhampton, Devizes

WILLAN, Group Capt. F. A., D.L., Bridges, Teffont, Salisbury

WILLIAMS, N. J., 57 Rotherwick Road, Hampstead Garden Suburb, London N.W.11

WILLOUGHBY, R. W. H., Langford Way, Berwick St. James, Salisbury

WILTSHIRE, D. C. S., Quintons, Walnut Close, Urchfont, Devizes

WILTSHIRE, Julian M., Ashlyns Cottage, Lybury Lane, Redbourn, Herts.

WORTHINGTON, B. S., Vale Lodge, Colnbrook, Bucks.

YOUNG, C. L. R., 25 Staveley Road, Chiswick, London W.4

UNITED KINGDOM INSTITUTIONS

Aberdeen. King's College Library

Aberystwyth. National Library of Wales

    ,, University College General Library

Bangor. University College of North Wales

Bath. General Reference Library

Birmingham. Central Public Library

    ,, University Library, Edgbaston

Bridgwater. Somerset County Library

Brighton. University of Sussex Library, Falmer

Bristol. City of Bristol Library

    ,, University Library

Cambridge. University Library

Coventry. University of Warwick Library

Devizes. Wiltshire Archaeological and Natural History Society

Dorchester. County of Dorset Library

Edinburgh. National Library of Scotland

    ,, University Library

Exeter. University Library

Glasgow. University Library

Gloucester. Bristol and Gloucestershire Archaeological Society

Hull. University of Kingston-upon-Hull Library

Leeds. University Library

Leicester. Univerity Library

Liverpool. University Library

London. British Museum

    ,, College of Arms

    ,, Guildhall Library

    ,, Inner Temple Library

    ,, Institute of Historical Research

    ,, London Library

    ,, Public Record Office

    ,, Royal Historical Society

    ,, Society of Antiquaries

    ,, Society of Genealogists

    ,, University of London Library

    ,, City of Westminster Public Library

Manchester. John Rylands Library

Marlborough. Adderley Library, Marlborough College

Norwich. University of East Anglia Library

Nottingham. University Library

Oxford. Bodleian Library
„ Exeter College Library
„ New College Library
Reading. Central Library
„ University Library
St. Andrews. University Library
Salisbury. Bourne Valley Historical Society, Allington
„ History Dept., College of Sarum St. Michael
„ Diocesan Record Office
„ The Museum
„ City of New Sarum Public Library
„ Royal Commission on Historical Monuments (England), Manor Road

Salisbury. Salisbury & South Wilts. College of Further Education
Sheffield. University Library
Southampton. University Library
Swansea. University College of Swansea Library
Swindon. Borough of Swindon Public Library
„ Swindon College Library
Taunton. Somerset Archaeological and Natural History Society
Trowbridge. Wiltshire County Library
„ Wiltshire Record Office, County Hall
„ The Wiltshire Times
York. University of York Library

OVERSEAS INSTITUTIONS

AUSTRALIA

Canberra. National Library of Australia
Melbourne. Baillieu Library, University of Melbourne
„ Victoria State Library
St. Lucia, Brisbane. Main Library, University of Queensland
Sydney. Fisher Library, University of Sydney

CANADA

Downsview, Ontario. York Universities Libraries
Kingston, Ontario. Queen's University
London, Ontario. Lawson Memorial Library, University of Western Ontario
Peterborough, Ontario. Dept. of History, Trent University
Toronto, Ontario. University of Toronto Library
Ottawa. Carleton University Library
St. John's, Newfoundland. M.U.N. Library, Memorial University of Newfoundland
Vancouver. Main Library, University of British Columbia
Victoria, B.C. McPherson Library, University of Victoria

DENMARK

Copenhagen. The Royal Library

REPUBLIC OF IRELAND

Dublin. National Library of Ireland
„ Trinity College Library

JAPAN

Osaka. Institute of Economic History, Kansai University
Sendai. Institute of Economic History, Tohoku University

NEW ZEALAND

Wellington. National Library of New Zealand

SWEDEN

Upsala. Kungl Universitetets Bibliotek (Royal University Library)

UNITED STATES OF AMERICA

Ann Arbor, Mich. General Library, University of Michigan
Athens, Georgia. University Libraries, University of Georgia
Baltimore, Md. Peabody Institute of the City of Baltimore
Bloomington, Ind. Indiana University Library
Boston, Mass. Public Library of the City of Boston
„ „ New England Historic Genealogical Society
Boulder, Col. University of Colorado Libraries
Buffalo, N.Y. Lockwood Memorial Library, State University of New York at Buffalo
Cambridge, Mass. Harvard Law School Library
„ „ Harvard College Library

Chicago, Ill. University of Chicago Library
„ „ Newberry Library
Cleveland, Ohio. Public Library
De Kalb, Ill. Northern University of Illinois, Swen Franklin Parson Library
East Lansing, Mich. Michigan State University Library
Haverford, Pa. Haverford College Library
Iowa City. State University of Iowa Library
Ithaca, N.Y. Cornell University Library
Las Cruces, New Mexico. New Mexico State University Library
Los Angeles, Cal. Public Library of Los Angeles
„ „ „. University Research Library, University of California
Minneapolis, Ma. Dept. of History, Minnesota University
Newark, Delaware. University of Delaware Library

New Haven, Conn. Yale University Library
New York. Columbia University of the City of New York
„ „ Public Library, City of New York
Notre Dame, Ind. Notre Dame University Memorial Library
Philadelphia, Pa. Pennsylvania University Library
Princeton, N.J. Princeton University Library
Salt Lake City, Utah. Genealogical Society of the Church of Latter Day Saints
San Marino, Cal. Henry E. Huntingdon Library
Stanford, Cal. Stanford University Library
Urbana, Ill. University of Illinois Library
Washington, D.C. Library of Congress
Winston-Salem, N.C. Wake Forest University Library

LIST OF PUBLICATIONS

The Wiltshire Record Society was founded in 1937, as the Records Branch of the Wiltshire Archaeological and Natural History Society, to promote the publication of the documentary sources for the history of Wiltshire. The annual subscription is £3. In return, a member receives a volume each year. Prospective members should apply to Mrs. N. D. Steele, 41 Castle Road, Salisbury. Many more members are needed.

The following volumes have been published. Price to members £3 and to non-members £4, postage extra. Available from the Hon. Treasurer, Mr. M. J. Lansdown, 37 Hilperton Road, Trowbridge, Wiltshire.

I *Abstract of Feet of Fines relating to Wiltshire for the reigns of Edward I and Edward II.* Edited by R. B. Pugh (1939)

II *Accounts of the Parliamentary Garrisons of Great Chalfield and Malmesbury, 1645–6.* Edited by J. H. P. Pafford (1940). Illustrated

III *Calendar of Antrobus Deeds before 1625.* Edited by R. B. Pugh (1947)

IV *Minutes of Proceedings in Sessions, 1563, 1574–92.* Edited by H. C. Johnson (1949)

V *List of Records of Wiltshire Boroughs before 1836.* Edited by M. G. Rathbone (1951)

VI *The Trowbridge Woollen Industry as illustrated by the Stock Books of John and Thomas Clark, 1804–24.* Edited by R. F. Beckingsale (1951). Illustrated

VII *Guild Stewards' Book of the Borough of Calne, 1561–1688.* Edited by A. W. Mabbs (1953)

VIII *Andrews and Dury's Map of Wiltshire, 1773.* A reduced facsimile in 'atlas' form, with an introduction by Elizabeth Crittall (1952)

IX *Surveys of the Manors of Philip, Earl of Pembroke and Montgomery, 1631–2.* Edited by E. Kerridge (1953)

X *Two Sixteenth Century Taxation Lists, 1545 and 1576.* Edited by G. D. Ramsay (1954)

XI *Wiltshire Quarter Sessions and Assizes, 1736.* Edited by J. P. M. Fowle (1955)

XII *Collectanea.* Edited by N. J. Williams, with a foreword by T. F. T. Plucknett (1956)

XIII *Progress Notes of Warden Woodward for the Wiltshire Estates of New College, 1659–75.* Edited by R. L. Rickard (1957). Illustrated

XIV *Accounts and Surveys of the Wiltshire Lands of Adam de Stratton, 1268–86.* Edited by M. W. Farr (1959)

XV *Tradesmen in Early-Stuart Wiltshire: A Miscellany.* Edited by N. J. Williams (1960)

XVI *Crown Pleas of the Wiltshire Eyre, 1249.* Edited by C. A. F. Meekings (1961)

XVII *Wiltshire Apprentices and their Masters, 1710–60.* Edited by Christabel Dale (1961)

XVIII *Hemingby's Register.* Edited by Helena M. Chew (1963)

XIX *Documents Illustrating the Wiltshire Textile Trades in the Eighteenth Century.* Edited by Julia de L. Mann (1964)

XX *The Diary of Thomas Naish.* Edited by Doreen Slatter (1965). Illustrated

XXI, XXII *The Rolls of Highworth Hundred, 1275–87.* Edited by Brenda Farr (1966, 1968). Map

XXIII *The Earl of Hertford's Lieutenancy Papers, 1603–12.* Edited by W. P. D. Murphy (1969). Illustrated

XXIV *Court Rolls of the Wiltshire Manors of Adam de Stratton.* Edited by R. B. Pugh (1970)

XXV *Abstracts of Wiltshire Inclosure Awards and Agreements.* Edited by R. E. Sandell (1971). Map

XXVI *Civil Pleas of the Wiltshire Eyre, 1249.* Edited by M. T. Clanchy (1971)

VOLUMES IN PREPARATION

Wiltshire Glebe Terriers, edited by D. A. Crowley; *Wiltshire Extents for Debts,* edited by Angela Conyers; *Salisbury General Entry Books,* edited by Alan Crossley; *The Wiltshire Forest Eyre, 1257,* edited by N. J. Williams; *The Charters of Lacock Abbey,* edited by K. H. Rogers; *Abstract of Feet of Fines relating to Wiltshire for the reign of Edward III,* edited by C. R. Elrington; *The Edington Cartulary,* edited by Janet Stevenson; *Wiltshire Tithe Awards,* edited by R. E. Sandell; *Salisbury Poor in the Early Seventeenth Century,* edited by P. A. Slack; *Wiltshire Clergy of the Seventeenth Century,* edited by Barrie Williams.

A leaflet giving fuller details may be obtained from Mrs. Steele.

Q.12. [a] Are there any chapels of ease in your parish? What are the names of them? [b] How often are there prayers and sermons in them? [c] Have they any estates or funds particularly appropriated to their maintenance? [d] How far distant are they from the parish church? [e] By whom are they served? [f] Have you any ruinated chapels in which there is no divine service performed?

Q.13. [a] Have you a true and perfect account or terrier of all houses, lands, tithes, pensions, and profits, which belong to you as minister of your parish? [b] Hath a duplicate thereof been laid up in the bishop's registry? [c] Hath there been, since that was done, any augmentation made of your living? [d] And hath an account of such augmentation been transmitted thither also?

Q.14. [a] Is there any free school, alms-house, hospital, or other charitable endowment in your parish? And for how many, and for what sort of persons? [b] Who was the founder? And who are the governors or trustees? [c] What are the revenues of it? Are they carefully preserved, and employed as they ought to be? Are the statutes and orders made concerning it well observed? [d] Have any lands or tenements been left for the repair of your church, or for any other pious use? [e] Who has the direction and management of such benefactions? And who takes an account of and conducts them?

Q.15. [a] Are the churchwardens in your parish chosen every year in the *Easter* week? [b] How are they chosen? By the minister and parishioners together, or one by the minister and the other by the parishioners?

Q.16. [a] Is there (or has there been founded) any public school in your parish? [b] Is there any charity school in your parish? How is it supported? By voluntary subscription, or by a settled endowment? Is it for boys or girls, and for how many? [c] What are the children taught? More particularly, [d] is care taken to instruct them in the principles of the Christian religion, and to bring them regularly to church? [e] And are they also lodged, fed, and clothed? [f] And how are they disposed of when they leave school? [g] Does your school flourish? And if not, for what reasons?

Q.17. [a] Do you constantly reside upon this cure, and in the house belonging to it? [b] If not, where, and at what distance from it, is your usual place of residence? [c] How long in each year are you absent? [d] And what is the reason for such absence?

Q.18. By whom, and to what uses, is the money given at the offertory disposed of?

Q.19. Is there any matter relating to your parish or chapelry of which it may be proper to give me information?

Q.20. What is your place of residence, and the nearest post town?

P.S. They who by illness, or any other just cause, are prevented from attending the visitation, are requested to send their answers by those persons who attend for them; or by the post, in covers, not weighing above two ounces, to the bishop, at *Mongewell-House*, Wallingford, Berks. It would be an additional satisfaction to the bishop, if his clergy, at the end of these queries, would write the dates of their collation, or institution; of their deacon's and priest's orders; and their degrees.